THE THIRD KEY

THE JEWISH COUPLE'S GUIDE TO FERTILITY

THE THIRD KEY

THE JEWISH COUPLE'S GUIDE TO FERTILITY

Rabbi Baruch Finkelstein and

Michal Finkelstein, RN, CNM

FELDHEIM PUBLISHERS
JERUSALEM NEW YORK

Also by the authors:

B'Sha'ah Tovah — The Jewish Woman's Clinical and Halachic Guide to Pregnancy and Childbirth (Jerusalem: Feldheim Publishers, 2001)

Readers are invited to contact the authors at:
thethirdkey@mail.com

Library of Congress Cataloging-in-Publication Data

Finkelstein, Baruch.
The third key : the Jewish couple's guide to fertility / Baruch Finkelstein, Michal Finkelstein.
p. cm.
Includes bibliographical references.
ISBN 1-58330-390-1
1. Infertility—Religious aspects—Judaism. 2. Fertility, Human. 3. Medical laws and legislation (Jewish law) 4. Ethics, Jewish. I. Finkelstein, Michal. II. Title.

BM538.H43F53 2003

296.7'4—dc22 2003049450

First published 2005

FELDHEIM PUBLISHERS
POB 43163 / Jerusalem, Israel

208 Airport Executive Park
Nanuet, NY 10954

www.feldheim.com

Printed in Israel

10 9 8 7 6 5 4 3 2 1

ב"ה

Rabbi Y. Belsky
506 EAST 7th STREET
BROOKLYN, NEW YORK 11218

ישראל הלוי בעלסקי
941 - 0112

The Third Key is a *tour de force* whose every page is educational and inspiring. My reading of the manuscript was well rewarded by the plethora of information and guidance in its carefully researched and brilliantly written pages, presented with remarkable sensitivity and delicacy. Its intended readership could be offered no less in light of the torment already endured by them in their quest for progeny.

Rochel Imeinu expressed their deep and wounded feelings in words whose passion cannot be exceeded: הבה לי בנים ואם אין מתה אנכי — "Give me children! If not it is as though I am dead." Perhaps one can explain these words on a simple yet striking level. Man has been granted by Hashem a certain measure of immortality by way of his children. Through them he transcends his own personal mortality and exists through the continuity of his generations. Through his children he lives forever, but ואם אין — without them, his death seems to be permanent and irrevocable.

The Navi addresses that despair with his enlightening and heartening message: ונתתי להם בביתי ובחומותי יד ושם טוב מבנים ומבנות. A person can leave a mark of permanence in the world more enduring and valuable than that of blood lineage. It will be as though the individual himself is still here — his very presence illuminating the world that he had affected so deeply.

This book covers every facet of these issues. The medical information is extremely helpful. The Halachos are carefully presented and are designed to lead the way to consultation with Rabbonim of stature who can give each individual personal guidance.

The chapters on Bitachon and Tefilla etc. are inspiring and restorative to the spirit. Broken hearts will be mended by reading this work and its advice will help many in discovering the path to the solving of their problems in the happiest form. Even those who have become overwhelmed by the futility of many failed attempts may find herein a spark of courage to try once more and with Hashem Yisborach's help achieve their dreams in that flash of triumph that only those who experienced it can fully understand.

The Third Key will also serve as a valuable guide to those who advise afflicted families, such as Rabbonim, guidance people and the like. It is more easily read than the finest professional material and much more helpful than most.

A word of caution: Many people are so humbled by the medical profession as to consider their every pronouncement and opinion as a heavenly oracle which must be accepted as fact and commandment. Mere opinions are assumed to be always based on careful study of professionally assembled data with hardly any margin for error. One must always be wary and cognizant of the human tendencies and failings of every segment of the population.

In light of this, careful assessment and cautious evaluation are in order whenever any major procedure is suggested. Listen to other opinions and think through everything with an open mind. A Rov with a sensitivity towards and an understanding of these issues will add a rational voice to the discussion and balance one's decision with the wisdom of the Torah.

Again, thanks and Brocho Vehatzlocho to the authors, R' Boruch Finkelstein and Mrs. Michal Finkelstein, for this *magnum opus*, and for being responsible and capable spokespeople for the Torah perspective.

Signed this 16th day of Shevat 5765 (corresponding to January 26, 2005) in Brooklyn, New York.

ישראל הלוי בעלסקי

Rabbi Yisroel Belsky

ביהמ"ד גבול יעבץ
ברוקלין, נוא יארק

דוד קאהן

I have read "The Third Key" from cover to cover and have found it to be an educational as well as an uplifting experience. It encompasses Halacha and Hashkafa, medicine and psychology, which throw light on the rocky road that many must take to become parents.

This sefer shall, without a doubt, give spiritual and emotional strength and sustenance to all that are "metzapim liyeshua".

Rabbi and Mrs. Baruch Finkelstein have done a great service, through their talents and efforts, to the entire Jewish community.

Rabbi David Cohen
13 Elul 5764

דוד קאהן

ביהמ"ד גבול יעבץ
ברוקלין, נוא יארק

בס"ד

לכל מאן דבעי לאודועי

קראתי ברוב עניין הספר "המפתח השלישי" מהרב והרבנית ברוך פינקלשטיין שיחיו דכבר איתמחו גברא ואיתמחי על ידי ספרם הראשון באנגלית "בשעה טובה".
הספר מלא על גדותיו בעניני הלכה והשקפה עם לרבות חכמת הרפואה ופסיכולוגיה המפיצות אור ונותנות חיזוק לאלו הנאחזים בסבך בעית ההולדה.

לענ"ד כדאי שכל מבין עם תלמידי ת"ח בני ובנות תורה הבאים לבנות בית בישראל לקרוא בספר זה, וימצאו בו חומר רב לחזק את ביתם.

והנני מברך להרב והרבנית פינקלשטיין שיפוצו מעינותיהם חוצה ושכל אשר יפנו ישכילו.

בכבוד ויקר
דוד קאהן
י"ג אלול תשס"ב

ב"ה

המרכז הרפואי שערי צדק, ירושלים | מסורת של מצוינות | 100 | 1902 2002 | A Tradition of Excellence | Shaare Zedek Medical Center, Jerusalem

מסונף לפקולטה למדעי הבריאות אוניברסיטת בן-גוריון בנגב | Affiliated with the Faculty of Health Sciences Ben-Gurion University of the Negev

פרופ' אברהם שטינברג
מנהל היחידה לאתיקה רפואית

מנחם אב, תשס"ד

לכבוד
הרב ברוך פינקלשטיין שליט"א
ומרת מיכל פינקלשטיין תי'
השלו' והברכה

נתכבדתי בקבלת כתב היד של ספרכם השני "The Third Key – The Jewish Couple's Guide to Fertility", המכיל אוצר בלום וחשוב בכל ההיבטים הנוגעים לבעיות פוריות של זוגות נשואים, ולפתרונות המודרניים לבעיות אלו.
כמעשיכם בספרכם הראשון "בשעה טובה – מדריך רפואי הלכתי להריון ולידה" כן מעשיכם בספר השני, מלאכת מחשבת של איסוף וסידור חומר רב ומגוון הנוגע להריון, ללידה ולבעיות פוריות מבחינה רפואית, פסיכולוגית, הלכתית ומחשבתית. הכל ערוך ומסודר בשפה ברורה ונעימה, בסדר נכון, ומתוך רגישות והתחשבות מירבית במצוקות ובבעיות הכרוכות בתהליכים מורכבים ועמוסי-רגשות.
דומה שאין שילוב מוצלח יותר ומתאים יותר לכתיבת שני הספרים הללו ממחברי ספרים אלו, הלוא המה הזוג הנכבד הרב ברוך פינקשלטיין שליט"א והאחות-המיילדת מרת מיכל פינקשלטיין תי', שמשלבים בצורה אופטימלית ידע מקצועי-רפואי רלוונטי עם ידע הלכתי-מחשבתי יהודי.
אמנם כבר כתב פוסק הדור מרן הגר"מ פיינשטיין זצ"ל, שגם כאשר יש היתר הלכתי לשימוש באמצעי מניעה הוא צריך להיות בצניעות, ללא פרסום, "שלא תדענה חברותיה מזה, כדי שלא יקלו נשים אחרות וכו', ומטעם זה אני מזהיר בכל פעם שמזדמנת אשה שמתירים לה בשביל סכנה, שיהא הדבר בצניעות גדולה" (שו"ת אגרות משה תאבהע"ז ח"ד סי' סז); "ועד עתה נהגתי שלא לענות במכתב בדברים אלו, אלא כשבאו אלי לשאול בעל פה, שאז הזהרתי וכו', אבל מכיוון שהוא ממקום רחוק שכרוך בהוצאות גדולות אני משיב, אבל סומך אני על כתר"ה שיהיה בצנעא ובאזהרות" (שו"ת אגרות משה תאבהע"ז ח"ג סי' כב); "וכן יש לכל רב מובהק להתנהג בזה, וסתם רבנים ח"ו להם להורות בעניין חמור זה" (שו"ת אגרות משה תאבהע"ז ח"א סוסי' סד. וראה עוד בשו"ת אגרות משה תאבהע"ז ח"א סי' סד); וכן כתב הגר"ש ואזנר שליט"א "אף שמאד מרבים לשאול בהלכה זו, מכל מקום אני מתרחק להשיב בכתב באורך בזה, שלא לפרסם היתרים למי שאסור להתיר לו" (שו"ת שבט הלוי ח"ג סי' קעז). ואף שדברים אלו נכתבו ביחס לשימוש באמצעי מניעת הריון, יש גם בנושאים הקשורים לטיפולי פוריות בעיות הלכתיות שבעבר הצניעות היתה יפה להם.
אכן, בימינו כמדומני שאין עוד אפשרות שלא לדון בפירוט ובהרחבה בכל הנושאים הללו, שכן הציבור הרחב חשוף למידע רב, לעתים קרובות מסולף ופוגע, באמצעי תיקשורת מודרניים כמו עתונות, רדיו, טלביזיה, ובעיקר אינטרנט. בתנאים כאלו נכון וחשוב לפרסם מידע עדכני, מהימן ומבוסס מבחינה מדעית-רפואית, ובעיקר בכל הנוגע לעמדת ההלכה וההשקפה היהודית בנושאים מורכבים ובעייתיים אלו. דווקא לאור ההמצאות והחידושים הרבים בתחום הפוריות, הפך הנושא לנפוץ ומעשי. לפיכך, בעקבות הפתיחות הרבה והדיונים הפומביים בנושא זה בשנים האחרונות, יש מקום להבהיר ולהעמיד על דיוקם ופירוטם את עמדת היהדות וההלכה.
לפיכך טוב עשו מחברי הספר שלפנינו על שכינסו, סדרו וערכו את כל החומר הנוגע לבעיות פוריות ופתרונן בסגנון בהיר וברגישות רבה, ובעיקר תוך ביסוס עמדת ההלכה וההשקפה היהודית על מקורות ההלכה והאמונה, תוך ציון מקורות רבים.
יישר כוחכם על התרומה הנכבדה שהרמתם לטובתם של הנזקקים לחידושי המדע והרפואה בתחום הפוריות, ויהי רצון שתזכו להפיץ מעיינותיכם חוצה, להרבות דעת ויראת ה', ותזכו להגדיל תורה ולהאדירה.

בברכה נאמנה,

אברהם שטינברג

ת.ד. 3235 ירושלים 91031 טל. 02-655 5111 פקס. 02-651 3946
P.O.B. 3235 Jerusalem Tel: 972-2-655 5111 Fax: 972-2-651 3946
www.szmc.org.il ע.ר. 580007557

Menachem Av 5764

Greetings,

It was a great honor and privilege to review the manuscript of your second book, *The Third Key: A Jewish Couple's Guide to Fertility*. The book is a treasure of information relating to problems of infertility and some of their modern solutions.

As in your previous work, *B'sha'ah Tovah: A Jewish Woman's Clinical and Halachic Guide to Pregnancy and Childbirth,* this book too is written in a very professional and well thought-out manner. [Your works comprise] an impressive collection of material relating to pregnancy, birth, and fertility issues. The fertility issues and their associated difficulties are treated from a medical, psychological, halachic, and philosophical perspective. The book is clearly written and a pleasure to read, and you have shown extra special sensitivity in dealing with the great hardships and difficulties involved in complex and emotionally-laden procedures.

It appears to me that as a team, the esteemed couple, Rav Baruch Finkelstein, *shlita,* and his wife, the nurse and midwife Mrs. Michal Finkelstein, complement each other in the most optimal manner. They combine professional knowledge of the relevant medical issues together with knowledge of the halachic and Jewish philosophical matters.

The primary halachic authority of our generation, haGaon haRav Moshe Feinstein, *zt"l,* has written that although there are circumstances in which the halachah permits practicing birth control, it must be handled in the most private and modest manner... (*Igros Moshe, Even haEzer,* vol. IV, letter 67). Furthermore, writes R' Moshe, "Until now I have been very careful not to put any of these things in writing. It has been my practice to discuss these issues only in person, and I have cautioned greatly against publicizing them..." (ibid., vol. I, letter 64). He also wrote, "These serious matters must be handled exclusively by a competent halachic authority, and ordinary Rabbanim should not rule in these matters" (ibid.). HaRav Shmuel haLevi Wosner, *shlita,* writes, "Although I have received many questions regarding these *halachos*, I try to avoid elaborating in writing, for these leniencies should not be publicized to those who may not use them" (*Shevet haLevi*, vol. III, chap. 177).

Although the above letters were all written regarding methods of birth control, the requirement of modesty and privacy applied in the past to fertility problems as well. However, it seems to me that in today's day and age, avoiding detailed discussion of these matters is no longer a valid option. Modern media has exposed the population at large to vast amounts of information via newspapers, radio, television, and most of all, the Internet. Quite often this information is distorted. Under these conditions, it is of the utmost importance to publicize information that is up-to-date, reliable, and with a strong medical foundation. Most important, the halachic and Jewish philosophical position on these complex and difficult issues must be made known to the public. It is precisely in light of new discoveries in the area of fertility that this issue has become very popular as well as practical. Given this openness as well as the many public forums on these issues in recent years, I feel it is absolutely essential to clarify and present the halachic perspective in precise detail.

The authors of this book have done a great service by organizing and presenting all the material related to fertility problems and their solutions in a clear and sensitive manner. The work presents the position of the halachah and Jewish thought as well as discussion on faith and belief, and includes a wealth of sources.

Congratulations on your great contribution on behalf of those in need of the latest medical breakthroughs in the area of fertility. May it be the will of the Almighty that "your springs will spread outwards" (*Mishlei* 5:16), to increase knowledge and fear of God, and that you merit elevating and glorifying the Torah.

With sincere blessings,
Avraham Steinberg
Director, Department of Medical Ethics
Shaare Zedek Medical Center, Jerusalem

ב"ה

Shaare Zedek Medical Center, Jerusalem
A Tradition of Excellence 100 מסורת של מצוינות
המרכז הרפואי שערי צדק, ירושלים
Affiliated with the Faculty of Health Sciences Ben-Gurion University of the Negev
מסונף לפקולטה למדעי הבריאות אוניברסיטת בן-גוריון בנגב
The Josef Nathanson IVF unit
יחידה להפריה חוץ גופית ע"ש יוסף נתנזון ז"ל
Prof. Ehud Margalioth Director
פרופ' אהוד מרגליות מנהל

I strongly recommend the book The Third Key written by Michal Finkelstein R.N., and her husband, Rabbi Baruch Finkelstein. I found the information in this book to be accurate, comprehensive, and up-to-date. I spent many hours with Mrs. Finkelstein discussing all the medical sections of this book and I have complete confidence in her knowledge and her ability to convey this information to her readership. This book will be a great benefit to all those who are seeking information on the fertility process.

Prof Ehud J. Margalioth

Director IVF Unit

Shaare Zedek Medical Center

ת.ד. 3235 ירושלים 91031 טל. 02-6666055 פקס. 02-6666211
P.O.B. 3235 Jerusalem 91031 Tel: 972-2-6666055 Fax: 972-2-6666211
E-mail: haran@szmc.org.il ע.ר. 580007557

PUAH INSTITUTE
Rabbi Menachem Burstein, Director

27 Tevet 5764

To our Honored Friends
HaRav and Mrs. Baruch Finkelstein

Greetings and blessings,

I was asked by the head of our institute's English department, haRav Gideon Weitzman, to review the manuscript of your new book dealing with the subject of fertility and the associated halachic issues. I am elated that you have published a book that serves as a guide for religious couples experiencing fertility difficulties. At our institute, we are all too aware of the pain and despair of these couples. Many turn to the Puah Institute in search of medical guidance as well as halachic rulings. It is of extreme importance that these couples have access to appropriately written material describing the medical procedures as well as the halachic issues.

A couple who reads this book will undergo treatment in a more confident and relaxed matter, and it will also be clear to them what the halachic issues are and when a Rabbinic authority must be consulted.

Just as your previous book was well-received by the public and has become a guiding light for thousands of couples on the subject of pregnancy, we pray that this work will find favor in the public eye and bring merit and blessing to you and your family.

With Torah blessings,
Rabbi Menachem Burstein

בס"ד
מכון פוע"ה - פוריות ורפואה עפ"י ההלכה.
Puah Institute - Fertility and Medicine in Accordance with Halacha
רח' עזריאל 19, ג. שאול, ירושלים 95477, טל' 02-6515050, פקס, 02-6517501
19, Azriel St. Givat Shaul, Jerusalem 95477, Tel: 02-6515050 Fax: 02-6517501
דואר אלקטרוני: **E-mail: info@puah.org.il** אתר: **Site: www.puah.org.il**

הרב מנחם בורשטין
ראש המכון

כ"ז טבת תשס"ד

Document8

לכבוד
ידידנו ומכובדנו
הרב ברוך פינקלשטין ורעיתו שליט"א
בית אל

רב ברכה ושלום,

בקשתי מראש המחלקה לאנגלית במכון הרב גדעון ויצמן שליט"א לעיין בעלי ההגהה של ספרך החדש בעניני פוריות והלכה ומאוד שמחתי שכבודו ורעיתו הוציאו ספר שהוא מדריך לזוגות דתיים הנתקלים בבעיות פוריות .
מי כמונו יודעים את הצער והחוסר האונים של זוגות אלו ורבים הזוגות השוחרים למכון פוע"ה ומבקשים גם הדרכה רפואית וגם פסק הלכתי. חשוב מאוד שיהיה לזוגות אלו גם חומר כתוב בטוב טעם ודעת על התהליכים הרופאים וכן רקע הלכתי.
זוג שיקרא ספר זה הוא יכנס לטיפולים בצורה בטוחה ורגועה יותר וגם יהיה ברור לו מה הם השאלות ההלכתיות ומתי הוא חייב לשאול רב.

כמו שספרכם הקודם התקבל בצבור באהדה גדולה והוא כמגדל אור לאלפי זוגות בכל הנושא של הריון אנו תפילה שגם ספר זה יהיה אהוב על הצבור ויעמוד לזכותו ולבני ביתו.

בברכת התורה ולומדיה,

הרב מנחם בורשטין
ראש המכון

Bar-Ilan University (RA)
School of Social Work
52900 Ramat-Gan, Israel

Tel: 972-3-5318355 טל'
Fax: 972-3-5347228 פקס.
E-Mail: swschool@mail.biu.ac.il

אוניברסיטת בר-אילן (ע"ר)
בי"ס לעבודה סוציאלית
רמת-גן 52900

Of the scores of books reaching the shelves each year which purport to shed new light on some aspect of human suffering, few contribute in any concrete way to substantive understanding or significant problem solving, In their latest volume, "The Third Key," Baruch and Michal Finkelstein have again shown that they are among those rare authors who not only are expert in their field, but who can also provide helpful information in a manner that is both respectful and compassionate.

The Finkelsteins fully explore the challenges faced by couples confronting the anguish and frustrations of infertility and do so from perspectives including each partner, the couple dynamic and the social context. Using traditional Jewish sources as their echoing theme, they provide a rich source of practical, emotional and spiritual guidance to those searching for explanations, support and specific advice. Their down-to-earth approach and readable style make this volume useful and available to a wide range of potential readers, including those unfamiliar with Jewish citations and concepts.

As an academic and marital therapist, I see this book as valuable for couples struggling to bring children into the world and for students and professionals seeking to understand this phenomenon and learn how best to be helpful. I would also recommend that family and friends, often puzzled by how to respond in a positive manner, be encouraged to make use of this unique resource.

We all look forward to the day when technology renders infertility a problem of only historical interest. Until that time, "The Third Key", is now and will remain an essential tool.

Dr. David S. Ribner

School of Social Work
Bar-Ilan University
Ramat Gan Israel

Marital Therapist
Jerusalem

To Cousin Amy

חנה בת מוטל ודישה
Toyen הי״ד
ד׳ תמוז תשל״ז – כ״ג אלול תשס״א

Taken from us
in the Twin Towers on Sept. 11, 2001.

The way you departed will never be forgotten,
The way you lived will always be remembered.

Your love, warmth, and beauty
will stay with us forever.

תנצב״ה

This book is dedicated to the memory
of our Uncle Nat

נחום בן ברוך
פינקלשטיין
י׳ מרחשון תרע״ב – ד׳ אלול תשס״ג

Dedicated brother, loving uncle.

You kept us together in hard times
and in good times.

We were all your children.

There was only one Uncle Nat.

תנצב״ה

Contents

Acknowledgments

WITH GRATITUDE TO THE Almighty Who has been so generous to us in so many ways, we have finally seen the fruit of our efforts in the "birth" of *The Third Key*. It has taken a long time.

Upon the publication of our first book, *B'sha'ah Tovah: A Jewish Woman's Clinical and Halachic Guide to Pregnancy and Childbirth* (Feldheim Publishers, 1993), we decided to continue jointly publishing works in the area of family health from a Torah perspective. With the encouragement of Marsi Tabak, former editor-in-chief of Feldheim Publishers (may God grant her a speedy and complete recovery), we began research on infertility. The initial steps in beginning this book were taken twelve years ago, but throughout all the interruptions, setbacks, additional research, complications, and changes, we never lost faith that this work would eventually see the light of day. ברוך שהחיינו וקיימנו והגיענו לזמן הזה.

It is our pleasure to thank all those who have contributed to this work. We would first like to thank all the couples who gave us their insights and perspectives on the topic: Some of them discussed various aspects of infertility with us, some read parts of the book and offered suggestions, and some wrote us letters about their infertility experiences. Sensitivity demands that their names remain confidential. We hope that when they see this book on people's shelves, they will get satisfaction in knowing that they were a part of it.

Our appreciation is also extended to the professionals who contributed to the book by reading the sections relevant to their fields of expertise:

To Rabbi Zev Leff of Moshav Matityahu, Israel, who read the Torah sections and graced this book with his introduction. His great *ahavas Yisrael* and his sterling erudition make it a privilege to know him.

We thank Professor Ehud Margalioth, director of the fertility clinic at Shaare Zedek Medical Center in Jerusalem, who sat with Michal for many days and reviewed every medical section of this book in its entirety, offering his recommendations and adding the practical professional advice that only someone of his stature and experience could do.

Many thanks to our good friend, former neighbor, and "role model," Dr. David Ribner, for reviewing the sections of this book which deal with the marital relationship and the psychological ramifications of infertility. Dr. Ribner is a prominent academic and an experienced marital therapist, and it gave us much confidence to know that he approved the book's content.

We thank our friends, Rabbis Gideon Wietzman and Menachem Burstein from Machon Puah in Jerusalem, for reading the entire book and offering suggestions on the halachic aspects. Machon Puah is a non-profit institute run according to halachah that helps many couples in their quest to have children. May God give them strength to continue their highly regarded work.

We are so greatly honored that Professor Avraham Steinberg of Shaare Zedek hospital took time out of his busy schedule to read the book and give his letter of recommendation. Professor Steinberg is an internationally renowned physician, academic scholar, and *talmid chacham*. His tremendous knowledge of both Torah and medicine is preceded only by the loving care with which he treats his patients. May the Almighty grant him many years of strength to continue his work in Torah and medicine.

Another great honor for this book and for us is the approbation of Rabbi David Cohen of Congregation Gvul Ya'avetz, Brooklyn, New York, who read the entire manuscript and offered his comments and suggestions. Rabbi Cohen spent a great deal of time with us over the phone, taking an interest in every aspect of the book. He is an immensely knowledgeable *talmid chacham* and *posek*, and one of the nicest people you could know. His recommendations and insights are included in the book, sometimes with his name and sometimes without. We thank Rabbi Cohen from the bottom of our heart.

ומחיל אל חיל, we also merited to have the involvement of Rabbi Yisroel Belsky, Rosh Yeshiva of Torah Vodaath in Brooklyn, New York. Rabbi Belsky advised us on how to relate to some of the book's more controversial halachic issues. Rabbi Belsky has studied the medical issues in depth and is extremely knowledgeable in these areas. He is very careful in his approach to rendering halachic decisions, weighing every question with the utmost care. He read over this book with great interest, for which we are most grateful to him. We were honored to receive his beautiful approbation.

The Jewish People are indeed fortunate to have two such *gedolim* in their midst.

Most of all, we would like to thank the editorial, design, and production staff at Feldheim Publishers, Jerusalem. They worked hard in turning our ideas into a book. First and foremost, our thanks go to R' Yaakov Feldheim, who took a personal interest in the content of this work. He believed in its importance *l'shem Shamayim*. Second, we would like to thank Joyce Bennett, who oversaw the editing process and who was consulted on some of the more sensitive aspects of this book. We would also like to thank Bracha Steinberg for her beautiful design of this book, as well as Michael Silverstein for his clear charts and gorgeous cover. It was a pleasure to work with each and every one of you.

We are especially grateful to our editor, Deena Nataf. Deena did much more than dot the i's and cross the t's. Her knowledge of Torah and her *chochmas chaim* contributed greatly to this book. There were times when working with Deena was reminiscent of banging out *sugiyos* with a *chavrusa* in the *beis midrash*. She had to deal with all of our changes and additions, and somehow she kept everything under control. It is hard to imagine how this work would have turned out without Deena's professional expertise and input.

May God grant all those at Feldheim Publishers the merit to continue to grace Jewish homes with timely, contemporary works of Torah — ויהא חלקנו בחלקם.

Michal and Baruch Finkelstein
Beit El, Israel
Rosh Chodesh Shevat 5765

Foreword
by Rabbi Zev Leff

THE MOTHER OF Rav Shmuel Wosner of Bnei Brak, Israel, used to pray: "Help me, God, until You help me. Help me cope with the problem until You remove it or correct it." In our daily *Shemoneh Esrei* prayer, the seventh blessing is the supplication for redemption. However, it isn't until the fourteenth and the fifteenth blessings that we actually ask for the rebuilding of Jerusalem and the Temple, and the coming of *Mashiach*. Rashi explains that the redemption referred to in the seventh blessing is the ongoing daily redemption that individuals need in their personal trials and tribulations until the ultimate Redemption, the *Geulah Sheleimah*, will finally come.

King Solomon relates in the book of *Mishlei* (12:25): "A person who has a worry that weighs heavily on his heart should minimize it and reduce it." The Talmudic Rabbis Rav Ami and Rav Assi offered two methods to accomplish this goal (*Yoma* 75a): first, try to remove it from the focus of your attention, and second, discuss the problem with others. Many infertile couples suffer from worry and emotional pain. Obviously, the most desirable way to remove this worry is to discover that a baby is on the way. However, until that blessing comes, couples must have a short-term plan for reducing their anguish.

Taking Rav Ami and Rav Assi's second suggestion has many benefits. Discussing one's troubles with sympathetic and empathetic listeners can bring solace as well as good advice. A shoulder to cry on, a person who will share your pain, will make you feel less alone. This will help lighten your load. Moreover, you will see how others have dealt with similar problems and have been successful in solving them, which will give you hope and strengthen your determination.

The Rabbis exhort us (*Pirkei Avos* 1:7): "Don't give up and despair because of misfortune." No matter how bad the situation gets, no matter how dismal it looks, a person should never give up hope. Every salvation comes to the world because people want it to come, because they look forward to it, and because they haven't given up hope. According to halachah, if one gives up hope in finding a lost article, that "separates" the item from him and makes it ownerless. Similarly, when a person gives up hope of salvation, he "separates" himself from that very salvation. A person can feel alone, abandoned, despondent, and hopeless. But when others strengthen him and give him encouragement, then they strengthen each other; each gives the other hope.

There is yet another benefit to discussing one's fertility problems, especially with others who are in a similar situation. The Talmud relates (*Shabbos* 31a) that when one faces the Heavenly Court he will be asked six questions. These questions correspond to the six orders of the Mishnah. The fourth question, corresponding to *seder Nezikin*, Damages, is, "Did you look forward to and anticipate God's ultimate salvation? Did you take care not to damage others, being concerned about their welfare?" — for ultimately that will bring salvation. Sharing the pain of one's infertility with others who are similarly suffering transfers one's concern for his own plight into a concern for the plight of others. And it also puts the concern into a more universal, selfless yearning, which is in itself a factor that will aid one to merit being blessed with children.

The Lakewood *mashgiach*, Rav Matisyahu Solomon, said that praying for others is a merit for receiving all things. We have all heard the famous *gemara*, "One who requests mercy (i.e. prays) for his fellowman, if he needs the same thing, he is answered first" (*Bava Kama* 92a). When it comes to fertility, this concept is even more potent. Avraham Avinu must have prayed heartfelt, tearful prayers for decades. Yet when was he answered? After he prayed for Avimelech and his family to have children. *That* prayer caused the change in Avraham's life; not the prayers that he prayed for himself. And later on, when Yitzchak has to pray for children, we read that "he stood opposite his wife" and prayed for her. Yitzchak learned from his father that it isn't enough to pray for himself. Instead he prayed not for himself to have children, but rather for his wife to have children, and those were the prayers that were answered.

One can long for children to fulfill his or her own innate parental instincts to nurture a child, as well as to achieve a sort of physical immortality. All these are positive motivations. However, one must also consider the more sublime and universal mandate to have children, the Divine command to be fruitful and multiply and fill the earth. God tells us through the prophet Yeshayahu, "I did not create [the earth] to be desolate, but rather to be populated" (*Yeshayahu* 45:18). One must yearn to produce additional "soldiers in God's army of servants" to fulfill His will and inhabit and perfect His world.

Consequently, the third question the Heavenly Court will ask, which corresponds to the order of *Nashim*, laws dealing with women, marriage, divorce, etc., is, "Did you occupy yourself with populating the world?" Not, "Did you have children?" for that is not totally in one's control. Rather, Did you make the attempt, did you concern yourself with bringing a new generation into the world, to populate the earth, to bring it closer to perfection?

In the last decade, medicine has advanced in the area of infertility in phenomenal ways. There are a host of procedures being done today to enable people to have children, who, fifty years ago, could not have done so without open miracles. This makes it much easier, because not everyone who needs a miracle will merit one!

Why did God specifically allow these breakthroughs in medicine and science to occur in our generation? About eighty years ago, the Chafetz Chaim observed that history was progressing much faster than it had ever done before. Governments were being toppled, states and countries were being created and changed; many things were happening as if the world were on "fast forward." What had previously taken hundreds of years was now happening within decades. The Chafetz Chaim explained that as we are getting closer and closer to the coming of *Mashiach,* God has a lot of "accounts to settle," and they have to be settled before *Mashiach* comes. So He is settling all these accounts very, very quickly.

And there is another account that has to be settled before *Mashiach* comes. The Sages relate (*Yevamos* 62a) that *Mashiach* will not come until all the souls that were created are brought into this physical world. God sees that it is getting close to the deadline and there are many souls in Heaven who haven't yet come into the world. So He has directed breakthroughs in science and medicine to make it possible to bring more and more of these souls into this world in a shorter amount of time, in order to bring *Mashiach* closer. This explains another interesting point, which is that those who need modern medical technology to conceive have a higher rate of multiple births — twins, triplets, and quadruplets. If God already made these procedures in order to bring these souls down, He apparently wants to bring down as many as He can at one time.

We learned above that Rav Ami and Rav Assi's first method for reducing and minimizing worry was to try to take it out of your mind, which means to direct your focus away from the worry, the trials and tribulations. A close reading of the original text shows that the rabbis didn't say to take the worry out of your heart but rather to take it off your mind. You can't take it out of your heart; it's always going to be there. But you *can* focus your mind, your intellect, on other things that reduce the pain in your heart.

There are various ways to accomplish this. The first is to recognize that having a child is not the only important aspect of your life. You must focus on the many other important parts of your life and personality as well. This idea is illustrated in the episode of Chanah (*I Shemuel,* chapter1). Chanah was so distraught because she didn't have children that she didn't want to eat. Her husband told her, "Chanah, why do you weep, and why do you not eat, and why is your heart troubled? Am I not better to you than ten children?" Then is says that after Chanah finished eating and drinking, she got up, still weeping, and went to cry her heart out to God. What caused her to change her mind and decide to eat?

Originally, Chanah felt that having a child was the only thing that made her life worthwhile, and if she couldn't have one then her life was worthless. Therefore, there was no reason to eat, for eating means that one is concerned about living. If life is worthless, then why bother eating? But then her husband essentially told her, "Chanah, there is more to our life than just our desire to have a child and our lack of children — we have each other. Am I not as important to you as at least ten children? This doesn't take away our desire to have children, but recognize the fact that there is something special about our being a married couple." When Chanah heard this, she realized that it was worthwhile to eat. It didn't take the pain out of her heart; she still wanted a child. Her husband could not take its place. But she did have a reason to eat, a reason to live.

A person who is childless should remember that they have been spared other suffering: there are those who can't find their mate, and suffer being alone. Others suffer from illnesses, or from domestic strife. Infertility is not the only focus in life; it is one focus among others. Most other aspects of your life probably bring you immense joy and fulfillment, not more pain.

Another way to reduce the pain in your heart is as follows: Remember that it is not only the final salvation and the realizing of your goal that is significant and should bring you happiness; the entire process of reaching that salvation is also significant and purposeful. The book *Sha'arei Teshuvah* (*Sha'ar* 2, paragraphs 3–5) says that when a person is delivered from a misfortune, he should not limit his thanks just for the deliverance, but he should thank God for the misfortune itself, because he gained from it. He should thank God for the benefits it brought him. True, the *Sha'arei Teshuvah* does not say that when a person is experiencing a misfortune he should thank God for it. That is beyond human capabilities — at least for most of us. But the *Sha'arei Teshuvah* does say that when you are delivered from the misfortune, you then must look back and appreciate that the misfortune was also for a purpose, it also served a good end, and it's also something for which to thank God. If one is still in the throes of his misfortune, he's not looking back, so he can't really thank God for it, but at least intellectually he can understand that in truth the misfortune is for a purpose and he is gaining from it. God is not intending to harm him, but rather to give him a test because He knows that person needs it, and He knows that he is going to gain from this test.

When Chanah thanked God for giving her a child, she opened her prayer with the following words: "*Ein tzur ke'Elokeinu*," there is no rock like God. The Rabbis comment (*Berachos* 10a), "Don't read *tzur* — rock, but *tzayar* — artist; there is no artist like God." Rav Shraga Feivel Mendlowitz, *zt"l*, explained this metaphor in the following way: If you take a kindergarten child and tell him to draw a picture of the person standing in front of him, he draws a circle for the head, a line down for the body, two lines out for arms, two lines down for legs, two dots for eyes, a dot in the middle for a nose, and a big smile and he's finished, and you know exactly what he's drawing every step of the way. However, if you tell Rembrandt to paint the same picture, he doesn't start with a circle on the canvas, he dabs some red paint here and black paint there. A novice who doesn't know anything about art will say to Rembrandt, "I hate to say this, but you just ruined this canvas. Red paint, black paint. I'll get you another canvas. Start again, make the circle and let's get on with it." Rembrandt will tell this person, "This painting is going to take me six months. If after six months you have any questions, please ask.

But at this point could you just sit quietly, have some patience, and wait until you see the whole picture." In six months when the picture is finished, the person will see that the red was needed for contrast, the black was needed for a shadow, and everything fits the picture beautifully. But if you don't see the whole picture, you can't appreciate its fragments.

So too, said Rav Shraga Feivel Mendlowitz, God is painting a beautiful panorama of history, and we are in the middle. We see blotches of red and blotches of black, blotches in Jewish history of holocausts, pogroms, and inquisitions. In our own personal life each one of us has a little part of that picture and we see in our part things we don't understand, things that look like a total mess, total destruction, totally negative. But God says, Wait — have a little faith and trust Me, I know what I'm painting. To you, it looks very destructive and negative. If you could see the finished picture, however, you would know that eventually everything is for the good. And that's why we say on what appears to be calamity, *Gam zu l'tova,* this is also for the good. We never say that we see it as good now; we can't. We see red blotches and black blotches; it looks like destruction. But *gam zu l'tova,* this is also for the good. I believe that the misfortune that I am going through has a purpose to it, and that God knows what that purpose is — and ultimately I will gain from it too.

The word *nes,* miracle, is composed of two letters, *nun* and *samech.* The *nun* is the first letter of *nefilah,* falling, while the *samech* represents the word *somech,* supporting. The *nes* is composed of both the fall and the support, not either one by itself. Both are important. Similarly, the *Chiddushei haRim* says that when a person thanks God for a salvation, he has to say both *Hallel* and *Hoda'ah. Hallel,* praise, is for the salvation. *Hoda'ah,* acknowledgment, is an admission that the misfortune was also necessary and that he gained from it.

Our matriarch Rachel cried for her children. How many tears do we shed that we think are wasted, destructive, negative? But the prophet (*Yirmeyahu* 31:14) tells us that our mother Rachel's tears bring hope and ultimately salvation. Tears are the oil that lubricates the salvation. Even tears, even misfortune and suffering, have a positive purpose.

People in our generation, even religious people, think that the purpose of life is to be "fulfilled." People of low spiritual stature want to be fulfilled in very crass ways, and people on a higher spiritual plane want to be fulfilled in more noble ways. But it all boils down to the same philosophy: My purpose in life is to be "fulfilled," and therefore I will seek fulfillment by any means. But this is not a Torah perspective! Our purpose in life is not to be fulfilled; rather, we were put on this earth to fulfill a purpose. How do we know what our purpose is? Young people may think that one day a little piece of paper is going to fall out of the heavens with their Divine mission and purpose written on it. Older people know that this doesn't happen.

Someone once asked me this question. He was a very fine man who was dying of a brain tumor. He was in his forties. The doctor said there was no more that medical science could do for him. He was fully conscious, walking around, but they told him that it was only a matter of time. He went home from the hospital knowing that he had only weeks to live. He called me and said, "Rabbi, I must speak to you." So I went to speak to him. It was right before Yom Kippur, and he told me the following: "I have no complaints against God. He gave me a beautiful life, a beautiful family. I've had a very special, fulfilling life, and I don't have any complaints if God feels that this is the amount of time that He wanted to give me. I only have thanks for what He gave me." You can see what kind of person this was. He said, however, that one thing was gnawing at him: "I want to know, Rabbi, did I fulfill my purpose, my mission in this world?" I told him, "Your mission and purpose in life is to face all of the situations that God brings you in this world, with your abilities, capabilities, and talents. Those who come in contact with you, those whom you can affect, those who affect you, where you live, the era in which you live — to take all these factors together and to take the responsibility to react in a way that you know the Torah wants you to react, that's your purpose. It's revealed to you second by second, day by day. God puts you in the place that He wants, with the circumstances that you have to face, with the problems that you are given, with the opportunities that you are given, and that is your mission and purpose. Live up to the situations that you are placed in. You can't control what comes your way — that's all in God's hands."

When we are young, we may think we can control our lives. But as we get older, we learn that there are many things we cannot control. Ultimately, we come to the realization that there is nothing in our control except how we react to and deal with the situations that we encounter in life.

The nine blessings that form the Rosh Hashanah *Musaf* service are based on Chanah's prayer. She mentions God's name nine times in that prayer. After Chanah had that child that she wanted so much, she looked back and she understood that God creates the framework, the parameters of one's life. When He didn't want her to have a child, she didn't, and she had to react to that in the proper way. And when He wanted her to have a child, she did, and now she had to react to that in the proper way.

Of those nine blessing, three are special additions. The first of those additional blessings is called *Malchuyos,* and it relates to God's royal sovereignty. God is the King, He "calls the shots," He creates the situations, the parameters. And only after that comes the second of these special additional blessings, *Zichronos,* Remembrances. We remind ourselves of how we are supposed to react within the situations that God gives us. And the way to do that is through the third of these special additional blessings, *Shofaros,* the sounding of the ram's horn — awakening ourselves and inspiring ourselves to function properly.

The Midrash relates (*Bereishis Rabbah* 58:3) that Rabbi Akiva was delivering a lesson and the audience started falling asleep. (Nothing has changed in two thousand years.) Rabbi Akiva wanted to wake them up, so he said, "Why did Queen Esther deserve to rule over 127 provinces? Because her great-great-grand-mother, our matriarch Sarah, lived 127 years. Therefore she ruled over 127 provinces." The students woke up.

What is the connection between Sarah's 127 years and Esther's 127 provinces? I think Rabbi Akiva was telling them the following: When it says that Sarah lived 127 years, it doesn't mean that mean that 127 years passed over her. But as our rabbis relate (Rashi, *Shemos* 23:1), all of Sarah's 127 years were equally for the good. This is impossible to understand literally. The 90 years that Sarah was barren were not equally as good as the day that Yitzchak Avinu was born or the day of his *bris*. The night that she was dragged to Pharaoh was not equally as good as the joyful days and nights that she had raising her son Yitzchak. It doesn't say that they all were equally good, but rather that they were all equally *for* the good. Sarah had the ability to control not the situations that came her way, but how she used them and reacted to them. And Sarah used even the most dire situation for the good. She didn't despair, she wasn't despondent, she didn't give up. She used every situation as a means for growth. She used all of them in a positive way.

Queen Esther had a miserable life. She was snatched from her home, she was forced to marry a non-Jew, she had children, the Sages tell us, who were brought up as non-Jews. One of them even became the king of Persia. Is that the *Yiddishe nachas* that Queen Esther wanted? And she was severed from the Jewish People. You would think that Esther would have been despondent, would have given up. But she looked at Sarah and said, if Sarah could make the best of every second of her life, then I can too. And she merited to rule over 127 provinces in a way that brought salvation to the Jewish People.

Take advantage of this precious book. It can serve as a "good friend," a sounding board. It is an excellent source of advice and strength, while its universal appeal makes one aware that others have the same trials and worries. Moreover, it gives you a broader view of your infertility and a more spiritual, selfless perspective. Utilize the Torah wisdom it conveys to focus your mind beyond your own infertility misfortune. Internalize its words of direction, comfort, enlightenment, and encouragement.

I commend the authors, Rabbi Baruch and Mrs. Michal Finkelstein, for a superb job. Their book is an excellent combination of medical and psychological information and advice bolstered by a firm, Torah-true outlook and perspective. May this book be as successful as their previous one on pregnancy and childbirth, *B'sha'ah Tovah,* serving as an invaluable aid to countless couples who will find in it enlightenment, comfort, and a source of strength and blessing. May the authors see much *nachas* from all their endeavors, and from all those who will benefit from this book and be blessed with the children they now yearn for.

With Torah blessings,
Rabbi Zev Leff
Moshav Matityahu

Preface

FERTILITY RESEARCH IS ARGUABLY the most dynamic area of medicine today. The study of fertility branches into numerous areas, and many of those areas are the focal point of ethical and theological debates.

Fertility research has even affected the political world, as the ethical debates concern government policy. The media has furnished us with headlines that raise many questions about scientific research and human limitations. We read of "miracle" babies born to 50- and 60-year-old mothers; of procedures that can enable couples to select embryos that do not carry genetic disorders; and the possibility that couples can choose the sex of their baby and even his or her eye color!

Yet behind all the razzmatazz of high-tech breakthroughs, and futuristic "Brave New World" scenarios, stands the reason for which all this technology is being developed — a barren couple whose interest is simply to hold their child in their arms. The desire of this couple to have a baby is an inherent aspiration that is fueled by society's expectations of them to build a family. Trying to have a baby will become a full-time occupation, and eventually can become an obsession. For those who strive to be parents, the ethical debates over the new technologies are dwarfed by the magnitude of their longing.

Today, for reasons that have not have been completely determined, infertility is on the rise. Approximately 10 to 15 percent of couples in America suffer from infertility. Studies confirm that infertility is a psychological crisis. The crisis affects both husband and wife, but it is usually the wife who is more profoundly affected.

There is an abundance of literature today dealing with both the medical aspects and the emotional anguish of infertility. If one performs a search on the Internet, he or she will find over four hundred and fifty book titles dealing with infertility — and the list grows monthly. Some of the books are written for professionals, some for laypeople. Some books are written by professionals, and others by laypeople who write about their personal experiences. The latter give the couple the comfort that they are not alone and that their feelings are not unusual. Their problems are the same as most couples who live with and try to overcome infertility. The fact that so many people who went through infertility feel the need to write about it shows that it is a singular and significant experience.

The infertile couple suffers in six areas:

◆ **Spiritually**: Desiring a child is natural and inherent in all of us. Being denied this natural "right" — or, as some professionals have called it, "the mandate to motherhood" — leaves a person feeling empty and unfulfilled, regardless of how successful they are in other areas of life.

◆ **Socially**: The couple feels alienated and isolated from the fertile world, which seems to emphasize the importance of raising children and to glorify the enjoyment of family life.

◆ **Theologically**: Couples, and especially religious couples, have trouble with the fact that the Almighty and Merciful God Who can create Heaven and earth, Who can split the sea and can stop the sun from setting, "cannot" give them a child. This is a great source of anguish and stress for them since they think they are being punished by God or that He hates them.

◆ **Psychologically**: Infertility causes tremendous feelings of jealousy and anger toward the fertile word, including fertile friends, neighbors, and siblings. Dealing with these extremely negative feelings is very difficult. Infertile women feel terrible for having these feelings. Because they have them, they are plagued by guilt and shame. Ridding themselves of these feelings is essential for their psychological well-being.

◆ **Physically**: Medical fertility procedures for the women are painful. They demand much of her time and take her away from her professional life.

◆ **Interpersonally**: The relationship between husband and wife is greatly affected. The couple quarrels. Intimacy is damaged.

When considering treatment of the infertile couple, not only is the clinical advice important, but advice on how to cope with the infertility — even after treatments are over and there is a positive result — is important as well.

Some people may think that once you finally have a baby, the ordeal is over. But the experience is never completely over. Although after one either has a child, adopts, or resolves to being childless — and although one can have a happy life in any of these circumstances — infertility will remain a part of every couple who went through it. It will always be remembered as a seminal phase in their lives. After going through the infertility experience, certain aspects of life become clearer than ever. God, one's life's priorities, friendships, family relationships, loneliness, hope, prayer, the beauty of a child, and life itself — they all take on a different meaning. There are certain things in life that only couples who went through infertility will ever understand.

These couples know exactly what we are talking about.

Introduction

THIS BOOK WAS WRITTEN as a guide to the childless couple who is seeking support and direction in achieving fertility. The couple interested in knowing the Torah's viewpoints regarding both clinical procedures and psychological aspects will find this book beneficial. We also believe that people who went through infertility in the past but now either have a child or have resolved to live a life without children will reap benefit from reading this book as well. This book should put much of their experience into perspective.

People who are close to childless couples should read this book too. They will gain much understanding of what their relatives or friends are going through. And finally, this book will be of benefit to rabbis, social workers, and anybody else interested in understanding the special situation that childless couples find themselves in. Even those who just want to get a fuller understanding of the Biblical personalities who suffered through infertility will benefit from this book.

OBJECTIVES

This book has a few objectives. One is to supply the reader with the most up-to-date fertility information possible together with the *halachos* that are relevant to the treatments and procedures.

Another is to show that the Torah and our many Jewish sources have much to say about infertility, and offer a great deal of support. Our Sages' wisdom and insight on the subject are a source of strength and encouragement. And there is much to learn from the many great *tzaddikim* who went through the same suffering that the average childless couple endures.

Finally, one of the aims of this book is to discuss significant theological issues and psychological/emotional aspects of infertility from a Torah perspective. These are discussed throughout the book.

WHAT WAS NOT INCLUDED IN THE BOOK

Even though financial issues are a major source of stress, we have chosen not to engage in any significant discussion about these concerns, as they vary from country to country, from insurance policy to insurance policy, and from couple to couple. We have also left out names and addresses of specific fertility clinics and support organizations, as well as names of rabbis who are known to be experts in the field. Since this information is constantly changing, any list would be outdated by the time this book hits the shelves. We are confident that you will find the right resource people and organizations for you and your specific situation.

HALACHAH

About the Halachah

The *halachos* that appear in this book are only *halachos* that pertain to fertility. Other *halachos* that may be indirectly relevant to this topic are not included. Most of the *halachos* are woven into the clinical sections of the book. Each halachah appears at the end of the discussion of each treatment. The *halachos* can be broken up into three categories: Those relating to the treatments themselves, *niddah* questions, and questions about treatments on Shabbos. In addition, there are also three chapters solely devoted to halachah. Chapter 5 discusses the mitzvah to be fruitful and multiply, chapter 21 explains the halachah regarding artificial insemination from the husband, and chapter 22 explains the *halachos* of third-party fertility. There are no special chapters explaining the laws of *niddah* or Shabbos; they are cited in concise form whenever relevant.

Why Ask the Rabbi?

The reader, while searching for halachic solutions in this book (and many other modern, practical halachic books, for that matter), may feel a bit disappointed when rather than getting a one-word, yes or no, forbidden or permissible answer, the only advice he receives is, ask your rabbi. "Great! I could have thought of that on my own," he thinks. Why do writers of practical halachah books constantly instruct their readers to ask their rabbi or a halachic authority?

Halachic books which are intended for readers with innumerable different levels of knowledge and background are not really books of *piskei halachah* (halachic rulings). Their purpose is to guide the reader in the halachic considerations of a question, and *general* halachic conclusions, but they are not meant to replace the ruling of a Rav. Nothing can replace that. The purpose is *education,* not authoritative *psak.*

The same way the medical sections in this book are not meant to replace the doctor, but rather to inform you of your medical options and to enhance your awareness, so too are the halachic sections of this book. Just as it would be unfathomable to only rely on this book without going to your doctor, so too is it unfathomable to rely on this book for your halachic solutions.

It is to your advantage to ask your rabbi a question only after you have a halachic background in the area you are asking about. You may even open up a dialogue about it. You will understand his ruling better if you are educated in the subject matter. Being educated will help you understand the rabbi's ruling.

Even when the halachah in this book seems black and white, it is still preferable to ask your rabbi. You can show him what was said in this book and ask him if he agrees. There may be some detail in your personal situation that cannot be taken into account in the book that may change the ruling for you. It is impossible to consider everybody's personal circumstances in a book, which is why you need a Rav.

Another reason why we suggest asking your rabbi is because of the constant change in and improvement of medical research and clinical technique. Especially in the area of infertility, treatment constantly changes and improves. One alteration in any procedure could affect the halachah. Since it is impossible to foresee all the changes, as well as differences in technical procedure between clinics, it is therefore recommended to check with your Rav. Parts of this book may become obsolete before we print the next, updated edition. The *halachos* in this book pertain to medical information known at the time of this writing — so always ask your Rav.

We are aware that there are people who live outside Torah communities, but are still concerned about doing the right thing. Not everybody has access to a Rav. So in writing the halachah, we took that into consideration as well. If you don't have a Rav, it is better to rely on the halachic sections in this book than to decide on your own. However, we strongly suggest that you find a Rav.

Halachic Considerations for this Book

In presenting the halachah in this book, we were confronted with the problem of deciding between the great *poskim*. Because of the dynamic nature of Jewish law, halachic opinions vary greatly. How could we determine what to write? At first, we thought we'd gear the halachah according to majority rules, but that wasn't possible. A majority opinion today may be a minority opinion ten years from now. And even if we were to decide based on the majority, how would we determine that majority?

We then thought to cite all the halachic opinions, leaving each problem with the suggestion, "Ask your Rav." But that didn't seem fair, since everyone knows that they could ask their Rav, and reading all the different opinions without any one prevailing *psak* would only confuse the reader even more. Even though we suggest many times to ask your Rav, we didn't do so to solve a halachic dispute.

Therefore, the decision was to pick one *posek* and cite his opinions throughout the book. In each case that he wrote about, whether he had a strict opinion or a lenient one, whether it was the majority opinion among the modern-day *poskim* or the minority opinion, he would be the *"posek"* of this book. For several reasons, we chose Rav Moshe Feinstein, *zt"l,* whose rulings are published in *Igros Moshe.* In the footnotes, sources for other opinions are cited. Also, in the three halachah chapters mentioned above (5, 21, and 22), the other opinions and their reasoning are brought down. In the clinical sections of the book where the practical halachah is found, the deciding *psak* is according to Rav Moshe. If your Rav has a different opinion, that is fine, but this book goes according to Rav Moshe Feinstein as he wrote in *Igros Moshe.* We pray to God that we understood him correctly. In cases where Rav Moshe didn't write on a particular subject, we cite other opinions.

THE DIFFERENCE BETWEEN THE DOCTOR, THE THERAPIST, AND THE RAV

In your attempts to achieve fertility there will be several professionals accompanying you along the way. There will be the medical professionals — doctors, nurses, lab technicians, pharmacists, dieticians, etc. There may be a therapist or group therapy leader, and there will be your religious guide — the rabbi.

Each one has a different function and don't expect one to know the work of the other. The doctor should not teach you halachah. Don't expect him or her to even be knowledgeable in halachah, and don't expect his or her suggestions to be necessarily halachically correct. It is better that the doctor only informs you of all your medical options and lets you get halachic guidance from your Rav. You need to bring the medical advice to the rabbi to see if the recommended procedures are halachically acceptable. You can then come back to the doctor and say either that a certain procedure is permitted, or that your religion doesn't allow it, so please let's go with another option.

If you go to a therapist for counseling, which during stressful times such as fertility treatments is recommended, you need to be aware that the therapist is not like your rabbi and his or her objectives differ from his. Many people go to both their religious leader and their therapist for counseling assuming that they are in the same profession, just wearing a different cap. That is not the case. Your therapist is trying to help you in certain areas and your Rav is trying to help you in others. Sometimes the Rav is interested in helping you the same way a therapist would help you, but he has a different perspective, and different resources to work with.

The goal of the therapist is to help you cope, or to feel positive about what you are doing and the choices you are making. That is very important. The Rav's objective, however, is to guide you to carry out God's will in the midst of this trying experience and to strengthen your faith and courage. You ask your rabbi, how do we serve God in our situation? You ask your therapist, how do we live day by day with all of the difficulties? To the rabbi, you ask, how do I strengthen my faith in God in light of the unpleasant events that have visited us? To the therapist you ask, how do we strengthen ourselves to get through this ordeal?

The therapist and the rabbi could work together very nicely, and they usually will, but they might not all the time. And the difference between "feeling good" and doing God's will should be clear to you. The therapist has the task of helping you cope with infertility within the halachic considerations and restrictions, and the Rav should try and help you in your faith and spiritual endeavors in light of your special situation.

Another difference is that the therapist will not let him- or herself get personally involved in the therapeutic relationship. In the counseling profession, getting emotionally involved in a patient's situation is not recommended for many reasons. However, the rabbi should and probably will feel more personally involved in your situation.

LEARNING FROM THE LIVES OF TZADDIKIM

Who Were Our Mothers and Fathers?

Throughout this book there is much analysis of the behavior of the patriarchs and the matriarchs, as well as some other important Biblical figures. This may lead the reader to think that we should look at these spiritual giants in the same way that we would look at anybody. We have problems, they had problems. They quarreled, were envious, became depressed, were revengeful, etc. There is no difference between them and us. They were human.

Yes, they were human, and that is what makes them so special. But they were in a completely different "spiritual league." The level that they reached is miles past any that we could even grasp. This is important for us to remember, especially today, for there are many people who view the righteous personalities of the Torah as "regular people," with normal lives, with common strengths and faults, just like us. In order that readers not misunderstand us and think we are relating to our matriarchs and patriarchs in such a light, we must emphasize this is not the intention of our words at all. While we are to learn from and be strengthend by their lives, we all must view our forefathers and foremothers as the spiritual giants that they were.

These people reached the level of prophecy. Their lives were recorded in God's Book, and they were selected to be the parents of God's Chosen Nation. Even though we read about their feelings, and sometimes even their mistakes — for *Chazal* never hesitate to point out the errors of the *tzaddikim* of the Torah — nevertheless, they were the feelings and mistakes of great people. Learning about Rachel's jealousy of Leah, for example, will teach us a great deal about jealousy as it relates to infertility. It is not meant to teach us that Rachel is "just like us."

A THOUSAND PICTURES

We wrote this book with a feeling of trepidation. Infertility is a sensitive topic, and we were afraid of saying "the wrong thing" and offending someone. In the initial stages of work on this book, when we were first exposed to the magnitude of the experience and the intensity of the feelings it engendered, there were times that we actually trembled — who were we to talk to people about a condition such as infertility?

They say a picture paints a thousand words, but similarly, just one word can paint a thousand pictures. We pray that we have chosen our words properly. We hope we haven't painted too dreary a picture or made too light of a somber crisis. Everyone reacts differently, and we did not know if we were addressing couples who took their infertility in stride, or couples who were devastated by it — or were we perhaps speaking to the people who fit in between those two extremes?

We read over everything many, many times, and tried to anticipate reactions. We gave out chapters to childless couples for feedback. We tried our best to combine practicality, analysis, truthfulness, support, and sensitivity. That isn't an easy juggling act, so we pray that we were successful. If there is anything in this book that you find is missing the point, or exaggerating a point; if there is anything at all that offends your sensitivities or hurts you, please forgive us.

It is our heartfelt prayer that you will learn from the clinical information in this book and that you will understand your options within the fertility maze. We hope you will be more aware of the halachic considerations, and will gather strength, encouragement, and awareness from our Sages and the Biblical commentators in dealing with the emotional aspects of this trying experience. But most of all, we hope that you won't need this book. *Halevai* you should only read it out of curiosity, out of an interest in a subject that with God's help will one day be only history.

May you be successful in all your endeavors and may the Holder of the three keys grant you your deepest wish. May you become parents.

1.
The Key to Life

It is impossible for there not to be miracles.

(*Midrash Shochar Tov* 106)

A FEW KEYS

THERE IS A *MIDRASH* ABOUT keys. The *midrash* has a couple of variations, although the gist of it, as you will see below, is that God Himself supervises and is responsible for three specific physical acts.

The Talmud in tractate *Ta'anis*[1] states: "Rabbi Yochanan says: 'There are three keys (*mafteichos*) in the hand of haKadosh Baruch Hu that were not given in the hand of a messenger. They are: the key to rain, the key to a woman giving birth, and the key to *techias ha-meisim* — the resurrection of the dead. The key to rain, as it is written, "The Eternal *will open* (*yiftach*) for you His good treasury...to give you rain in its time"[2]; the key to a woman giving birth...as it is written, "God remembered Rachel, and He heard her and *He opened* (*vayiftach*) her womb"[3]; the key to *techias ha-meisim*...as it is written: "And you will know that I am your God as *I open*

1. 2a.
2. *Devarim* 28:12.
3. *Bereishis* 30:22.

(*b'fitchi*) your burial places."[4]"

In *Devarim Rabbah*[5] on the verse, "The Eternal will open for you His good treasury...to give you rain in its time," the version is: "What is the meaning of 'will open?' Rabbi Yochanan said, 'There are three keys in the hand of haKadosh Baruch Hu and no creation has control over them, not (even) an angel, and they are: the key to *techias ha-meisim*, the key to infertility (*akarus*),[6] and the key to rain.'"

The version in *Bereishis Rabbah*[7] is: "Rabbi Tanchuma in the name of Rav Bibi said, 'There are three keys in the hand of haKadosh Baruch Hu: the key to burial places (resurrection), the key to rain, and the key to the womb.'"

There is a version in *Osiyos d'Rabbi Akiva* (Midrashic literature) that says that God holds the key to a woman.[8] In *Pirkei d'Rabbi Eliezer* it says, "He holds the key to the treasury of souls."[9]

Basically, it is the same *midrash* with slight variations. There are differences in the order and differences in the wording. Excluding *Osiyos d'Rabbi Akiva* and *Pirkei d'Rabbi Eliezer*, the remaining three versions are similar in style. The Talmud lists: rain, a woman giving birth, and the resurrection. *Devarim Rabbah* has the opposite order: the resurrection, infertility, and rain. In *Bereishis Rabbah* the order is again different: the resurrection, rain, and a woman's womb.

The reason for the variations in the order is simple: it

---

4. *Yechezkel* 37:13.

5. 7:6, in *Parashas Ki Savo.*

6. This is also the version in *Midrash Tanchuma* (Buber edition), *Vayera* 35. See also *Midrash Tanchuma* (Buber), *Vayetze* 17, in the name of Rabbi Yochanan: "There are four keys in the hand... the key to infertility.

7. 73:4.

8. *Osiyos d'Rabbi Akiva, os zayin.*

9. *Pirkei d'Rebbi Eliezer* 44.

serves the purposes of each version. The tractate *Ta'anis* begins with the prayer for rain, so the version in the Talmud starts with rain, for that is the main subject. It then goes to "a woman giving birth," and ends with a future event. The *midrashim* had different purposes, as they were originally sermons delivered in the synagogue. The speaker's intention is to end with the point of his message, in order to make an impact on his audience. Both *Devarim Rabbah* and *Bereishis Rabbah* begin with resurrection. The reason for this is that each speaker wanted to begin his point with the obvious. It is obvious that only God holds the key to the resurrection, for it will be a supernatural occurrence. In *Devarim Rabbah*, the sermon was on the verse about rain, so the speaker ended his sermon with rain. In *Bereishis Rabbah* the aim of the speaker was to discuss Rachel's giving birth to Yosef, so his third key was the key to the womb. And since this book is about fertility, we have called it *The Third Key*.

The designation of this key is different in each *midrash*. It is called the key to a *chayah* – a woman giving birth, the key to *akarus* — barrenness or infertility, the key to the womb,[10] the key to a woman, and finally the key to the treasury of souls.

All of the above expressions have one thing in common, and that is that they are all another name for the key to the beginning of life. They are the same key. So whether it is called the key to a woman giving birth (*chayah*) or the key to infertility (*akarus*), it is just another word for the same idea. The Scriptural source for this key is the same in all the versions: "God remembered Rachel, and He heard her and *He opened*

---

10. See Tosafos on *Niddah* 16b, which explains that while there may be an angel responsible for pregnancy, birth is only in the hands of God. Even the *gemara* there tells us that the angel goes to God and asks Him about the personality of the fetus. In other words, only God gives permission for everything that will happen.

(*vayiftach*) her womb." In other words, the source comes from the story of an infertile woman who after many good deeds and much prayer finally gave birth.

The other two keys are also keys to life. One key is the key to rain, without which there would be no life, and the other is the key to the next life – the resurrection. The Gemara brings down another opinion which says that there is yet another key, and that is the key to livelihood. The Gemara then asks, "Why didn't Rabbi Yochanan [in *Ta'anis* 2a] count the fourth key?" The answer the Gemara gives is that the key of livelihood is included in the key of rain.[11] This makes sense, since in those days especially, people lived in an agricultural economy. Therefore, rain and livelihood were interlocked. So the bottom line of all these *midrashim* is that the keys to "life" are solely in the hands of the Al-mighty.[12]

GOD'S OCCUPATION

An aristocrat once asked Rabbi Yosi bar Chalafta, "In how many days did your God create the world?" He answered,

---

11. *Taanis* 2b. In Babylonia, Rabbi Yochanan's version was the accepted one, and in Eretz Yisrael the original version of four keys was accepted. *Bereishis Rabbah* mentions the key to livelihood in its list as "some say."

12. There is another interesting parallel to rain and fertility. We will discuss the teaching of *Chazal*, "Why were the patriarchs sterile? Because God craves the prayers of the righteous" (*Yevamos* 64a). The same teaching is by rain as well. The Talmud finds a contradiction between two verses concerning creation: "One verse says, 'The land sprouted vegetation' (*Bereishis* 1:12), referring to the third day, whereas another verse, when speaking of the sixth day, says, 'None...of the plants of the field [had] yet sprouted' (*Bereishis* 2:5). This teaches us that the plants commenced to grow but stopped just before they were about to break through the soil, until Adam came and prayed for rain for them; and when rain fell they sprouted forth. This teaches you that the Holy One, blessed be He, craves the prayers of the righteous" (*Chullin* 60b).

"In six days." She then asked, "What does God do since the days of Creation?" He answered that God is making *shidduchim* (matches). The aristocrat, trying to prove that this occupation wasn't so difficult, tried to play matchmaker on a grand scale with a thousand of her servants. It ended in disaster, as in the morning her servants were found with black eyes, bruised heads, and broken legs. She then called for Rabbi Yosi bar Chalafta and said, "There is no God like your God. Your Torah is truthful, praiseworthy, and beautiful."[13]

What is the meaning of this *midrash*? We know that God doesn't only make matches. He controls wars, establishes kingdoms, manages the weather, moves the solar systems, judges humanity, rules over the world, and directs history. He also makes matches.

Why did the question of the aristocrat begin with the six days of Creation? If the purpose of the *midrash* was to show how difficult it is to make a successful *shidduch,* then why was it connected to Creation?

Marriage is a direct continuation of the six days of the creation of the physical world. Only through loving couples does God want the world to continue. *Shidduchim* are a precondition for the fulfillment of the mitzvah to be fruitful and multiply, and that commandment is the fulfillment of the maintenance of God's world. The *midrash*'s intention was to illustrate that the whole topic of *kiyum olam* — the maintenance and advance of the universe — is solely controlled by the Almighty. Even the meeting of a man's mate is manipulated by God. From the *shidduch* to the pregnancy to the birth, God is making it happen.

---

13. *Bereishis Rabbah* 68:4.

KEYS TO MIRACLES

Why did *Chazal* use the analogy of a key? The fact that there is a key suggests that there is a room or a chest that contains valuables. If there is something that even God keeps under lock and key, imagine how precious it is. The need for a key also tells us that the contents of the treasury needs to be taken out.

Both the *midrash* about the *shidduchim* and the *midrash* about the keys are telling us the answer to two questions about *kiyum olam*, the continuation of creation: Who makes it happen? and How does it happen? The continuation of creation is in the hands of God, and it happens through marriage and having children. God said to man, "Be fruitful and multiply, populate the earth and take control of it."[14] With that mandate, God made us partners with Him in continuing the process of the creation of the world. But God holds the key.

Each time a new life is created, God opens His treasury that holds the fertile power of a man and a woman. Every time a woman gets pregnant it is a miracle; God is opening up His treasury of souls. Every time it rains, God is making it rain. He is opening up the treasury that holds the fertile powers of the world. Fertility is the force that is the extension of God's creation. He opens up the treasury that holds life.

God supervises everything, but some things are more precious to Him than others. Concerning conception, pregnancy, and birth, God is involved in the process, for He is the exclusive holder of the key to life.

This book was written with the aim of helping childless couples be more educated and active in their quest to become parents. The God-fearing Jew also wants to know how to go about it within the parameters of halachah and to understand

---

14. *Bereishis* 1:28.

the entire experience from a Torah viewpoint. We live in a great day and age. HaKadosh Baruch Hu has opened up the wellsprings of wisdom, and today so much of what was impossible years ago is now routinely part of life. Medicine has developed by leaps and bounds. The field of fertility especially has seen advances that once were considered science fiction. One might say that since man is now able to produce life in a test tube, it appears as if the key to life is finally in the hands of man. This is not so. The key is always in the hand of God, the same way that the key to livelihood is always in the hand of God. Just as a man who cultivates the soil or gives someone else a job does not hold the key to livelihood, neither do the fertility specialists hold the key to fertility. The laboratory facilitates the meeting of the egg and the sperm and helps create suitable conditions for the embryo to survive before implantation. Yet there is still no guarantee that there will be a pregnancy. God is the only One Who develops that meeting of egg and sperm into a living soul.[15]

---

15. A woman who is experiencing infertility certainly merits special *hashgachah* (Divine supervision and care). Two sources prove this. There is an alternative source from *Chazal* that suggests that there is an angel who is appointed over attraction and pregnancy (*Niddah* 16b). According to this source, it isn't God Himself Who supervises attraction and pregnancy, but a special angel. This source brings down the level of *hashgachah* that God has over the start of a new life.

We must point out that there are two different approaches by *Chazal*; one says that there is an angel appointed over attraction and pregnancy, and the other says that it is so important to God, that only He holds the key. Tosafos on *Niddah* 16b answers this contradiction by saying that there is an angel appointed over pregnancy but not over birth. This answer does not seem to take into account the more obscure Midrashic sources that we have cited. Yet even according to the opinion that an angel is appointed over pregnancy, pregnancy of the infertile is only from God, as it says, "And God remembered Sarah" — Sarah was remembered by God Himself and not by an angel. The verse about Sarah teaches us about all childless women.

Rain — the resource for sustaining life in the present; resurrection — the mechanism for our future lives; and fertility — the creation of new life, are all miracles that occur when God decides that it is the right time for them to happen. Only the One Who said *v'hayah ha-olam* — "There will be a universe" — only the One Who holds the third key, can say whether and when there will be a child.

The second source is from the source of the three keys, for from where do *Chazal* learn that only God has the key to birth? From the verse that says, "God remembered Rachel, and He heard her and *He opened* (*vayiftach*) her womb." So the idea of God's special *hashgachah* is derived from the childless who finally gave birth.

2.
In the Clefts of the Rock

Infertility is always with me. Sometimes it is right below my skin and sometimes it is tucked deeply inside of me. I experience pangs of jealousy when I see a pregnant woman and anger when I see unfit parents with their children. My husband and I have been married for seven years; we are *ba'alei teshuvah.* I work as a professional for a large company. I have found that I have a "dual personality." On one side is my life as a wife and homemaker in the Jewish community, and on the other is my life as a well-paid professional in a male-dominated industry. This dichotomy helps me to cope since I can surround myself with work several hours a day. However, when a colleague announces a pregnancy or passes around pictures of his or her children, all the pain and anger rush to the surface.

(Ruth, age 31)

INTRODUCTION

WHEN A COUPLE marries they usually expect that in a short time they will be parents. They don't anticipate for a moment that they will fall into the category of the small but, sadly, growing number of couples who have difficulty with fertility. It isn't supposed to be this way.

What was supposed to be so simple and natural becomes a draining, obsessive venture. Infertility is a psychological crisis. According to a study that compared the emotional distress of women with infertility to fertile women who were facing medical diagnoses of heart disease or cancer, or who were HIV positive, the infertile women showed equivalent levels of depression and anxiety to women with these life-threatening diseases.[1] According to Dr. Aline Zoldbord, a psychologist who specializes in counseling childless couples, the anger and sense of unfairness that infertile women feel is even stronger than the anger and resentment that cancer and AIDS patients endure.[2]

Childless couples are racked with grief, fear, anxiety, obsession, depression, envy, isolation and alienation, rage, guilt and blame.[3] Psychologists say that the infertile couple will respond to their predicament in the same way a mourner responds. Upon grasping their new situation they will first be in shock. "It must be a bad dream." A life without having children is too dreadful to imagine, so it can't be. The next phase is depression. A strong feeling of despondency will overcome the couple. They feel lost and powerless. The options for having a child — artificial insemination, IVF, surrogates, adoption — are frightening. After depression comes anger. The couple become angry at themselves and anything they might have done in the past to contribute to this problem, be it physical or spiritual. They are angry with each other, angry at every pregnant woman in sight, and angry with God. Only after that comes the phase of acceptance.[4]

The Torah reveals a feeling of irrational despair through

---

1. Study by A. Domar, P. Zuttermeister, and R. Friedman, 1993. Cited in Helen A. Carcio, RNC, ANP, MS, *Management of the Infertile Woman* (Philadelphia: Lippincott Publishers, 1998), p. 300.

2. Aline P. Zoldbord, *Men, Women, and Infertility* (New York: Lexington Books, 1993), p. 112.

3. Ibid., p. 3.

4. Orit Luria, *Children of Love* (Kfar Saba: Arye Nir Publishers, 2000), pp.

Rachel's supplication to Yaakov, "Give me children — or else I die!"[5] According to the Ramban, Rachel was so distraught that she was threatening suicide.[6] And we find a tone of recluse depression through the portrayal of Chanah: "She wept, and would not eat."[7]

WHY DO WE WANT CHILDREN?

Why is the desire to have children so strong that it evokes such intense emotions? Our longing for children is so great that it could actually lead to the halachic category of *pikuach nefesh,* a life-threatening situation.[8] Furthermore, through the ages, women have put themselves in danger in order to have children.

Why do we want children so much? One might think that it is because we want to fulfill the mitzvah to "be fruitful and multiply,"[9] but this can't be, because the halachic obligation is only upon men.[10] Women feel the anxiety of infertility more than men; non-Jewish women suffer from infertility as well as

---

18–19 (Hebrew).

5. *Bereishis* 30:1.

6. Ramban, ibid.

7. *I Shemuel* 1:7.

8. See the end of the essay by Rabbi Yigal Shafran called *"Tipul Poriut baShabbat,"* in *Techumin,* vol. xvii. The emotional state of an infertile woman could sometimes be considered a situation of *pikuach nefesh.* See also the wording of Rav Shlomo Zalman Auerbach in his response to why he would allow certain procedures even though he would generally be against them in *Noam,* vol. I (exerpts from this were printed in *Otzar haPoskim,* 20:10.) And whom do we have greater to testify to the devastating feeling of being without child than our mother Rachel: "Give me children — or else I die."

9. *Bereishis* 1:28.

10. *Shulchan Aruch, Even haEzer* 1:13.

Jewish women, without the halachic commitment.[11] So what is it that makes us want children so badly that not having them makes us feel as depressed as women in life-threatening situations?

A man, and on a stronger level a woman, needs to produce offspring, to care for somebody. As Rabbi Eliyahu E. Dessler writes: "We all want children. Two motives may be distinguished here. We want children to give us a sense of community; we feel that death is not quite so final if we have left children behind us. But perhaps an even stronger motive is the need to have someone on whom to lavish our love and affection."[12] This desire for children is something inborn in us. Perhaps it is an innate expression of emulating God.

Psychologists say that there are two distinct desires for fertility. Both men and women share one, but only women feel the other. Both men and women desire a child to care for, to raise the best way they can. But women also have a desire to be pregnant. This desire is so strong that a woman who can't become pregnant will even be envious of women who miscarry.[13] Dr. M. Mazor notes that women at support group meetings were jealous of other group members' miscarriages, for at least pregnancy had been attained even if not completed.[14] Women who don't have eggs anymore will seek an egg donor, so they can at least carry a pregnancy. And even though they know that they are not going to be the genetic

---

11. All the research in this field done by Mazor (1978), Menning (1977), and others, which determined the magnitude of the infertile couple's stress, was not done on Orthodox couples.

12. Rabbi Eliyahu E. Dessler, *Strive for Truth!*, vol. I (Jerusalem: Feldheim Publishers, 1988), p. 126.

13. *Men, Women, and Infertility*, p. 114.

14. M. Mazor, "Emotional Reactions to Infertility," p. 43. Paper presented at the 133rd annual meeting of the American Psychiatric Association, San Francisco (1980).

mother of the child, they can at least be the gestational mother. For many women, this option is preferable over adoption. We see the desire for pregnancy in the Torah as well.

The Torah says, "There should not be a barren woman or a *meshakeilah* amongst you."[15] This is the blessing that God gives the Jewish People. What is a *meshakeilah*? Rashi says that it is a woman who either miscarries or buries her children.[16] The *berachah* is easily understood. If we do the will of God, we won't have the anguish of being barren or burying our children. But why does Rashi explain that a *meshakeilah* is also a woman who has repeated miscarriages? Isn't it enough to say that you won't bury your children? Furthermore, if miscarrying is its own tragedy, and therefore needs to be mentioned, wouldn't we think that miscarrying is more a problem of infertility than of burying children? After all, the child wasn't born yet! There is not yet the emotional connection to a fetus as there is to a living child. Rashi should have included miscarriages with barrenness. Why then was the condition of miscarrying put in the category of death rather than the category of infertility?

In relating the story of the birth of Yitzchak, the Torah says: "And God remembered Sarah as He had said, and God did unto Sarah as He had spoken."[17] Why did the Torah say "as He had said" and "as He had spoken," when either one would have sufficed? What do these extra words teach us?

Rashi explains that "as He had said" refers to her pregnancy, and "as He had spoken" refers to the birth.[18] Yet this does not fully answer the question. If God fulfilled His promise regarding the birth, surely a pregnancy must precede it. If

---

15. *Shemos* 23:26.
16. Rashi, ibid.
17. Bereishis 21:1.
18. Rashi, ibid.

so, why would there be a separate mention of pregnancy? Why did God promise Sarah both a birth and a pregnancy? The answer is because women desire to be pregnant. So part of what God promised Sarah was not only the birth of a child, but the pregnancy as well.

Rivkah shared the same desire for pregnancy. She referred to her unusual pregnancy by saying, "*Lamah zeh anochi* — Why is this for me?"[19] Rashi interprets this as, "Why did I crave to be pregnant?"[20] Rashi's use of the term "pregnant" as opposed to "have children" implies that Rivkah also had a special desire to be pregnant.

When Chanah was depressed, Elkanah tried to comfort her by saying, "I am better to you than ten children."[21] He thought that what Chanah needed was to have someone whom she could shower with unconditional love; that is why she wanted children. So he told her that their love was even stronger than children. He may have succeeded in convincing Chanah of that, but he didn't realize that women have a biological need to be pregnant. So she was still depressed.[22] Elkanah tried to make her happy, but he couldn't. He gave her extra gifts, but that didn't make her happy either. Dr. Alice Domar relates the testimony of a woman who said about her husband, "He felt so helpless — he'd try to buy me things or do things for me, but nothing made me feel better."[23]

That is why Rashi put the problem of miscarriages together with *meshakeilos*, because being pregnant is something to covet. The desire to have children is not only psychological,

---

19. *Bereishis* 25:22.

20. Rashi, ibid.

21. *I Shemuel* 1:8.

22. Netziv, *Bereishis* 30:1.

23. Alice Domar, *Conquering Infertility* (New York: Viking Press, 2002), p. 12. See also p. 105 (of the same book) for a similar account.

but for a woman it is physiological as well.

GETTING READY

Infertility assaults several aspects of our lives. It affects our relationship with our spouse. It can cause tension with parents and in-laws. It alienates us from our social circles. We see the world through "infertility-colored glasses." Everybody seems to be pregnant or pushing a baby carriage. News of a friend's pregnancy or birth of their child can evoke anger and envy. "Isn't there anything else to talk about other than a birth experience, diapers and schools?" "Does every man have to dance with his child on his shoulders on Simchas Torah?"

If you have just embarked on this journey, you will need to be emotionally prepared to weather the storm. You will need to be educated in the many facets of the medical treatments. Understanding your options will help you determine what you want to do. Much of the anxiety of the infertile couple is the lack of control they have over their lives. Knowledge will give you a sense of control.

It is strongly recommended that right at the start of seeking medical intervention you find a support group that will share information with you. You may even want to consider some kind of private counseling. Don't be so sure that you won't need it. The stress that this experience will place on you is far greater than you can imagine.

Every couple will need some extra help. Don't be embarrassed to look for support. It is better to start out with the right kind of support than to wait until you absolutely need it to heal a lot of hurt that could have been avoided if you had had proper counseling from the outset. So from the initial assessment of your infertility, you need to begin to become educated and to look for the right kind of support counseling to help you get through this.

Couples can be obsessed with theological questions. Why is this happening to us? Is it a punishment? Is this God's will? Why doesn't God answer my prayers? How do I rid myself of envy? Discussing these questions will help you cope with your situation.

If you are in the midst of the infertility experience, you need to strengthen and organize your knowledge to help you continue. Even if you are finished with the ordeal, with or without a child, understanding such a monumental phase in your life will help put it in perspective for you.

Infertility Will End

You also need to believe that infertility will end. You will not suffer from infertility forever. If you are in the midst of the infertility crisis, don't think that the intensity of the emotional anguish will last forever. Infertility is a passing phase. There are three possible endings to your infertility saga: Either you will give birth, naturally or through medical intervention; you will adopt; or you will resolve to live without children. So if you are in the midst of the infertility crisis now, don't think that you will feel like this forever. There will be an end to this situation, one way or another. You will ultimately live with peace of mind and yes, even happiness.[24]

TORAH: THE SOURCE OF OUR STRENGTH

The source of every believing Jew's strength is our Torah. Our Torah is not only a book of laws and ancient stories, it is a liv-

---

24. Alice Domar writes in *Conquering Infertility*, p. 91: "A few years ago, Canadian researchers looked at women in their sixties and seventies who had struggled with infertility when they were younger. A third of the women had biological children, a third had adopted, and a third had remained child-free. The researchers examined the women and found that their psychological profiles were identical. They were all equally happy. And they had survived their infertility just fine."

ing Torah that can give us guidance and strength through all of life's challenges. The Torah contends with the subject of infertility through the lives of certain Biblical characters, and the Midrash expands the list. In the Tanach the infertile women are: Sarah,[25] Rivkah,[26] Rachel,[27] the mother of Shimshon,[28] Chanah,[29] according to some opinions Michal (either with secondary infertility or with primary infertility),[30] and the Shunamite woman.[31] According to *Chazal*, Leah was infertile[32] (but was cured of her infertility because God wanted her to be

---

25. *Bereishis* 11:30. She is the first to be noted as childless. The Torah also tells of the women in the house of Avimelech as being infertile (*Bereishis* 19:17-18). However, this was, in the words of the Torah, because the king took Sarah. They probably had not been infertile before that.

26. *Bereishis* 25:21.

27. Ibid. 29:31.

28. *Shofetim* 13:2.

29. *I Shemuel* 1:2.

30. *II Shemuel* 6:23. Michal was not included in the *midrash* that lists the seven barren women, among them the Land of Israel during the Jews' exile (see *Yalkut Shimoni, Tehillim* 873), because the *midrash* only lists those women who were barren and ultimately had their own children and became happy. Michal either had children and then became infertile, or she never had her own children, or she had a child and died in childbirth. See *Sanhedrin* 19b. According to Philo and Joseph Flavius (Josephus), the daughter of Pharaoh was infertile and that is why she took baby Moses for a son. Philo, S. Rappaport, *Aggada und Exegese bei Flavius Josephus* (Vienna, 1930), pp. 27, 115.

31. *II Melachim* 4:14.

32. *Midrash Tanchuma, Vayera* 17. See the commentary *Anaf Yosef*, which brings other *midrashim* that say that Leah was infertile. Although *Yalkut Reuveni, seder Vayechi* says that Leah wasn't infertile, Leah certainly had secondary infertility, as the verse says, "She then stopped bearing children" (*Bereishis* 29:35). It is difficult to know if the *midrashim* that considered Leah barren were referring to her secondary infertility, or if she was born with fertility problems. For more on Biblical and Talmudic figures who were barren according to some opinions, see Yael Levin Katz, *HaAkarut b'Aggadah*, p. 81,*Teudah* 13, Tel Aviv University, 5757.

loved by Yaakov[33]) and Ruth was infertile.[34] Men who were infertile according to *Chazal* were Avraham,[35] Yitzchak,[36] Boaz,[37] and possibly Shimshon's father.[38] This book will show how these great figures dealt with their infertility, and how everything that they endured is relevant to our lives as well. Just being able to relate to their feelings should give us strength as well as validate our feelings throughout the journey of infertility. We will see how some of them were strong in some areas and weak in others. We will see ourselves in some of them and we will learn about coping from them. God wanted us to know what they went through so that we can learn from them and apply the lessons to our lives.

THE CLEFTS OF THE ROCK

On the verse in *Shir haShirim* (2:14), "My dove in the clefts of the rock, in the secret places of the terrace, show Me your appearance, and let Me hear your voice; for your voice is sweet, and your appearance is beautiful," *Chazal* tell us that the dove refers to our matriarchs who were barren.[39] God says to them, "Show Me your appearance, and let Me hear your voice; for your voice is sweet, and your appearance is beautiful."

The verse doesn't only refer to the matriarchs, it refers to everybody going through infertility, for a dove symbolizes the

---

33. See *Bereishis Rabbah* 71:1.

34. *Yalkut Shimoni, Ruth* 606: "Boaz was eighty years old and didn't have children. Ruth was forty years old and didn't have children."

35. *Yevamos* 64a.

36. Ibid.

37. *Yalkut Shimoni, Ruth* 606.

38. *Shofetim* 13:2. See chapter 15 for further discussion on this.

39. *Shir haShirim Rabbah* 2:30.

Jewish People.[40] The dove is hiding in the clefts of the rock. A rock doesn't bear fruit. The dove is hiding in its clefts from the hawks, all the circumstantial injuries that emerge with infertility: your neighbor's prying comments, the damaged intimate life with your spouse, and your anger and envy toward the fertile world. The feelings that accompany infertility are in the secret places of the terrace, they are hidden deep within you, kept secret from the rest of the world. The Divine reason for your infertility is in such secret places that even the dove is unknowing. So God says, Show Me your appearance — your anguish.[41] Let Me hear your voice — your supplication.[42] For your voice is sweet — speak to Me, pray to Me. I want a relationship with you. I love for you to talk to Me about it. And your appearance is beautiful — don't think that you are a sinner and therefore have not yet had children, don't think you have to hide from Me. Don't be afraid anymore. You are beautiful.

---

40. Ibid.

41. Netziv, *Shir haShirim* 2:14.

42. Ibid., and *Eitz Yosef* on *Shir haShirim Rabbah* 2:30.

3.
Infertility: An Introduction

A person doesn't bruise a finger without
it being decreed from Heaven.

(*Chullin* 7b)

INFERTILITY IS DEFINED as the failure to achieve pregnancy after a full year of marital relations without the use of birth control. According to medical research, the average length of time needed to achieve conception for a normal couple at the age of peak fertility (25 years of age) is 5.3 months. Twenty-five percent of couples will have achieved pregnancy after one month of unprotected intercourse, 63 percent by the end of six months, 75 percent by the end of nine months, and 80 percent by the end of twelve months. For another 10 percent (making a total of 90 percent), conception will occur within the six months after the arbitrary limit of a year, without medical supervision.[1]

Fertility rates are at their peak in men and women at age 25. Beyond that point, fertility rates begin to decline with age.[2]

Statistics show that about one-third of women who defer pregnancy until their mid-to late 30's will have infertility

---

1. A. Spira, "Epidemiology of Human Reproduction," *Human Reproduction*, 1:111–115, 1986.

2. B.M. van Noord-Zaadstra, C.W. Looman, et al., "Delaying Childbearing: Effect of Age on Fecundity and Outcome of Pregnancy," *BMJ*, 1991: 302: 1361-1365.

problems.[3] Medical data supports evidence for a decline in fertility with advancing age.

Unfortunately the rate of infertility in the general population is growing. Now at about 10 to 15 percent, infertility may be attributed to some of the following causes:

- Delayed age of childbearing
- Epidemic venereal diseases
- Possible exposure to toxins in the workplace and the environment

IS THERE A PROBLEM?

At exactly which point a couple may suspect a problem and choose to investigate is an individual decision based on many factors. A couple may not be so anxious to begin a family, thereby delaying medical investigation. A couple may consider themselves very young and not be concerned that it is taking extra time for the wife to become pregnant. Or conversely, family or peer pressure may cause a couple to seek medical advice sooner than the average.

It is common medical practice for a couple who have had regular marital relations for at least one year without conception, to begin a fertility evaluation. If the woman is over 35, the fertility evaluation should begin after six months. If there are suspected fertility problems then the evaluation should not be delayed. A couple should consult with their Rav before beginning any invasive testing; however, a simple medical consultation would not necessitate advice from a halachic authority.

Throughout this book, we will attempt to answer questions about your reproductive health and examine the causes

---

3. Leon Speroff, *Clinical Gynecologic Endocrinology and Infertility*, sixth edition (Baltimore: Lippincott, 1999), p. 515.

of infertility in men and women. We will offer you guidelines for choosing a doctor and a fertility clinic. You will have a clearer understanding of what to expect from doctors' examinations, invasive testing, and possible treatment options.

In Summary

Some facts about infertility:

- Infertility is defined as the inability to conceive after one year of unprotected intercourse.
- Infertility effects about 10 to 15 percent of all couples worldwide.
- Fertility peaks at age 25 in both men and women.
- Fertility potential in women over the age of 35 drops dramatically.
- Many factors influence a couple's plan to seek medical assistance:
  — Age
  — Family or peer pressure
  — Religious orientation
  — Fear of the unknown
  — Finances

4.
Anatomy and Physiology

There are 248 positive mitzvos in the Torah corresponding to the limbs of a man. Every day they cry out to man, "Do for us so you will live in our merit!"

(*Tanchuma Ki Savo* 106)

FERTILITY IS THE ability to conceive and produce children; the union of sperm and egg to bring forth life. Of course, this brief definition is an over-simplification of the intricate fertilization process that requires normal anatomical, physiological, and hormonal components. After reading this section, you will begin to understand how each element of fertilization is interdependent with the other, and only when certain biological interactions are completed is the stage set for fertilization to take place. We will now take you through the ABCs of the reproductive system.

Beginning with the sixth to seventh week in the life of an embryo, the anatomical components of reproduction in males and females begin to form. They continue to grow and develop throughout adolescence as a person matures into adulthood. Any problems along the way can unfortunately contribute to infertility. Let's take a look at specific reproductive organs (anatomy) and how they function (physiology).

A WOMAN'S ANATOMY

In a woman, the proper development of the uterus, fallopian

tubes, ovaries, and birth canal (vagina) are essential in order to ensure fertility.

FEMALE ANATOMY

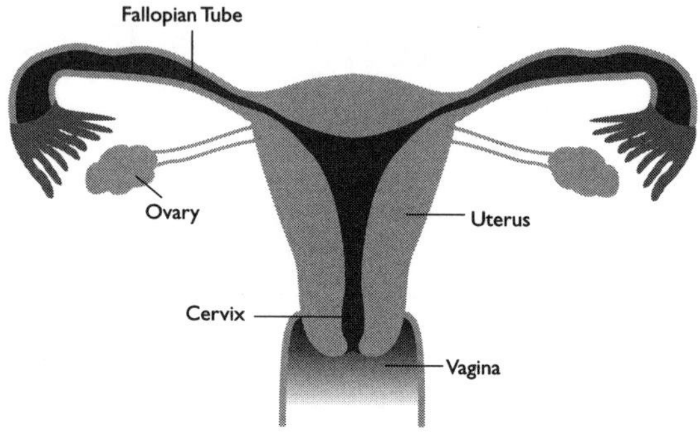

The *ovaries* are almond-shaped organs located on each side of the uterus. Already in the fetal stage, the ovaries contain several million *oocytes* (immature eggs) located in fluid-filled *follicle cells*. These follicle cells are like egg crates safeguarding the eggs. Despite the enormous quantity of eggs which are potentially available by the time a girl reaches puberty, normal degeneration decreases the number to about 400,000. From the onset of puberty, hormones influence only a portion of these follicles to grow and develop, resulting in the release of one egg (*ovum)* each month. This is known as *ovulation*. A menstrual cycle in which no follicle ruptures and releases an egg is referred to as an *anovulatory cycle.* Over the thirty to forty reproductive years, only about 400 of the 400,000 follicles mature into eggs and are released from the ovary. (That means the average woman can potentially menstruate around 400 times.) The ovaries are also involved in the transmission of hormonal messages that affect the entire reproductive system.

Once the egg is released from the ovary, it travels through

one of the *fallopian tubes* on its way to the uterus. There are two fallopian tubes, shaped like trumpets branching forth from either side of the uterus. Each tube is long and narrow with fringed, finger-like openings draped over the ovaries. When an ovum is released by one of the ovaries it gently sweeps the egg into a fallopian tube, where fertilization may take place. If the egg is not fertilized then it will degenerate and be reabsorbed in the body. Since the fallopian tube is similar to a tunnel, if one part is too narrow or obstructed, then the sperm and egg cannot meet and fertilization will not take place. This can result in *mechanical infertility*.

The *uterus* is a hollow, muscular, pear-shaped organ located in the pelvis between the bladder and the rectum. The uterus expands fivefold from the size of a small pear to a watermelon during pregnancy. The inner lining of the uterus is called the *endometrium*. Throughout the menstrual cycle the endometrium, under hormonal influence, transforms its consistency from being thin and smooth before ovulation to becoming thick with expanded blood vessels after ovulation. At this point the uterine lining is like a quilted cushion, for the purpose of receiving the embryo for implantation. The fertilized ovum embeds in the uterus, which cuddles and protects the developing embryo.

If fertilization does not take place, part of the endometrium falls away at the end of each menstrual cycle causing the bleeding we call a *period*. The endometrium is now thin and ready again to be built up and enriched to receive a fertilized egg for implantation. Simply put, this four-week menstrual cycle is a repetitive building up and sloughing off of the endometrium. If fertilization occurs, then this cycle is disrupted and the pregnancy develops.

The bottom of the uterus narrows to form the *cervix,* which connects the uterus with the *vagina*. The cervix functions both as a gateway, dilating during labor to allow a baby to be born, and as a secretory organ, secreting mucus in different consistencies as a direct result of hormonal influence. During certain points in the menstrual cycle, cervical mucus can be hostile to sperm, actually preventing most of the sperm from passing the cervix, whereas during ovulation cervical mucus contains 98 percent water, making it sperm-friendly. This increases the chance of fertilization during ovulation. This time span, of about thirty-six hours, is aptly referred to as the "window of fertility."

OVULATION, FERTILIZATION and IMPLANTATION

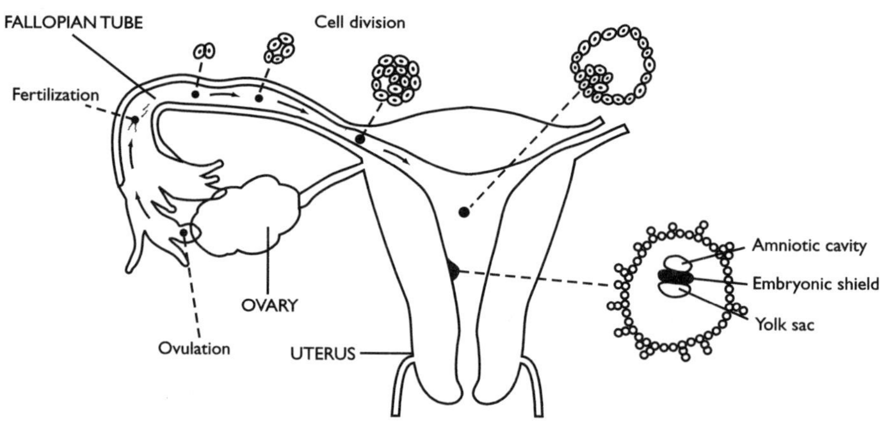

Oogenesis is the process where primary oocytes (immature egg cells) develop into a mature *ovum*, (plural=ova). The egg or female gamete carries twenty-three chromosomes, one of which is an "X" sex chromosome. Surrounding the ovum is a thick, transparent membrane, the *zona pellucida*. The zona prevents the penetration of more than one sperm at the time of fertilization. Following ovulation, the unfertilized ovum has a life span of about twenty-four hours, while the sperm can stay alive for seventy-two hours.

Hormonal Bureaucracy

A hormone is an organic secretion that acts on specific cells, prompting them to perform particular tasks. Hormones are very powerful, and minute quantities can produce some profound effects. Throughout the male and female life cycle, hormones are secreted in varied amounts, inducing diverse bodily reactions. In men and in women, there exists hormonal communication between the brain and the testes (in the male) or the ovaries (in the female), which stimulates and regulates the production of hormones needed for normal sexual development and function.

In the brain of both sexes, hormonal fireworks are constantly flaring. The portion of the brain that most concerns us is the *hypothalamus* and *pituitary gland.* The hypothalamus produces *gonadotropin-releasing hormone* (GnRH) that in turn stimulates its partner, the pituitary gland, to produce and release two important hormones, that you'll consistently hear about, *follicle-stimulation hormone* (FSH) and *luteinizing hormone* (LH).

In technical terms, which you will probably never use, this is referred to as the *hypothalamic-pituitary-gonadal axis.* The hypothalamus and pituitary glands send and receive signals to and from the ovaries or testes (*gonads*). This is a complex system of positive and negative feedback ensuring that a delicate hormonal balance is maintained.

In women, specific combinations of hormones influence ovulation and menstruation, and support pregnancy and lactation. The hormonal relay system continues with FSH and LH stimulating the ovaries to produce *estrogen* and *progesterone.* Specifically, FSH stimulates the follicles in the ovaries to develop and secrete estrogen from the ovaries. LH is responsible for the final maturation of the ovum and its release from the ovary. That spot on the ovary from which the egg is released is called the *corpus luteum*. Upon ovulation, the corpus luteum begins to produce progesterone.

Estrogen is primarily responsible for the stimulation and development of accessory reproductive organs (uterus, fallopian tubes, ovaries and vagina) and for the growth and maintenance of the secondary sex characteristics (hair distribution, body shape). *Estradiol* is the major form of estrogen secreted by the ovary. The secretion of estrogen varies throughout the menstrual cycle. After the reproductive years, estrogen secretion declines dramatically, and a woman enters menopause.

Progesterone is found in very small amounts during the first half of the menstrual cycle. It is released by the corpus luteum, the adrenal glands, and the placenta in a pregnant woman. The two hormones work together, with estrogen beginning the preparation of the uterus to receive the fertilized ovum while progesterone completes that preparation and creates a suitable site in the uterus for implantation and development of the embryo. Progesterone preserves the rich vascular buildup of the endometrium throughout pregnancy. Progesterone is sometimes referred to as the hormone of pregnancy.

In Summary

The main structures of the female reproductive system are:

- Ovaries
- Fallopian tubes
- Uterus
- Cervix
- Vagina

The three main controls of female hormonal functions are:

- Hypothalamus (GnRH)
- Pituitary gland (FSH and LH)
- Ovaries (estrogen and progesterone)

To help better explain hormonal influence on the menstrual cycle, we will use a 28-day cycle to illustrate the delicate body changes which occur throughout the month.

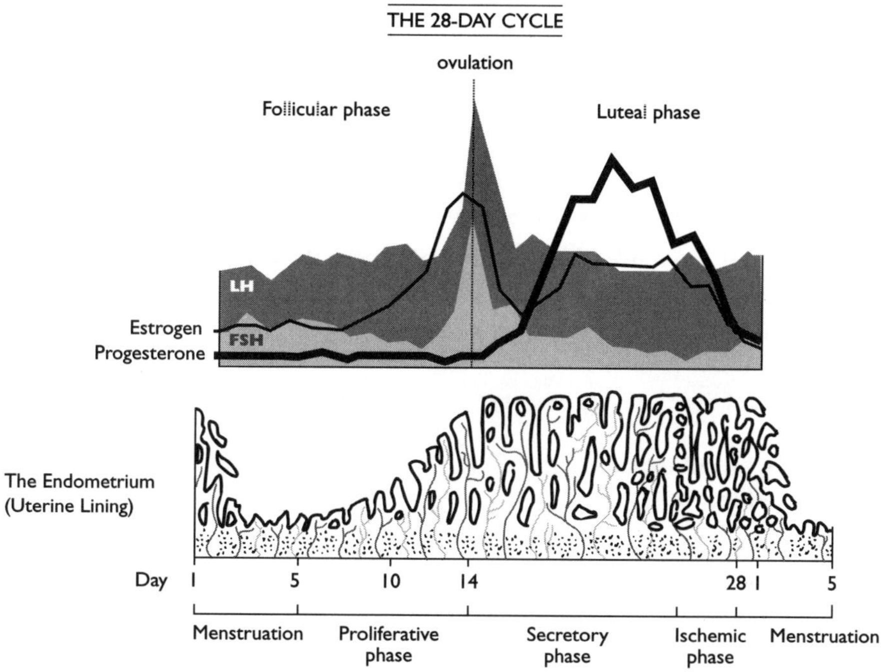

For example, using a 28-day cycle:

Days 1–5

Menstrual bleeding, estrogen and progesterone are low, FSH and LH are at mid-range.

Days 5/6-10

Estrogen begins to rise, FSH begins to fall.

Day 11 or 12

Preceding ovulation — LH surges upward, estrogen continues to rise, progesterone levels start to rise and FSH falls to its lowest level. The next day or two, we witness LH and estrogen reaching their highest levels, with FSH making a tremendous comeback and peaking a day later.

Day 14 (approximately)

LH, FSH, and estrogen fall and several hours later a mature ovum is released from the ovary. Progesterone continues to rise, peaking on day 22 and falling immediately prior to menstruation if conception does not occur. Progesterone will remain elevated if conception occurs.

A MAN'S ANATOMY

Plenty of men are squeamish when it comes to learning about the intricate workings of their bodies (especially this part of the body), but it's important to hear this side of the story too!

The male reproductive system includes the *hypothalamic-pituitary-testes axis* as well as the primary reproductive organs, the *testes* (plural=testes; singular=testis). The testes are located outside the body in a sac, called the *scrotum.* The groundwork for a male's reproductive function is set during his fetal development. From conception, the male is defined by his chromosomal makeup of "XY," and from forty days afterward the embryonic cells differentiate into the precursors of the male anatomy. During the ninth month of gestation the testes descend from inside the fetal abdomen and suspend outside the body in the scrotum.

Inside each testis is a factory of ducts, tubes, and cords. The average testicular volume is 20 cc in healthy young men and decreases in elderly men. Normal longitudinal length of the testis is approximately 4.5 to 5.1 cm. Measurement of testicular size is critical in evaluating the man, since the sperm-producing region of the testis occupies approximately 80 percent of testicular volume. The temperature inside the testes is 1 to 2.5 degrees Fahrenheit below body temperature in normal men. Increased scrotal temperatures can temporarily or permanently destroy sperm production.

In the testes, the first structures of sperm production (*spermatogenesis*) are tightly packed coils called *seminiferous tubules*. In the base of the tubules are germ cells which are immature sperm cells. A cycle of sperm production takes about seventy-two days. Nutritional and environmental support of the germ cells are provided by *peritubular cells* and *Sertoli cells*. In tiny spaces between the seminiferous tubules are scattered clusters of *Leydig cells*. These are endocrine (hormone) cells responsible for the production of male sex hormones – primarily *testosterone*.

MALE ANATOMY

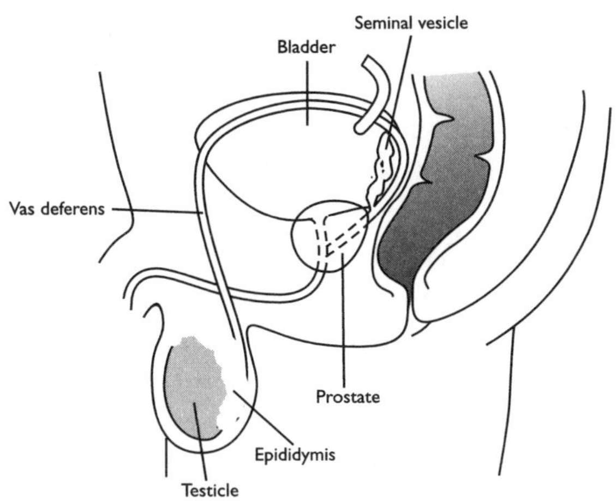

Once it is produced, the sperm then migrates into the next structure, the *epididymis.* The epididymis is made up of narrow, coiled tubes found in the uppermost part of the testes. Not only a storage facility for sperm, the epididymis provides the environment for sperm to undergo an additional maturation process, thereby acquiring the capacities for both progressive motility and fertility.

From the epididymis, the sperm leave the testes through the *ductus deferens* into the *vas deferens* (vasa), which carries sperm up through the *inguinal canal* (the groin region) into the abdominal cavity, behind the bladder (referred to as the *retroperitoneal area* of the body).

Continuing on their journey, the sperm travel by way of the *seminal vesicle.* The seminal vesicle produces fructose, which gives sperm energy, and other substances that comprise the *seminal fluid (semen).* Also contributing to the composition of semen is the *ejaculatory duct,* which leads into the *prostate gland.* The *bulbourethral glands (Cowper's glands),* which lie adjacent to the prostate, provide mucus along with prostatic secretions, protecting the sperm against the acidity of the female reproductive tract and maintaining the proper consistency of the seminal fluid.

Ejaculation occurs when the seminal fluid is propelled forward by action of the *bulbocavernosus muscle* toward the *urethra* (the urethra is the structure that transports urine from the bladder to the exterior). The urethra serves a dual function of passing urine and transporting semen. An internal sphincter (made up of muscle fibers which can close an opening) stimulated during sexual excitement contracts, preventing both urination and *retrograde ejaculation* (semen flowing to the bladder). The semen is transported to the outside of the penis through the urethral opening (*meatus).* The nervous system's control of the sphincter can be disrupted as a result of certain medications, illness, spinal cord injury, or prostate surgery.

Spermatozoa (singular=spermatozoon)/sperm are the male gametes contained in semen. The *spermatogonia* — germ cells in the seminiferous tubules — give rise to spermacytes through a process of maturation division (meiosis), eventually maturing into spermatozoa. Each sperm cell has twenty-three chromosomes, one of which is either an "X" or "Y" sex chromosome. The male sex chromosome determines the sex of the child, as it will combine with the female "X" sex chromosome. An "XX" combine is female, an "XY" combine is male.

The sperm is made up of *head, neck, body,* and *tail.* The sperm resembles an arrow. *Chazal* tell us that semen that does not "shoot out like an arrow" will not fertilize.[1] The simple explanation is that if the ejaculate is not forceful enough, fertilization may not be achieved. Let us suggest that *Chazal* was also referring to the form of the sperm as being relevant to its capacity to fertilize. Therefore, if the sperm is not in the shape of an arrow, it will not fertilize.

SPERM SHAPES

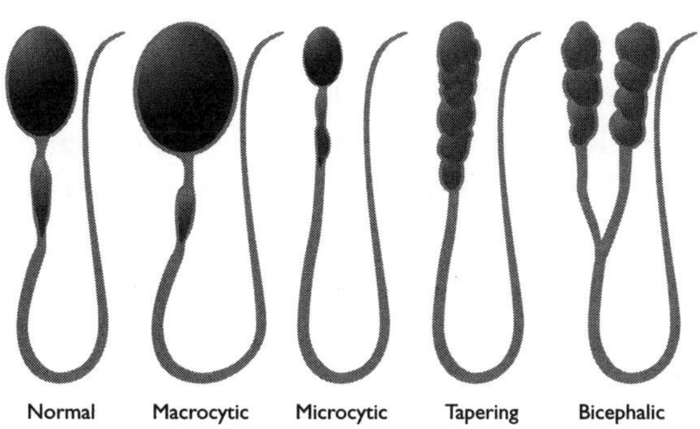

1. *Yevamos* 80a; *Niddah* 43a.

Over the top of the sperm head is the *acrosomal cap* (*acrosome*), which is responsible for boring through the zona pellucida to fertilize the ovum. Upon penetration, there are discarded enzyme fragments. Remaining signs of fragmentation are significant when evaluating the quality of fertilized eggs during assisted reproductive techniques. Sperm has an average life span of about seventy-two hours. This was also known to *Chazal*, as the Gemara says, "Sperm can live for three days and after that they degenerate."[2] Only one sperm cell will penetrate the egg. *Chazal* tell us that only the strongest sperm cell will achieve this goal.[3]

As in the female, a functioning hormonal axis (hypothalamus-pituitary-testes) is essential in the male. In the brain, the hypothalamus produces GnRH (gonadotropin-releasing hormone) by pulstile release. The pituitary, influenced by the hypothalamus, produces two gonadotropic hormones, *luteinizing hormone* (LH) and *follicle-stimulating hormone* (FSH). LH and FSH are differentially regulated by hormonal and other factors.

LH stimulates the Leydig cells inside the testes to produce testosterone, the "male hormone" responsible for the development and maintenance of many physical characteristics. When testosterone reaches a certain level in the body, a signal is sent back to the hypothalamus and the pituitary to reduce the amount of LH produced. Testosterone reaches a maximum concentration during the second or third decade of life, then reaches a plateau, and declines thereafter. Additionally, annual and daily rhythms in testosterone concentration occur, typically with a testosterone peak in the early morning. Interestingly, excessive testosterone levels, associated with certain types of hormone therapy, may paradoxically result in

2. *Shabbos* 86a.
3. *Niddah* 31a.

increased feminization from conversion of male hormones to estrogens (aromatization).

Prolactin (PRL) is another pituitary hormone that can affect fertility by decreasing LH production, resulting in a decrease in testosterone and subsequently decreased libido.

FSH secretion is influenced by the Sertoli cells of the seminiferous tubules and by a substance called *inhibin.* Inhibin is a glycoprotein hormone produced mainly by the Sertoli cells of the testes under the influence of FSH, and is itself involved in the feedback regulation of FSH. Inhibin is suppressed in infertile men and correlates with sperm concentration and spermatogenesis in infertile men.[4]

In Summary

The main structures of the male reproductive system within the testes are:

- Seminiferous tubules
- Epididymis
- Vas deferens
- Seminal vesicle
- Ejaculatory duct
- Prostate
- Urethra

The three main controls of male hormonal functions are:

- Hypothalamus (GnRH)
- Pituitary gland (FSH and LH)
- Testes (spermatogenesis and testosterone)

---

4. M. Fujusama and T. Yazazki, "Serum Inhibin in Infertile Men," *Archives of Andrology* 47:191-194, 2001.

5.

The Mitzvah to Have Children

Therefore a man shall leave his father and his mother and cling to his wife, that they may become one flesh.

(*Bereishis* 2:24)

INTRODUCTION: A BLESSING AND A MITZVAH

God created man in His [designated] mold, [and] He created him, with God's form; He created them male and female. God blessed them and God said to them, "*Pru Urvu* — Be fruitful and multiply, populate the earth and take control of it...."[1]

IN THIS PASSAGE GOD blessed and commanded mankind to procreate. There is a unique blend of blessing and mitzvah in this verse. God also blessed the fish and the birds that they should be fruitful and multiply,[2] but the blessing obviously did not include a commandment. Man's mitzvah is evident from the difference in the wording between the two blessings. Regarding the fish and birds it says, "God blessed them saying, 'Be fruitful and multiply....'"[3] But for man it states, "God blessed them and God said to them...." "God said to them"

1. *Bereishis* 1:27–28.
2. *Bereishis* 1:22.
3. Ibid.

means that He commanded them.[4] After the Flood, when humanity began again from a single family, God repeated: "Be fruitful and multiply."[5]

What is the significance of a blessing? A blessing is Divine sanction for success. As the simple meaning of the blessing, "May you be blessed in the city, may you be blessed in the field,"[6] is that you should be successful in the city and in the field, so too the meaning of the blessing to be fruitful and multiply is that you should be successful in populating the world. God promises mankind that he will be successful in populating the world and continuing the human race.

The blessing is obviously a general promise that the human species will continue, from generation to generation. However, at the same time, God commands the Jewish People to take a proactive role in this Divine plan, so He commanded us to intentionally bring children into the world as the fulfillment of it. One who deliberately refrains from the mitzvah of procreation is compared to one who spills blood and diminishes the Divine image.[7] Others say that he causes the Divine presence to depart from Israel. As God said to Avraham, "I will set up My covenant between Me and you and your descendants after you, throughout their generations, as an everlasting covenant, [that I will] act as God for you and for your seed after you."[8] Where there exists "seed after you," the Divine Presence dwells.[9]

The blessing to have children is a commandment, and the fulfillment of the commandment is a blessing.

---

4. *Netziv, Bereishis* 1:28.
5. *Bereishis* 9:7.
6. *Devarim* 28:6.
7. Tosefta *Yevamos* 8:5.
8. *Bereishis* 17:7.
9. *Yevamos* 64a.

FULFILLING THE MITZVAH

Chazal[10] teach that according to Beis Shammai the minimal requirement to fulfill the mitzvah of *Pru Urvu* is to beget two male children. They learn this from Moshe Rabbeinu, who had two sons. Beis Hillel says that having one male and one female child fulfills the mitzvah, as it says, "He created them male and female."[11] Another version in the Tosefta says that according to Beis Shammai the requirement is one male and one female child, and according to Beis Hillel it is either one male or one female child.[12] In practice, the halachah is as Beis Hillel says in the Mishnah, i.e. that one should have at least one male and one female child, providing that they too are able to have children.[13]

If by having two children one can fulfill the mitzvah to be fruitful and multiply, why, then, do religious couples see it as a religious duty to have more than two children? The Talmud quotes Rabbi Yehoshua as saying that if a person had children when he was young he should have them also when he is older, for the verse says, "In the morning sow your seeds and in the evening do not rest your hand. For you do not know which shall prosper, whether this or that, or whether they shall both be good."[14] We view each child as a blessing, as a whole world. Just like you wouldn't want to stop receiving blessings of another kind, you wouldn't want to stop receiving more children. Even though it may entail a lot of hard work as well as physical, emotional, and financial resources, it is worth it.

---

10. Mishnah, *Yevamos* 6:6 and Tosefta *Yevamos* 8:3.
11. *Bereishis* 1:27.
12. Tosefta *Yevamos* 8:3.
13. *Shulchan Aruch, Even haEzer* 1:5.
14. *Yevamos* 62b quoting from *Koheles* 11:6.

There is another concept connected to the mitzvah of "Be fruitful and multiply," called "*Lasheves*" — settling or populating the earth. This is derived from the words of the prophet Yeshayahu, where he says, "[God] did not create the world to be barren, but rather **to be settled** (*lasheves*)."[15] This verse supports the idea behind the mitzvah of *Pru Urvu*. So even if someone did not fulfill his obligation to have a boy and a girl, but instead had, for instance, eight boys, or only one girl, he still helped settle the earth.

BE FRUITFUL AND MULTIPLY: MAN AND WOMAN

The technical mitzvah to have children is on the man. A woman is not obligated to have children.[16] (The Mishnah does bring the opinion of Rabbi Yochanan ben Berokah, who says that both man and woman are commanded to have children, but the practical halachah goes according to the first opinion in the Mishnah that only a man is commanded.[17]) This is learned from the verse, "Be fruitful and multiply, populate the earth and conquer [take control of] it." The commandment "Be fruitful and multiply" is connected to the rest of the verse, "and conquer it." Since it is a man who conquers and not a woman, the commandment "Be fruitful and multiply" refers

---

15. *Yeshayahu* 45:18.

16. *Shulchan Aruch, Even haEzer* 1:13. See *Aruch haShulchan, Even haEzer* 1:4, "[God] did not create the world to be barren, but rather to be settled" (*Yeshayahu* 45:18). See *Teshuvos haRan* chap. 32, who says that for a woman, having children is optional and not obligatory. She also receives reward for assisting her husband in the fulfillment of his mitzvah. According to Tosafos on *Gittin* 45b ("*lo tehei*"), a woman is obligated in the mitzvah of *Lasheves* (settling or populating the earth). And Tosafos on *Shabbos* 100b ("*ve'ha-tanya*") says she is obligated in the mitzvah of "In the evening do not rest your hand" (*Koheles* 11:6). See *Beis Yitzchak, Even haEzer*, chap. 91, for more on this.

17. Mishnah, *Yevamos*, end of chap. 6. See also *Yevamos* 65b.

only to the one who conquers – the man.[18]

One reason that only the man is commanded to have children is because by nature women want to have children, so they don't need a commandment. Another reason is that since there is a certain amount of danger in childbirth, the Torah therefore doesn't command a woman to put herself in a situation of possible danger.[19] If a woman on her own is willing to become pregnant it is her choice, but she shouldn't feel forced to do so by the Torah. Of course, by having children, a woman actively participates in the mitzvah — although she is not commanded. A woman also performs the mitzvah of assisting her husband in his mitzvah of *Pru Urvu* (see note 16).

A woman shouldn't feel cheated that she is not obligated in the mitzvah of *Pru Urvu*. Without doubt, she is the one who bears the burden of the mitzvah. She goes through the pregnancy and the birth, and is the main caregiver at least during the early years of the child's life (the physically more demanding stage). There is a saying in the Talmud, "According to the pain is the reward."[20]

There are some who are of the opinion that although women are exempt from the technical mitzvah of *Pru Urvu*, they are commanded in the fulfillment of *Lasheves* (see note 16).

If a woman was commanded to have children the same way a man was commanded, then her conclusion might be that her primary goal in life is to have children. She may feel that if she cannot fulfill her religious obligation to produce a child then her life is meaningless. Many women who suffer from infertility have that feeling anyway. A commandment to have children will only give that feeling religious justification.

---

18. Ibid. See also *Otzar haPoskim*.
19. *Meshech Chochmah, Bereishis* 9:7.
20. *Pirkei Avos* 5:26.

That could be devastating, for a religious person believes that his or her mission in this world is to serve God, and that is the reason he or she was born. If a woman cannot fulfill the basic commandment, then her whole reason for being born will be a waste.

However, a woman is not specifically commanded to have children! From this we learn that she can serve God and fulfill her mission in life in many other ways.

Had women, who are naturally inclined to want children both biologically and psychologically, had a religious commandment on top of that, the combination would be unbearable if the goal couldn't be achieved.

So God, in His wisdom, commanded the man, who is not biologically and psychologically compelled to want children, to have children. And the woman, who is biologically and psychologically compelled to want children, is religiously exempt from the mitzvah to be fruitful and multiply. As a couple, they complement each other, one with the natural tendency and one with the religious obligation to have children.

"BE FRUITFUL AND MULTIPLY" THROUGH MEDICAL INTERVENTION

Does a man fulfill his halachic obligation to be fruitful and multiply if he fathers a child through artificial insemination or in vitro fertilization (IVF)?

As is to be expected, there are different opinions. Some say that the man did not fulfill the mitzvah, for it was not performed in the natural way.[21] Others say that he did fulfill the

---

21. Rabbi Ben Tzion Uziel, *Mishpetei Uziel, Even haEzer* 19.

mitzvah, since the end result is that a child was born.[22]

There are basically three major sources for the *poskim* to render their opinions on this subject.

The Talmudic source is in tractate *Chagigah.* There the Gemara asks a question, "If a virgin gets pregnant can she marry a High Priest?" The Gemara explains how this is possible. We suspect that she was impregnated in a bathtub.[23] The explanation is that a man was previously in the bathtub and left some semen there. After that, the girl went into the bathtub and was impregnated by the semen. Let us disregard for a moment the likelihood of such a case. The important thing is that this *gemara* is the source for doctor-assisted pregnancy. We see from here that Judaism relates to the possibility of pregnancy achieved through means other than intercourse.

The second source for medically assisted fertility is a tradition about Ben Sira, author of a "book of wisdom" highly regarded by our Sages. According to this tradition, cited in *Likutei Maharil,*[24] Ben Sira's mother was impregnated in the bathtub from the semen of the prophet Yirmeyahu. (The name Sira has the numerical equivalent of the name Yirmeyahu.)

The third source is the *Beis Shemuel,* which proves from a halachah of Rabbeinu Peretz's in the latter's glosses to the halachic work, *Sefer Halachos Ketanos* — or more commonly known as the *Semak* — that the child of a woman impregnated from a man's semen not through regular intercourse is considered that man's child, and he fulfills the mitzvah of *Pru Urvu.*

---

22. See *Chelkas Mechokek, Even haEzer* 1:8, who asks this question, and *Beis Shemuel* 1:10, who proves that the child is considered his in every aspect.

23. *Chagigah* 16a.

24. Maharil (*Minhagim*), *Likutim, d.h.* (ג). See also *Otzar haMidrashim* (Eisenstein ed.), p. 35.

Rabbeinu Peretz says that a woman should be careful not to sit on the sheets of another man, lest she become pregnant from the semen that is left there, yet she may sit on the sheets of her husband, even when she is a *niddah*.

Rabbeinu Peretz cautions women not to sit on the sheets of another man not because she would be considered an adulterous woman, for if that would be true, she would have to be careful not to sit on the sheets of her husband when she is a *niddah* — lest she become pregnant and the child would be considered a *"ben niddah."* Rather, the reason is that the child might never be aware of who his father is and may eventually marry his half-sister without knowing it. We see from here that the child born to a woman who sat on a strange man's sheets is connected biologically to the depositor of the sperm (yet she is not considered adulterous). His other children are relatives of this child. Therefore, because the child is considered in every aspect the offspring of the man who left the sperm, the latter has indeed fulfilled the mitzvah of *Pru Urvu*.[25]

Some *poskim* are of the opinion that in the case of a bathtub, the man who left the semen would not fulfill his obligation in *Pru Urvu*, because he did not do it with the intention of bringing a child into the world. However, a man who deliberately produced semen for the purpose of having a child, even though he did not do it in the usual way, has fulfilled his mitzvah to be fruitful and multiply.[26] Other *poskim* say that although according to many opinions he did not fulfill the technical mitzvah of *Pru Urvu*, he nevertheless fulfilled his obli-

---

25. *Beis Shemuel, Even haEzer* 1:10.

26. Rav Y. Baumel, *Emek Halachah*, chap. 68; Rav Tzvi Pesach Frank, *Har Tzvi*, on the Tur, chap. 1; Rabbi Y. Y. Weiss, *Minchas Yitzchak*, vol. I, chap. 50, 6; *Igros Moshe, Even haEzer*, vol. II, chap. 18. *Yabia Omer*, vol. II, chap. 1. See also *Otzar haPoskim* 1:42.

gation to populate the world.[27]

Most of the *poskim*, including Rav Moshe Feinstein,[28] are of the opinion that one does fulfill the mitzvah of *Pru Urvu* with artificial insemination. The same is true for IVF.[29] So if you merit having a child through assisted fertility, you should feel confident that you fulfilled the mitzvah. Naturally, you will then be obligated in all the mitzvos of a father toward his child.[30]

FERTILITY TREATMENTS: OPTIONAL OR OBLIGATORY?

Now that we have established that according to most opinions one does fulfill the mitzvah of "Be fruitful and multiply" through assisted fertility, we must deal with the next step. Is it a requirement to seek high-tech medical intervention in order to fulfill the mitzvah? On one hand, it is such an important mitzvah that one might think it cannot possibly be ignored. If in our generation the possibility of medically assisted fertility exists, it would seem almost criminal not to take advantage of the wisdom that God bestowed on man.

However, the Torah only obligates us to do mitzvos in the

---

27. See *Emek Halachah*, chap. 68, cited in *Otzar haPoskim* 23:17. See also Rabbi Yisrael Ariel, *BeOhelah shel Torah, Even haEzer*, chap. 69.

28. *Igros Moshe, Even haEzer*, vol. II, chap. 18. See also Rav Ovadiah Yosef in *Yabia Omer*, ibid.

29. Rav Ovadiah Yosef, brought down from Professor Avraham Sofer, *Nishmas Avraham, Even haEzer* 1. See also Rav Avigdor Nebenzahl in *Assiah*, vol. V. Rav Waldenberg in *Tzitz Eliezer*, vol. XVI, holds that one does not fulfill the mitzvah of *Pru Urvu* through IVF. So does Rav Moshe Sternbuch in *BeShvilei haRefuah* 5747, pp. 29–36.

30. As the *Beis Shemuel* says, "He is his son in every aspect." See Rabbi Yehoshua Ze'ev Zand, *Birkas haBanim*, pp. 181–183 (Jerusalem: Institute of Halachah and Refuah, 1994), which discusses some of these aspects.

natural, standard way.[31] A man must try to have children. This means he must marry and have intimate relations with his wife. He does not need to go through fertility treatments if he doesn't want to.

A woman also does not need to go through these treatments to assist her husband in fulfilling his commandment to be fruitful and multiply. She also is only obligated to have a normal intimate relationship with her husband, but she can't be forced to undergo fertility treatments if she doesn't want to. Rav Moshe Feinstein writes that the mitzvah to be fruitful and multiply is not having children, but rather having intimate relations that hopefully will bring children.[32] A person is obligated to have marital relations at least until he has a son and a daughter. (After that, the laws of intimacy have a different halachic requirement.)

In the major responsa literature on the topic of medically assisted fertility, there is no discussion of an obligation to seek out this technology. Rather, the question is asked, if a couple want to undergo fertility treatments, are they permitted to do so? Therefore, if you don't want to go through fertility treatments, or if you want to discontinue them, don't feel obligated from a religious perspective to either begin or continue them. The halachah does not obligate you to do so. Fertility treatments are optional. Yet if you have children as a result of them, you have fulfilled the mitzvah of *Lasheves* and *Pru Urvu*.

Although medical intervention may not be an obligation, we see from *Chazal* that Sarah and Rachel were rewarded with children of their own because they gave their maidservants to

31. See Rabbi Malkiel Tzvi haLevi Tannenbaum, *Divrei Malkiel*, vol. IV, chap. 107.

32. *Igros Moshe, Even haEzer*, vol. II, chap. 18.

their husbands.[33] Why was this such a great deed? It may be because Sarah and Rachel did all they could to have children. In those days there were no fertility clinics, so all they were able to do was to give a surrogate to their husbands.[34] Nowadays we can go to a fertility clinic, and perhaps in the merit of our doing all that is possible in the modern world, God will grant us a child.

---

33. See *Midrash Tanchuma, Vayera* 14 concerning Sarah, and see *Bereishis Rabbah* 73:4 concerning Rachel.

34. Rachel and Leah also made use of *duda'im* as a "fertility drug." See chapter 7.

6.
What Could Be Wrong?

God tests the righteous;
everyone according to his ability.
(Yalkut Shimoni, I Shemuel 89)

CAUSES OF INFERTILITY

WHY THE TWO OF you have yet to conceive and bear a child may become clearer as we classify the causes of infertility.

When divided between husband and wife, the categories of infertility break down to the following:[1]

MALE-FEMALE FACTOR INFERTILITY

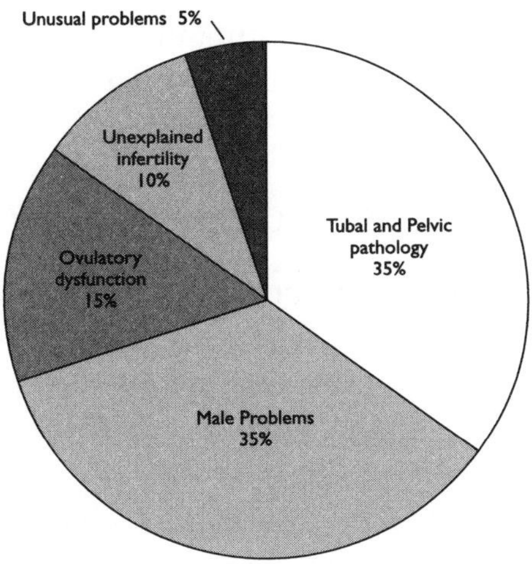

1. Leon Speroff, *Clinical Gynecologic Endocrinology and Infertility* (6th ed.) (Baltimore: Lippincott, Williams and Wilkins, 1999), p. 1021.

- Female problems — 50%
- Male problems — 35%
- Unexplained infertility — 10%
- Unusual problems — 5%

Infertility in women is itself broken down into the following groups:

- Tubal and pelvic pathology — 40%
- Ovulatory dysfunction — 40%
- Unexplained infertility — 10%
- Unusual problems — 10%

Infertility in men is broken down into the following groups:

- Structural abnormalities
- Sperm production disorders
- Ejaculatory disturbances
- Immunologic disorders

We will now discuss each category in detail to help clarify if a problem exists and what course of diagnosis your doctor may follow. You can look up unfamiliar terms in chapter 4, "Anatomy and Physiology," or in Appendix C, "Glossary of Medical Terms" (page 458).

FEMALE-FACTOR INFERTILITY

Tubal and Pelvic Factors

This category includes problems with the fallopian tubes, the uterus, the cervix, and the vagina. Difficulties in conception can be due to obstruction in the pathway of the fallopian tubes, structural abnormalities of the uterus, or cervical factors.

Obstruction of the fallopian tubes is referred to as *mechanical factor infertility*. Mechanical factor infertility is any physical barrier that prevents sperm meeting egg, fertilization, or implantation of the fertilized ovum in the uterus, from taking place. Obstructions come in the form of adhesions inside or around the reproductive organs, endometriosis, or organ malformations.

Pelvic adhesions are fibrous bands of scar tissue which clog and occlude partially or wholly the fallopian tubes or wrap around the tubes, ovaries, and other internal organs, interfering with their function. Adhesions can be caused by infections in the pelvic area, or in the peritoneal area (abdomen); for example, a ruptured appendix, ectopic pregnancy, or scarring from bleeding related to abdominal surgery.

Pelvic Inflammatory Disease (PID) is any infection, chronic or acute, of the fallopian tubes, ovaries, cervix, or uterus that extends to the connective tissue and uterine ligaments. Though PID is usually venereal in origin (sexually transmitted gonorrhea or chlamydia), widespread pelvic infections can also be caused by a ruptured appendix or by contaminated medical procedures. If an infection is diagnosed and treated in the early stages this prevents PID from spreading up a woman's reproductive tract and affecting her fertility.

Symptoms may include: purulent discharge, low-grade fever, and lower abdominal pain. Treatment is commonly antibiotics, bed-rest, and analgesics for pain relief. Often, a woman will be hospitalized in order to receive intravenous antibiotics that are selected specifically to treat the bacterial infection, as intravenous (IV) antibiotic therapy is more effective than just taking pills at home. PID endangers a woman's fertility, and if it recurs can often create mechanical infertility problems.

Endometriosis is the presence of endometrial tissue outside the lining of the uterine cavity. "Ectopic" or misplaced tissue is found in the pelvic area; usually around the ovaries, outside of the uterus, and the surrounding ligaments. In severe cases, endometrial implants can spread to the bowel or bladder. This disease is progressive and destructive, can be painful, and can interfere with fertility. Endometriosis occurs in mild to severe forms in 10 percent of all women, usually between the ages of thirty and forty, and especially in women who delay child-bearing.[2] Generally, this condition is not found in women under the age of twenty, but becomes progressively worse during the childbearing years, and subsides after menopause.

Although the actual cause of endometriosis is unknown, it does run in families. It is thought that during menstruation, the fallopian tubes expel endometrial fragments from the uterine lining, which implant on the ovaries and the surrounding tissues (pelvic peritoneum). This is referred to as *retrograde menstruation.* Though it occurs in varying degrees in every woman, the endometrial fragments are cleaned up by most women's natural defense system.

Why some women have a predisposition to endometriosis is not known. Some medical researchers think that a faulty immunological response in women with endometriosis may play a part in the development of the disease. Others theorize that endometriosis is a birth defect where endometrial cells normally found in the uterus are misplaced during fetal development. These cells lie dormant until puberty and thereafter are stimulated by hormones. When there is monthly bleeding from the lining of the uterus, these endometrial implants also bleed.

According to the American Society of Reproductive Medicine (ASRM), severity of endometriosis is categorized as:

- **Stage I (minimal):** Superficial endometriosis in the peritoneum and on one ovary, along with filmy adhesions.

- **Stage II (mild):** Deep endometriosis in the peritoneum with superficial endometrial implants on both ovaries with filmy adhesions.

---

2. D.W. Cramer, "Epidemiology of Endometriosis," in E.A. Wilson, ed., *Endometriosis* (New York: Alan R. Liss Inc., 1987), pp. 5–22.

◆ **Stage III (moderate):** Superficial or deep endometriosis in the peritoneum, partial obliteration of the culdesac (occlusion and destruction of the pouch-like area between the rectum and the uterus), adhesions on the fallopian tubes, and deep endometriosis on one or both ovaries.

◆ **Stage IV-A (severe):** Endometriosis in the peritoneum, deep endometriosis and adhesions on one ovary , with dense adhesions on one tube.

◆ **Stage IV-B (severe):** Deep endometriosis in the peritoneum, complete obliteration of the culdesac, deep endometriosis of both ovaries, with at least one tube with dense adhesions.[3]

How is Fertility Affected?

The endometrial implants make tucks and kinks on the surface of the pelvic organs. After monthly bleeding, scar tissue often develops. This buildup of scar tissue interferes with organ function and the fallopian tubes' ability to "pick up" an ovum and transport it. Expecting the reproductive organs to function properly in this scenario is like expecting a runner to sprint in thick mud.

Fertility may also be affected by an inflammatory response in the lining of the pelvic cavity, fallopian tubes, and uterus, which interferes with fertilization and implantation.

The main presenting symptoms of endometriosis are painful menstruation (*dysmenorrhea*) and painful intercourse (*dyspareunia*). Secondary symptoms include cramping and pain in the lower abdomen, lower back, legs, and thighs from five to seven days before the onset of menstruation and lasting for two to three days following menstruation. There may be intermittent monthly bleeding (i.e. spotting between peri-

---

3. Revised American Society for Reproductive Medicine classification of endometriosis: 1996. American Society for Reproductive Medicine.

ods). In some cases, however, infertility may in fact be the only symptom. Upon internal pelvic examination, nodules or thickening of the uterine and ovarian ligaments may be felt. The most reliable diagnosis is made though laparoscopy. This procedure enables visualization of the endometriosis and the extent of the damage. (See pages 191–192 for a thorough explanation of laparoscopy).

Treatment for endometriosis depends upon the severity of the disease, i.e. exactly how widespread the organ involvement. Another factor involved in the choice of treatment is whether the woman wants to become pregnant now or in the future. The three major treatment choices are medical, surgical, or a combination of the two.

Danazol was the original drug to specifically treat endometriosis. An oral medication, it inhibits ovulation and menstruation, thus preventing the progression of endometriosis and in some cases causing the implants to recede. Ovulation usually returns within six weeks upon cessation of danazol, although the endometriosis can return and grow again as well. Side effects of danazol can include facial hair growth, oily skin, fatigue, emotional fluctuations, hot flashes, and weight gain.

Oral contraceptives (i.e. birth control pills) can also provide temporary relief from the symptoms of endometriosis. Hormonal therapy disrupts the cycle of stimulation and bleeding.

GnRH analogs are the leading drugs of choice in the treatment of endometriosis. They reduce estrogen levels, which helps implants shrink in size. As a result, painful symptoms are reduced. GnRH analogs are injected or inhaled with a nasal spray. Common side effects include hot flashes, dryness in the vagina, and decreased sex drive. A small amount of bone loss may occur, which can be restored upon cessation of treatment.

Many physicians opt for surgical treatment for moderate

to severe endometriosis. During surgery, the surgeon will try to remove endometrial cysts and break apart adhesions to restore normal anatomy and reproductive function.

Since medical treatment for endometriosis is suppressive rather than curative, the goal of improving fertility is a medical-surgical combination. For about three months, a woman is treated with GnRH analogs, and then laparoscopic surgery is done to remove the shrunken, softer implants.[4]

In the most severe cases, a total hysterectomy may be the only course of treatment for endometriosis.

It is often recommended that once the endometriosis is in remission, pregnancy not be delayed, and if possible, that a woman have a few pregnancies close together so the endometriosis cannot develop anew.

Malformations of the reproductive organs can be a possible cause of infertility. More often, however, malformations of, for instance, the uterus, may result in repeated miscarriages or premature labor. A woman can be born with developmental defects of the reproductive organs. For example, her uterus can be heart-shaped with a septum (line of tissue) partially or totally separating its two sides. If a woman is unable to carry a pregnancy to term, then she would be a candidate for corrective surgery. Operative hysteroscopy (see pages 188–191 for an explanation of this procedure) increases the chances of positive results.

One major cause of epidemic structural organ malformations was the misuse of *diethylstilbestrol* (DES). DES is a type of synthetic estrogen. This drug was dispensed in the 1950's and early 1960's as a "miracle" drug to treat an array of gynecological and obstetrical ailments, such as menstrual disorders, nausea and vomiting in pregnancy, prevention of mis-

---

4. O. Muneyyrici-Delate, "Hormonal Treatment of Bilateral Tube Obstruction, *International Journal of Fertility* 44:204–208, 1999.

carriages, toxemia, and diabetes. Doctors were so infatuated with DES, that unfortunately its use spread to treating normal pregnancies to "improve" their outcome. Only after much research did the Food and Drug Administration in the United States ban its use in preventing spontaneous abortion.

The disastrous use of DES created gynecological and fertility problems for the childbearing generation of the 70's, 80's, and 90's. DES harmed not only the pregnant mothers themselves, but caused even more damage to the female fetuses they were carrying. 70 to 90 percent of DES daughters have abnormal cell structure in the vagina and cervix.[5]

Another result of DES, *adenosis*, causes production of copious secretions and contributes to infection. Menstrual irregularities are common, along with an increased risk of vaginal and cervical cancer. Most DES daughters have deformities of the uterus, cervix, and fallopian tubes. Infertility runs as high as 33 percent in DES daughters, as opposed to 14 percent in the general population.

There is controversy whether sons born to DES mothers have greater incidence of urinary and reproductive tract abnormalities, testicular tumors, psychiatric problems, or gender identity problems than the general population.

DES is one of the major tragedies of modern medicine. The medical establishment and laypeople alike have perhaps learned to avoid overzealous and irresponsible use of medications. We have been given the gift of medical technology; we just have to be moderate in our use of it in order to reap its benefits.

Asherman's Syndrome are adhesions inside the uterus. These adhesions can be caused by the *dilation and cutterage*

---

5. R.J. Apfel and S.M. Fisher, *To Do No Harm: DES and the Dilemmas of Modern Medicine* (New Haven and London: Yale University Press, 1984).

(D&C) procedure or associated infection, resulting in the inner walls of the uterus literally sticking together. One major symptom of Asherman's Syndrome is little or no menstrual bleeding. Treatment involves dilation of the cervix and lysis (cutting or separating) of intrauterine adhesions. The woman then receives large doses of estrogen to help rebuild the endometrial lining. Following this procedure, 70 to 80 percent of patients are able to carry a pregnancy to term.

Leiomyomata, or fibroids, are benign tumors of the uterine smooth muscle. Fibroid growths can arise in different parts of the uterus. Fertility be affected depending on the type and location of the growths. The three most common types of fibroids are *submucosal* (in the uterine muscle), *intramural* (within the walls of the uterus), and *serosal* (serum-filled growths). [See diagram.] Submucosal myomas can be associated with infertility, because they interfere with implantation. In some pregnancies, myomas are present but do not usually interfere with the pregnancy.

FIBROID TUMORS

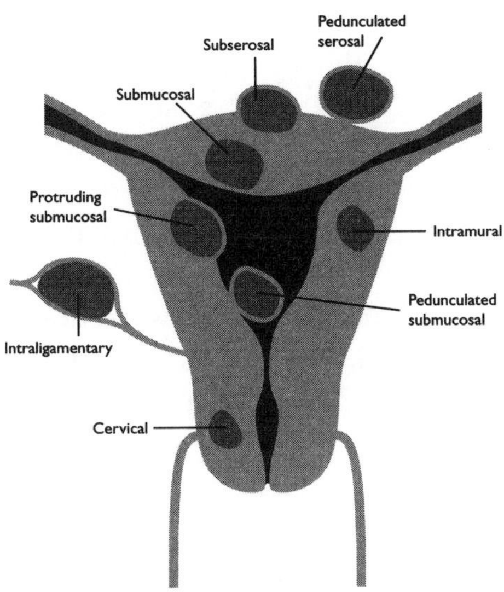

The major symptoms associated with myomas are heavy menstrual bleeding and the physical effects produced by larger tumors such as bloating, pressure, and gastro-intestinal involvement. It is often possible just to remove the myoma (*myomectomy*) while leaving the uterus intact. This can be done by way of abdominal surgery or operative hysteroscopy. Medical therapy with hormone antagonists can temporarily reduce symptoms and reduce myoma size. The peak incidence of myomas is at age 45, and 17 percent of all hysterectomies are performed because of them.[6]

As mentioned earlier, any psychological or physical problem which prevents normal marital relations is obviously a potential mechanical cause of infertility.

Cervical Factor

Though the cervix is small in size, tucked at the bottom of the uterus, its function is enormous. The proper functioning of the cervix during pregnancy and childbirth is crucial to ensure a successful outcome. The cervix's role is such that 10 to 15 percent of fertility problems can be related to cervical abnormalities. Hormones in the bloodstream directly affect the quality and consistency of the mucus secreted by the cervical glands, which aid in the sperm's journey toward their goal. Clear, watery mucus is normally secreted by the cervix around the time of ovulation, while other times during the menstrual cycle the mucus is thicker and less permeable, which threatens sperm survival and prevents the passage of sperm.

Laboratory cultures of cervical secretions may be done if infection is suspected. *Cervicitis* is a chronic bacterial or viral infection of the cervix causing secretions of increased viscosity (thickness), interfering with sperm survival. If after treatment with antibiotics the cervix continues to secrete overly thick

6. D.W. Cramer, "Epidemiology of Myomas," *Seminars in Reproductive Endocrinology* 10:320, 1992.

mucus, estrogen given on day 5 through day 13 of the menstrual cycle can improve the quality of cervical mucus.

Ovarian Factor

Problems with the ovaries and ovulation are the second largest category of infertility. This category includes infertility caused by hormonal disturbances. Though you may menstruate it does not guarantee that you ovulate each month as well. Women who menstruate regularly may have a few random cycles without ovulation. *Anovulation* is the medical term for lack of ovulation. The incidence of anovulatory cycles increases with a woman's age, especially when approaching menopause.

Normal ovulation requires coordination of the reproductive system at all levels. Irregularities in the menstrual pattern and ovulation can be related to premature menopause or other hormonal disruptions. The hypothalamic-pituitary axis and ovarian function must both be intact for the system to work. To pinpoint the cause of ovarian problems is not so simple. Groups of tests will be needed to provide a specific diagnosis.

The most positive proof of ovulation is pregnancy, but strong evidence of ovulation is provided by regular menses, elevations in basal body temperatures, elevation of serum (blood) progesterone levels, or through ultrasonic visualization.

The following are different causes of hormonal disturbance and anovulation:

◆ **Polycystic ovary (PCO)** (Stein-Leventhal Syndrome) is associated with persistent anovulation. Hormones are constant, not fluctuating as in a regular menstrual cycle. This steady, never-ending flow of hormones causes ova (eggs) to develop up to a point, but the ovary cannot release them when they mature. Fluid-filled cysts develop on the ovaries as a result of arrested development of the ova (*atresia*). Upon manual examination, the ovaries are found to be two to three times larger than normal. Women with PCO are often diagnosed with elevated insulin levels (*hyperinsulinism*), and their bodies are resistent to normal levels of insulin (*insulin resistance*) for glucose metabolism. Excess male hormones are also produced. Since the hormones are totally out of whack, acne and obesity are common symptoms of PCO, along with excessive hair growth (*hirsutism*) and little or no menstrual bleeding. Though infertility is the result of this syndrome, the most dangerous threat of PCO is the constant high level of estrogen that influences the buildup of the uterine lining without its being shed during menstruation. This can cause abnormal growths and even cancer of the uterus. Women suffering from PCO also have a higher chance of developing diabetes and heart disease (*atherosclerosis*) at an older age.

◆ **Premature Ovarian Failure (POF)** is the loss of ovarian function in women younger than 40 years. The ovaries fail to produce follicles or eggs, and menstrual periods become irregular and eventually stop. Ovarian failure is normal at the average age of 51 or so. But when a younger woman goes through the process of menopause prematurely, a couple's plans for children may not be realized. Approximately 1 percent of women will experience ovarian failure before the age of 40, and in women who have never menstruated spontaneously (*primary amenorrhea*) the prevalence ranges from 10 to 28 percent.[7]

There are a few theories about what causes POF. Thyroid deficiency and diabetes have been shown to predispose women to POF. Ovarian failure may also be rooted in an inherited chromosomal abnormality, which can be diagnosed

7. J.N. Anasti, M.R. Flack, "The Use of Gonadotropin Receptors in Premature Ovarian Failure," *Journal of Clinical Endocrinology Metabolism* 80:824, 1995.

through karyotype determination (a blood test which gives the complete analysis of a cell's chromosomes). The best prospect for couples with a diagnosis of POF is treatment with donated oocytes.

There have been cases of spontaneous pregnancy in women after being diagnosed with premature ovarian failure. This is apparently due to occasional ovulatory cycles, even though ovulation was assumed to have ceased.

◆ **Luteal Phase Defect (LPD)** can interfere with implantation when the corpus luteum fails to secrete adequate progesterone after ovulation, or when the endometrium does not thicken and develop sufficiently in response to progesterone. The luteal phase is normally twelve to fourteen days between ovulation and menstruation. In a short luteal phase there are not enough days between ovulation and the beginning of the menses in order for the fertilized egg to implant before the uterine lining is sloughed off. Inadequate luteal phase can occur in all women, but has been implicated in 4 percent of infertile women and in 5 percent of women with a history of recurrent abortions.[8]

LPD is usually diagnosed by endometrial biopsy (see pages 185–186), which shows at least a three-day lag in the endometrium's development when compared with corresponding dates of the menstrual cycle. Elevated prolactin levels (another pituitary hormone), hypothyroidism, decreased levels of FSH or LH, and use of the fertility drug clomiphene citrate have been linked to luteal phase defects.

◆ **Short menstrual cycles** can interfere with conception, as ovulation will precede a woman's *mikveh* date. In other words, she ovulates too soon because she has a menstrual cy-

---

8. A.J. Peters, R.P. Lloyd, "Prevalence of Out-of-Phase Endometrial Biopsy Specimens," *American Journal of Obstetrics and Gynecology* 73:88, 1992.

cle of less than twenty-seven days. By the time she has gone to the *mikveh*, the egg is no longer viable and capable of being fertilized. Medication can lengthen the cycle.

If a woman has a short cycle and is ovulating during her seven clean days, it is permissible, with the consent of a rabbi, to perform a *hefsek taharah* after waiting only four days (instead of the usual five[9]) after her period began — if she doesn't see any blood.[10] If she needs to begin counting the seven clean days even before that, she should consult with her Rav.[11]

◆ **Luteinized unruptured follicle (LUF)** is a syndrome where the ovarian follicle develops, but the egg is not released. LUF can only be diagnosed by ultrasound, as LH levels and basal body temperature indicate that ovulation has occurred. Nonsteroidal anti-inflammatory drugs can increase the incidence of LUF. Therefore, ibuprofen, indomethacin, naproxen, and pseudoephedrine hydrochloride (Dristan) should be avoided if LUF is suspected.

◆ **Radiation and chemotherapy** to treat cancer can temporarily or permanently damage the ovaries. The effect of radiation is dependent upon age, X-ray dose, and the target of the treatment. When the radiation field excludes the pelvis, a lead shield can be used to protect the ovaries. The younger the woman is when exposed to radiation treatment, the better the

---

9. The Ashkenazic practice is to wait five days from the beginning of the cycle until performing a *hefsek taharah* — if no blood is seen. Many Sephardic women wait four days — again, if no blood is seen.

10. *Tzitz Eliezer,* vol. IX, chap. 51, 7:2.

11. See *Har Tzvi, Yoreh De'ah,* chap. 157; *Igros Moshe, Yoreh De'ah,* vol. II, chap. 84; *Tzitz Eliezer,* vol. IV, chap. 92. See also Rav Mordechai Eliyahu, *Darchei Taharah* (Jerusalem: Succath David, 5746), p. 138. For a fascinating take on the limitations of the halachah of the seven clean days in a situation where it conflicts with the mitzvah of *Pru Urvu* or *shalom bayis,* see the end of the essay by Rav Yisrael Ze'ev Gustman, *"Sfeika deRabbanan leKula v'Dinei Minhag," Kuntris Shiurim — Kiddushin,* p. 356.

chances that normal ovarian function will return.

Ovarian function can resume after years of ammenorrhea, or damage from treatment may not appear until later in the form of premature ovarian failure. If pregnancy does occur, the risk of congenital abnormalities is no greater than normal.[12] Chemotherapy is often more damaging to the whole body. Different chemotherapy agents are more toxic to the ovaries than others.

Medical researchers are still working on ways to preserve a woman's fertility after cancer treatment, but the real hope may lie with harvesting and freezing oocytes prior to radiation and/or chemotherapy. There have been increasingly positive results with the freezing of oocytes and ovarian tissue. Any woman undergoing cancer therapy should investigate the possibilities available to her before initiating treatment.

The Thyroid and Fertility

Just when you thought things were beginning to become clear, we have to add a small section about a hormone that can complicate things in a big way. The *thyroid* affects fertility, but the problems it causes are often relatively easy to treat.

The thyroid gland is an H-shaped organ located in the neck, sitting astride the trachea, connecting at the larynx. The thyroid produces, stores, and releases thyroid hormones. Iodine, which is available from vegetable and seafood sources, is essential for the synthesis of thyroid hormones. The major hormones of the thyroid are *thyroxine* (T4) and *triiodothyronine* (T3), which in turn are regulated by *thyroid-stimulating hormone* (TSH) from the pituitary gland. To confuse matters further, these hormones are stimulated by *thyrotropin-releasing hormone* (TRH), which is secreted by the hypothalamus. These

---

12. B.L. Madsen, L. Giudice, "Radiation-Induced Premature Menopause: a Misconception," *International Journal of Oncology, Biology, and Physiology* 32:1461, 1995.

components make up the *thyroid axis*:

- *Hypothalamus* (in the brain) — TRH
- *Pituitary gland* (in the brain) — TSH
- *Thyroid gland* (in the neck) — T3 and T4

Estrogen influences TRH to stimulate TSH levels. Therefore, we see more thyroid imbalances in women than in men. TRH also stimulates *prolactin* secretion by the pituitary. We will discuss prolactin and its effect on fertility in the next section.

Thyroid function not only affects fertility, but a person's overall health as well. An underactive thyroid, *hypothyroidism*, and an overactive thyroid, *hyperthyroidism*, can be diagnosed by testing the blood levels of T3, T4, and TSH.

Hypothyroidism has no specific cause, although it is thought to be an autoimmune reaction. Menstrual irregularities and bleeding problems are common in hypothyroid women. Overall, metabolism is slowed and symptoms such as constipation, cold intolerance, decreased energy, fatigue, depression, poor memory, water retention, and low-body temperature are observed. If hypothyroidism is severe, a *goiter* (an enlargement of the thyroid gland) may develop. Elevated TSH and low T4 will confirm the diagnosis.

Initial treatment is pretty standard with synthetic thyroxine, T4, given daily. This usually sets the thyroid axis on track in approximately six to eight weeks.

Hyperthyroidism is also referred to as thyrotoxicosis. Menstrual changes may or may not occur. Classic symptoms of hyperthyroidism are nervousness, heat intolerance, weight loss, sweating, palpitations, and diarrhea. In more severe cases, *Grave's Disease,* protruding eyes with swelling around the eye-sockets, can develop. Some hyperthyroid conditions produce a goiter as well. A low TSH with elevated T3 and T4 levels in the blood confirms the diagnosis.

Initial treatment is the administration of antithyroid drugs followed by radioactive iodine treatment. A woman should not be pregnant and pregnancy should be postponed for at least six months if radioactive iodine is used.

Prolactin and Fertility

Prolactin is a hormone secreted by the pituitary gland that stimulates the secretion of milk and sustains lactation (breastfeeding). The production of prolactin is controlled by the hypothalamus through the influence of *dopamine.* In the brain, dopamine also influences the production of *epinephrine,* a hormone which directly affects heart-rate and blood pressure. Thus we again see the interdependence of different hormones and organic substances (those made by the human body) working together to make our bodies function normally. Excessive estrogen and an underactive thyroid can elevate prolactin levels (*hyperprolactinemia*) in the blood. Rarely, tumors of the pituitary gland can also raise prolactin levels.

A major symptom of hyperprolactinemia is *glactorrhea* (inappropriate milk secretion from the breasts). Any discharge of milk from one or both breasts in a non-pregnant woman or in a woman twelve months after childbirth or weaning her baby is considered abnormal and needs to be investigated. Additional symptoms include menstrual disturbances and lack of ovulation.

The Adrenal Gland Connection

The adrenal gland is the organ that sits on top of each kidney. The gland has two parts: the cortex and the medulla. The adrenal cortex secretes hormones — corticosteroids and androgens (male hormones). The adrenal medulla makes epinephrine and norepinephrine.

In normal, healthy men we will find a small amount of female hormones and the opposite is true for women. However, when a woman's adrenal cortex produces excessive amounts of androgens, ovulatory disturbances will result. Elevated male hormones will also trigger excessive body hair, oily skin, and acne. Adrenal hyperactivity is measured by elevated levels of *dehydroepiandrosterone sulfate* (DHEAS), and is often a reaction to the hormonal environment of anovulation. Elevated male hormones are often seen in women with polycystic ovarian syndrome (PCO), and will be concurrently treated during ovulation induction.

Chromosomal Disorders

Turner's syndrome (TS) is a chromosomal abnormality in which a female infant is born with only one X-chromosome (45X), instead of the usual two, or in which there is a structural abberation on one of the (46XX) chromosomes. TS effects one in every three thousand females, preventing proper ovarian development and causing infertility. Physical features of TS include:

- Short stature
- Webbed neck
- Low hairline at the back of the head
- Abnormal bone development
- Lack of breast development
- Absence of menstruation

A karyotype will reveal the absence of an X-chromosome. In some TS girls there are two X-chromosomes, but one is misshapen or missing a piece. Growth hormones can improve growth, and estrogen replacement therapy will stimulate breast development and menstrual periods. Assisted reproductive technologies (ovum donation) can help women with TS become pregnant and have children.

Immunological Problems

It is theorized that a woman may create antibodies against her husband's sperm or even the man himself may produce antibodies that attack his own sperm. An *antibody* is a protein substance produced by the body in response to a foreign invader (*antigen*). Through an immunological "error," antibodies are produced against the sperm. This results in damaged or dead sperm. Sperm may lump together, *agglutination*, by the heads or tails, or no sperm are found alive upon analysis. Agglutination occurs on occasions in many individuals, but if present in repeated sperm specimens, it may represent an autoimmune reaction or signal the presence of infection.

Research has targeted two different categories of immunological interference with male and female fertility: *Autoimmunity* (self antigens) and *Alloimmunity* (foreign antigens).

The category of autoimmunity contains diseases or symptoms in which the body reacts against its own tissues. Normally, a healthy pregnancy requires the formation of blocking factors that prevent maternal rejection of the baby she is carrying. Autoimmunity may result in allergy or autoimmune disease. These diseases include arthritis, ITP (a blood clotting disorder), or systemic lupus erythematosus.

In cases of recurrent miscarriages and a high rate of second-semester fetal deaths, antiphospholipid antibodies (APA) found in a woman's blood may point to an autoimmunity disorder. These antibodies are directed against a developing pregnancy, leading to vasoconstriction and thrombosis (narrowing of the blood vessels and blood clotting). This of course affects placental function and the oxygen and blood supply to the fetus. The preferred treatment in the case of significant levels (titers) of antiphospholipid antibodies consists of the combination of low-dose aspirin (80 mg daily), low-dose heparin (Clexan, a common blood thinner), or low molecular weight heparin (Enoxaparin, Fragmin) as soon as pregnancy is diagnosed.[13]

---

13. R. Rai, H. Cohen, M. Dave, and L. Regan, "Randomized Controlled Trial of Aspirin and Aspirin Plus Heparin in Pregnant Women with Recurrent Miscarriage Associated with Phospholipid Antibodies (or

Alloimmunity refers to all causes of pregnancy losses related to an abnormal immune response to antigens on placental or fetal tissues. Some couples have repetitive miscarriages due to a condition that does not allow the mother to make blocking antibodies. The use of steroids has not been shown to be effective in preventing alloimmunity.

Immunotherapy (treatment of alloimmunity) remains experimental, with potential risks of adverse consequences on the immune systems of both the mother and the child. Women with recurrent miscarriages have been treated with infusions of their partner's lymphocytes (a component of blood) in order to stimulate antibody formation, thereby causing the mother to produce a favorable maternal immune response which protects the developing embryo. Various fertility centers around the world offer these experimental treatments.[14]

There have been a few reported cases of pregnancy in couples suffering repeated pregnancy loss, as a result of treatment with in vitro fertilization (IVF), or with the use of donor eggs and IVF.[15]

Recurrent Miscarriages

Miscarriage occurs in 10 to 15 percent of all pregnancies. *Recurrent pregnancy loss* (RPL), which is also known by the medical term "*habitual abortion,*" is defined as three consecutive pregnancy losses before twenty weeks' gestation. This woman does not have a problem conceiving but she cannot carry the baby to term.

Antiphospholipid Antibodies)," *British Medical Journal* 314:253,1997.

14. J.S. Hill, "Immunotherapy for Recurrent Pregnancy Loss: Standard of Care or Buyer Beware," *Journal of the Society of Gynecological Investigation* 4:267, 1997.

15. J. Remohi, E. Gallardo, and M. Levy, "Oocyte Donation in Women with Recurrent Pregnancy Loss," *Human Reproduction* 11:2048, 1996.

Recurrent pregnancy losses can be classified into the following categories:

- Normal statistics
- Genetic factors
- Environmental factors
- Endocrine factors
- Anatomical causes
- Infection
- Thrombophilia
- Immunologic problems

Approximately 80 percent of pregnancy losses occur in the first twelve weeks of pregnancy.[16] The incidence of miscarriage increases with maternal age, reaching 26 percent in women over 40.[17]

Genetic Factors

Nearly 70 percent of miscarriages in early pregnancy are due to chromosomal anomalies.[18] Most couples go on to deliver a healthy child after an uneventful subsequent pregnancy, as the couple is chromosomally normal and the fetal chromosomal abnormality is a random event.

With a history of three consecutive miscarriages it is recommended to karyotype both parents, and if there is an aborted fetus in late pregnancy to karyotype, the fetus is tested as well. However, most embryonic losses (miscarriage up to the 12th week of pregnancy) are more likely to be karyotypically abnormal, whereas fetal losses (from after the

---

16. *Clinical Gynecologic Endocrinology and Infertility*, p. 1044.

17. J. Deaton, G. Honore, "Early Transvaginal Ultrasound," *Human Reproduction* 12:2820, 1997.

18. D. Bettio, S. Guerneri, "Prevalence and Distribution of Chromosome Abnormalities in a Sample of First-Trimester Abortions," *Human Reproduction* 2:735, 1987.

12th week) are usually karyotypically normal.[19]

Environmental Factors

Smoking, alcohol, and heavy coffee consumption have been linked to increased risk of recurrent pregnancy loss.[20] Certain pesticides, environmental pollutants, and chemicals in the workplace can also influence pregnancy health. Video display terminals and exposure to the accompanying electromagnetic fields do not increase risk of abortion.[21]

Endocrine Factors

Mild endocrine disease as well as thyroid imbalances or diabetes have not been implicated in repeated pregnancy losses. Inadequete luteal phase has been associated with recurrent miscarriages and may be helped with administration of clomiphene (see Ovulation Induction, page 275ff). Testing blood levels of TSH and prolactin, and performing a luteal phase assessment, may point to an endocrine factor.

Anatomical Causes

Approximately 12 to 15 percent of women with recurrent miscarriages have a uterine malformation which impairs uterine vascularization (formation of blood vessels) and limits the space in which the fetus can grow. A septate uterus (having a line of tissue dividing the uterus longitudinally in half) is the most frequent anatomic abnormality associated with early miscarriages, and surgical repair with hysteroscopy has met

---

19. L. Baker, R. Farquharson, "Types of Pregnancy Loss in Recurrent Miscarriage," *Human Reproduction* 5:1345, 2002.

20. B. Armstrong, A. McDonald, "Cigarette, Alcohol, and Coffee Consumption and Spontaneous Abortion," *American Journal of Public Health* 82:85, 1992.

21. B. Grajewski, T. Schnorr, "Video Display Terminals and the Risk of Spontaneous Abortion," *New England Journal of Medicine* 324:727, 1991.

with good success.[22] Diagnosis of uterine abnormalities is made after vaginal ultrasound with saline instillation.

Second and third trimester loss can often be attributed to an acquired anatomical problem of the cervix called *cervical incompetence,* where the cervix has difficulty remaining closed throughout pregnancy. This may be due to trauma to the cervix as a consequence of repeated intentional abortions, other damage inflicted on the cervix, or a congenital malformation of the cervix. A diagnosis of cervical incompetence is made on the basis of a miscarriage in the second trimester or a premature delivery in the third trimester of pregnancy. Unfortunately, a woman has to go through this difficult experience before the diagnosis of cervical incompetence is made. Treatment involves surgical closure (*cerclage*) of the cervix in the fourteenth week of pregnancy. This is an attempt to reinforce the cervix so it will remain closed until the thirty-sixth week, when the sutures are removed.

Repeated pregnancy loss can be devastating and frustrating to the couple, and to the clinician as well. Research is constantly being done to prevent this problem. The couple should receive proper medical and emotional support during this difficult time. In fact, with continued attempts at conception, 70 to 75 percent of these couples will have a successful outcome without having been able to identify the cause of the RPLs.[23]

Infection

There has been a good deal of research into the possibility of bacterial or viral infections causing repeated pregnancy loses, however no hard evidence has been shown to date. Maternal

---

22. D. Daly, D. Maier, "Hysteroscopic Metoplasty," *Obstetrics and Gynecology* 73:201, 1989.
23. K. Clifford, R. Rai, "Future Pregnancy Outcome in Unexplained Recurrent First Trimester Miscarriage," *Human Reproduction* 12:387, 1997.

infections during pregnancy (FIRS – *fetal inflammatory response syndrome*) have been linked to single spontaneous miscarriages, late pregnancy loss, premature delivery, and infant abnormalities.

Thrombophilia

Thrombosis is the formation of a blood clot. After injury our body prevents hemorrhage by the mechanism of blood coagulation and clotting. However, a predisposition for clotting and the formation of an overabundance of blood clots during pregnancy can adversely effect outcome. Thrombophilia can be inherited or acquired, and has been positively linked to repeated pregnancy loss. A healthy woman suffering repeated miscarriages should be screened (through a blood test) for the following clotting factor abnormalites:

- Antithrombin III deficiency
- Protein C deficiency
- Protein S deficiency
- Factor V Leiden mutation
- MTHFR gene mutation
- Prothrombin gene mutation
- Antiphospholipid syndrome

A positive result warrants treatment with low molecular weight heparin once pregnancy is diagnosed.

Immunologic Problems

As discussed above, a woman having either autoimmunity, where her body creates a response against itself, or alloimmunity, where her body relates to the pregnancy as a foreign invader, may suffer from repeated miscarriages. A woman with abnormal levels of anticardiolipin antibody, lupus anticoagulant, or prolonged prothrombin time may be a candidate for low-dose aspirin and heparin therapy.

Unexplained Infertility

With the constant advances in fertility research, categorizing the causes of infertility has become more specific and comprehensive. Twenty years ago, even ovulation problems were difficult to manage; now, they are fairly easily treated. There were many cases of unexplained infertility where a couple seemed to have no specific fertility problem, yet pregnancy did not happen. Though unexplained infertility covers 10 percent of the infertility breakdown, this category is filled with various "suspected problems," which for one reason or another are treated successfully with assisted reproductive techniques (see chapter 20).

In Summary

The causes of female-factor infertility are:

Tubal and Pelvic Pathology:

- Mechanical factor
- Structural abnormalities
- Infections past or present

Ovarian Factor:

- PCO
- POF
- Luteal phase defect (LPD)
- Damage to ovaries
- Thyroid problems
- Elevated prolactin
- Excessive androgens
- Chromosomal disorders (Turner's syndrome)

Unusual Problems:

- Immunological problems (autoimmunity/alloimmunity)

- Recurrent miscarriages

Unexplained Infertility

FEMALE-FACTOR INFERTILITY

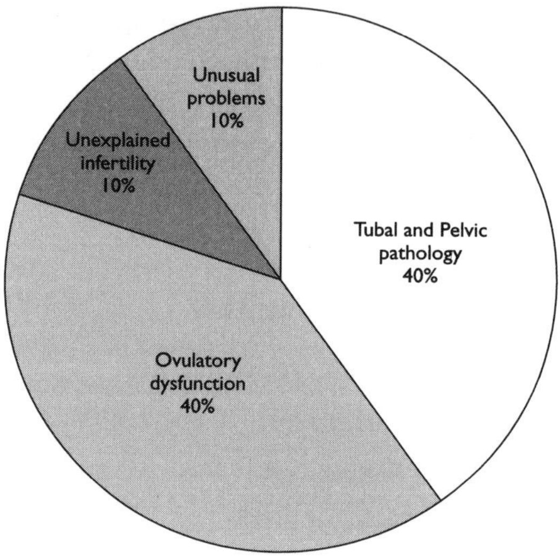

MALE-FACTOR INFERTILITY

In at least half of all cases of infertility, a male-factor is a major or contributing cause. There may be structural problems that a man was born with (congenital) or that were acquired as a result of illness or trauma. Hormonal imbalances upsetting the hypothalamic-pituitary-gonadal axis can impair a man's fertility as well. A man's job, lifestyle, and environment can also be detrimental to his reproductive health. We will now review the various categories of male-factor infertility.

Structural Problems

Varicocele is the most common identifiable cause of infertility in men. This is a condition of enlarged veins in the scrotum that causes abnormalities in the temperature regulation of the testes. Enzymes that are responsible for both sperm and hormone (testosterone) production have an optimal temperature at which they operate effectively. If this temperature is elevated by even one degree, sperm and testosterone production are adversely effected. Testicular temperatures are normally 1 to 2.5 degrees Fahrenheit below body temperature.[24]

Varicoceles can cause pain or a feeling of heaviness on the affected side. They are usually located on the left side because of the anatomical location and circulation of the *spermatic vein*, which supplies the scrotum and the testes with their blood supply. It is theorized that varicoceles exert their effects by raising testicular temperature, because of increased blood flow and blood pooling in those veins. The larger the varicocele, the greater its influence on fertility.

Approximately 25 percent of infertile males have a varicocele. Ten to fifteen percent of males in the general population have a varicocele but only in those with a subnormal sperm analysis (low sperm count) is definitive diagnosis and treatment necessary. Very small varicoceles, which are diagnosed solely by ultrasound, are not considered a significant impediment to fertility.

Sometimes, varicoceles can be detected in adolescence before fertility is even an issue. A symptomatic varicocele (i.e. one which causes pain or a feeling of heaviness on the affected side) should not remain untreated. Varicoceles cause progressive testicular damage over time. It appears that surgical repair of varicoceles not only halts this decline in testicular function, but often reverses it.[25]

According to Dr. Marc Goldstein of the Cornell Institute

---

24. P. Walsh, A. Retik. *Cambell's Urology* (7th ed.) (Philadelphia: W.B. Sanders, 1998).

25. A. Zini, M. Buckspan, "Loss of Left Testicular Volume ... Correlation with Grade of Varicocele," *Archives of Andrology* 41: 37, 1998.

for Reproductive Medicine, the average sperm count after repair of large varicoceles has been shown to increase by 60 to 80 percent.

A study by the WHO (World Health Organization) comparing men who had varicocele surgery to the control group (no surgery) showed that the pregnancy rate in couples in which the men underwent surgery was three times higher than the rate for couples in which the male partner did not undergo surgery.

Undescended testes (*cryptorchidism*) is a developmental defect where the testes fail to descend into the scrotum before birth. Since the testes usually descend into the scrotum during the eighth or ninth month of gestation (pregnancy), cryptorchidism occurs most commonly in premature newborns (30 percent of premature males), but in only 3 percent of males born at term. In 80 percent of those infants, the testes descend spontaneously during the first year of life.[26]

Those boys whose testes remain undescended will require surgical correction (*orchiopexy*) to reposition the testes in the scrotum. This relatively simple, outpatient surgical procedure is done by the age of six. However, if cryptorchidism is left untreated, sterility can result and the risk of testicular cancer increases.

Blockages and Obstructions

A second major cause of infertility in men is blockages or obstructions of the male reproductive tract. Men with a zero sperm count (*azoospermia*), where no sperm are found in the ejaculate, are divided into two broad groups:

- **Obstructive azoospermia:** Men who have an obstruction or blockage in the epididymis and vas deferens so

26. *Diseases,* The Nurse's Reference Library (Springhouse, PA: Intermed Communications, Inc., 1983), p. 1010.

the sperm can't get out. Obstruction of the ductal system is responsible for approximately 40 percent of cases of azoospermia.[27]

- **Non-obstructive azoospermia (NOA):** Men who have a production problem preventing them from making sperm.

Blockage can be caused by a urinary tract infection or by the sexually transmitted diseases chlamydia and gonorrhea. Bacteria can infect the epididymis, causing scarring and blockage, which inhibits sperm from leaving the duct.

Vasectomy is the most common cause of blockage. In this "male birth control" procedure, the vas deferens are surgically severed, obstructing the outflow of sperm and causing sterility. Some men regret having this operation which up until a few years ago was largely irreversible. Now, with specialized microscopic surgery (vasectomy reversal), the majority of these men can have their fertility restored.[28]

There is a hereditary, genetic cause of obstructive azoospermia as well. Approximately 1 percent of infertile men are born with *congenital absence of the vas deferens* (CAVD). There are no artificial replacement tubes for the vas deferens available, but many of these men can be helped with sperm retrieval, ICSI, and in vitro fertilization (see chapters 17 and 20). Of men with CAVD, 76 percent have a detectable cystic fibrosis gene mutation (CFTR).[29] A man carrying the CFTR gene does not have any other symptoms himself, but if his wife is also a carrier of the cystic fibrosis gene, the risk of having a child affected by cystic fibrosis is 50 percent. It is recom-

---

27. J.P. Jarow, M.A. Espeland, "Evaluation of the Azoospermic Patient," *Journal of Urology* 142: 62, 1989.
28. M. Goldstein, "Vasectomy Reversal: The Microdot Method," *Journal of Urology* 159:188, 1998.
29. Z. Mak, K. Jarvi, "Genetics of Male Infertility," *Journal of Urology* 156:1245, 1996.

mended that when genetic abnormalities are found, the couple should be referred for genetic counseling prior to attempts at assisted conception.

Chromosomal Abnormalities

Chromosomal abnormalities may or may not be identified at birth. Sometimes, only at the time of puberty or when a man wants a family, do these abnormalities come to light. Hormone supplementation may help to provide a man with a normal "manly" appearance, but not necessarily assist in sperm production.

Klinefelter's Syndrome is the most common chromosomal abnormality (1 per 500 newborns) associated with testicular dysfunction. It is characterized by a 47 XXY karyotype instead of the normal male 46 XY-chromosomes. In this syndrome, the Y-chromosome carrying the genes responsible for producing sperm is missing, and an extra X-chromosome is in its place. Although no sperm is found in the ejaculate, patchy areas of sperm production (spermatogenesis) can often be found within the testicle and withdrawn microsurgically and used for fertilization.[30] While appearing masculine, men with Klinefelter's can receive treatment with testosterone to improve sexual drive. Genetic testing can diagnose this problem.

A newer form of genetic testing, *preimplantation genetic diagnosis* (PGD), offers an alternative to advising a couple to terminate a pregnancy with a fetus at risk of carrying a genetic disease. PGD is a genetic analysis of one or a few cells biopsied from an embryo obtained through IVF. The cell is tested for genetic abnormalities before being returned to the uterus for implantation. (See chapter 20 for more information on PGD.)

Kartagener's Syndrome is an autosomal (non-sex-determining chromosome) recessive disorder which manifests itself in

---

30. C. Roresta, C. Galezzi, "Analysis of Meiosis in Intratesticular Germ Cells," *Journal of Clinical Endocrinology and Metabolism* 84, 1999.

men, causing frequent upper respiratory tract infections, sinusitis, and infertility by compromising sperm motility (movement). An estimated 1 in 5000 men referred to fertility clinics suffer from this syndrome, which is treatable with micromanipulation techniques (see chapter 17).[31]

Young's Syndrome is another disorder associated with frequent respiratory infections, which causes epididymal obstruction due to copious secretions.

Sertoli Cell-Only Syndrome is a congenital absence of the spermatogonia (mother cells) which are essential to sperm production. Sertoli cells maintain the environment for sperm production, but their presence alone will not produce sperm.

Endocrine Disorders

Endocrine disorders may express themselves with delayed or incomplete sexual development or with precocious sexual puberty (rapid, premature development). This disrupted hormonal axis is readily diagnosed with blood tests.

Congenital or *Acquired Adrenal Hyperplasia* (CAH) causes the adrenal glands (located above the kidneys) to produce too much testosterone. These males present with a history of accelerated bone growth and development of secondary sex characteristics. Their testes remain infantile in size. Treatement with glucocorticoids (steroids) can prevent excessive androgen (male hormone) production and allow the establishment of a normal hypothalamic-pituitary-gonadal axis, i.e. endocrine function.

Illness or Infection

Illness or infection is either an acute situation (where a person is suffering from an infection at the time of examination) or a past illness (such as post-puberty mumps or cancer) that continues to af-

---

31. R. Elliason, B. Mossberg, "The Immobile Cilia Syndrome," *New England Journal of Medicine* 297:1, 1977.

fect fertility. Antibiotic treatment given simultaneously to both spouses is often prescribed to treat active infections.

Infection anywhere in the body or any illness associated with a persistent high fever can depress sperm production. Once an infection is cleared up, sperm production usually returns to normal within three months.[32] Therefore, sperm analysis often reflects what happened in the body one or two months ago and not what is going on the day of the analysis. This is because approximately seventy-two days are required to produce sperm, which is followed by an additional period of transport and storage.

Untreated gonorrhea or tuberculosis can cause damage to the epididymis. Prostate infections, which are rare in young men, temporarily lower the sperm count. Any symptoms of discharge from the urethra, sharp twinges or dull aches around the testicles, or a dull backache, should be brought to the attention of a physician.

Mumps occurring before puberty will rarely effect the testes. However, mumps can cause fertility damage in 25 percent of the males who come down with the illness after puberty. Coming down with mumps during adolescence is fairly uncommon with the widespread use of vaccinations. Your immunization records should show that you received the MMR (Measles, Mumps, and Rubella) vaccine at 12 to 15 months of age and again in first grade. *Orchitis* (inflammation of a testicle) due to mumps may permanently affect one or both of the testicles, destroying the spermatogonia.

Sperm Production and Cancer

Sperm production cells are extremely vulnerable to chemotherapy treatments. Sometimes a man can regain fertility after completing lifesaving treatments, but this cannot be as-

32. J.M. Bedford, "The Contraceptive Potential of Fertilization," *Human Reproduction* 9:842, 1994.

sured. Therefore, before a man begins a course of chemotherapy for the very first time, he should consult both his doctor and his Rav about the possibility of providing sperm and banking it for future use.

Tumors, benign or cancerous, in the brain (hypothalamus/pituitary) or in the reproductive organs, mainly the testes, can also cause fertility problems. Hormonal deficiencies in a sexually mature man suggest a possible pituitary tumor or other pituitary or hypothalamic damage. Other symptoms may include headaches, visual disturbances, or discharge from the breasts.

Testicular cancerous tumors are the most common cancer in men between the ages of 15 and 35. Following treatment, sperm production may take four to five years to return to precancerous levels.[33]

Previous Surgery

Previous surgery of the scrotum may have caused blockage of or damage to the mechanisms of sperm production and delivery. Surgery for undescended testes or *testicular torsion* (twisting) in the past may have inadvertently harmed testicular function.

Men who have undergone testicular biopsy or vasectomy, or who have a history of testicular torsion or trauma, have a higher incidence of forming *antisperm antibodies.* Sperm autoimmunity causes decreased sperm movement due to clumping or immobilization of spermatozoa, and reduces the fertilizing capacity of the sperm. Antibodies can be detected in the blood, seminal plasma, and directly on the sperm. Micromanipulation techniques combined with IVF has been effective in overcoming this problem (see chapter 17).

---

33. H.R. Orecklin, J.T. Kaufman, "Fertility in Patients Treated for Malignant Testicular Tumors," *Journal of Urology* 109:293, 1973.

Trauma and the Environment

A toxic environment or an incident of trauma to the reproductive organs can cause fertility problems in men on either a short-term basis or sometimes even permanently.

An accident may have caused irreparable damage to the testes. Temporary loss or reduction of fertility function can be due to fluctuating circumstances that a man can actively reverse. Avoiding excess heat to the scrotum, frequent and excessively hot baths or Jacuzzis, long hours of sitting, and overly tight underwear can be helpful in raising a low sperm count. Though not widely practiced, application of a cooling pouch to the scrotum has been suggested as a treatment for male infertility.[34]

Recreational drugs, alcohol consumption, and heavy smoking are habits that men who want to father healthy children should try to avoid, as they can depress sperm count. Along with illicit drug use, some prescription medications such as cemetidine, nitrofurantain, and various other blood pressure remedies can cause difficulty in sexual performance. In addition, certain anti-depressant medications have been linked with sexual dysfunction. Consult your physician about changing certain prescribed medications that may be affecting sexual performance.

There is also increasing evidence that cigarette smoking can depress sperm motility.[35] Additionally, it appears that cigarette smoking in the presence of varicocele has a greater adverse effect than either factor alone.[36]

Suspected environmental toxins, especially in the work-

---

34. A.I. Sealfon, A. Toth, A.W. Zorgniotti, "Chronic Scrotal Hypothermia as a Treatment for Poor Semen Quality," *Lancet* I:904, 1980.

35. R.J. Stillman, M.J. Rosenberg, B.P. Sachs, "Smoking and Reproduction," *Fertility and Sterility* 46:545, 1986.

36. B.C.H Peng, P. Tomashefsky, "The Cofactor Effect," *Fertility and Sterility* 54: 143, 1990.

place, should be avoided by men with a lowered sperm count. Exposure to radiation or industrial toxins, and even living in an area of high altitude, can temporarily lower sperm production. Anyone undergoing X-rays should have their reproductive organs shielded with a lead apron.[37]

Coital timing, i.e. the frequency of intercourse, can directly affect the amount and quality of sperm. For example, long periods of abstinence will give greater amounts of sperm and volume of semen, but this does not necessarily improve the fertility potential of the sperm. (Too large a semen volume can interfere with fertility.) Very frequent intercourse will reduce sperm counts. During certain phases of treatment it is often recommended to time intercourse every other day.

The use of certain lubricants such as baby oil, K-Y Jelly, or Vaseline can destroy sperm. Specially prescribed solutions or peanut, safflower, or vegetable oil are better lubricant options.

Ejaculation Disorders

Ejaculation disorders may be because of anatomical defects in the urinary or reproductive (*urogenital*) tract or problems with the nerves that control the muscles involved in ejaculation. The disorder could also have a psychological cause.

Some of the main types of ejaculation disorders are:

- **Retrograde ejaculation**, in which the semen backs up into the bladder instead of exiting out through the urethra. Prior surgery on the bladder, prostate or colon may have injured the muscles involved in ejaculation. There may also be nervous system involvement.

- **Anejaculation**, where no semen is expelled at all. This is a result of nerve damage associated with spinal cord injury, neurological disorders such as multiple sclerosis, diabetes, or

37. O.P. Ledholm, J. Ranstam, "Depressed Semen Quality: A Study over Two Decades," *Archives of Andrology* 12:113, 1984.

certain types of surgery.

◆ **Delayed ejaculation**, in which ejaculation occurs only after a prolonged period of time. Certain types of anti-depressant medications or neurological disorders may be the cause.

◆ **Premature ejaculation**, which occurs most commonly in men under the age of 40. Ejaculation occurs involuntarily before the penetration. This may be related to sexual technique, psychological factors, or in some cases a neurological source.

◆ **Impotence**, which is a problem achieving or maintaining an erection. Medical conditions in which blood flow is impeded such as high blood pressure, circulatory problems, or diabetes may cause impotence. Neurological and psychological causes have been implicated as well. Stress, depression, and relationship problems also have an effect. Sexual dysfunction can be attributed to a combination of causes and often consultation with a competent sexologist can be helpful.

Viagra (*sildenafil*) is a medication that can increase erectile function in cases of impotence. Not without serious side effects, treatment with Viagra should only be done under the supervision of a doctor.

In Summary

The causes of male-factor infertility can be classified in the following categories:

Structural:

- Varicocele
- Undescended testes
- Obstructive azoospermia
  - Vasectomy
  - Congenital absence of vas deferens (CAVD)
- Infections

- Previous surgery or injury

Sperm production:

- Non-obstructive azoospermia
- Chromosomal abnormalities
- Endocrine disorders
- Cancer treatments
- Trauma and the environment

Ejaculation disorders (physical and psychological):

- Ejaculation disorders
- Impotence

Immunological:

- Anti-sperm antibodies

MALE-FACTOR INFERTILITY

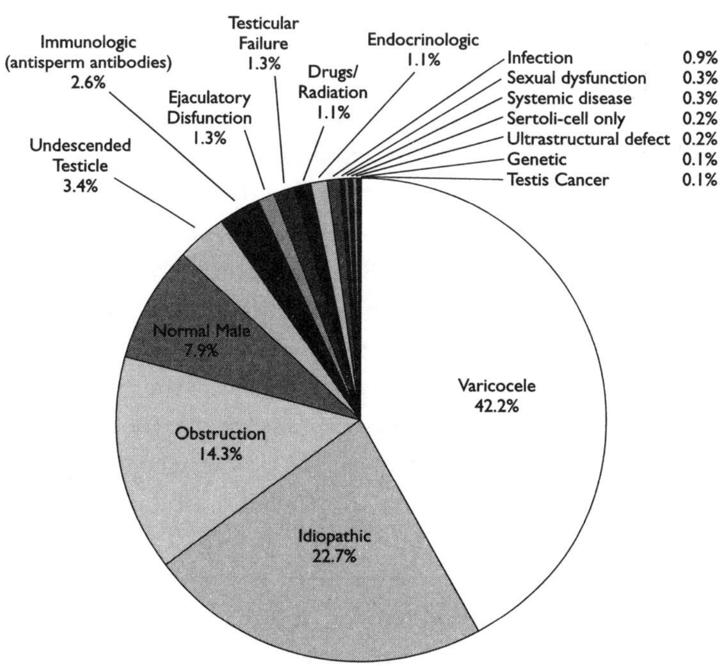

Hopefully, this review of potential causes of fertility problems will guide you in understanding care goals set for you by your doctor. It will also assist you in being assertive and knowledgeable patient-consumers, which can only improve your chances of conception. Now that you have more of a clue of what is going on, you will be better able to understand your preliminary medical examination (see chapters 12 and 13).

SECONDARY INFERTILITY

Secondary infertility applies to a man or a woman who has parented a child in the past and now cannot conceive after one year of unprotected intercourse. Although a man has successfully impregnated a woman or a woman has given birth before, he or she can develop infertility over time.

Secondary infertility is very distressing and often comes as a surprise to a couple whose previous pregnancy was conceived simply and without medical intervention. Couples with secondary infertility, with a child or children at home, are viewed differently by couples suffering from primary infertility. On one hand, they are already parents, but on the other, they have unfulfilled hopes and dreams of a larger family. Some people may make insensitive comments such as, "be grateful for what you have." But for a couple with secondary infertility their disappointment is immense.

How can secondary infertility develop? People change, conditions fluctuate, and we grow older. Life may be more stressful, our work environment may make us sick, or one spouse may be ill. Some of the causes of primary infertility can evolve after a period of time to affect previously fertile couples. Some couples may have been originally subfertile but were "lucky" and conceived anyway. A husband or wife may have been injured and suffer lingering physical consequences. Or simply, there are new marital partners. The following are some of the common causes of female and male secondary infertility.

In the woman:

- Premature ovarian failure
- Advanced age / menopause
- Endometriosis
- Tubal damage due to infection or a previous ectopic pregnancy
- Thyroid problems or other hormonal disturbances
- Consequences of chemotherapy or radiation treatment
- Trauma to or disease of the reproductive organs

In the man:

- Reduced sperm count
- Cumulative damage to the testes as a result of environmental toxins or drug abuse
- Erectile dysfunction or impotence
- Trauma to or disease of the reproductive organs
- Varicocele

Evaluation and treatment may proceed at a more rapid pace for couples with secondary infertility, as the couples are usually older than those with primary infertility. Diagnosis and treatment options are similar for most couples with either primary or secondary infertility problems. Therefore, anyone suffering from infertility — either primary or secondary — should refer to the chapters in this book on causes and treatments.

7. Children of Avraham and Sarah: Bitachon and Infertility

He who trusts in the Lord shall
be surrounded by kindness.
(*Tehillim* 32:10)

PREFACE

WE WROTE THE following chapter hoping to give readers the encouragement needed to take on the challenges of their special situation.

This book addresses two distinct approaches to the subject of *bitachon*, faith. One approach is to understand *bitachon* on its simplest level, which is that one has faith that God will supply whatever he needs. The other approach to *bitachon* is that whatever happens is God's will.

Those who subscribe to the first approach fully believe that God will grant them what they are praying for. Those who subscribe to the second approach do not believe (although they hope) that what they request will necessarily be granted; rather, they accept everything, good or bad, as God's will, and whatever happens is the ultimate good even if they don't understand it.

We had been under the impression that Judaism understands *bitachon* only according to the second approach. However, after studying the wealth of Rabbinic sources on the subject of *bitachon* in our research for this work, we see that the first approach is valid as well.

There is a problem in relating to this topic in a book like this. We are used to hearing about *bitachon* in general or collective terms. The Jewish People have *bitachon* that the *Mashiach* will come; that the troubles we suffer in Israel are for the best, and that eventually we will see the good in our suffering.

It is easier to have *bitachon* regarding things that seem totally out of our control. Ask any God-fearing Jew, and he will tell you that he has *bitachon* in God. God controls the world, so we have faith that He is taking care of business.

We know that God has promised us that our nation will be redeemed, but to believe that God will redeem us from our individual suffering takes a lot more faith. As Rabbi Yochanan said in the name of Rabbi Akiva, "Every *tzarah* (suffering) of an individual is considered a true *tzarah*. But every *tzarah* that is not of an individual [i.e. a collective *tzarah*] is not considered a true *tzarah*."[1]

We have *bitachon* on a collective level because we are all part of Jewish national destiny. It is not personal redemption we are looking for; it is national redemption we seek. Once we talk about *bitachon* on a personal level, however, the idea becomes more challenging. When you are singled out, when you have to hope and pray for something that not everyone has to request, faith becomes a tougher challenge. This is true in all personal areas, such as livelihood, health, success in childrearing, marital harmony, etc. And when it comes to infertility, when emotions are high and people's feelings fragile, the subject of *bitachon* becomes even more difficult to approach.[2]

Some childless couples may have already dealt with the

---

1. *Devarim Rabbah* 2:22.

2. For example, in this chapter we bring a story of a woman who displayed her faith in a complete way (see pp. 94–95). Some readers

subject of *bitachon* in their own minds and may have come to their own conclusions. Perhaps they have spoken with a rabbi and were given direction as to how to approach the topic. Maybe they have done their own reading and research on *bitachon*. Therefore, reading something in this book contrary to what they have already read or heard may upset them or cause them to feel resentment. Because of this, we want the reader to be aware of the two approaches to *bitachon* even before we start dealing with the topic. If we mention an approach to *bitachon* that is different from the way you may have previously thought, you may feel that your entire religiosity is being assaulted.

Which approach do you embrace? If you embrace the first approach — i.e. that God will grant you what you want, then what happens if you never receive your blessing? How are you supposed to come to terms with all those years that you had faith that God would grant you your heart's desire? However, if you embrace the second approach — i.e. that what you want will not necessarily be granted by God but whatever is granted is His will — then aren't you really just protecting yourself from disappointment? Aren't you holding back from completely putting your faith in the Lord? Is this, at least at the outset, a lack of faith that God *does* want to grant you your wishes?

At first glance, these two approaches to faith seem contradictory. How do we understand them?

There are different ways to understand the compatibility

---

might react negatively to that story, for almost nobody today would do what she did. Interestingly, the story appeared in a published *dvar Torah* about faith in God in the wake of the wave of terrorism that has smitten God's Chosen People in these early years of the third millennium. In that context, probably nobody reacted emotionally from the story. Here, however, when it applies to infertility, it will have a different effect.

of the two approaches to *bitachon*. One way is to use the analogy of an athlete. Every coach will tell you that on a high competitive level, the mental attitude of the athlete is what will give him the competitive edge over his rival. When athletes are basically equal in physical ability, victory will come to the one who wants it more, who believes in himself more.

If a boxer goes into the ring and is not entirely convinced that he will win, he has already lost. If the swimmer standing on the diving block is not sure that this time he will achieve his best time ever, he will not win that race. You have to believe in yourself 100 percent that you will win.

The problem is that your rival believes the same thing. He also "knows" that he will win. But only one can win. What happens at the end of the match or the race? How do you handle losing when you were so sure that you were going to win? How do you go into your next match? Will you be wiser, less sure that you will win, or do you still need to believe with all your heart that you will triumph?

Every coach will tell you that you must be sure that you will see victory every single time. If not, you have no chance of winning. So again you believe and set yourself up for possible disappointment. After a loss, the athlete must accept the fact that he lost. Between competitions, he must realize that not everyone can win. But still, at the next match he must again be 100 percent sure that he will defeat his opponents. The athlete must convince himself of this before every tournament.

The same is true for the believing Jew. When one is lacking something important, he must pray to God and be sure that God will grant him what he needs (first approach). However, if his wish isn't granted, he must accept the fact that God feels it is best for him not to attain it (second approach). And the next time he prays for his heart's desire, he should again have the faith that God will answer his prayer and give him what he needs. But if he is again disappointed, he must again accept the fact that this is God's will. In other words, the requesting stage demands of us complete faith that God will grant us our needs; the outcome demands our faith that everything that happens is God's will.

There is another way of reconciling the two approaches to faith. To have *bitachon* requires that you must be sure that God will fulfill your needs. However, you might not necessarily get what you want; perhaps what you wanted is not what you need, and only God can know this. So when you approach God with a request, you must have complete faith that He will answer you — although the answer might not be the one you had hoped for. You have *bitachon* that God will fulfill your true needs.

A third way to understand how both approaches to *bitachon* work is by seeing that people generally employ one of the two approaches intuitively. Before this book was published, we gave chapters out to various childless couples, and to couples who went through infertility treatments, for comments and recommendations. One woman told us that she read the chapters on *bitachon,* as well as the last chapter of the book, and saw the apparent contradiction in the two approaches to faith. We discussed the subject for some time. She then said that during all the treatments, she took the more cautious approach — hoping that they would receive good news, but believing that everything was God's will and perhaps parenthood for her and her husband was not meant to be. Her husband, on the other hand, was totally sure from the beginning that they would be parents. He never doubted it. He wouldn't even *consider* the possibility that they wouldn't have children. She would actually get angry at him, saying things like, "How can you be so sure, what if it won't work out, how do you know," etc. But he just kept on being sure that they would eventually become parents.

Perhaps there are two types of personalities. One puts his faith in God and has no doubt that God will fulfill his needs. The other is not so certain of the outcome, yet believes that whatever happens is for the best.

Discussing this topic with two psychologists (who specialize in infertility counseling), we found that their philosophies, and their advice to clients, could fit into the two categories mentioned. One therapist, Dr. Sara Barris, practices along the lines of the second approach to *bitachon*, advising her clients to have faith in "the process" but not necessarily in the outcome. In other words, don't set yourselves up for disappointment. Another therapist, Dr. Orit Luria, embraces the first approach, that you must have total faith that you are going to win.[3] If there is disappointment, think of it as just losing the battle but not the war.

If you embrace the second approach of *bitachon* that everything is God's will, then if you have a negative result from treatment you will be able to handle it — for you realize that God didn't yet will that treatment to work. But if you feel that God will certainly grant you what you ask for, then handling disappointment will be difficult unless you look at it as merely a lost battle and not a lost war. Rabbi David Cohen commented that the one who takes on this approach must be prepared to face an elevated level of disappointment if there is no blessing in the end. He also holds that this attitude is appropriate only for those who live their lives with a consistently equivalent level of *bitachon* in every situation. He therefore recommends the approach of Dr. Barris for most people.

Dr. Luria explains her position by saying that one who goes into these difficult and trying fertility treatments with

---

3. See this idea expressed in her Hebrew book, *Children of Love*, p. 150.

the attitude of maybe it will work, maybe it won't, will not be able to muster up the strength to continue treatments if the first treatment fails. She feels that you have to have the approach that you will see victory, in order to be strong enough to keep on going. Only after, if you don't see a blessing from your efforts, *r"l*, should you resort to the other type of *bitachon*.

Dr. Alice Domar recommends that before every treatment, you plan a back-up strategy.[4] If Plan A doesn't work, then go to Plan B. If Plan B doesn't work, then resort to the next strategy.

We recommend that you plan for the long term, not just for the next procedure. In other words, say to yourself: *I know I will defeat this infertility; I don't know when or how, but I know that God is going to get me through it*. That way, if your next treatment fails, you still have the strength to fight on. You are at war, and don't give up after losing one battle. In the end you will win the war. You must have faith in defeating the infertility, albeit not necessarily tomorrow.

If you read this chapter on *bitachon*, which deals more with the first approach to faith, yet feel that real *bitachon* is expressed in the second approach, you will find it discussed more at length in the final chapter of the book. However, while reading the present chapter, remember the analogy of the athlete. Realize that there are two valid approaches concerning faith, and one of them will be right for you.

INTRODUCTION

Throughout our history, the trademark of every Jew has been *bitachon*, the faith that God is with us. Before Yehoshua led the Jewish People into the Land of Israel, God said to him, "Be

---

4. *Conquering Infertility*, p. 217.

strong and brave".[5] Have faith! Moreover, the words of King David are the affirmation of every Jew: "Even though I walk in the dark wilderness, I will fear no evil."[6] Simply stated, I will have faith. *Bitachon* in God is our shelter from the storm.

The decision to pursue medical intervention to fulfill your desire to have children will require many resources: knowledge, financing, flexible work schedules, etc., but most of all you will need faith. Without faith in God the road will be too difficult to travel.

As a believing Jew, trust in God will become an integral part of your treatment. There will be you and your spouse, the healthcare professionals, and the Almighty. Belief in God will be a tremendous advantage. By believing that God is with you, you will always have hope. You will never be alone. The Talmud says that there are three partners in the birth of every child: his mother, his father, and God.[7] Just as God is your partner in the birth of your child, He is also your partner during the infertility treatments.

HOPE AND FAITH

It is common to use the words "hope" and "faith" interchangeably (in this chapter too the words will be used interchangeably), although there can be a difference between them. Hope is the wish for something to transpire in the future. It ends with the wish; there is no reason to believe that it will eventually happen. It is the way a gambler hopes that his horse will win, or the way we hope for pleasant weather when we schedule an outdoor event. Hope is looking forward to something.

---

5. *Yehoshua* 1:6.
6. *Tehillim* 23:4.
7. *Niddah* 31a.

Faith, however, is strengthening the wish into a belief that it will happen. Merely hoping that you will have a baby means that you are not inclined to give credence to the success; you just wish it would happen. Faith means that you believe that you will be successful because there is a Power Who will make the outcome favorable. Without God, all we have is hope. With God, we have *bitachon*. The word *bitachon* is derived from the Hebrew root which denotes security or being sure. We are sure it will happen. Too many people understand the concept of *bitachon* as hope. They are optimistic. This is good, but it is not enough. Real *bitachon* is being *batuach* — sure that it will happen.

The following Chassidic story is told:

> Two disciples of a Rebbe, one of whom was childless, would always visit their master during the festival of Sukkos. Every year they lodged at the inn of a childless couple. One year the owner of the inn requested that the disciples ask their Rebbe to pray that his wife become pregnant, and of course they agreed. The innkeeper's wife began strolling around the inn with a brand new baby carriage in anticipation of her new baby.
>
> The next year, when the two disciples arrived at the inn, they were invited to the *bris* of the son of the innkeeper. One chassid received the honor of *kvatter* and the other received the honor of *sandek*. But the *sandek* could not hold back his tears as he held the baby for the circumcision.
>
> When he met the Rebbe the next day, he expressed his anguish. "This couple, whom the Rebbe doesn't even know, asked the Rebbe only one time to pray for them, and they bore a child. I have been asking the Rebbe to pray for my wife to have a child for fifteen years, and we are still childless!" he said.
>
> The Rebbe held his hand and said, "But in all those fifteen long years that you have been asking me to pray for

you, did you ever buy a baby carriage?"

[Of course, in modern times, we wouldn't recommend that anyone do this. Bringing a baby carriage into your home before you have a child will only cause extra anxiety. And if your treatments are unsuccessful, the baby carriage will be a thorn in your eyes. This story is told here to illustrate what level of faith one must reach, but it doesn't mean that we have all reached that level. Also, we have to remember that in those days, there was no medical intervention to assist that couple. Therefore, all they had was their faith; and buying the baby carriage was the only *hishtadlus* that they could have done. Today, a true expression of such faith would embrace the spiritual with the practical, and our *hishtadlus* would be to seek fertility assistance.]

We need to believe that God will help us, with a level of certainty — *betach*. We have no doubt in our minds that He will answer us favorably. Faith in the future means that you believe you will obtain that which you are lacking, because the God Who created the heavens and the earth will see to it that success is achieved.

HOPE IN TOMORROW, FAITH IN THE FUTURE

Faith in a better tomorrow is what keeps all of mankind alive. Without faith, the human spirit could not exist. As the Talmud says, "As long as a man lives, he has hope."[8] Without faith in the future, no revolution in any area of life could ever have taken place. No political change could have occurred, nor could a discovery in science have been made; and no new land would have ever been explored. Faith is what advances the world toward the Messianic period.

Losing faith is a weakness of the human spirit. When one

---

8. Yerushalmi *Berachos* 9a.

loses faith he is essentially saying, God doesn't care about me enough to help me. But God is capable of doing anything, and God loves all His children and wants only the best for each one of them. Faith is the belief that God is capable of making anything happen; it is the belief that God hears our prayers and is sensitive to our needs.

Chazal tell us that our matriarch Sarah never lost her hope of having a child. On the verse, "And God remembered Sarah as He had said,"[9] the Rabbis explain that Sarah said to herself, "What! Am I going to lose my hope? No! Rather I will be delighted with my God, and I will rejoice with the Lord, my Savior." So God said to Sarah, "Because you didn't lose your hope, I won't let your hope fail." Rather, "And God remembered Sarah."[10]

It is human nature for a person to believe that he will be saved from his suffering, as the Midrash says, "King David said that there is hope for everything. The poor man hopes to be rich, the weak man hopes to be strong, the sick man hopes to be healthy."[11]

Some people might tend to protect themselves from pain by not getting their hopes up too much regarding their heart's desires; this way they will not suffer so much when the results of their efforts are disappointing. This may work, and may even be the recommended strategy by psychologists. However, it is not *Chazal*'s approach! *Chazal* tell us not to give up hope, "even if the sharp blade is on your neck."

It is not easy to achieve this level of *bitachon*. It is like the mitzvah of loving your fellow Jew; it is easy to talk about, yet difficult to really do.

Obviously your *bitachon* has to be realistic. If you are lack-

---

9. *Bereishis* 21:1.

10. *Bereishis Rabbah* 53:3.

11. *Midrash Tanchuma, Vezos haBerachah* 6.

ing a uterus, for example, be practical about your expectations. If your biological clock is winding down, don't expect a family of twelve biological kids. The reason that we shouldn't expect supernatural miracles is explained in chapter 14. When you are disappointed, you must learn how to see God's will in the outcome. We will discuss this further in chapter 24.

Chanah achieved such a level of greatness because her desire for a child showed she still had faith in the future. And thus she merited having a son — the prophet Shemuel — who brought a new sense of leadership, unity, and spiritual renaissance to the Jewish People.

THE PARAGON OF FAITH

The ability to have faith through infertility is the prime test of *bitachon*. We are a people who descended from an infertile couple who distinguished themselves with *bitachon* that they would have a baby, when it was impossible by natural means. When you begin your infertility treatments, you should do it with the confidence that you will triumph. The fire of victory should burn in your heart, for you know that God is with you, just like He was with Avraham and Sarah.

Avraham Avinu is considered the quintessential "man of faith." Where did Avraham come shining through with his unyielding faith in God? It was his belief that he and Sarah would have a child. As it is written, "And He [God] took him outside and said, 'Gaze to the heavens and count the stars; if you are able to count them...so shall your offspring be.' And he [Avraham] believed in God."[12]

For a man of a hundred years and a woman of ninety years to have a child was impossible. Medicine was primitive. There were no doctors to rely on. A cure from an advanced

12. *Bereishis* 15:5–6.

medical research center was unfathomable. Yet Avraham still believed that if God said he would have a child, then he would indeed have one. So when God told him that he would have a child, he laughed. That laughter was not laughter of cynicism but laughter of joy. That laughter was so beautiful to God that He told Avraham to name his newborn baby Yitzchak, a name that would reflect the happiness of his faith. The name Yitzchak is derived from the Hebrew root which denotes laughter — but it is in the future tense. Hence the name Yitzchak means, "he will laugh." This reflected Avraham's faith. Avraham laughed from happiness, for he believed that in the near future he would laugh the laughter of joy at being a father.

KINDNESS, NOT PAYBACK

Even if you perceive that your level of piety is wanting, you should never relinquish your reliance on God. God helps all of His children, and believing this is the key to *bitachon*. Thinking that God will refuse you because you are not deserving of His help demonstrates a lack of faith. Your wish stays on the level of hope, not *bitachon*. When we ask for God's help, we are imploring Him for unconditional kindness. We are not asking God to grant our wishes because we have done this or that mitzvah. We are not asking for payback. If we could just understand this point, we would understand the most essential quality of faith. As King David said, "There are those who have confidence in their good deeds. There are those who rely on the actions of their fathers. And I have faith in You, even though I do not have good deeds."[13]

Consider the implications of the alternative. If we would only ask for Divine intervention based on our good deeds,

---

13. *Midrash Shochar Tov, Tehillim* 141.

then those who would be beseeching God's help would essentially be saying that they are righteous. And based on their level of devoutness, they "deserve" an affirmative response to their supplication. This is flagrantly presumptuous. In addition to that, if we are requesting something from God based upon our behavior, then God can inspect all of our deeds. Nobody would be able to stand up to that. It is to our advantage to beg for unconditional love and kindness, rather than payback for our merits.

The Chafetz Chaim said in the name of the Gra that the quality of *bitachon* is not conditional on our merits. Even a person who is not proper in his behavior, but strengthens his faith in God, merits God's protection and salvation by virtue of his faith. This is learned from the verse in *Tehillim*, "The eye of God is upon those who fear Him, to those who await His kindness."[14] The verse clearly describes two classifications, those who fear God, and those who look forward to His kindness, even if they are not God-fearing.[15] Furthermore, Rav Moshe Feinstein said that all prayers are accepted, even those said by sinners.[16]

God told Moshe, "I shall show favor when I wish to show favor."[17] *Chazal* say that this means that God will specifically show mercy even to people who appear undeserving.[18]

This idea, according to Rashi, is the meaning of the Talmud's statement that one who extends his prayer and expects to be answered because of it will have heartache. This is be-

---

14. *Tehillim* 33:18.

15. *Shem Olam, Kuntress Nefutzos Yisrael*, chap. 8. (For more sources proving this point, see *Beis Yechezkel*, by Rabbi Moshe Yechiel haLevi Tzuriel, *Sha'ar Bitachon*, pp. 171–174.)

16. *Igros Moshe, Yoreh De'ah*, vol. VIII, 276.

17. *Shemos* 33:19.

18. *Berachos* 7a.

cause he thought that as a reward for his long prayer he would be answered.[19] In reality, we are answered because God grants us *chesed*.

When God promised Avraham that he would have a child, the verse says: "He [Avraham] believed in God, and he considered it as righteousness."[20] Who considered it as righteousness? According to the Ramban, it was Avraham who felt it was the righteous kindness of God to grant him a child.[21] He did not feel that he earned a child based on his good deeds, and thus considered it unconditional love and kindness. So if Avraham felt the promise of a child to be a gift of kindness and not a reward for his good deeds, who are we to think that our deeds could merit us such a gift?

We are all deficient in something. If you feel that your sins will prevent you from attaining your deepest desires, then you will never be able to pray. You will give up hope. Your bond with God will come to a stifling halt, and that will be the greatest loss of all.

The Torah should be our life, but an insufficient level of Torah observance should not prevent us from putting our trust in the Almighty. A child may misbehave. Even when the parent is angry with the child, if the child is in pain or in trouble, he always knows that he can go to his parents for help. The child will not hesitate to say, "Mommy, Daddy, I'm hurting." He trusts his parents. He knows that his parents are always there for him. We are all God's children. He is always there for us.

The verse from *Shir haShirim*, "My dove in the clefts of the rock, in the secret places of the terrace, show Me your appearance, and let Me hear your voice; for your voice is sweet, and

---

19. *Berachos* 32b, 55a. See Rashi ad loc., *d.h. U'me-ayin ba.*
20. *Bereishis* 15:6.
21. Ramban, ibid.

your appearance is beautiful,"[22] teaches us that God is always yearning to hear our prayers. For we are the dove, hidden in the rock from the predators, all of our troubles. Even when we are concealed in the rock — which can also indicate that we are on a low spiritual level — God still says, "show Me your appearance, and let Me hear your voice [in prayer]; for your voice is sweet, and your appearance is beautiful."

THE CLOUD AND THE FIRE

The book of *Shemos* is the story of exile and suffering, and of freedom and redemption. It is the chronicle of the birth of a nation, a special nation, bound to the Creator of the world. *Sefer Shemos* is the fulfillment of the promise to a childless Avraham that his children will be many, and that they will be taken out of slavery and given a great reward. The story of *Shemos* is the Divine model of *hashgachah,* providence. God keeps His promises, and watches over the nation that bears His name.

The book closes with a description of the *anan* — the heavenly cloud that protected and guided the people through all their travels: "For the cloud of the Eternal was above the Dwelling during the day, and at night there would be a fire, visible to all the House of Israel, throughout all their journeys."[23] The Netziv expounds on the Scripture's emphasis, *all* their journeys. God's protection and care of the Jewish People was ceaseless, whether the people were going against His will or whether they were fulfilling it. God was always with them.[24]

The cloud offered protection from the hot rays of the

---

22. *Shir haShirim* 2:14.

23. *Shemos* 40:38.

24. *Ha'amek Davar, Shemos* 40:38.

desert sun and the fire illuminated the darkness of the night. The cloud represents protection; the fire symbolizes direction. God's protection and guidance of the Jewish People were ceaseless, as well as "visible to all the House of Israel." We have to do our part, and that is to look in the direction of God for His providence.

We are a nation whose origin is the fulfillment of a promise to a barren couple that they would have a child. Their belief in the fulfillment of that promise is embedded in the souls of all of us. No matter what spiritual level we may be on, no matter what we did in our past, as long as we look to the cloud and the fire, as long as we anticipate God's protection and seek His direction, the Heavenly cloud and the light will always be with us. And God-willing, we too will merit the blessing of children.

BITACHON AND HISHTADLUS — FAITH AND EFFORT

There is a classic dynamic between *bitachon*, how much we should rely on God, and *hishtadlus*, how much effort we should put into helping ourselves. Should we just sit back and relinquish our troubles to the Almighty, or should we attempt to solve our problems through all known physical means? Reams of philosophical literature deal with this quandary, providing convincing arguments on both sides. Judaism's approach to medical issues and other challenges in life is that we should rely on God while seeking practical solutions to our problems. Notice that trust in God is not the secondary component, but rather the main factor. We see that the matriarchs did whatever they could to have children. They gave their maidservants to their husbands so that the maidservants could bear children for them. Rachel and Leah "did business" over Reuven's *duda'im* because it was a plant thought to be good for fertility.

When we seek any type of help, we must still put our faith in God that He is the One Who will provide whatever we are lacking. Regarding infertility, we must view the doctor as the emissary of God. The doctor is not the one who will bring us our salvation; rather, he is the "human tool," so to speak, of the Almighty. It is only the Almighty Who can give us what we are lacking.

We need to have *bitachon* in our *hishtadlus* as well. In other words, we need to have faith that we are doing the right thing by our *hishtadlus*. *Bitachon* means security. We need to be secure in our efforts that we are doing everything we can. This is having *bitachon* in the process, rather than *bitachon* in the results. We do our part to achieve our goal, and the results we leave to God. If God wills it, it will be, but at least we know that we did our part. God can never come to us with a "complaint," as it were, that we didn't do what was in our power to do.

King David tells us how far this feeling of faith in God, as opposed to faith in man, goes. It is written in *Tehillim*, "It is better *lachasos* — to trust — in God, *mibtoach* — than to trust — in man."[25] What is the difference between these two Hebrew words, *lachasos* and *mibtoach* (whose infinitive is *livtoach*), which both mean "trust"? Rashi explains that the latter is a very strong type of trust. It means to be certain. The former denotes a weaker type of trust.[26] The Gra explains that *livtoach* is when someone pledges something to you. *Lachasos* is trust without receiving a pledge.[27] King David is saying that it is better to take refuge in the shade of God (according to Rashi), or to rely on God without any guarantees (according to the

---

25. *Tehillim* 118:8.
26. Rashi, ibid.
27. Gra, *Mishlei* 14:26.

Gra), than to trust in the assurances of a person.[28]

Some say this was the mistake that Yosef made when he trusted in Pharaoh's head butler. It appeared as if he was putting more trust in the butler than in God, as if only then he had a chance to be redeemed from prison. The Chazon Ish explains that Yosef's sin was that he knew the butler would not help him, yet he asked him anyway.[29] This actually shows a lack of *bitachon,* for he did what is called a *ma'aseh yiush.* Yosef's sin, as interpreted by the Chazon Ish, teaches us that all of our efforts, our *hishtadlus,* should be serious. We should avoid far-fetched undertakings to achieve our coveted goal. We should refrain from superstitious acts and amulets that do not have basis in our Torah or in Jewish tradition. We should never forget that our faith is in God, not in good-luck charms. We explore approved means to have children only while realizing that they are merely the mechanisms through which God will grant His blessing.

BELIEF IN MIRACLES

Earlier we mentioned Avraham and Sarah as a standard of *bitachon,* for they had faith when it was "medically impossible" for them to have children. Avraham and Sarah had reached tremendously high levels of faith by believing that they would have a child.

Rashi regards the words, "And He considered it as righteousness,"[30] to mean that God considered it as righteousness on Avraham's part to believe in Him.[31] Why? What is so special about Avraham's believing that God could grant him a

---

28. See the Malbim, who explains it differently.

29. *Emunah u'Vitachon,* chap. 2, number 6.

30. *Bereishis* 15:6.

31. Rashi, ibid. This is a different explanation from the Ramban that was cited earlier.

child in his old age?[32] Avraham believed in God before. Why was Avraham's faith in God when it came to granting him a child, more praiseworthy?

We know that God does miracles that are outside of the bounds of nature, and we know that God can do anything He wants; but *how* do we know this?

The answer to this question lies in what God Himself said to Moshe Rabbeinu: "I am God, *Yud-hei-vav-hei.* And I appeared to your forefathers, Avraham, Yitzchak and Yaakov, as *El Shaddai;* but My name *Yud-hei-vav-hei* I did not make known to them."[33]

The name *Yud-hei-vav-hei* portrays God as the God Who can execute miracles outside the realm of nature, simply because He is Master of the universe. Knowing *Yud-hei-vav-hei* is knowing God as the One Who will change the laws of nature, such as splitting the sea, to save us.[34] The name *El Shaddai,* however, depicts God as the God of nature, Who conducts the world and assists us from within nature's boundaries. To the patriarchs, God appeared as *El Shaddai;* the miracles they saw and experienced were performed within its laws.

Every Jew knows that God is capable of doing anything. But the reason that this is such a central notion of our belief is because of the Exodus from Egypt. Avraham, however, came to believe in God on his own. Through his own philosophic inquiry, and not through experiencing supernatural miracles, he came to the conclusion that there is a Master of all things, that there is a Divine Power Who moves the universe, a Creator and Sustainer. Unlike us, Avraham's knowledge was

---

32. This question is asked by many commentators.

33. *Shemos* 6:2–3.

34. Although God is referred to as *Yud-hei-vav-hei* even in the book of *Bereishis,* it wasn't until the Exodus from Egypt that God *revealed* Himself in the world as *Yud-hei-vav-hei.* See *Shemos* 6:2–3, and Rashi ad loc.

within the parameters of *El Shaddai,* the God Who controls and supervises the universe through nature. He never experienced God as One Who changes nature to perform any phenomenon.[35]

The Torah tells us that Sarah was post-menopausal,[36] and *Chazal* say that Sarah didn't even have a womb.[37] The only way Sarah could have had a child was through a supernatural occurrence. Avraham and Sarah lived before God split the sea and brought the manna. They had no encounter with miracles outside the realm of nature. Without a promise from God that they would have a child, they would have had no way of even entertaining that possibility. When God said that they would have a child, they trusted Him. They knew that a child would be born to them.

This is what it means when it says that Sarah laughed when she heard from her three guests that in another year she would have a child. The verse says, "Now Avraham and Sarah were old, advanced in years; Sarah had ceased having a woman's cycle. And Sarah laughed about herself, saying, 'After I have become withered will I [now] have smooth skin? And my husband is [also] old!'"[38] When Sarah laughed, it appeared that she was lacking faith. And even God said to Avraham, "Why did Sarah laugh?...Is anything beyond God?"[39] Sarah believed that God would give her a child somehow, but she couldn't figure out how. She believed God could make anything happen, but couldn't comprehend how a supernatural miracle works. The Seforno suggests that she envi-

---

35. We are referring here only to the miracles Avraham experienced that are depicted in the Torah, not those described in the Midrash.

36. *Bereishis* 18:11.

37. *Yevamos* 64b.

38. Ibid., verses 11–12.

39. Ibid., verses 13–14.

sioned something like *techias ha-meisim* — the resurrection of the dead.[40]

When God said, "Why did Sarah laugh?" He was asking, why didn't she believe that supernatural miracles could be achieved, in her case through pregnancy? Sarah claimed that she didn't laugh, meaning that she never lost her belief that she could have a child. Yet she was rebuked — "No you laughed" — because she didn't believe that the laws of nature could be changed. So Sarah always believed that she would have a child, but she just couldn't understand how it would happen.

Avraham's trust in God went through a similar process. Avraham looked up at the sky and said to God that having children was not "in the stars" for him.[41] In those days, the stars were the means through which people perceived their *mazal* — their destiny. Therefore, this was Avraham's way of saying that there was no "scientific," natural way for him to have a child.[42] That is also why Avraham never prayed until this point for a child,[43] for he thought that if it wasn't in your nature to have a child, then you simply couldn't have one.

Our Sages teach that God said to Avraham, "Abandon your theories of astrology!" Don't put all your faith in the scientific knowledge of your day and age. I can give you a child even though you cannot naturally have one. I will change your name from Avram to Avraham, for now you are not only the "father of Aram" (Avram), but the "father of many nations" (Avraham). You have a new purpose in the world. Nature deals you certain conditions, and takes nothing else into account. I am the Creator of everything and I am changing

---

40. Seforno, *Bereishis* 18:12.
41. Rashi, *Bereishis* 15:5.
42. See *Tiferes Yisrael* at the end of *Kiddushin*, Boaz.
43. See also the commentary *Melo haOmer*, cited in *Ma'ayanah shel Torah*.

your *mazal*, as I am changing your name, for you have a purpose in life, and in your case it is to have a child, and to be a father of many nations.

And Avraham believed. He believed, even though the birth of a child contradicted the principles of nature, and even though there was no proof that God would change the laws of nature to perform a miracle.

So although you may not have received a personal pledge from God that you will have a child, you know that He can make anything happen. He can split the sea, He can stop the sun. He can give Avraham and Sarah a child. He can give you a child too. Pray with confidence, not just with hope, that God will answer your prayers, and do all the procedures that you need to do, for that is *bitachon*.

ZION AND THE BARREN WOMAN

You do have reason to believe that God will take away your infertility. First of all, the Midrash tells us of God's promise that He will remember the childless: "In the future I will turn the seas into dry land. I already did through Moshe and the splitting of the sea. In the future I will remember childless women. I already did, as it says, "God remembered Sarah."[44] [The Midrash compares Sarah's pregnancy to the splitting of the sea, as they were both miracles that defied nature. In order to attain "credibility" for the future, as it were, God has to "prove" that He can do it. So He says, "I already did."[45]]

Secondly, another *midrash* tells us that concerning a barren woman, if the Torah uses the word *ein* (she doesn't have)

---

44. *Vayikra Rabbah* 27:4; a similar version appears in *Koheles Rabbah* 3:1.

45. The idea that God "proves" his ability to fulfill promises is common in midrashic literature. See also *Midrash Aggadah, Bereishis* 30:22 (Buber ed.): "Ephraim, who is the grandson of Rachel, bears testimony that God answers the barren."

concerning her infertility,[46] the meaning is that she will ultimately have a child.[47]

Our prophets compared the Land of Israel throughout the Jews' exile to a barren woman.[48] Accordingly, concerning the Land of Israel the prophet says, *doresh **ein** lah* "No one cares."[49] We have a guarantee that God will bring the redemption and the Land of Israel will see her children return to her, as it says, *U'va l'Tzion go'el*, "And the redeemer will come to Zion."[50] This constant association between barren women and Zion begs a deep connection between the two.[51] If the prophets constantly felt the need to compare Zion to a barren woman, it is because Zion is in pain throughout the exile, just as a barren woman is in pain throughout her infertility.

We all believe that God will bring the redemption, and that He will bring an end to the pain of the barren Zion. This is the type of *bitachon*, mentioned earlier, that we all subscribe to. There is no believing Jew who doesn't believe in the salvation of the Jewish People and the ultimate redemption of the Land of Israel. We just don't know when it will come. We hope that it will happen today, tomorrow, this month, this year. When it doesn't happen, we tell ourselves that it will happen tomorrow. It will happen when God wants it to happen. And we hope to be there when it does happen.

Zion suffered like a barren woman, and barren women

---

46. Regarding Sarah, see *Bereishis* 11:30 (***ein** lah valad*); regarding Chanah, see *I Shemuel* 1:2 (***ein** yeladim*).

47. *Bereishis Rabbah* 38:14 (end of *Parashas Noach*).

48. Even when the Midrash lists seven barren women, it lists Zion as one of them. *Midrash Aggadah, Bereishis* 53 (Buber ed.); *Pesikta d'Rav Kahana* 20 (Mandelbaum ed.).

49. *Yirmeyahu* 30:17.

50. *Yeshayahu* 59:20.

51. See *Pesikta d'Rav Kahana* 22:2 (Mandelbaum ed.). It is a *gezerah shavah*.

will be redeemed just like Zion. We must have faith in that, just as we have faith in the final redemption. We don't know when it will happen, but we do know that it will happen: "Sing, O barren one, you who does not bear; break forth into singing, and cry aloud, you who did not travail with child: for more will be the children of the desolate... says the Lord."[52] This is God's promise to Zion. What God promises Zion, he promises barren women. You have every reason to believe that God will bring an end to infertility. We just don't know when. Let us hope that it will be soon.

52. *Yeshayahu* 54:1.

8. Improving Fertility

God is my rock and my redeemer.
(*Tehillim* 19:15)

OUR REPRODUCTIVE SYSTEM is very delicate. It is vulnerable to our physical and psychological health, the lifestyle we practice, and the environment we live in. Reproduction is a secondary function, not necessary for preservation of daily life. Therefore, our body will shunt its available resources first to those essential body systems required for survival, and only afterwards tap into our reserves to support reproductive and other secondary functions. To support life, the circulatory, respiratory, and nervous systems will continue to function even if we are not at our optimum health.

The reproductive system is a mirror of our general health and well being. For instance, a man who is ill may have a reduced sperm count. Stress and lack of sleep in women can cause irregular periods. Since hormones are solely produced in our bodies, their imbalance often reflects impaired health. A person may feel fine, but have a dietary deficiency or suffer some kind of hormonal imbalance that only becomes evident when trying to conceive.

The causes of infertility are numerous, and in response, there are a variety of treatment options available. Medications or invasive procedures, though sometimes necessary, should not always be a first resort in fertility treatment. Most couples would prefer to approach their fertility problems naturally, while avoiding expensive treatments and their accompanying side effects. If we could some how improve our health to the most optimal level, maybe as a result we could overcome some obstacles interfering with fertility.

There are health factors we have no control over, such as heredity, birth defects, accidents, or childhood diseases. However, we can optimize our options by implementing positive changes in our daily lives. Now is the time to catch any emerging physical problems before they can seriously effect your health when you are older.

Whether or not you have ever thought about leading a "healthy lifestyle," let's take a look at some relatively simple ideas that may affect your physical health — changes you can make in your life that may benefit your general health and increase fertility.

MODERN OR TALMUDIC REMEDIES?

People have always looked for remedies that would assist fertility. The Talmud mentions some of them. Today, however, we should not rely on the remedies of the Talmud unless there is modern scientific support validating those ancient remedies. Even in the time of Tosafos (twelfth century), the Rabbis said that the medicines of the Talmud were not suitable for the present day.[1] Some say that one who does rely on them should be excommunicated, for it will bring people to think negatively about *Chazal* — if they think that *Chazal* made incorrect statements in this area, then they might think that *Chazal*'s statements in other areas are mistaken as well.[2]

According to some opinions, the reason that what *Chazal*

---

1. Tosafos, *Mo'ed Katan* 11a.

2. See Prof. Avraham Steinberg, *Encyclopedia of Jewish Medical Ethics* (Jerusalem: The Schlesinger Institute for Medical Halachic Research at Shaare Zedek Medical Center, 1988), vol. II, pp. 244–282. In the English

said regarding health issues and medicine isn't relevant today is because nature has changed since Talmudic times. What was true back then may not be true today.[3] Another reason is that we are not sure anymore about what exactly *Chazal* were referring to. Perhaps the plant that we recognize today according to a particular name was a different plant altogether back then. Even if it was the same plant or herb, we don't know how much to use, which part of the plant to use, with what mixture it should be used, how it should be prepared, and so on.[4]

In this book, we note those medical opinions and remedies of *Chazal* for which there is modern, scientific support. *Chazal* would want us to rely on our own modern medicine rather than on their own understanding of science in their time.[5]

However, for educational purposes only, the following are some things that *Chazal* saw as either decreasing or increasing male fertility.

Things that decrease male fertility: Salt, famine, leprosy, sleeping on the ground, beer and other alcoholic beverages, and bad wine. Also, waiting when one feels the need to urinate.

Things that increase male fertility: red meat, dairy products, eggs, certain beans, garlic, *esrogim* (citrons), and old wine.

---

edition of the book (Jerusalem: Feldheim Publishers and Shaare Zedek Medical Center, 2003), this appears in vol. I, pp. 151–160.

3. See Igros Moshe, *Choshen Mishpat*, vol. II, chap. 73,4.

4. *Chavas Yair*, chap. 234.

5. *Responsa Rav Sherira Gaon*, in *Otzar haGeonim, Gittin*, p. 152; Rambam, *Guide to the Perplexed*, section 3, chap. 14.

NUTRITION AND FERTILITY

Body Fat: Too Much or Too Little

Malnutrition has been linked to decreased reproductive function. You don't have to look like you are starving to death in order to be classified as malnourished. Not eating a balanced diet of protein, carbohydrates, fats, and daily portions of fruits and vegetables could put you in this category. Being very thin may be the style for some, but will not necessarily work for you if you want to have children. Underweight women do not produce enough estrogen to support their reproductive function.[6]

Conversely, obesity has been implicated in infertility as well. Being overweight leads to all sorts of health problems, which are then treated with medications that can interfere with fertility and sexual function. High blood pressure medications are notorious for interfering with a man's sexual performance. Sometimes, a man can avoid having to take medicine for high blood pressure by keeping his blood pressure normal through eating properly, losing extra weight, and exercising moderately during his fathering years. Often a family physician will give a person a trial period of time to improve his diet and increase his physical activity in order to lower his blood pressure naturally before resorting to pills. Motivation such as fear of disease or a desire for children is a great incentive that often works!

Maturity-onset diabetes, which has also been implicated in reduced sexual function, can be avoided, or at least delayed. The same grace period of trial self-help is usually extended to men with a diagnosis of borderline diabetes. A man should do all that he can to get himself in shape on his own

---

6. R.E. Frisch, "Body Fat and Reproductive Ability," *Seminars in Reproductive Endocrinology* 3:45, 1985.

before the doctor has to step in. Utilizing dieticians, personal trainers, and weight-loss support groups can help. Often a person's supplemental insurance will cover these added health expenses.

In overweight women, the over-production of insulin can throw hormones out of balance and prevent conception. Obesity, polycystic ovaries, and insulin resistance have been proven to be a vicious cycle interfering with conception. Even losing ten to twenty pounds can get your hormone production back in sync. Obesity in women is associated with decreased likelihood of conceiving, and these women often require much higher doses of fertility drugs during the course of ovarian stimulation treatments.[7] Drastic weight fluctuations and fad dieting must be avoided. Consult a professional dietician or weight-loss group.

Diet and Reproduction

Certain foods effect estrogen levels. Protein consumption is an important component in a balanced diet. But where does that protein come from? In western countries, it is common to treat livestock not only with hormones to increase milk production (for dairy cows) but with growth hormones to increase body mass before slaughter. These hormones filter down to us humans and effect sperm counts and hormone balance in males and females.[8] In the past decade we have also increased our consumption of soy-based products such as vegetarian patties, sausages, *phytoestrogens* in plant products, and soybean oil. Increased intake of these foods has been implicated in disrupt-

---

7. C. DiCarlo, F. Zullo, "Superovulation with u-FSH, Correlations with Body Mass Index and Body Fat Distribution," *Gynecologic Endocrinology* 10:17–21, 1996.

8. R. Sharpe, "Lifestyle and Environmental Contribution to Male Infertility," *British Medical Bulletin* 56 (No. 3); pp. 630–642, 2000.

ing estrogen production and balance in men and women.[9] Are we suggesting that you eliminate protein from the diet? No, of course not! But if you suspect you may have fertility problems due to hormone imbalance, then eating untreated meat products and eliminating soy products may be helpful. Along these lines, avoiding MSG and other artificial food additives can reduce unwanted chemical reactions in the body. *Acrylamide*, a chemical by-product in fried and oven-baked foods, especially potato chips and French fries, has received world-wide attention. The US Food and Drug Administration (FDA) is conducting tests to see what can be done to reduce or eliminate this chemical since it can cause cancer, neurological damage, and infertility.

Another common addition to our diet is caffeine. Soft drinks, coffee, tea, chocolate, and even some pain relievers keep us peppy during the day and awake at night. Unfortunately, caffeine has been linked to increased risk of miscarriages and reduces the likelihood of conception in women after just one cup of coffee per day.[10]

We know that too much dietary fat and unnatural food additives are not good for us. Should we make up for deficiencies in our diet with additional vitamins and minerals? Healthy people who eat a balanced diet do not need to take vitamin supplements. The American Dietary Association recommends us to eat at least five servings of fruit and vegetables a day in order to obtain the vitamins we need. Nutritional information to promote good health can be easily obtained from a number of sources as well as from your doctor or a profes-

---

9. A.M. Andersson, N.E. Skakkebaek, "Exposure to Exogenous Estrogens in Food: Possible Impact on Human Development and Health," *European Journal of Endocrinology* 140:477–85, 1999.

10. M. Brachs, L. Dulgosz, "Coffee Decreases Fertility," *Epidemiologic Review*, vol. 14, p. 83, 1992.

sional dietician. Some health professionals suggest that supplementing our daily diet with vitamins and minerals will improve our health in general and fertility in particular. This may be one natural way to improve our chances of conception. In the next section we will review some of the research which shows the influence of nutritional supplementation on fertility.

Fat-Soluble and Water-Soluble Vitamins

Excess fat-soluble vitamins (vitamins A, D, E, and K) build up in the body, as opposed to water-soluble vitamins (vitamins B and C), which are excreted by the body in the urine. Therefore, the possibility of toxicity from too much supplementation can be a problem with vitamins A, D, E, and K. A person needs to be careful not to exceed the recommended daily allowance of different vitamins and minerals, which can in itself be harmful.

◆ **Vitamin E:** Vitamin E has an important function as an antioxidant, which means that it literally keeps the waste products that float inside our body from harming our health. Vitamin E supplements of 400 IU per day have been shown to increase sperm parameters (number, shape, motility).[11] Vitamin E supplements of 500 IU per day has been shown to increase endometrial thickness in women unresponsive to additional estrogen.[12]

◆ **Vitamin C:** Known for fighting infections and keeping colds away, vitamin C (ascorbic acid) also keeps our skin, teeth, bones, and cartilage strong. Implicated in protecting the

---

11. B. Bartoov, M. Geva, N. Zabludovsky, "The Effect of Antioxidant Treatment on Human Spermatozoa and Fertilization Rate," *Fertility and Sterility* 66:430–4, 1996.

12. N.L. Bataille, F. Olivennes, "Thin Endometrium Improvement by Combined Pentoxifylline and Vitamin E," *Human Reproduction* vol. 17, no. 5, pp. 5:1249–1253, 2002.

body against damage from cell destruction (free-radical damage), supplementation of 500 mg per day improves the quality of sperm in smokers.[13] In all men, vitamin C has been shown to increase sperm counts and reduce clumping. Women can also benefit from vitamin C, but one should not exceed 1000 mg per day during pregnancy.

◆ **Vitamin B12:** For the prevention of anemia, vitamin B12 is acquired primarily from animal products and synthesized in the small intestine. As opposed to iron-deficiency anemia, pernicious anemia has been linked to increased number of miscarriages, failure to ovulate, and implantation failure. Many women have been successfully treated with vitamin B12, immediately becoming pregnant and delivering at term.[14] Regular intake of meat, fish, eggs, and milk usually supply enough vitamin B12. A simple blood test will rule out any deficiency. An interesting note: too much vitamin C can interfere with B12 metabolism.

◆ **Folic Acid:** Vitamin B9, or folacin, is needed for cell growth and reproduction. It functions with vitamins B12 and C in the breakdown of proteins and in the making of hemoglobin. The World Health Organization and various national nutritional organizations recommend that every woman in her childbearing years take a daily 400 mcg supplement of folic acid, before becoming pregnant, to prevent anemia and reduce the risks of birth defects and miscarriage.[15]

◆ **Vitamin B6:** Vitamin B6, or pyridoxine, is part of the

---

13. E.B. Dawson, W.A. Harris, "Effect of Ascorbic Acid Supplementation on the Sperm Quality of Smokers," *Fertility and Sterility* 58:1034–9, 1992.

14. M. Bennet, "Vitamin B12 Deficiency, Infertility and Recurrent Fetal Loss," *Journal of Reproductive Medicine* 46:209–212, 2001.

15. H. Bellet, I. Quere, "Case Report With Recurrent Miscarriages," *Fertility and Sterility* vol. 69, no. 1, pp. 152–154, 1998.

B-complex vitamin group. It is needed to break down amino acids (proteins) and to make antibodies, and for glucose metabolism and red blood cell synthesis. During pregnancy and nursing, the body requires greater amounts of vitamin B6, while certain hormone treatments interfere with its absorption in the body. According to Karen Bradstreet, author of *Overcoming Infertility Naturally* (Pleasant Grove, UT: Woodland Books, 1995), vitamin B6 is an infertile woman's best friend. She recommends B6 supplementation as a natural way to correct estrogen and progesterone imbalances. She goes on to quote a study which demonstrates vitamin B6's ability to lower an elevated prolactin level, thus improving fertility.[16] Vitamin B6 has also been recommended to treat nausea and vomiting during the first trimester of pregnancy. It is advised not to exceed 200 mg of B6 daily.

Foods rich in the B vitamins are milk, yeast, whole grains, organ meats, beans, green vegetables, eggs, carrots, bananas, nuts, oranges, whole wheat. Heat and prolonged cooking, especially cooking with water, can destroy vitamins in food. Symptoms of deficiencies in the B family of vitamins include: mouth and tongue sores, cracking at corners of the mouth, fatigue, sleep disturbances, nausea, diarrhea, depression, and irritability. Vitamin B deficiencies in men have been shown to damage the testes and other reproductive organs.[17] Although vitamin B is water-soluble and excesses are excreted through the urine, it is unwise to consume more than necessary.

Minerals

We are familiar with the importance of vitamins, but what exactly are minerals and what do they do for the body? Minerals are substances found naturally in the

16. Wright, Jonathan, *Dr. Wright's Book of Nutritional Therapy*, (Emmaus, PA: Rodale Press, Inc., 1979).

17. D. Calloway, "Nutrition and Reproductive Function in Men," *Reviews in Clinical Nutrution* 53:373, 1983.

ground and in the food we eat. Minerals are important in regulating many body functions such as nerve responses, muscle contractions, food metabolism, electrolyte balance, and the making of hormones. Supplementation of certain minerals may be helpful in improving fertility.

- **Selenium:** An additional 200 mcg a day can significantly increase sperm motility.[18] As there are no particular selenium-rich foods, one must take this compound as a supplement. However, excessive consumption of selenium supplements can have a harmful effect on semen quality and can be toxic above recommended levels.

- **Zinc:** A lack of zinc can effect normal sperm production. For men with a low testosterone level, zinc supplements of 20 mg per day may raise testosterone levels and increase sperm production.[19] Zinc is also required for normal functioning of the hypothalamic-pituitary-gonadal axis. Leydig cell synthesis of testosterone is dependent on adequate dietary zinc. A zinc deficiency can cause testicular failure.[20]

Zinc-rich foods are eggs, nuts, cereals, and wheat germ.

Herbs and Fertility

Most alternative approaches to fertility take a step back from the mechanics of fertilization to address the overall state of the body. The *holistic* approach treats the entire body as a whole in order to remedy any imbalance no matter how small. If one part is not well, it affects the entire person and therefore the entire person must be treated. For example, if the body is not producing viable

---

18. A. MacPherson, R. Scott, "The Effect of Oral Selenium Supplementation on Human Sperm Motility," *British Journal of Urology* 8:276–80, 1998.

19. R. Hartoma, A. Netter, "Effect of Zinc Administration on Plasma Testosterone and Sperm Count," *Archology of Andrology* 7:69–73, 1981.

20. C. Hunt, P. Johnson, "Effects of Dietary Zinc Depletion on Seminal Volume," *American Journal of Nutrition* 56:148–157, 1992.

eggs, perhaps the blood supply to the ovaries has been impaired by any number of factors. The problem could be alleviated by improving circulation, building blood (iron levels), and improving digestion. If there is a hormone imbalance, added nourishment to the organs that regulate that balance may help.

Herbs are reputed to strengthen organ systems and improve their function, without harmful side effects. Various herbs can be taken in the form of drops, pellets under the tongue, or as tea infusions. However, it's always best to check with a doctor before doing this.

- **False unicorn root:** This has a long history as a fertility herb. Ten drops in the morning reportedly improves ovarian function. For use up until the twelfth week of pregnancy.
- **Dong quai root:** A Chinese herb commonly used to build up the female system by enhancing the utilization of estrogen. Recommended dosage: 20 to 30 drops three times a day until conception.
- **Raspberry leaf:** Strengthens reproductive organs, supports digestion, supplies a wide array of vitamins and minerals. Two 50 mg capsules a day strengthens the uterine lining and may lengthen the luteal phase.

There are many other herbs that may help enhance your fertility and health in general. Seek professional advice before embarking on any nutritional program and never exceed the recommended dosage.

To prepare an infusion, fill a clean, wide-mouthed jar one-third full with dried herbs, fill to the top with boiling water, cap, and steep for at least four hours. Strain and drink one cup per day. Refrigerate the rest. When reheating, do not allow to boil.

ENVIRONMENT AND FERTILITY

While striving to make positive lifestyle changes to improve our fertility, there are elements in our enviroment that bear a second look. The definition of "environment" is the many factors, including physical and psychological, which affect the life of a person. The air we breathe, the water we drink, the atmosphere in our home, neighborhood, and workplace can affect our fertility. So it is only logical that if we suspect a health problem, especially one as elusive as infertility, we should avoid those influences that are detrimental to our health.

Obviously smoking is bad for our lungs, but it can also damage our fertility. Sperm parameters are worsened in men who smoke, and couples undergoing assisted reproductive techniques are less successful if one of the spouses is a smoker. Premature ovarian failure is accelerated in women who smoke.[21]

Alcohol is associated with many factors that influence fertility and pregnancy, from male sexual dysfunction to miscarriage and birth defects to children.[22]

Athletic teenagers and young adults who use growth hormones or steroids to build muscle and strength may inadvertently be harming their fertility. In addition to potential liver and muscular-skeletal damage, long-term impact of an irreversible nature due to the use of these substances is still under investigation.[23]

Ingestion of mercury, lead poisoning, exposure to pesti-

---

21. G. Conway, "Premature Ovarian Failure," *British Medical Bulletin* 56:643–649, 2000.

22. H.J. Goverde, H.S. Deffer, "Semen Quality and Frequency of Smoking and Alcohol Consumption," *International Journal of Fertility* 40:135–138, 1995.

23. I.P. Huhtaniemi, "Anabolic-Androgenic Steroids — A Double Edged Sword," *International Journal of Andrology* 17:57–62, 1994.

cides, and toxic chemicals in the workplace have also been implicated in harming fertility.[24] Environmental pollutants can have a cumulative effect, thereby causing secondary infertility. Miscarriages and birth defects have been linked to hazardous work environments due to chemical, electromagnetic, or radiation exposure.[25] If you have any doubts regarding possible toxic exposure, your local municipality or national environmental protection agency should be able to provide you with information.

For information on the effects of stress on fertility please see chapter 10.

Many physical and psychological factors effecting fertility are not in our control. However, we can make an effort to change those things that are within our power to change, thus laying the groundwork for improving fertility with or without medical intervention.

In Summary

Our fertility is a mirror of our health and vulnerable to influences from both inside and outside our body. We can improve our fertility potential by:

- A balanced diet
- Body Mass Index (BMI) within normal range
- Prevention and treatment of diabetes and high blood pressure
- Avoidance of unhealthy food additives, drugs, and alcohol

---

24. R.K. Juhler, S.B. Larsen, "Human Semen Quality In Relation to Dietary Pesticide Exposure and Organic Diet," *Archives of Environmental Contamination and Toxicology* 15:151–158, 1999.

25. G. Huel, D. Mergler, "Evidence For Adverse Reproductive Outcomes Among Women Microelectronic Assembly Workers," *British Journal of Independent Medicine* 47:400–404, 1990.

- Addition of certain vitamins, minerals, and herbs to our diet

SEGULOS

A *segulah* is an endeavor which is useful for improving one's condition, or guarding oneself from harm. Its power is mystical. But we must not confuse a *segulah* with mere superstition. In fact, most real *segulos* are either mitzvos or accepted traditional Jewish customs.

Superstition is the irrational belief that an object, action, or circumstance not logically related to a problem at hand can influence its solution. There are many people who are looking for that "one special *segulah*" to help them conceive, just as others are looking for a *segulah* for livelihood. One must be careful, however. Not every *segulah* is indeed valid. We must always question the validity of unusual suggestions or *segulos* — especially those that negate halachah.[26]

You must never allow your faith in *segulos* to obfuscate your belief in God or to relegate it to just another way to "cover your bases" or "hedge your bets," as it were. We believe in God, not merely because we were told that He helps; rather, we believe in Him because we know that He exists, because He took us out of Egypt with great miracles and gave us the Torah. This tradition was handed down from father to son, from generation to generation, in an unbroken chain.

---

26. For instance, we came across a book on *hilchos niddah* that suggested a fertility *segulah* involving eating the stomach of a rabbit. As rabbits are not kosher, performing this *segulah* would clearly be against halachah.

One may wonder how this *segulah* came to be mentioned in a Jewish book. *Tosefta Atikta* 5:19, p. 206, says that Shimshon's mother was advised by someone to eat a hare's stomach as a *segulah* for fertility. Perhaps that was the prevailing belief in the pagan society in which Shimshon's mother lived. Unfortunately, it got filtered down to other books and sources.

If you place even a little bit of faith in amulets or other such things, you detract from your belief in the One and only Holder of the key. One of the thirteen foundations of belief established by the Rambam is that we don't pray to God through an intermediary. We believe that God hears us directly; irrational faith in the power of some object is contrary to this belief. It might cause you to ascribe equal validity to wearing a red string, drinking special water, wearing a rabbit's foot — and praying!

God wants us to have a relationship with Him; we do this through prayer and mitzvah observance. Therefore, for a *segulah* to be even considered, it must accomplish this goal of drawing us closer to God. It must create or enhance our relationship with Him.

Certain mitzvos may bring help or healing to specific areas of our lives. For instance, *Chazal* tell us that charity saves from death; that eating three meals on Shabbos saves us from the calamities prophesied about the future; that saying the *Ashrei* prayer three times a day guarantees us a place in the World to Come.

We relate to certain customs as *segulos*, too. The Gemara says, "*Simana milsa*" — a sign means something. We have apples and honey on Rosh Hashanah in order to have a sweet year. This type of sign helps us think positively toward the coming year; it shows our faith in God that He will bless us with a good year.

If you have heard of a specific *segulah* for having children, consult your Rav as to its validity before you embrace it. There may be certain prayers that are especially efficacious to help you accomplish your goal. Consult your Rav concerning which prayers are appropriate for your specific need.

Some readers may object to our approach. They may say, "If doing certain *segulos* makes people happy, let them do it. It doesn't hurt." Our intention here is not to take away people's faith, but rather to help guide it to the one place where it should be directed: straight to the Almighty. We should put our faith only in God and in nothing or no one else.

Prayer and mitzvos are the *segulos* of Israel. They were given to us by the One and only the Holder of the key.

The following is a partial list of some real *segulos*, some of which will be expanded upon in chapter 9.[27] All of them will accomplish the goal of a traditional Jewish *segulah* — to get closer to God.

◆ **Living in Eretz Yisrael.** Living in the Land of Israel is a *segulah* for having children. We learn this from our patriarch Avraham. *Chazal* tell us that Avraham was infertile, yet when he moved to Eretz Yisrael he merited having a child from Hagar. [Sarah's infertility was more severe and therefore needed more Divine intervention.] This *segulah* even has halachic ramifications, as Jewish law states that if a couple has been married for ten years and have not had a child, they should divorce; but if they move to Eretz Yisrael, then the counting of the ten years starts over again. According to the Rosh, in the merit of living in Eretz Yisrael they will have children.[28] The *Matanos Kehunah* on *Bereishis Rabbah* says that infertility can be caused by the sin of living outside the Land of Israel.[29]

There is a connection between Eretz Yisrael and children, in that when God promised Avraham children, it was connected to the promise of possessing the Land of Israel. Both the Land and the continuing generations symbolize the future

---

27. For more on *segulos*, see *Chasam Sofer, Yoreh De'ah* 101; *Chazon Ish, Yoreh De'ah* 5:3 and *Nashim* 12:7; *Tzitz Eliezer*, vol. X, chap. 25:19, 4.

28. Rosh, *Yevamos* 64a.

29. *Matanos Kehunah* on *Bereishis Rabbah* 45:3. See his commentary, where he brings a proof from the Mizrachi on Rashi.

of the Jewish People.[30]

◆ **Fulfilling the mitzvos, especially *Shiluach haKen*, sending away the mother bird.** If a person chances upon a nest and sees the mother bird sitting on either the eggs or the chicks, and he wants to take the eggs or chicks for himself, he must send away the mother bird first.[31] The Midrash says,[32] "One who does one mitzvah, (God) does good for him and grants him long life. God said: If you fulfilled the mitzvah of sending away the mother bird, even if you were infertile and cannot give birth, *chayechah* (I promise) that I will grant you children, as it says (*Devarim* 22:7), 'Send away (the mother bird).' If you did this, 'then you may take the children for yourself.'"

Although this special mitzvah usually does not come our way, we are citing it here because it is one of only two mitzvos cited by *Chazal* as having a direct influence on fertility.

◆ **Observing "חנ"ה," the mitzvos of taking *challah*, observing *niddah* (the laws of Family Purity), and lighting Shabbos candles.** These mitzvos are directly linked to a woman's femininity. Taking *challah* symbolizes the mitzvah of *chesed*, for when the Temple stood, a woman would give the *challah* (a piece of her dough) to a Kohen. Fulfilling the laws of *niddah* sanctifies Jewish marriage.[33] And lighting the Shabbos candles represents the light of Torah that a woman brings into her home.[34]

These three mitzvos are *Chazal*'s advice for ensuring a safe

---

30. See, for example, *Bereishis* 17:2–8.

31. *Devarim* 22:6–7.

32. *Yalkut Shimoni, Ki Seitzei* 930.

33. See *Baraisa Niddah* 2:6: Rabbi Chiya says in the name of Rabbi Chanina ben Dosa, "You find concerning the matriarchs that they would keep the laws of *niddah* and were immediately answered...."

34. See chapter 11 of *B'Sha'ah Tovah* by these same authors (Jerusalem: Feldheim Publishers, 2001), for a more complete explanation of this idea.

birth, and they are also relevant to a woman who desires children. As we discussed in the first chapter of this book, the key that God holds is called variously "the key to a woman giving birth," "the key to infertility," and "the key to the womb." It is the same key. Fertility is connected to a woman's femininity, and meticulous fulfillment of these three mitzvos, which are the three spiritual expressions of a woman's femininity, will hopefully bring God's mercy to grant a woman a child — the tangible fulfillment of her femininity.

If you normally buy *challos* for Shabbos and Fesivals, perhaps you can begin to bake your own in order to fulfill the mitzvah of setting aside *challah,* a portion of the dough.[35] Be careful with the laws of *niddah,*[36] and when you light Shabbos candles, say a special prayer for having children.

◆ **Judging people favorably.** Our Sages teach: If we judge others favorably, God will judge us favorably. The opening chapters of the Chafetz Chaim's classic work, *Shemiras haLashon,* address this question and demonstrate how this is so.

◆ **Making His will your will, so that He will make your will His will (*Pirkei Avos* 2:4).** Being careful in mitzvah observance is the way to make God's will your will.

◆ **A *tzaddik*'s blessing.** Traditional Jews have always gone to a *tzaddik,* a righteous, pious person, to request that he pray for them. Already from the book of *Bereishis,* we see that the righteous were given this trust:[37]

"Avraham gave everything he had to Yitzchak" (*Bereishis*

---

35. Consult your Rav regarding the amount of flour which requires the "taking of *challah*" from it.

36. See *Baraisa Niddah* 5:6. "Sarah was barren, but since she kept the laws of *niddah* she was immediately answered."

37. See Rabbi Yaakov Hillel, *Faith and Folly* (Jerusalem: Feldheim Publishers, 1990), pp. 110–112.

25:5). He gave him as a legacy the power to bless others. God had told Avraham, "Be a source of blessing" (*Bereishis* 12:2) — the blessings are entrusted to your hands to bless whomever you wish. And Avraham gave this power to Yitzchak.[38]

Furthermore, the Gemara says, "The *tzaddik* decrees and God fulfills."[39]

◆ **Praying.** Because God answers your prayers. See the next chapter, on prayer.

---

38. Rashi, *Bereishis* 25:5.

39. See *Shabbos* 59b, *Ta'anis* 23a, and *Sotah* 12a.

9.
Infertility and Prayer

And God heard her, and opened her womb.
(*Bereishis* 30:22)

When God sees a grieving soul, who does good deeds and prays before Him,and says, "for Your Name's sake, be kind to me," God opens His treasures, and grants him.
(*Midrash Tanchuma, Ha'azinu* 5)

CREATING A RELATIONSHIP WITH GOD

The Snake and the Dust

The Torah tells us that God punished the snake for causing Adam and Eve to eat from the Tree of Knowledge, by forcing him to move on his belly and to eat dust the rest of his days. The *Chiddushei haRim* asks: If the snake has to crawl on his belly and eat dust, he never has to search for his food. What kind of punishment is that? The answer is that if he never has to search for his nourishment, he never needs God. He never needs to develop a relationship of dependency on his Creator. There is no greater punishment than that.[1] On the other hand, the greatest blessing is a situation in which we need to feel dependent on the Almighty.

Developing a relationship with and fulfilling the will of the Creator of the world is the goal of our life; it is the purpose of our doing mitzvos. Sometimes, in order to encourage this

1. *Chiddushei haRim, Bereishis* 3:14, quoted in *Ma'ayanah shel Torah.*

kind of relationship with His children, God creates a situation of discomfort, sometimes even pain and suffering. As undesirable as pain and suffering is, it can be the vehicle for us to connect with God in a way that is even stronger than mitzvos.

The Gemara says that God looked to find the proper trait for the Jewish People, and the most appropriate one that He found was the trait of poverty.[2] It is not that God wants Jews to suffer, but that He wants a relationship with us. It is human nature to forget about God when things are going well. When people are content with their lives, when they have their health and livelihood, they sometimes forget that they still need Him. So God, in His desire for a relationship with His children, gives them reasons to connect with Him. He gives them poverty; He gives them a reason to pray.

Prayer and Our Matriarchs

The supplication of the barren woman has always been the paradigm for prayer. The essential laws of the *Shemoneh Esrei* are derived from Chanah's plea for a child.[3] Her prayer is the prayer that every Jew should try to emulate. It was the pain of infertility that enabled Chanah to reach such a strong bond with God. Infertility, as painful and undesirable as it is, contains the hidden blessing of drawing us closer to our Father in Heaven.

The most important component of prayer is the feeling of loss or lack. *Chazal* ask, Why were the matriarchs barren? They answer that they were barren because God craves the prayers of the righteous.[4] The matriarchs were wealthy and beautiful; they had to have something lacking in their lives in order for them to feel dependent on God. So God prevented them from

2. *Chagigah* 9b.
3. *Berachos* 31a–b.
4. *Shir haShirim Rabbah* 2:14, *Bereishis Rabbah* 45:5.

having children, which enabled them to have a relationship with Him through their prayers.[5]

The same is true of our patriarchs. *Chazal* tell us that they too were infertile, the reason being so that they should pray, because God craves the prayers of the righteous.[6] We see this from the way the Torah worded the verse in which Yitzchak prayed for Rivkah to have a baby. The verse says, "And Yitzchak prayed to God, opposite his wife, because she was barren."[7] However, the verse should have said something like, "And behold, Rivkah was barren, so Yitzchak prayed." That would have suggested that a situation came up that needed prayer, so Yitzchak prayed. But the Torah first expresses the fact that Yitzchak prayed, which suggests that God's desire for Yitzchak's prayers was the reason that the couple was infertile.[8]

This idea can apply to all of us. The verse in *Shir haShirim* says, "My dove in the clefts of the rock, in the secret places of the terrace, show Me your appearance, and let Me hear your voice; for your voice is sweet, and your appearance is beautiful." As mentioned earlier, *Chazal* say this verse alludes to our matriarchs and to every Jew who is infertile, for God craves their prayers. In the verse, God asks to see the dove's appearance and then to hear its voice. Then the order switches, as it says first "for your voice is sweet" and then "your appearance is beautiful." Why the change in order? The answer may be

---

5. *Midrash Tanchuma, Toldos* 9: "Why were the mothers barren? R' Levi in the name of Rabbi Shila from Kfar Timra and Rabbi Hilbo in the name of Rabbi Yochanan said, 'God craves their prayers. God said, they are wealthy and pretty. If I give them children they will never pray to Me.'" Another version of this *midrash* can be found in *Midrash haGadol, Bereishis* 25:21. More on this subject appears in chapter 15.

6. *Yevamos* 64a.

7. *Bereishis* 25:21.

8. *Torah Temimah, Bereishis* 25:21, *os yud-gimmel*.

because, according to the commentaries, "your appearance" means your sorrows. The voice refers to prayer. The order is changed so that the prayer (voice) comes first, because that is the important part. For that is why sorrows come, in order that God should hear our prayers.

This same teaching, that God craves the prayers of the righteous, is found concerning rain as well. The Talmud[9] finds a contradiction between two verses concerning Creation: "One verse says, 'The land sprouted vegetation,'[10] referring to the third day, whereas another verse, when speaking of the sixth day, says, 'None of the trees of the field were yet on the land.'[11] This teaches us that the plants commenced to grow but stopped just before they were about to break through the soil, until Adam came and prayed for rain for them; and when rain fell they sprouted forth. This teaches you that the Holy One, blessed be He, craves the prayers of the righteous." God could have had the earth's vegetation already grow on the third day of Creation, but He wanted man to need it, to ask for it, so He stopped it right before it was about to sprout, so that man would pray for it. With this, God instilled in man the need to pray, in order that we could have a connection to Him.

If such *tzaddikim* as the patriarchs and the matriarchs needed a painful reason to pray and strengthen their connection with God, how much more so do we need something lacking in our lives that will cause us to pray and realize our dependency on the Almighty.

Not only is prayer the means to an end (i.e. fertility), but infertility can also be a means to an end — prayer. Praying is an act of bonding with God, the essence of our existence.

---

9. *Chullin* 60b.

10. *Bereishis* 1:12.

11. *Bereishis* 2:5.

The Lesson of Birkas haMazon

Concerning *Birkas haMazon* (Grace after Meals), the *Meshech Chochmah* makes the following observation: The Torah only commands us to bless God *after* we eat. (The blessing that we say before eating is a Rabbinic edict.) Why did the Torah command us to thank God for our nourishment only after we eat? If we think about it, it would seem more logical to say a blessing before we eat.

The *Meshech Chochmah* answers that it is human nature to beseech God when one is hungry; however, when one is satisfied he tends to forget God. The Torah therefore requires us to bless God for our nourishment after we are satisfied.[12] The relationship of dependency on God must continue even after the desired request is achieved. The same level of connection that was achieved during the entreaty should be maintained after the prayer was answered.

Chanah, whose prayer was answered, still prayed as strongly after Shemuel was born as she did when she felt the pain of being childless. Her prayer of gratitude is distinctly introduced, "And Chanah then prayed and said...."[13] This prayer is so powerful that both the weekday *Amidah* and the Rosh Hashanah *Amidah* are modeled after it.[14] Both prayers of Chanah are recorded in the Tanach to teach us that how we pray after we are answered, after we are satisfied, is as important as how we pray before we receive what we need.

Chanah's Promise

The content of our prayer should express the idea that we want to continue strengthening our relationship with God even after we receive what we request.

---

12. *Meshech Chochmah, Devarim* 8:10.
13. *I Shemuel* 2:1.
14. *Midrash Tanchuma, Vayera* 1; *Berachos* 31a–b.

When Chanah asked for a child, she promised to offer him to God. Therefore, when Shemuel was born, he worked in the Tabernacle at Shilo. This teaches us that we should want to raise our children in a way that they will also have a strong relationship with God. You should not ask for a child for selfish reasons, but rather in order to give God another servant, who will get close to Him as well as bring your whole family closer to Him.

We are not bargaining with God. We are not saying, if you do X, then we will do Y. We pray to God with all our heart. We are making His will our will. We are asking for the knowledge to see God in every aspect of our life. We are developing a relationship with the Almighty, and regardless of the outcome of our prayers we will continue to strengthen our relationship with Him. In our prayers, we should request a child that the parents, the Jewish People, and the Almighty will be proud of.

PRACTICAL ADVICE

"And Avraham Prayed"

"And Avraham prayed to God, and God cured Avimelech and his wife and his maidservants; and they bore children. For the Lord had firmly closed up every womb of Avimelech's household, because of Sarah, Avraham's wife. And God remembered Sarah as He had said, and God did unto Sarah as He had spoken."[15] *Chazal* learn from here that when one prays on behalf of his fellowman for something he himself needs, he is answered first.[16] Therefore, one should pray for others. Pray for other childless couples to have children.

Moreover, when we pray we should always pray as part of the collective soul of the Jewish People. When Elisha the

---

15. *Bereishis* 20:17–21:1.
16. *Bava Kama* 92a.

prophet said to the Shunamite woman that he would pray specifically for her, he asked her what it was that she wanted him to say to the King (i.e. God). She answered him that she sits "among [her] own people."[17] In other words, she said to him, don't single me out — just leave me as part of the Jewish People. Therefore, when you do pray for yourself or for anyone else, you should ask that your request be granted from among the Jewish People. You could say something like, "Grant me a child, among the other barren couples of the Jewish People."

When, How, and Where to Pray

The Talmud says that on Rosh Hashanah, the matriarchs and Chanah were remembered.[18] Consequently, Rosh Hashanah is a good time to pray for children.

One can pray any time for a child; you do not need a specific time, or a special insertion in a structured prayer. It is best, though, to pray from within a regular, legislated prayer such as the *Shemoneh Esrei.*[19] You can add your personal prayer in the blessing, "*Shome'a tefillah,* right before "*Ki Atah shome'a*" toward the end of the blessing. You can also add your special request right before the blessing *Elokai netzor,* or toward the end of it, after "*hoshia yemincha Va'aneini.*" In those places you can open your heart and ask God for what you desire. A woman can also pray for a child when she lights Shabbos candles, takes *challah,* and goes to the *mikveh,* as these are considered auspicious times for women to pray that their children be enlightened with Torah.

You can pray in any place that is respectable and clean. It is best for a man to pray in a synagogue with a *minyan.* If this

17. *II Melachim* 4:13.
18. *Rosh Hashanah* 11a.
19. Netziv, *Shir haShirim* 2:14.

cannot be done, then he can pray by himself. If he wants to add special prayers to have children, then he may. A woman does not need a *minyan*, so praying from the home is a naturally good place for her. She can pray in a synagogue if she chooses to do so.

There are people who go to special places to pray for fertility. Of course, the Kosel, the Western Wall, always remains the holiest spot to pray. Rachel's Tomb is also a traditional place to pray for a child, for our mother Rachel was childless. The Me'aras haMachpelah in Hebron, where our patriarchs and matriarchs are buried, is another good choice, for Sarah, Rivkah, and Leah were barren as well. Some people may want to go to Tel Shilo (about 20 miles north of Jerusalem), for this is the place where Chanah's prayer for a child was answered. Additionally, many people go to the graves of *tzaddikim*.

A Tzaddik's Prayer

Although someone else's prayer on your behalf should never replace your own prayers, the Gemara does tell us that when a person is ill he should go to a *tzaddik*, so that the *tzaddik* will pray for him or her. This seems like a logical step since the *tzaddik* is on a high spiritual level, and his prayer would seem to be more effective. However, when a person is ill the *Shechinah* is with him. Moreover, if the *Shechinah* is with him, then the sick person is also on a high spiritual level. Why then does he or she require the *tzaddik*'s prayer?

A story is told that a man once came to the Chafetz Chaim to ask him to pray for his sister. Although the Chafetz Chaim was very old, he cried to God with all his might to bring a speedy recovery to the girl. Tears streamed down his face as he prayed for her. The man later reflected that although he loved his sister very much, and although she was his own flesh and blood, he still couldn't bring himself to cry over her predicament. The Chafetz Chaim, however, cried for her after hearing the story only once.

The *tzaddik*'s prayer is effective not only because he is on a higher spiritual level; it is effective because of the strong *ahavas Yisrael* that he has for each and every Jew. The *tzaddik* literally puts himself in the position of the ill person, feeling their pain and suffering. Consequently, he receives the same level of the *Shechinah*'s presence as the ill person, attaining the highest level of prayer. It is therefore most beneficial to beseech the prayer of the righteous.

Couples with fertility problems might want to go to a *tzaddik* too, to ask him to pray for them. Although many people may not understand the pain that you are going through, the *tzaddik* not only understands your pain, but he feels it, too.

WHEN PRAYERS SEEM UNANSWERED

There is a famous quote from the father of Nachshon Wachsman. When Nachshon, a young Israeli soldier, was kidnapped by Arab terrorists, practically the entire Jewish People united in prayer for his salvation. The Israeli army attempted a daring rescue, and almost succeeded, but the young soldier was murdered before they could get to him. Nachshon's father was asked, "How could it be that all the prayers that were said for Nachshon's sake weren't answered? Doesn't God answer prayers?" Mr. Wachsman's answer is a lesson in Jewish belief. He said, "When I prayed to God for [other things], He answered me.... I asked for my son's life, and He said no. *No* is also an answer." God always answers us. We might not understand His answer, but we believe that God hears our prayers, and answers each prayer in the way that He deems appropriate.

Avraham prayed to God not to destroy the city of Sedom, but God destroyed it anyway. On the surface it appears that Avraham's prayer was unanswered. However, the *Pri Tzaddik* says that Avraham's prayer for the salvation of Sedom is what ultimately brought King David into the world. For although Avraham's prayer did not save Sedom, it helped save Lot. From Lot came Moab, from Moab came Ruth, and from Ruth came King David. King David was "found" in Sedom,[20] and the prayer of Avraham found him.[21] From King David the Messiah will come. Pray with all your heart, for the power of prayer is beyond our comprehension. You may pray for a child, and ultimately save the world. "God is close to all those who call to Him, to all those who call Him with *emes* — sincerity."[22]

Never Give Up One should never give up praying. Even if you decide to discontinue medical procedures, you should never stop praying. *Chazal* tell us that if your prayer was not answered, you should pray again and again until you are answered. The reason is, as we mentioned before, that the purpose of prayer is to build a relationship with God.

Even if the doctors tell you that there is no chance of having a child, you should still believe that it is possible. As long as you can pray, you can still have hope. The *Pri Tzaddik* points out that Moshe Rabbeinu still prayed to enter the Land of Israel, even though God specifically told him that he would not be able to.[23]

The Torah relates the following story: "In those days Chizkiyahu fell mortally sick. And the prophet Yeshayahu the

---

20. This is an allusion to *Bereishis* 19:15, where it refers to Lot's two daughters "who are found" in Sedom. Ultimately, King David — a descendant of one of those daughters — is "found" by God (see *Tehillim* 89:21) and anointed as king and progenitor of the Messiah.

21. *Pri Tzaddik, Vayera, os hei.*

22. *Tehillim* 145:18.

23. *Pri Tzaddik, Va'eschanan, os gimmel.*

son of Amotz came and said to him, 'Thus says the Lord, Set your house in order: for you shall die, and not live.' Then Chizkiyahu turned his face toward the wall and prayed to the Lord, and said, 'Remember now, O Lord I beseech You, how I have walked before You in truth and with a perfect heart, and have done that which is good in Your sight.' And Chizkiyahu wept exceedingly. Then came the word of the Lord to Yeshayahu, saying, 'Go, and say to Chizkiyahu, thus says the Lord, the God of David your father, I have heard your prayer, I have seen your tears: behold, I will add to your days fifteen years.'"[24]

This story teaches us that even when God decrees the death of a person, that person can change the decree through prayer. *Chazal* tell us that it was Chizkiyahu's faith that enabled the prayer to be effective. His prayer was not a last-ditch effort. He prayed with the full belief that he could change the decree against him. The Talmud says that Chizkiyahu said to Yeshayahu, "Forget your prophecy; it is a tradition from my father's house, that even if the sharp blade is on your neck, never give up hope of being saved."[25]

Rabbeinu Tzadok haKohen from Lublin asks why Chizkiyahu needed the tradition of his father's house. He could have learned the same lesson from Moshe Rabbeinu. Rabbeinu Tzadok answers that from Moshe, one can only learn that even when all seems lost, one is obligated to pray, but the prayer may not be effective. From Chizkiyahu's father's house — i.e. his ancestor King David, however, we learn that even after a decree has been issued, one still has the power to change it. This is illustrated in the episode concerning

---

24. *Yeshayahu* 38:1–5.
25. *Berachos* 10a.

Bat-Sheva.[26] King David himself ruled that he was guilty and therefore worthy of death, and this is also what was determined in Heaven; yet he prayed with all his heart, and was forgiven for his sin.[27] So Chizkiyahu knew that through prayer he could change his destiny.

Psychologists recommend prayer to give people a feeling of comfort, a feeling that they are doing all that they can in a difficult situation. It gives them confidence. That sounds very nice, but of course it is not the Jewish approach. We don't pray because it is a "feel good" technique. Prayer is neither meditation nor a hobby. It is not a vent to ease emotional suffering. Prayer, if taken seriously, is an active response to whatever problem arises. It is not a last resort. It is a proactive process for attaining that which is meaningful to us. It is a petition to the One Who can make anything happen. Simply put, we pray because God listens. He listens to all of us. You don't have to be a *tzaddik* for God to answer your prayer. Your need, sincerity, and recognition that you are not in control are enough.

We need to pray with confidence that God hears our prayer and is interested in what is best for each one of us. We say every day in the *Shemoneh Esrei,* "For He hears the prayers of *every mouth"* — *kol peh.*[28] "Every mouth" means all of us.

The Ramban explains that Yaakov was angry at Rachel for saying to him, "Give me children, for if not I am dead,"[29] because she thought that since Yaakov was such a righteous man, only his prayer for children would be effective. But Yaakov wanted Rachel to pray too. Even though, as we said earlier, it is beneficial to have a *tzaddik* pray for you, it does not

---

26. See *II Shemuel* 11–12.
27. *Otzar haMachshavah shel Rav Tzadok,* p. 166.
28. Nusach Sefarad.
29. *Bereishis* 30:1.

take the place of your own prayer. Nobody's prayer can ever be stronger than your own. In the end it was Rachel's prayers for a child that were answered. Prior to the birth of Yosef, the Torah says, "And God remembered Rachel, and God heard her [prayers],[30] and opened her womb."[31]

A couple once came to the famous *Chozeh* of Lublin. "We beg the Rebbe to pray to God for us that we should have a child," they said.

"Fine!" responded the Rebbe. "But you will have to pay me a thousand rubles."

"A thousand rubles! If we sold our house and gave you everything we had, we couldn't come up with such a sum."

The Rebbe was insistent. "One thousand rubles, not one ruble less."

The man's face was pale. He could never pay that kind of money. How would he ever have a child, he thought. "Let's go," said the man's wife. "We don't need this Rebbe — we can pray to God ourselves. God will see how distraught we are, and He will surely answer us."

"Finally!" smiled the *Chozeh*. "Sometimes this is what it takes for people to realize that they don't need 'the Rebbe,' they can pray to God themselves."

---

30. See the Netziv, *Ha'amek Davar, Bereishis* 30:22.

31. *Bereishis* 30:22; see also Ramban ad loc.

10. "Upon Tranquil Waters": The Stress Factor

We are not supposed to wait for the next world until we can be happy. There is a way to find joy even amidst the suffering of this world – through belief in the World to Come. The stronger our belief in it, the more we can accept and rejoice in the trials of this world – because we believe, we know, that their ultimate purpose is good. We discover the real good that is in this world.

(Rebbe Nachman of Breslav, *Garden of the Souls*)

THE EYE OF THE STORM

YOU DON'T HAVE TO BE a neuroendocrinologist, a psychologist, or a behavioral scientist, to realize the effects that emotions have on our bodies. A large number of acute ailments and chronic diseases are influenced by our psychological state of health. When we are excited, our heart beats faster and our bodies are primed for action. When frightened, we may perspire profusely and even lose control of our excretory sphincters. When we are depressed, we may suffer from lack of energy to do anything but sleep. It is obvious that our fluctuating mental state brings forth myriad physical symptoms.

The main control of our physical/psychological mechanism lies within the central nervous system — the brain and the spinal cord. Our brain sends signals through the spinal cord to various nerve receptors that lie on internal organs and muscles. These signals are either voluntary or involuntary. For instance, we may consciously regulate our breathing while exercising, but most of the time, we don't even think about when and how to take our next breath.

As important as it is, and as widespread as its actions are, the nervous system does not, however, control everything. Another control system, the endocrine system, promotes actions that are also vital to our well-being. The endocrine system secretes hormones that affect many cell activities, thereby performing a parallel function to the nervous system. There are four main categories of hormonal function:

- **Energy supply.** Hormones help control the digestive system, regulating metabolism and energy released from foodstuffs after they have been digested and have entered the bloodstream.
- **Fluid and electrolyte balance.** Hormones help control the metabolism of water and electrolytes, regulating the balance of sodium, potassium, calcium, phosphorus, and water in the body.
- **Body functions.** Hormones help regulate such basic aspects of life as growth, development, and reproduction.
- **Physical and psychological stressors.** Hormones help us cope with adverse conditions or stresses, including such adversities as cold, heat, dehydration, trauma, blood loss, and emotional stress.

As we mentioned in chapter 4, the hypothalamus is located in the brain. It coordinates nervous system function with hormonal function, influencing the bodily processes of reproduction, temperature, sleep, and appetite. It is also the director of the hormonal axis comprised of the hypothalamus, the pituitary, and the gonads (testes or ovaries). No body process is totally independent of another. This clearly demonstrates the interdependent relationship that exists between the physical, psychological, and reproductive health of our body.

The Emotional Trigger

A certain percentage of infertility cannot be solved in the doctor's office. There are many cases of couples who went through years of treatments, and after they stopped the treatments — and resolved that they would not be parents — suddenly were blessed with a child.

Some studies suggest that relaxing is the key to success. The data on the relationship between stress reduction and increased conception rates is not yet conclusive; however, it makes sense. Psychogenic causes of infertility, i.e. those originating from emotional factors, have traditionally been considered when no mechanical, organic or medical explanation can be identified. The increasing ability to diagnose underlying causes of infertility has decreased the number of such patients to fewer than 5 percent of the infertility population.[1] Nevertheless many couples have aspects of their infertility that remain unexplained.

Infertility is considered a major life stressor. As stated in chapter 2, one study compared the emotional distress of infertile women to fertile women who were facing medical diagnoses of heart disease or cancer, or who were HIV-positive. Infertile women showed equivalent levels of depression and anxiety to women with these life-threatening diseases.[2]

Infertile couples often report that the experience of infertility is more devastating than any previous life experience, in-

---

1. A. Shushan, V. Eisenberg, and J. Schenker, "Research on Stress as a Contributor to Infertility," *Fertility and Sterility* 64 (1995), pp. 459–469.

2. A. Domar, P. Zuttermeister, and R. Friedman, "The Psychological Impact of Infertility," *Journal of Psychosomatic Obstetrics and Gynecology* 14 (1993), pp. 45–52.

cluding divorce or the loss of a parent.[3]

It is possible that the relationship between stress and infertility is bi-directional. Infertility may cause stress, which may in turn contribute to infertility.[4]

The question is, what comes first, infertility that leads to stress or stress that leads to infertility?

Research has shown that stress affects reproductive function. For instance, stress increases the levels of *cortisol* (a steroid secreted by the adrenal glands in response to stimulation from the pituitary), which in turn disrupts normal ovulation by lowering estrogen and progesterone levels in the bloodstream. It is commonly known that emotional stress can wreak havoc on a regular menstrual cycle. Weight loss is known to be associated with an increase in cortisol production and a decrease in thyroid function.[5]

When the body is under physical stress from eating disorders, strenuous athletic training, or illness, reproductive function is suspended in order to support necessary body functions. In men, stress has not only been implicated in sexual dysfunction but with the interference of normal sperm production.[6]

---

3. P. Mahlstedt, S. MacDuff, and J. Bernstein, "Emotional Factors and the In Vitro Fertilization and Embryo Transfer Process," *Journal of In Vitro Fertilization and Embryo Transfer* 4 (1987), p. 232.

4. Helen A. Carcio, RNC, ANP, MS, *Management of the Infertile Woman* Philadelphia: Lippincott Publishers, 1998), p. 304. The author bases her information on studies of stress in women undergoing fertility treatments by K. Demyttenaere, S.P. Ni, O. Steeno, and P. Koninckx, from "Anxiety and Conception," *Journal of Psychosomatic Obstetrics and Gynecology* 1988.

5. R.S. Ahima and D. Prabakren, "Neuroendocrine Response to Fasting," *Nature* 382:250, 1996.

6. A. Aqarwal, "Oxidative Stress in Male Fertility," *Urology News* Cleveland Clinic Foundation, vol. 6, 1999.

The Connection between Thought and Conception

There is an obvious connection between sexual function and thought. A man cannot perform sexually if his thoughts are elsewhere. If he is not aroused in his thoughts, he will be unable to be aroused physically. Even Hebrew, our holy tongue, reflects this, as the word for "thought," ***hirhur,*** and the root of the verb "to conceive," ***harah,*** contain the same Hebrew letters. Furthermore, the Ra'avad in his book *Ba'alai Nefesh* teaches the importance of having holy thoughts during marital relations, for our thoughts will have an influence on the personality of the child conceived from that act of coition. Many of the *halachos* concerning intimacy point to the same idea. For instance, it is said that a man shouldn't have relations with his wife if they constantly quarrel, for this would be considered *znus* — promiscuity, since there is no love between them. The Ra'avad says that the children born from that act will be rebellious and nefarious.[7]

DEALING WITH STRESS

In a study by Dr. Alice Domar at the Beth Israel Deaconess medical center in Boston,[8] infertility patients were enrolled in a ten-week program promoting relaxation response training and cognitive and behavioral coping strategies. An average of 34 percent of the 110 participants conceived within six months of completing the program. Women who underwent in vitro fertilization (IVF) treatment during or immediately after completion of the program showed a 37 percent conception rate for that cycle, approximately twice the then national rate.

---

7. See *Nedarim* 20b and *Ba'alai Nefesh, Sha'ar haKedushah.*

8. A. Domar, M. Seibel, and H. Benson, "The Mind/Body Program for Infertility: A New Treatment Program for Women with Infertility," *Fertility and Sterility,* 53 (1990), pp. 246–249.

Begin a Relaxation Plan as Early as Possible

The theory that stress may contribute to infertility leads to the hypothesis that stress reduction might improve conception rates. Several studies support this.[9] It is therefore recommended that you do something significant to work on stress reduction even while you are going through the early phases of infertility treatment. You may choose counseling, deep muscle relaxation therapy, prescribed drugs from a doctor, walks in the park, an exercise class, or whatever you need to make you feel more at ease. Husband and wife should embrace a significant relaxation technique. You only stand to benefit psychologically from this, and it may even substantially assist in the success of the treatment.

Even if you are only just embarking on the path of fertility treatments, it is not too soon to look into counseling and other techniques that will help you cope. Don't wait until you reach the point that you are suffering from serious stress. This is not intended to frighten you; it is just to make you aware of the real difficulties that await you. Plan for a rough road ahead. Be prepared. Be smart.

REDUCING STRESS

Get Physically Active

Sitting around, moping, and becoming a bundle of nerves just makes us even more miserable. Dormancy slows circulation. Physical activity, on the other hand, increases the production of *endorphins,* a compound of amino acids produced in the pituitary gland which enhance the body's feeling of well-being and act on the nervous system to reduce pain. Endorphins influence the menstrual cycle and LH release.[10]

---

9. Ibid.

10. R.L. Goodman, D.B. Parfitt, "Endogenous Opiod Peptides Control

An overstressed body is resistant to the benefits of endorphins. This contributes to insomnia, sexual dysfunction, irritable bowel syndrome, and a host of other conditions. Therefore, it follows that a little exercise goes a long way in helping our bodies and minds and improving our fertility.

We've all heard that exercise, even a moderate amount, reduces stress and makes us feel better. But which activity is right for you depends both on your personality and on the level of stress you may be feeling. Minimally, twenty minutes of brisk walking, three times a week, is considered beneficial. But that's only a starting point.

To receive cardiovascular benefits, a more rigorous, lengthier aerobic activity is needed to raise your pulse and to work up a sweat. Combining some running with your walking will accomplish that, or walking very quickly for forty minutes, four times a week. Swimming or a low-impact aerobic class followed by stretching can be lots of fun.

Sometimes we have to go even further to burn off extra stress with more aggressive exercise. Kickboxing can pound out a lot of frustration. A professionally supervised weight-training program is very invigorating, and it builds muscle strength and flexibility. For a more mellow approach, water aerobics can help you relax. The natural "high" you get after a workout is therapeutic and a welcome relief from all of life's stresses, not just the fertility treatments. (Remember to always check with your doctor before starting any new exercise program.)

Appreciate Nature: *Mah Rabu Ma'asecha, Hashem* Increasing your contact with nature can be quite soothing and refreshing. Together or alone, looking at the ocean, walking in the woods, watch-

---

GnRH Pulses," *Endocrinology* 136:2412, 1995.

ing clouds in the sky, or even eating lunch outdoors will put you in touch with a natural, growing, and cyclic perspective of life. Visit the zoo or a local botanical garden. Working in your own garden is a productive way of combining love of nature with exercise.

Give Yourself a Lift

Nurture yourself: go shopping, get a massage, go to a show or a concert. Perform an act of *chesed*. Doing something nice for someone, even a stranger, is good both for you and for him. Smile and say "Good morning" to the store cashier or postal clerk. You'll both feel better. Even if you are feeling absolutely miserable, getting out, keeping busy, and relating to others will automatically raise your spirits a few notches.

Keep a Journal

Just sit and write. You don't have to show it to anyone. Putting thoughts on paper can help you organize them as well as keep things in perspective. You may find a creative side to yourself that you never knew existed. You could even illustrate your journal as well. Sometimes it's easier to write than to talk about your feelings. Try different venues — by the beach or in the park. Having trouble sleeping? Writing may help.

Try Something New

Your time together as a couple shouldn't be only fertility-related. Have you thought about studying Torah together, taking walks together, attending a lecture series? Setting a regular time for such activities together provides a nice change from routine as well as a pleasurable time.

Do you recall a time when both of you would talk and the time just flew by? How hours seemed like seconds even when there wasn't anything special to do or to talk about? Once you start fertility treatments it is hard to remember what it was like before your concerns focused solely on ovulation and sperm counts. You got married because you wanted to be together always. By setting aside blocks of time together that are unrelated to infertility, you will simply enjoy each other's company, as you used to. Make sure you talk about something other than infertility during those times as well.

Additional Strategies to Reduce Stress

The following are just a few suggestions that may help take the edge off your stress and anxiety.

◆ **Education:** You will benefit from being fully informed about the diagnostic process, the effects of medication, and the course of treatment. Instead of feeling victimized and helpless, you can take an active part in treatment decisions if you are knowledgeable about your fertility problems. For many, this information is most effective when updated at each appointment and supplemented by reading material. Keeping a record of questions between appointments will reduce the anxiety of not remembering what you wanted to talk about during each visit.

◆ **Teamwork:** Although infertility is a couple's, not an individual's, problem, spouses move through the infertility experience at different rates. Keeping the lines of communication open, with or without professional guidance, reduces the marital stress that often accompanies fertility treatment.

◆ **Avoiding stressful situations:** You should not feel guilty about wanting to avoid stressful situations such as attending a *bris* or other family events that highlight the pain of infertility. You may feel pressure to conduct your lives as though there is no private pain, but this is a difficult act to keep up. An event that may bother one spouse may not even faze the other; therefore, you have to coordinate your plans. Perhaps only one of you will attend an event. You don't owe anyone an explanation, but if you feel you must tell people why you're not coming to an event, discuss your strategy and excuses ahead of time.

Talk to God Never stop talking to God. Talk to Him about your infertility, and about everything else as well. In addition to praying from a *siddur*, there is benefit in simply conversing with God. Sit at home and open up to Him. Tell God everything you feel.

Verbally expressing your thoughts and feelings will make you feel better. It will give you a sense of control, for you are doing everything possible by letting the One Who can make anything happen know what you are feeling. This may seem a bit awkward at first, but after a while you will get the hang of it. This is not only an effective way to pray, it is also a great way to relieve the stress and sense of loneliness that come with difficult situations. It will make you more aware that God is with you.

Tehillim Reading *Tehillim* (Psalms) on a regular basis is strongly recommended. Somehow every emotion that any person, in any situation, would feel is expressed in *Tehillim*. By reading *Tehillim*, you will see that everything you feel — joy, sorrow, frustration, humiliation, anger, sadness, regret, everything — King David felt as well. Did you ever hear a sermon in shul, or even a song, and feel that the Rabbi or the singer was speaking directly to you? Something struck a chord, and gave you some degree of comfort immediately. It is comforting to have our feelings validated. The verses of *Tehillim* do this in the most profound way.

For example, in the frenzy of infertility treatments, when emotions and negative feelings are usually at their highest, these words speak as if the patient were saying them him/herself:

"...Be gracious unto me, O Eternal, for I am in distress;

> wasted away by grief is my eye, my soul and my stomach.
>
> For consumed in sorrow is my life, and my years are sighing; through my iniquity has my strength failed, and my bones have wasted away.
>
> Because of all my tormentors I have become a disgrace, and to my neighbors exceedingly so, and a fright to those who know me; those who see me outside move away from me.
>
> I am forgotten like the dead from the heart; I have become like a lost vessel.
>
> For I have heard the slander of the multitude, terror all around; when they took counsel against me, they conspired to take my life.
>
> As for me, in You have I trust, O Eternal; I said, "You are my God."
>
> In Your hand is my destiny; deliver me from the hand of my enemies and from my pursuers.
>
> Let your countenance shine upon Your servant; deliver me in Your kindness...[11]

Jews throughout the ages have been comforted by the sacred words of *Tehillim*. Contemplating their meaning and conversing thus with God will give you a sense of hope and an acceptance of His will simultaneously.

---

11. *Tehillim* 31:10–17.

11. Choosing a Caregiver

Incline Your ear to me in the day
when I call, answer me speedily.
(*Tehillim* 102:3)

CHOOSING A FERTILITY SPECIALIST

ONCE YOU SUSPECT THAT there may be a fertility problem, how do you choose the right doctor or move on to other doctors or clinics until you find the right one for you? It's like any *shidduch* — there has to be "chemistry." Fertility treatment is a long and involved process. It is painful both physically and emotionally. Therefore, selecting the right physician is crucial to your being able to survive the long road ahead. Even before the first medical examination, you'll have a gut feeling whether the three of you can work together. In a short time, you will hopefully build a trusting and open dialogue.

Many spouses are reluctant to talk about their physical relationship with each other, let alone with a third party. This total stranger will eventually become privy to some of the most intimate details of your sexual relationship. He or she should be able to put the two of you at ease with this part of the infertility workup. The doctor needs to take a delicate approach, both being modest and helping you not be embarrassed. That's why only the most compassionate and empathetic physicians should be fertility specialists. Deciding who that will be for you is no easy task.

The auxiliary staff with whom the doctor surrounds himself is important to you as well. You want to feel comfortable with the people who draw your blood and perform other laboratory functions. You will get well-acquainted with the ultrasound technicians and the nurses who give injections and additional instructions. The doctor's office assistants, especially whoever is in charge of answering the phone and scheduling appointments, should be people you feel comfortable with.

Your doctor, whether he or she works alone, with a group of physicians, or in a clinic with a large staff, will be the team leader. This means that decisions involving your care will be largely up to him or her. This is a monumental responsibility. What qualities should you look for, when shopping for "Dr. Right"? Here are a few points to consider.

◆ **Connections.** Is your doctor connected with a major fertility clinic or hospital? Your first step is often an appointment at the gynecologist's office. Perhaps there is just a small problem requiring little or no treatment. More often, unfortunately, blood tests and more invasive diagnostic procedures will be required. Therefore, the average gynecologist is not equipped to handle more than a simple exam and initial fertility testing. A larger fertility clinic associated with a major hospital or university can offer the best options and the latest innovations for care. You want and deserve the most up-to-date treatment you can get.

◆ **Expertise.** Does the doctor you are considering have training beyond that required of certified obstetricians and gynecologists? The field of infertility is a specialty requiring years of advanced training beyond medical school and OB/GYN residency. You wouldn't go to an optometrist seeking eye-laser surgery or to a general surgeon for a face-lift. Fertility diagnostics and procedures are complex and often full of tedious details. You want an experienced and professional approach to your fertility problem.

◆ **Personality.** Whatever you want to call it — bedside manner, compassion, patience, or *mentschlichkeit* — you want a doctor whom you like and trust. Don't put up with an abrupt manner or a know-it-all attitude. You want someone who talks *to* you, not *at* you, and includes you in decisions about your care. The doctor-patient relationship during fertility treatment is more intense and sensitive than in most other fields of medicine. Your doctor's involvement may last for weeks, months, or even years. Treatment is difficult, with many psychological and physical highs and lows. Are you comfortable working closely together? Can you ask questions without being made to feel stupid? Does your doctor explain each step well? Are you made to feel you are "just another infertile couple," or does your doctor make you feel important and special? Is he encouraging and positive, yet honest with you? How you feel and how you are made to feel are significant components in the roller-coaster world of infertility treatment.

◆ **Availability.** Of course you're not the doctor's only patients, but when you are together in the office or during a test or treatment, you want his undivided attention. Emergencies happen, but your time is precious too. If he seems preoccupied with other cases, always in a hurry, difficult to reach by phone or beeper even after-hours, maybe he isn't the right doctor after all.

CHOOSING A FERTILITY CLINIC

If you have decided to work with a larger fertility medical practice, whether it be private or associated with a specific hospital or university, there are things to be aware of. Picking the doctor to be in charge of your care is one step. But how do you decide if the setting he practices in is right for you? Larger clinics are staffed by many people with varied responsibilities. There will be laboratory and ultrasound technicians and nurses who specialize in fertility treatment. In addition, you will come across psychological and social service consultants. They can be very helpful during this stressful time. You need to ask yourselves if you are receiving the best care options and benefiting from the latest innovations in fertility technology without sacrificing a personal and friendly atmosphere. Are you just a case number, or does the staff remember your names? A successful fertility practice can feel like family and friends who are supportive and understanding. This is important for being able to emotionally survive the rigors of daily blood tests and ultrasounds, as well as weekly pelvic examinations and periodic sperm collection.

Competition is fierce, so each doctor or clinic will be vying for your business. Consequently, they will emphatically inform you that they should be entrusted with your care. Statistics are often coated in confusing medical jargon. Here are some examples of common categories used to evaluate fertility success rates of Assisted Reproductive Technology (attempts at IVF versus results). You'll understand these terms better after reading the chapter on Assisted Reproductive Technology (chapter 20).

- **Live births per cycle.** Also referred to as the "take-home baby rate," this is the percentage of healthy children born per ovulatory cycle. Multiple births are counted as one pregnancy. This calculation is usually the most accurate — and incidentally, very similar at most fertility centers.
- **Pregnancies per cycle.** This is the percentage of ovulatory cycles resulting in diagnosed pregnancies. This rate is always higher than the rate of live births per

cycle, because unfortunately not all pregnancies result in a healthy baby being born.

- **Live births per egg retrieval.** Also usually a higher rate than live births per cycle, this is the number of live, healthy births as a result of harvesting eggs from a woman for in vitro fertilization (IVF). This rate does not include cancellations of care midway through a cycle due to technical difficulties or illness.
- **Live births per embryo transfer.** This is the number of live births from a procedure where an egg is fertilized outside the woman's body and transferred back to her. This rate does not include cycles where eggs were not successfully transferred.
- **Pregnancies per embryo transfer.** This is an unrealistically high statistic related to the number of times a pregnancy test is positive after an embryo transfer.

When evaluating a clinic's statistics, ask how they were calculated. Also inquire about the center's cycle cancellation rate, which refers to the number of cycles which had to be interrupted before completion — usually due to an increased risk of ovarian hyperstimulation, or less commonly due to a dosage error or a technical mix-up on the part of the couple. These statistics are considered public domain — available to anyone who requests them. There are many state laws that enforce full disclosure and the public's right to know. If a doctor or a clinic hesitates to reveal their records, you would be wise to doubt the quality of the care they give.

Last but certainly not least for Jewish couples is how your doctor or clinic relates to the halachic considerations involved in your care. When the doctors, nurses, and laboratory personnel are aware of how important it is that all procedures be done in accordance with Jewish Law, then the course of treatment will be all that much easier and less stressful. When you feel that all your needs are being met, then, God willing, this feeling of confidence will bring you closer to your goal — having a child.

"But they're so nice" is not a sufficient reason to stay with a fertility group when you've given them a fair chance and still have not seen results. Referrals from acquaintances are helpful, but just as important is how your doctor relates to you. If you have any hesitations about the quality of your care, you must bring them up to your doctor. If this makes you uncomfortable, then this is also a sign that you should consider switching clinics.

Remember: you are not married to your doctor or your fertility clinic. You are not in debt to anyone! A baby is what you want. Previous records of examinations, ultrasounds, and lab results are your personal property and can be transferred to whatever doctor or facility you choose. A doctor can often use your previous diagnostic workups without repeating costly and painful new tests. Repeated exams are not always required and will not necessarily show anything different. New treatments can be initiated on the basis of previous test results.

Changing treatment venues two or three times is not uncommon. However, going from one doctor or fertility clinic to another is costly in both time and money, in addition to being emotionally and physically exhausting.

Modern medicine is big business and infertility is an especially lucrative field. We are inundated with advertisements in newspapers and magazines, and on the radio, of overjoyed parents praising one fertility clinic or another. This serves the positive purpose of bringing the issue of infertility out in the open, but we have to be careful not to be falsely impressed by misleading statistics or sentimental pictures.

Choosing a fertility practice is similar to many other business transactions you might enter into, as it is about commitment, provision of services, and expenditure. Therefore, it is wise to remember the phrase, "Proceed with Caution."

In Summary

Fertility care is a team approach. In choosing the right caregiver, you want someone who is:

- Easy to talk to
- Well-connected to fertility professionals and institutions
- An expert in his/her field
- A positive person
- Available to you during non-office hours

In choosing a clinic, you should look for:

- Professionalism
- Good success rates
- Modern and clean
- A personal approach to you

Before you agree to any treatment, your uncompromising adherence to halachah should be well-understood by both the caregiver and the clinic staff.

FAITH IN THE ALMIGHTY OR THE DOCTOR?

Some God-fearing Jews ask, Why should I go to the doctor for checkups if haKadosh Baruch Hu controls everything in my life? Isn't it more appropriate to pray to God for good health rather than rely on the wisdom of mortal men?

This question is found in Rabbinic literature as well. The Rambam admonishes those who say that a sick person who goes to a doctor to be healed is demonstrating a lack of faith in God. According to the Rambam, this is like saying that one who eats bread in order to relieve the "disease" called hunger is also demonstrating a lack of faith, because the person should have prayed to the Almighty and relied on Him to cure the hunger.[1]

The Ramban, on the other hand, says that in days of yore the *tzaddikim* did not go to doctors, but to the Prophets.[2] In other words, physical ailments can be cured by strengthening our spirituality.

However, the halachah clearly follows the Rambam, determining that one should go to doctors not only to cure illness but also to prevent it.[3] Even the Ramban would agree that only a select group of very pious individuals could rely on their spirituality and refrain from visiting a doctor. Most people are not on that spiritual plane, however, and modern medicine, while not perfect, is generally effective. The *Birkei Yosef* writes, "Today one should not rely on a miracle. A sick person is required to act according to the ways of the world and call a doctor. And no one has permission to deviate from the custom of the world."[4]

The *Shevet Yehudah* says, "A sick person is strongly obligated to seek out a good doctor and medicines. And whoever is lax in doing so and relies on a miracle, saying that God will send his cure, is considered foolish. He is being negligent with his own body, and in the future he will have to face judgment for doing so."[5]

This does not contradict our faith in the Almighty. Of course we believe that our good health is in the hands of God.

---

1. Rambam, Mishnah *Pesachim* 4:10.
2. Ramban, *Vayikra* 26:11.
3. See the following in the *Tzitz Eliezer*: vol. V, *Ramat Rachel*, chaps. 1, 20, and 21; and vol. X:25, chap. 30.
4. *Birkei Yosef, Yoreh De'ah* 336:2.
5. *Shevet Yehudah, Yoreh De'ah* 336.

Medicine and the advice of doctors are merely the tools that we must use in seeking a cure. Together with this, we must also pray to God that the medicine and treatment will be beneficial to us.

Another question is sometimes asked: If God made us ill, wouldn't it be considered interference with His will if we cure the illness? God obviously had a reason for making us sick.

The following *midrash*[6] provides an answer: Rabbi Yishmael, Rabbi Akiva, and a companion were walking along together in Jerusalem. They met a sick person who asked them, "Rabbis, how can I be healed?" The Sages gave him medical advice that would cure him.

The man asked, "Who made me ill?" And they answered, "God." The sick man then questioned their interference with the will of God.

The Sages responded by asking the man his occupation. He showed them his scythe and replied that he was a farmer. The Rabbis then asked, "Who created the vineyard?" And the farmer responded that God had created the vineyard. "Then aren't you interfering with something that is not yours?" asked the Rabbis. "God created it and you are taking the fruits." The farmer replied that if he were not to use his scythe to clear his land, or if he didn't plow, fertilize, or weed, then nothing would grow.

The Sages then admonished the farmer, referring to the verse in *Tehillim* (103:15): "As for man, his days are like grass." A man is like a tree which requires the farmer's care. If the farmer were not to weed and plow, the tree would not grow. And even once it grows, it still requires irrigation and fertilization. So it is with the human body. The medicine can be compared to fertilizer, and the doctor can be compared to the farmer.

---

6. *Midrash Shemuel, parashah* 4.

THE CORRECT BALANCE

Those who rely on a miracle for their good health are considered foolish. Those who think their good health depends on modern medicine and does not ultimately lie in the hands of God are also foolish. We must choose between the two extremes and find the Golden Path.

The Chazon Ish related to this dilemma in the following letter:

> Concerning myself, I consider the physical effort to maintain good health to be both an obligation and a mitzvah. It is one of the requirements dictated by the Creator for self-perfection. It is recorded that the *Amora'im* [Rabbis of the Talmudic period] went to doctors of other nations to become cured. It is evident that much of plant and animal life serves medicinal purposes. Also, gates of wisdom were created for all to contemplate and achieve understanding. However, the ways of the Divine may bypass natural laws as well as the efforts man puts into using them. What is needed is the correct balance. Deviation from the true path is not acceptable — whether it is to rely on the level of faith which I have honestly reached, or to believe too much in the natural order.[7]

The correct balance between human effort and faith in the Divine is an essential value of Judaism. This applies not only to matters of health, but to all aspects of our lives. There is no contradiction. These activities complement one another. On one hand, our Sages tell us that a *talmid chacham* should not live in a city that does not have a doctor.[8] On the other hand, they also tell us that when the Jewish People raise their eyes to Heaven and submit their hearts to God, they will be healed.[9]

---

7. *Chazon Ish, Letters,* vol. 1, letter #136.
8. *Sanhedrin* 17b.
9. *Rosh Hashanah* 29a.

12.
The Woman's Initial Fertility Evaluation

Every place you walk, God is with you.
(*Devarim Rabbah* 2)

THE FIRST LEVEL OF TESTING IN THE WOMAN'S FERTILITY WORKUP

SINCE A WOMAN'S FERTILITY is a mirror of her general health, it is essential to do an overall examination of her past and present physical health. We can't just look at one organ of the body or test one particular physiologic process, as every part of a person's body is dependent on the other. A complete evaluation is necessary to combine the pictures of the puzzle in order to determine the best course of treatment.

In this section, we will discuss the woman's preliminary physical examinations and their relationship to infertility. The general sequence of the initial exam is as follows:

- Past medical history
- Present health status
- Physical examination: observation
- External examination
- Gynecologic examination
- Internal examination
- Initial laboratory tests

Past Medical History

The first time you are examined will usually be in the gynecologist's office. Many events in your past medical history can give direction to any fertility workup.

The following are basic areas of exploration:

Menstrual History

When did menstruation start? Were periods regular, painful? At what age did physical development begin? Your answers may point to problems with ovulation.

Childhood Illness or Injury

Any history of severe illness, abdominal injury, or abdominal surgery are important for your doctor to know. A ruptured appendix or any other abdominal infection due to surgery can cause adhesions (scarring) on the internal organs, which affects fertility. Any past sexual abuse or trauma is significant. Any head injury or vision disturbances may point to problems of the brain, the hypothalamus, or the pituitary gland in particular.

Family History

Are there any close relatives who are also having problems with infertility, male sterility, or delayed or underdeveloped physical characteristics? This may point to chromosomal abnormalities. Did your mother take DES during her pregnancy? DES was given to millions of pregnant women during the 1960's and caused their daughters to be born with uterine and cervical malformations and questionable fertility potential.

Sexual History

Though a personal and sensitive area, questions about a couple's intimate relations such as frequency of intercourse, presence of pain, and perhaps even about sexual technique will be asked. There are even some couples whose infertility may be due to the fact they have not even consummated their marriage! One condition that interferes with intimate relations is a psycho-physiological condition called *vaginismus*. This causes a woman to involuntarily contract her thigh, pelvic, and perineal muscles, preventing intimacy, thereby making intercourse nearly impossible. Fortunately, vaginismus can be cured, with an almost 100 percent success rate, with short-term psychological counseling and behavioral conditioning.

Gynecological and Obstetrical History

Previous encounters with venereal disease, rape, or abuse can contribute to fertility difficulties. Structural damage could have been caused to the reproductive organs.

Have you ever become pregnant, had a miscarriage or abortion, or given birth? If so, your problem of infertility is referred to as *secondary infertility*, as you have "proven" yourself to be capable of conceiving and carrying a pregnancy in the past. (*Primary infertility* refers to a woman who has never conceived.) Your hormonal makeup can change. You may have had some sort of physical trauma, disease, or infection that may have caused structural damage to the reproductive organs. Your husband may now have a low sperm count also related to trauma or illness. Many problems can arise in either spouse that can change a once fertile situation to less than optimum.

Present Health Status

Complaints of any lower abdominal pain, milky discharge from the breasts, or overabundance of facial or body hair may point to hormonal imbalances. Current illness or medication taken on a regular basis can affect one's fertility as can obesity or severe underweight. It is important for the doctor to know about the characteristics of your menstrual cycle. Are periods regular, how often, how many days in length? Is menstruation painful? At what point in your cycle do you go to the *mikveh*? Do you feel any mild, lower abdominal pain in the middle of the cycle? (This phenomenon is called *mittleschmerz* — when a woman feels minor pangs due to the buildup of fluid in the ovarian follicle immediately prior to ovulation.) Some women feel mittleschmerz, while others do not. Both scenarios are normal.

Physical Exam: Observation

The first part of the physical exam is a "hands-off" observation of your general appearance. Excess weight, acne, or overabundance of facial and body hair may suggest a hormonal imbalance. Bulging eyes, agitation, or over-tiredness may be indicative of a problem with the thyroid gland that can throw the hormonal axis off track.

Your height and weight are measured to evaluate your body structure. BMI, *body mass index*, is used as a standard of measurement. BMI is the ratio of weight divided by height squared (in metric units):

$$\text{BMI} = \text{kilograms}/\text{meters}^2$$

For example, take a woman who weighs 70 kg and is 1.7 meters (1 meter, 70 cm) tall:

$$\text{BMI} = 70/(1.7)^2$$
$$\text{BMI} = 24.2$$

A BMI over 27 necessitates medical intervention. Optimal BMI for adults is 20 to 24. A high BMI is associated with decreased likelihood of conceiving, with obese women requiring higher doses of hormones to induce ovulation.[1]

Conversely, severe underweight (in anorexics and serious

1. C. DiCarlo, F. Zullo, "Superovulation Correlations with Body Mass Index and Body Fat Distribution," *Gynecological Endocrinology* 10:17–21, 1996.

athletes) can cause the cessation of menstruation. The lack of fatty tissue on the body interferes with the production of estrogen, which is essential for menstrual function.

External Examination

This initial exam serves to evaluate a woman's general health and ability to carry a future pregnancy. The breasts are examined for any lumps and for discharge from the nipples. A woman who is not nursing or pregnant should not have any discharge from the breasts. The medical term for this is *glactorrhea,* which is a sign of excess prolactin, a hormone produced in the pituitary gland. Excess prolactin (*hyperprolactinemia*) interferes with fertility and can be easily diagnosed with a blood test.

The eyes and field of vision are examined for signs of increased intracranial pressure, which could point to a pituitary growth.

The abdomen is palpated for enlargement of the liver or spleen, as well as the lower abdomen for any unusual growths over the reproductive organs.

Gynecologic Examination

If this is your first gynecologic examination, it can be rather humiliating. As embarrassing as it seems to be, your physician is discreetly trying to do his or her best to help you. For most women it gets easier every time.

The external genitalia are examined for any malformations. If the *hymen* (the excess tissue partially or fully covering the vaginal opening) is still intact, then proper penetration, i.e. regular intercourse, may not have occurred. This is an uncommon but possible cause of infertility.

Untreated infections can cause *pelvic inflammatory disease* (PID). PID can interfere with fertility, damaging the internal reproductive organs, especially the fallopian tubes.

All women have various clear-white, vaginal discharges throughout the month. This is considered totally normal as long as symptoms of itching, burning, pain, or an offensive odor do not accompany the discharge. More often than not, itching and irritation are a sign of a simple yeast (candida) infection, which can be quickly treated in a few days and is not considered dangerous, only bothersome.

An infectious discharge from the vagina may be noted. If the causative organism (bacterial infection) is unknown, then a culture can be sent to the laboratory to correctly identify the cause.

Internal Examination

The doctor will be able to view the vagina and cervix with the aid of a *speculum*. A speculum is two metal or plastic tongs that hold the walls of the vagina open, enabling better visualization of the cervix and vaginal walls. A red and irritated cervix may be a sign of *cervicitis*, an infection of the cervix. A cervical infection can produce a discharge that acts as a barrier against sperm. During this initial examination the cervical mucus is observed and its characteristics (amount, thickness, and stretchability) are noted, in order to compare its qualities to the specific time in the woman's menstrual cycle. A standard pelvic exam with a speculum would not render a woman a *niddah*. If, however, if any bleeding occurs, consult a Rav.

A *Pap Smear* may also be done at this time. A few cells from the cervix are gently removed with a small brush. (If any bleeding should occur, this will usually not render a woman a *niddah*. However, if a woman does bleed, a Rav should be consulted.) The cells from the cervix are examined microscopically for any signs of precancerous or cancerous changes in the cellular composition. The gynecological exam may include a *colposcopy*, which enlists the aid of a cervical microscope to view the cervix more closely.

The speculum is withdrawn after a very short time, one to two minutes, and does not cause discomfort if a woman is relaxed. The physician then proceeds to the *bimanual examination* (pelvic exam), inserting two fingers into the vagina and leaving the other hand on the lower abdomen. The doctor then palpates for masses or tenderness next to the areas of the uterus, ovaries, and fallopian tubes. Varied levels of discomfort along with reported pain during menstruation and/or marital relations may aid in the diagnosis of *endometriosis,* an excess of endometrial tissue growing outside of the uterus.

A cyst or a tumor on an ovary or in the uterus may be palpated and warrants further investigation. If the internal pelvic organs are felt to be stiff and immobile, then *pelvic adhesions,* scarring around the internal organs due to previous surgery or infection, may be present. Blocked fallopian tubes, due to pelvic adhesions or other circumstances, are a major cause of infertility in women. Mechanical infertility (obstruction of the fallopian tubes) cannot be diagnosed during an internal exam, but only through special X-ray studies or surgical evaluation (hysteroscopy or laparoscopy).

Initial Laboratory Tests

Laboratory analysis of the blood is also part of the initial evaluation. You can expect your blood to be tested for:

- Hemoglobin (iron level)
- Glucose (to rule out diabetes)
- HIV (AIDS)

In addition, the following *hormonal assays* will be performed in the blood analysis:

- Estrogen (E2)
- Progesterone
- FSH
- LH
- Testosterone
- DHEAS (a hormone produced by the ovaries and adre-

nal glands that when elevated produces male hormone effects)
- Prolactin
- Thyroid: T3 triiodothyronine, T4 thyroxine, and TSH

Testing of the Menstrual Cycle — Was There Ovulation?

Hormonal assays give an accurate assessment of hormonal function during the menstrual cycle and whether ovulation took place. Blood will be tested three times during the cycle.

- **Day 3 to 5** (approximately) — beginning of the cycle
- **Day 13, 14, or 15** — ovulation — midway through the cycle
- **Day 21** (approximately) — toward the end of the cycle

See Appendix A, "Index of Laboratory Values," page 446.

LH, FSH, estrogen, and progesterone are tested to see whether their levels match the normal levels for that point in the cycle when the blood was drawn. Any abnormal results will guide the physician in prescribing the proper recipe of hormone supplements to induce ovulation (if that is the problem) and/or to put the cycle into "sync." In chapter 17, we will discuss which medications or synthetic hormones can be used to influence the menstrual cycle.

The results of these initial examinations will enable you to proceed toward the second level of the fertility investigation.

THE SECOND LEVEL OF TESTING IN THE WOMAN'S FERTILITY WORKUP

Although individual doctors and fertility centers have their own preferences as to the order in which different tests will be done, we will attempt to present a thorough explanation of the tests a woman is likely to encounter during the second stage of the fertility workup. A busy month-long series of fertility tests may look like this (explanations follow):

- **Basal body temperature (BBT).** This should be taken throughout the cycle. A sustained elevation in the curve in the second half of the cycle is consistent with ovulation.

- **Hysterosalpingography (HSG).** This X ray of the uterus and tubes should be taken after menstruation ends and before ovulation. To be sure of avoiding ovulation, day 10 or 11 of the cycle would be the last day for taking the X ray.

- **Postcoital test (PCT).** This microscopic examination of sperm in cervical mucus is usually scheduled between days 12 and 15 of a 28-day cycle.

- **Progesterone blood assays and additional blood tests.** Progesterone in the bloodstream is measured around the time of greatest progesterone production, between cycle days 19 and 24. In addition, other blood tests might be taken if an immune disorder is suspected.

- **Endometrial biopsy.** The tissue lining the uterus should have the structure of secretory endometrium, best developed after cycle day 18 until the onset of menstruation.

A woman's fertility status is substantially clarified after these five examinations, in addition to other common diagnostic procedures.

Ovulation Prediction: Basal Body Temperature (BBT)

Basal body temperature measures the body's metabolic rate, which is defined as the amount of energy needed for maintenance of life when a person is at digestive, physical, and emotional rest. The normal temperature of human beings is usually considered to be 98.6°F (37°C), but it actually fluctuates around 98°F at rest. Measuring BBT each day and keeping a chart is an inexpensive, noninvasive way of recording the rise and fall of a woman's resting temperature throughout her menstrual cycle. Fluctuations in basal body temperature during the monthly cycle can help pinpoint subtle hormonal changes in the body signifying the follicular phase, the presence or absence of ovulation, and the luteal phase. The BBT chart can also provide a visual guide for the scheduling of tests and procedures, while documenting menstrual cycle symptoms, and timing intimate relations.

Directions for BBT

Use a standard oral, mercury thermometer. There are special BBT thermometers that display very slight incremental changes in temperature and are easier to read. Keep it by the bedside, along with pen and paper. Remember to shake it down *after* each use, as even that slight activity can alter the temperature of the body if done right before taking one's temperature. Temperature should be taken immediately upon awakening, and before getting out of bed. The thermometer should be placed under the tongue for three minutes.

Besides recording the temperature, it is also important to document factors that can alter the BBT. These include inadequate sleep (less than six hours), travel, alcohol consumption the evening before, use of electric blanket or heated water bed, emotional upset, illness, or using the bathroom during the early morning hours. Plot the daily temperatures on a chart and record menstruation, along with observable signs of ovulation which include mittelschmerz or the presence of wet, watery vaginal discharge. A new chart (see example, page 175) should be started on the first day of every monthly cycle.

Implications

During the first half of the menstrual cycle, before ovulation, BBT can range from 97.2° to 97.4°F. It will rise 0.4° to 0.8°, to above 98°F, conforming with ovulation, where it will remain the rest of the cycle. It may drop slightly before ovulation (*nadir* — a lower point before a significant rise), but is often difficult to see on the BBT chart. The temperature usually remains elevated for ten to fourteen days and then drops one to two days before menstruation, as the progesterone level falls.

BBT will remain elevated beyond the expected *menses* (menstruation) if a woman is pregnant, due to the continuing influence of progesterone. This prolonged temperature elevation can be used as an indicator of a possible pregnancy. Increased levels of progesterone cause body temperature to rise as progesterone acts on the hypothalamus, the thermo-regulatory center of the brain.

The goal of measuring BBT each morning is to establish a monthly cyclic pattern and therefore predict the approximate time of ovulation. Resultant graphs are referred to as displaying either a *biphasic pattern* (having fluctuating points) or a *monophasic pattern* (points forming a relatively straight line). In the body, the lutenizing hormone peaks (*LH surge*), causing a small dip in and then the elevation of basal body temperature within two days of the LH surge. The onset of the LH surge is a reliable indicator of ovulation, with the LH peak occurring 24 to 36 hours prior to the ovarian follicle rupture. The LH surge lasts about 48 to 50 hours and influences the progesterone level to rise, which then acts as a negative feedback to terminate the LH surge.[2]

BBT testing is more difficult than it sounds. Some women see no temperature change or record erratic temperature changes not associated with ovulation. One of the major drawbacks of the BBT chart is that it predicts the day of the LH

---

2. C.A. Eddy, C.J. Pauerstein, "Temporal Relationships of Estrogen, Progesterone, and Luteinizing Hormone Levels," *American Journal of Obstetrics and Gynecology* 130:876, 1978.

surge only within two to three days. Nevertheless, BBT is helpful as a preliminary indicator of ovulation and as a tool for advising couples about the timing of intercourse. Couples are usually advised to have intimate relations every other day from three to four days before ovulation or from *mikveh* night, until at least two days after the estimated time of ovulation. Couples should try not to be fixated with temperature-taking, as the general trend of a few months of BBT charts is usually sufficient to set a reliable monthly pattern.[3]

(EXAMPLE OF) BASAL BODY TEMPERATURE (BBT) CHART

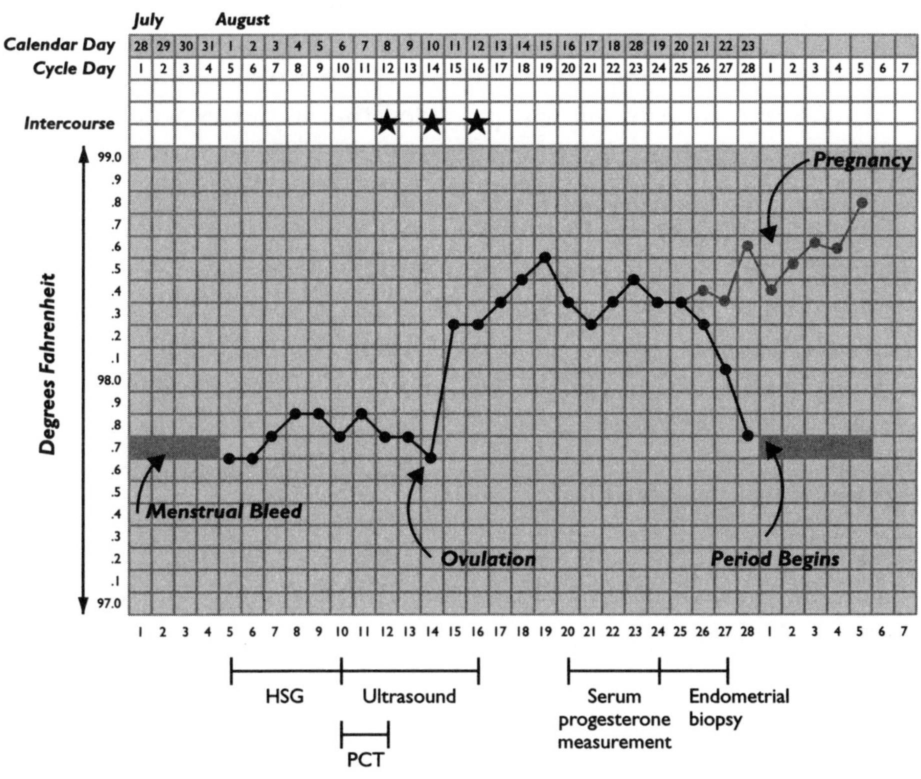

(SCHEDULE OF EVALUATION)

3. *Clinical Gynecologic Endocrinology and Infertility*, p. 1028.

Home Ovulation Prediction Kits

In addition to measuring BBT but short of invasive blood tests and ultrasounds to predict ovulation, there are a few "at home" ways of predicting the time of ovulation. LH surge can be measured in the urine between 0 and 21 hours after the LH surge would be measured in the blood. Therefore, beginning on about day 12 of the menstrual cycle, it is recommended to test the second urine of the day (within an hour of the first void). Only a few drops of urine are needed. Ninety-five percent of the time, ovulation can be expected to occur within 24 to 48 hours, plus or minus 6 hours, following a positive test result.[4]

Another at-home urinary LH analysis works along the same principle. A monitor is provided that indicates when a woman is at her peak fertility potential. There are also at-home testing kits to detect rising LH levels in the saliva.

Self-examination of cervical mucus can also help you determine if you are ovulating. Cervical secretions change throughout the cycle, and with pending ovulation, you should be able to stretch the mucus up to 8 to 10 cm between your fingers. The mucus at the time of ovulation should be thin, watery, and clear.

Hysterosalpingography

Hysterosalpingography (HSG) is an X ray of the uterus and fallopian tubes. Your doctor will recommend this test if he suspects a blockage in your fallopian tubes or a structural problem in the uterus. HSG is routinely performed not only to evaluate tubal patency (unblocked fallopian tubes) but also to diagnose abnormalities of or masses in the uterus.

---

4. K.L. Deaton, R. Clark, "The Value of Urinary Luteinizing Hormone Versus Human Chorionic Gonadotropin Timing," *Fertility and Sterility* 68:43–47, 1997.

The exam takes place in a regular X-ray room, while a woman lies on a examination table. A speculum is inserted into the vagina and the cervix is cleaned with an antiseptic. A long, thin instrument called a *tenaculum* is inserted into the vagina. Similar to slender, rounded, kitchen tongs, the tenaculum grasps the cervix, holding it in place, and the speculum is then removed. Contrast medium (3 to 6 cc) is then injected through a thin catheter past the cervix. (The catheter and tenaculum are then removed.) X-ray movies are taken as the dye flows from the uterus and through the fallopian tubes. Three films are usually taken; a preliminary one before the dye is injected, a second film showing the spill of dye from one or both tubes, and third, a delayed picture as the dye flows through the peritoneal (abdominal) cavity. The test takes about fifteen minutes.

HYSTEROSALPINGOGRAPHY (HSG)

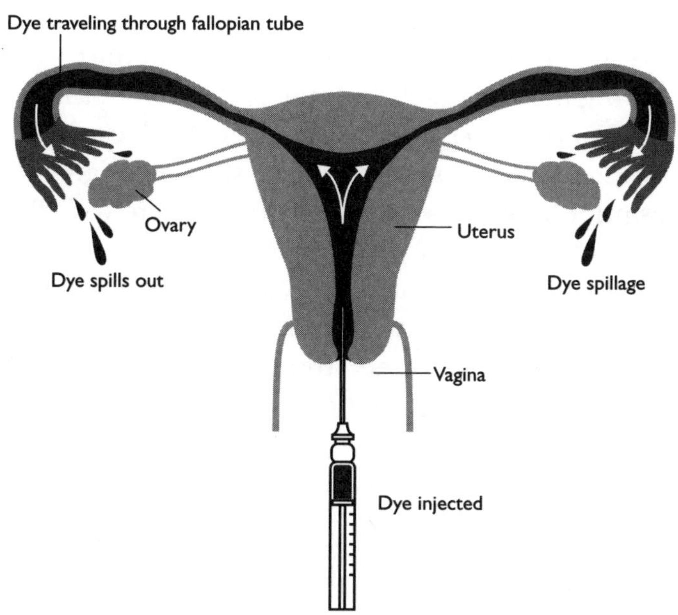

The HSG is valued by many as a therapeutic procedure in treating infertility as well. The following are theories of the HSG's therapeutic action:

- It may rinse the tubes, dislodging mucus plugs.
- It may straighten the tubes and thus break down peritoneal adhesions.
- It may stimulate function of the tubes.

A conception rate of 41.3 percent within one year of HSG with oil-based dye has been seen, with most pregnancies occurring within seven months.[5]

For couples with unexplained secondary infertility and normal tubes, pregnancy rates have been found to be improved by up to 79 percent within just four months of an HSG with oil-based dye.[6]

A water-soluble dye is substituted in a patient who may be at risk for pelvic inflammatory disease. The HSG may be bypassed altogether if active PID is suspected.

Some women feel absolutely no pain or discomfort from this X ray, while others complain bitterly about the cramp-like pains during the introduction of the of the dye. Spasms of the uterus and/or the tubes from a reaction to the dye are possible. Therefore, an anti-spasmodic drug or sedative is given thirty minutes prior to the X ray. Spasms can interfere with the passage of the dye and cause discomfort.

HSG is an integral diagnostic tool for evaluating tubal function as well as the contour of the uterus and uterine cavity. Cervical continence (the strength of the cervix) is also evaluated based on the amount of dye that can be seen spill-

---

5. H.W. Gillespie, "The Therapeutic Aspect of Hysterosalpingography," *British Journal of Radiology* 38:301, 1995.

6. D. Nugent, A. Watson, "A Randomized Controlled Trial of Tubal Flushing with Lipiodol for Unexplained Infertility," *Fertility and Sterility* vol. 77, 2:238, 2002.

ing from the cervix. The results of the HSG can help direct continued fertility treatment.

- **Normal:** Both tubes patent with free spill (i.e. the dye is seen to flow through the uterus and out through the tubes) and the tubal mucosal pattern appears normal.

  Plan of action: IUI (intrauterine insemination), ovulation induction

- **Suspicious:** Unilateral or bilateral tubal occlusion, proximal (end closest to the uterus) or distal (the end of the fallopian tube closest to the ovary); with or without unilateral or bilateral spill, or insufficient information about tubal mucosal pattern.

  Plan of action: Laparoscopy

- **Abnormal:** Both tubes have distinct distal tubal occlusions with or without dilatation.

  Plan of Action: Hysteroscopy, Laparoscopy. Based upon the results — proceed to microsurgery or IVF-ET (in vitro fertilization - embryo transfer).

Special Note on HSG

The use of a tenaculum to hold the cervix still during the HSG may cause bleeding to the outside of the cervix. This in itself would not render a woman a *niddah*. However, the HSG could cause bleeding, either from the uterus or the cervix. As it is difficult to differentiate between bleeding from the cervix and bleeding from the uterus, the woman would be considered a *niddah*. However, the HSG is usually done during the seven clean days. Hence, once the bleeding stops, a woman should do a new *hefsek taharah* and begin counting the seven clean days again. You should consult your Rav because the circumstances will not be the same for any two women.

Alternatives to HSG and Ultrasound

The following are two fairly new ways to evaluate the uterus and the fallopian tubes.

Sonohysterography (SHG)

An ultrasound of the uterus and the fallopian tubes is done while observing the passage of saline. Some prefer the SHG over the HSG as no contrast medium is used and there is no need for X rays. It can be performed in the office as opposed to a radiology center. For a more thorough evaluation of the fallopian tubes, however, a HSG is considered to be more precise in diagnosing tubal problems.

Salpingography

Also referred to as a *falloscopy*, this is an endoscopic procedure where a salpingoscope or falloscope is inserted vaginally through the cervix to observe the insides of the fallopian tubes. Referred to as tubal cannulation or tubal catheterization, the narrow scope's curved tip can irrigate the tubes with saline, or its inflatable balloon tip can be used to clear minor occlusions in the tubes (as in heart angioplasty). There is no incision in a tubal catheterization as opposed to a laparascopy. Local anesthesia of the cervix along with sedation is all that is required in this diagnostic/therapeutic procedure, which lasts for thirty to forty-five minutes. Normal activities can be resumed the next day.

Risks of this procedure include infection or perforation of the fallopian tube. Salpingography has met limited success in opening tubal occlusions in the proximal tube (closest to the uterus).

Tubal Reconstruction

There are surgical techniques for repairing damaged or blocked tubes. Surgery is performed with microsurgical or laser techniques. Microsurgery is performed on an outpatient basis through a laparoscopy, with a recovery period of a few days. If a more major surgical approach with an abdominal incision (laparotomy) is necessary, a hospital stay of about two days is required. Each procedure is done under general anesthesia and last for about two hours. Depending on the extent of tubal damage, tubal reconstruction results in pregnancy rates of about 40 to 60 percent, with an ectopic pregnancy rate of about 10 percent.

The following are the different techniques and procedures of tubal reconstruction:

- **Salpingolysis** — A technique for cutting away adhesions from the tubes.
- **Fimbriolysis** — A technique used to remove adhesions from the fimbriated (distal) end of the tube (the end nearest the ovary).
- **Fimbrioplasty** — A procedure to repair damaged fimbria and a blocked fallopian tube.
- **Salpingostomy** — A procedure performed to open a tube that is blocked at the fimbriated end.
- **Tubal Anastomosis** — Most commonly done for women who want to reverse a tubal ligation (a birth control method that severs the fallopian tubes). The blocked portion of the tube is removed and the opened ends are rejoined.

The decision whether or not to undergo tubal surgery depends on many factors: maternal age, quality of the husband's sperm, and the seriousness of the occlusion. For some, the possibility of a successful outcome that would enable the couple to conceive spontaneously without any further medical intervention will be the deciding factor. For others, other contributing infertility issues in either the woman or the man may influence a couple to bypass surgical repair and move on to assisted reproductive techniques (IVF).

Postcoital Test (PCT)

This is a basic test of cervical function and the presence of sperm which can be done in either the initial or the second stage of the fertility workup. The PCT is usually timed to parallel the LH surge (a day or two before ovulation). This time can be approximated by measuring basal body temperature, measuring LH levels in the blood, with at-home ovulation prediction kits, or by ultrasonic monitoring of the ovaries. A couple is required to have relations late at night or early in the morning, two to eight hours prior to the examination. It is also suggested that the couple abstain from intercourse for forty-eight hours before the PCT. At the clinic the woman undergoes an examination similar to a standard pelvic exam. She lies down while a speculum is placed in her vagina. Visual examination reveals the cervical mucus mixed with sperm, the majority of which can be found pooled next to the cervix. It is painlessly withdrawn with a small needle-less syringe. (Enough sperm remains in the body, thus allowing for conception.) The mucus is then put on a microscopic slide and observed for the following qualities that point to pending ovulation:

- **Amount.** Increased amount of mucus more than other times during the month.
- **Spinbarkeit.** Around the time of ovulation, stretchability (spinbarkeit) increases and thickness (viscosity) decreases. This is assessed as the mucus is withdrawn from the cervix. Elasticity of 8 to 10 cm or more is considered normal.
- **Ferning.** Crystallization, as seen under the microscope,

creates the appearance of a fern-shaped leaf in the mucus which is caused by increased levels of salt and water interacting with the glycoproteins found in the mucus during this time. This is a presumptive sign of estrogen production which increases at midcycle and stimulates the cervical glands.

Within 24 to 48 hours after ovulation, rising progesterone levels cause a marked decrease in the quantity of cervical mucus and an increase in mucosal viscosity and cellularity (an increase in the number of cells), and a consequent decrease in sperm survival. Spinbarkeit and ferning are absent after ovulation.

◆ **Sperm motility.** The amount of sperm found near the cervix should remain constant during the first 24 hours after relations. To check this, the mucus containing the sperm is placed on a microscopic slide within a small area and viewed at a magnification of 400. This is called a high power field (HPF). Live sperm found on the small area of the slide is very significant. For one, it shows that the cervical mucus is conducive to sperm survival, largely ruling out pH problems (mucus that is too acidic — below a pH of 7.0) or immunologic causes of infertility. Dead or immobile (shaking) sperm will be found when a man or woman produce antibodies which attack and immobilize the sperm.

The PCT can be a good indication of a normal sperm count. Twenty-one or more sperm per HPF is almost always associated with a sperm count above 20 million per ml.[7] However, the postcoital test cannot be considered a substitute for semen analysis, which gives more specific information on sperm characteristics and which is essential to conclusively evaluate sperm function and quality. Sperm antibody testing should also be done when the sperm are found to be dead or

---

7. N.T. Jette, R.H. Glass, "Prognostic Value of the Postcoital Test," *Fertility and Sterility* 23:29, 1972.

shaking in place. And of course, if no sperm is found in the cervical mucus, then further evaluation of the male is essential. PCT is commonly repeated two or three times to achieve more conclusive results.

Additional Blood Tests

What, more blood tests?! You may wonder what else there is to test for, but there are many other things to check.

Besides repeating 3-day FSH levels, and testing estrogen and progesterone levels in response to treatment, additional blood tests will be taken. Moreover, if an immune disorder is suspected, more specific blood studies will be done. A list of the latter follows.

- **Anticardiolipin antibodies:** High titers may point to a coagulation problem or an autoimmune disease.
- **Antithyroid antibodies:** High titers represent thyroid disease.
- **Lupus anticoagulant:** Detects cells demonstrating an autoimmune illness such as Systemic Lupus Erythematosus (SLE), which compromises the immune system.
- **Protein C:** Protein C is produced in the liver and acts as a potent anticoagulant. Deficiencies of protein C may be acquired or congenital.
- **Antinuclear antibodies:** In response to SLE or other autoimmune illnesses, the body perceives its own cells as foreign invaders and produces antinuclear antibodies (ANA).
- **Fibrinogen:** Measures the protein involved in the blood clotting process.
- **Prothrombin time:** Tests the amount of time the body takes to form clots as a response to cell or tissue damage.
- **Partial prothrombin time:** Evaluates clotting factors.

Taking a Closer Look at Ovarian Function: The Role of Inhibin B

There exists a reciprocal relationship between FSH and inhibin (see chapter 4). FSH stimulates the secretion of inhibin from the ovaries and FSH in turn is suppressed by inhibin. A blood test indicating this balance provides another diagnostic tool of ovarian function by measuring FSH, inhibin, and estrogen in the bloodstream. Decreasing levels of inhibin B may have a role as an early indicator of decreasing ovarian reserve before any change in FSH levels is observed.[8]

Endometrial Biopsy

Many physicians feel that the most reliable assessment of ovulation and the luteal phase requires the performing of an endometrial biopsy. A simple blood test to rule out pregnancy (Beta HCG) may be performed the day before. This procedure is performed on an outpatient basis, in the clinic or physician's office, sometime after day 19 of the woman's menstrual cycle and up until two to three days before the onset of menstruation.

ENDOMETRIAL BIOPSY

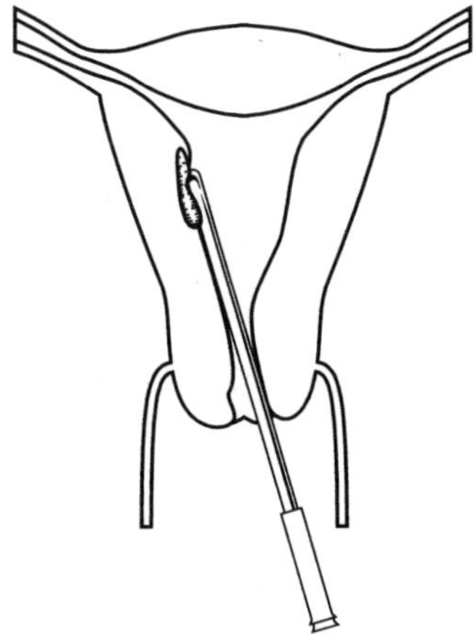

A small hollow tube is passed into the uterus by way of the cervix. Small scrapings of the endometrium (the inner lining of the uterus) are removed and sent to the laboratory for testing. The tissue sample is microscopically examined and "dated" to see whether its characteristics match the timeframe

8. M. Blauer, H. Tinkenen, "Correlation between Serum Inhibin B and Other Indicators of Ovarian Function," *Obstetrics and Gynecology* 94:109 –113, 2001.

in the menstrual cycle when the biopsy was done. This will confirm that the consistency of the endometrium is developed sufficiently to allow implantation and growth of an embryo. No anesthesia is necessary for an endometrial biopsy as the test is not painful, although some cramping and bleeding may occur as a result. Any bleeding would render a woman a *niddah*.

Other Available Tests

There are other tests available that your doctor might recommend be done. Some are invasive and others are not. Below we will list the different tests and describe how they are performed, as well as give you an idea of when and why they might be indicated.

Progestational Challenge Test

The *progestational challenge test* is done to test ovarian function in cases of *amenorrhea* (no menstrual bleeding). There are some women who have fully functioning ovaries, but do not have periods. The test is performed by giving the woman progesterone and seeing if it causes her to have a period. There are different ways of administering progesterone. The most common method is to take medroxyprogesterone acetate, 10 mg daily, by mouth, for five days. The woman is advised to take the medication at the same time each day to keep the hormone level constant and prevent breakthrough bleeding (spotting). This simple procedure can often set a woman's cycle on track. In addition, it can be done at any time, as the woman does not have a menstrual cycle.

Within two to seven days after taking the last progesterone pill, a woman will either bleed, demonstrating that there is ovarian function albeit with stimulation, or not bleed (called a negative withdrawal response), demonstrating a need for a further evaluation.

Clomiphene Citrate Challenge Test

The *clomiphene citrate challenge test* (CCCT) is another tool used to determine ovarian reserve (the ovary's ability to produce mature eggs as a result of hormonal stimulation). It is more accurate in assessing ovarian function than just measuring FSH in the blood on day 3 of the cycle. Clomiphene citrate, 100 mg, is taken on days 5 to 9 of the cycle. FSH is measured on day 3 and day 10. If the FSH is greater than 15 IU/L on either day, it is considered abnormal and indicative of diminished ovarian reserve. A day-3 FSH level blood test and a CCCT are considered part of a standard fertility workup for a woman over age 35.

Ultrasound

Ultrasonic monitoring (sonography) plays an integral role in diagnostic and follow-up care during fertility treatment. Ultrasounds are routinely performed to diagnose disease and structural problems in all parts of the body. In a gynecologic ultrasound, intermittent sound waves from the ultrasound's transducer (the tip of the ultrasound that touches the patient) are projected toward the pelvic area. The sound waves bounce off the various bone, organ, and tissue structures in the pelvis and are then converted into images and displayed on a television screen. Various shades of light and dark reflect the thickness of the structures. Ultrasound is considered much safer than standard X rays, as radiation is not used. Long-term detrimental effects of ultrasonic monitoring have not been detected in over thirty-five years of its use in medicine.[9]

The transducer comes in many shapes and sizes to accommodate the type of examination required. The vaginal transducer has made ultrasonic monitoring of ovulation, for

9. American Institute of Ultrasound in Medicine: "Bioeffects — Considerations for the Safety of Diagnostic Ultrasound," *Journal of Ultrasound Medicine* 1988;7 (Supplement); S1–S38.

instance, much easier. Before the routine use of vaginal ultrasound, women were required to have abdominal ultrasound and hence had to drink over a liter of fluid before the exam. A vaginal ultrasound eliminates that discomfort, plus gives an even clearer picture of the reproductive organs. The vaginal transducer is long and narrow and lubricated at the tip to make the examination easy and painless. It presses up against the cervix in order to get the closest picture possible. Vaginal ultrasound is useful in observing the ovaries preceding ovulation, measuring endometrial thickness to assess possible luteal phase defects, and monitoring early pregnancies before the twelfth week. We will discuss, in chapter 17, the various ultrasonic measurements, and their relationship to specific medical treatments.

Hysteroscopy

Hysteroscopy can be done throughout the menstrual cycle but is usually carried out within a couple of days following the cessation of menstrual bleeding.

There are several indications for the use of hysteroscopy to aid in diagnosing causes of infertility. By viewing the inside of the uterus, hysteroscopy provides valuable information concerning the quality and characteristics of the endometrium. Hysteroscopy can magnify the area under examination, to view mucosal patterns, blood vessels, tissue color, and details of lesions within the cervical canal or uterine cavity. Diagnosing abnormalities of the uterine lining is particularly important before beginning any series of in vitro procedures, as a major cause of failure in IVF is not a problem with fertilization, but the inability of the embryo to implant in the uterus. Hysteroscopy is also useful in the evaluation of women experiencing repeated spontaneous abortions. This procedure is recommended if the hysterosalpingogram (HSG) is abnormal. Intrauterine adhesions, uterine polyps, and myomas (tumors of the muscular tissue of the uterus) can usually be seen. Accurate assessment and diagnosis can be made of uterine malformations. Patency of the fallopian tubes (i.e. they are unblocked) is confirmed by the passage of CO^2 bubbles or another distention medium from the uterus to the tubes.

How Is It Done?

A long, narrow instrument called a *hysteroscope* is passed through the cervix toward the uterus. Carbon dioxide (CO^2) or another distention medium is simultaneously pumped through the instrument, which slightly dilates the cervical opening (*os*) and distends the uterus for examination. Distention to separate the walls of the uterus allows for adequate visualization. The type of distention medium is chosen for its compatibility with whichever hysteroscopic procedure is planned. Carbon dioxide or saline is ideal for diagnostic hysteroscopy. Hyskon, a crystal clear medium that does not mix with blood, and glycin, an oily substance, are well-suited for operative hysteroscopy.

As the physician looks through the opposite end of the hysteroscope (similar to a telescope, encased in a sheath), the cervix and uterus are scanned and observed for any abnormalities. The hysteroscope offers the possibility of obtaining visually directed biopsies for studying endometrial development.

Longitudinal channels in the telescope are divided between viewing, medium installation, and operating. Instruments can be slid through the hysteroscopic channel for intrauterine surgery enabling the operative hysteroscope to grasp, cut, perform a biopsy, and cauterize to cut off bleeding. Fiberoptic lasers are also used for operative procedures. Performing operative procedures with operative hysteroscopy eliminates the need for an abdominal incision and the recuperative process abdominal surgery entails. Operative hysteroscopy can be done to remove a myoma (benign tumor of the uterus), take out a polyp, cut away adhesions from previous surgeries or endometriosis, or repair uterine malformations. A still camera or a video can be attached to the eyepiece for documentation.

Hysteroscopy can be carried out in three different settings:

- **Doctor's office:** Diagnosis only, without anesthesia or with mild sedation or local anesthesia (paracervical block — injection at the cervix). A 3 to 4 mm hysteroscope is used, which usually requires no dilation of the cervix before the procedure.
- **Outpatient unit:** Diagnostic with or without minor interventions, with local or general anesthesia. A 6.5 mm hysteroscope is used, requiring manual dilation of the cervix.
- **Operating room:** Diagnostic or operative hysterocopy can be performed in combination with other procedures. Local, epidural, or general anesthesia is used. A 7 to 10 mm hysteroscope is used.

Side effects include tenderness in the lower abdomen, cramping, mild uterine bleeding, and aching in the shoulders as the gas used to distend the uterus slowly dissipates.

Hysteroscopy carries a minor risk of cervical lacerations or uterine perforations. An infection rate of 1.5 percent is seen and is easily treated with antibiotics.[10]

According to halachah, bleeding as a result of this procedure would render a woman a *niddah*. However, in this case

---

10. A. Agostini and L. Cravello, "Postoperative Infection and Surgical Hysteroscopy," *Fertility and Sterility* 77:4, 2002.

we recommend that you consult a Rav.

Laparoscopy

Laparoscopy is the direct visualization of the pelvic organs through the abdomen. Laparoscopy is done for observation, treatment, and surgical purposes.

During the past few years, laparoscopy has become one of the most frequently performed operations in gynecology. Laparoscopy has reduced the need for laparotomy (surgically opening the abdomen to perform surgery) in all fields of medicine. Major surgeries are now considered minor procedures since the advent and perfection of laparoscopic surgery. Although laparoscopy is performed under general anesthesia, the incision sites are only millimeters in length, requiring minimal repair and recovery, and since major muscles are not affected, recovery time is much quicker than with laparotomy. Most laparoscopies, whether diagnostic or surgical, can be done on an outpatient basis or with only an overnight hospitalization.

How Is It Done?

A small (2 cm) incision is made next to the umbilicus. The laparoscope, a long and narrow stainless steel tube, is inserted through the incision. Similar to a telescope, the laparoscope enables the physician to view the outside of the internal organs closely. The abdominal cavity is distended with about 3 liters of carbon dioxide or other gas, in order to push aside the abdominal organs from the pelvic cavity. With a clear view, the doctor can examine the ovaries, fallopian tubes, and other reproductive organs. With insertion of an additional one to four trocars (sharp-pointed surgical instruments with a cannula) into other small abdominal incisions, treatments and surgery can be performed. Dye can be injected through the cervix and be observed passing through the uterus and out the fallopian tubes to assess uterine or tubal abnormalities. Often, a laparoscopy will be combined with a hysteroscopy.

Definitive diagnosis of endometriosis and pelvic adhesions are routinely made with laparoscopy. Treatment to cut away adhesions or clear blockages, with scalpel, scissors, or even laser, can be done with the laparoscope.

Risks include trauma to internal organs (perforation of the bowel, bladder, or ureter) upon insertion of the laparoscope, reactions to anesthesia, or infection. The incidence of these severe side effects are rare. Commonly, a woman can expect to feel soreness at the incision sites, cramping or aching in the shoulders and neck from the CO^2 gas, and mild vaginal bleeding. A woman should feel progressively better every day, with full recovery in about five days. She should report signs of fever, continuous abdominal pain, or increased vaginal bleeding to her doctor. If bleeding should occur, you should consult a Rav, who will then speak with your doctor about the specific details of the procedure in order to determine if you are a *niddah*.

In Summary

The aim of a woman's fertility evaluation is to start slowly and add one piece of the puzzle at a time.

Level I evaluation:

- Interview and general examination
- Gynecologic examination
- Blood test/urinalysis

Level II evaluation:

- BBT
- HSG
- PCT

- Endometrial biopsy

Based on the results, addtional tests will be done:

- Progesterone between days 19 and 24
- FSH day 3
- Immunological assays
- CCCT

A woman may expect to undergo:

- Ultrasound
- Hysteroscopy
- Laparoscopy

Goals:

- Definitive diagnosis
- Plan of care

13. The Man's Initial Fertility Evaluation

The Holy One, blessed is He, said:
"There is no illness without a remedy."
(*Midrash Tanchuma, Yisro* 8)

IF YOU'RE LIKE MOST MEN, you have to be feeling pretty sick to go to the doctor, let alone do any type of medical testing. Since infertility is a "couple's issue," however, it is therefore essential that you undergo a complete fertility evaluation in order for you and your wife to receive complete and successful treatment.

According to the American Urological Association, the purpose of the male fertility evaluation is to identify:

- Potentially correctable conditions
- Irreversible conditions that are amenable to assisted reproductive techniques (ARTs)
- Irreversible conditions that are not amenable to ARTs, but for which donor insemination or adoption are possible
- Life- or health-threatening conditions that may underlie the infertility and require medical attention
- Genetic abnormalities that may affect the health of the offspring if ARTs are to be used[1]

---

1. I. Sharlip, J. Jarow, "Best Practice Policies for Male Infertility: Recommendations from the Practice Guidelines Committee of the American Urological Association, Inc.," *Fertility and Sterility* vol. 77, no. 5, 2002.

THE FIRST LEVEL OF TESTING IN THE MAN'S FERTILITY WORKUP

Past Medical History

As with your wife, the preliminary exam begins with a through review of your medical history. Factors influencing fertility include:

◆ Age — spermatogenesis is reduced by half in men over the age of 50.[2]

◆ Occupation — certain environmental pollutants in the workplace can interfere with fertility.

◆ Childhood illness, undescended testes, history of surgery, radiation or chemotherapy, traumatic injury, or infection that could disrupt sperm production and testicular function. Additional pertinent information should include family reproductive history, current illness, or the current use of any medication.

◆ Any details about your sexual habits or sexual relationship that may be pertinent to the fertility investigation should be discussed with your doctor. This may be uncomfortable, so perhaps you may want to meet with the physician in private. Of course there should be total honesty between you and your wife, but realistically this may not always be possible. If you ever fathered a child in a previous relationship, for example, this would be important information to disclose to your doctor.

Physical Examination

After the history is taken, you will undergo a complete physical examination. Observation of hair distribution, sexual maturity, and body shape is made in order to rule out hormonal or chromosomal abnormalities. Location of the urinary opening (*meatus*) is

---

2. J.B. Kerr, "Ultrastructure of the Seminiferous Epithelium and Intertubular Tissue of the Testes," *Journal of Electronic Microscopic Technology* 19:215–240, 1991.

evaluated. If the opening is on the underside of the penis (*hypospadias*) it can interfere with placement of the sperm alongside the cervix, which in turn can reduce chances of conception.

Symptoms of burning upon urination, or irritation or redness around the meatus, could signal an inflammatory or infectious process. Any purulent discharge or lesion will be noted. Semen or prostatic (from the prostate) secretions will be cultured if infection is suspected. Mycoplasma and chlamydia are the most common infecting organisms.

The testes will be palpated for any lumps or hard spots. Descent of the testes into the scrotum is verified at this time. The doctor will ask you to stand up and bear down, as a bulging vein(s) in the testicle may indicate a varicocele.

The doctor will then insert his finger into the rectum to exam the prostate gland. The prostate is located a few inches above the anal opening. Upon examination, the prostate is palpated to note shape and size in order to rule out the possibility of a tumor or infection.

Urinalysis and Blood Tests

A complete urinalysis may reveal infection of the urethra or prostate. Reduced semen volume and large amounts of sperm in the urine may indicate retrograde ejaculation.

Any man suspected of a fertility problem will have blood assays to evaluate levels of testosterone, FSH, LH, TSH, and prolactin.

Various results may include:

- **Testosterone low:** Delayed puberty, decreased libido (sex drive), impotence.
- **FSH and LH low** (*hypogonatrophic hypogonadism*)**:** Hypothalamic insufficiency, incomplete sexual maturation.
- **FSH and LH low / prolactin high:** Pituitary damage, pituitary tumor.

- **FSH and LH high:** Testicular dysfunction, *azoospermic* (no sperm production), *oligospermic* (reduced amount of sperm). FSH elevated to three times the normal value usually makes a poor prognosis.
- **TSH high:** Hypothyroidism.
- **TSH low:** Hyperthyroidism.

THE SECOND LEVEL OF TESTING IN THE MAN'S FERTILITY WORKUP

Based on the initial fertility evaluation, this next level of tests will hopefully complete the evaluation and give your doctor specific treatment options.

Semen Analysis

The semen analysis, or sperm count, can be performed at any time during the fertility investigation. It is considered the most significant diagnostic study of the male's fertility function. Sometimes the semen analysis is delayed and a normal postcoital test (PCT — the extraction and analysis of sperm from the woman after normal relations) is relied upon instead. The semen analysis is much more comprehensive, as it tests other characteristics of sperm that are not evaluated in the PCT.

If your doctor would like to skip over the PCT and do the semen analysis instead, you may want to suggest the possibility of doing a PCT first. Halachically, it is the preferred method, as it does not entail the problem of wasting seed. If your doctor feels that a semen analysis is necessary even at this point, you should consult a Rav.

The procedure for the semen analysis is as follows: A man is asked to abstain from intercourse for two to three days prior to collection of the specimen. Although not the method of collecting sperm from a halachic point of view, the general protocol is for a man to provide a specimen in a special container by means of self-stimulation. Many clinics and doctor's offices provide a private room for this, but it is also possible to obtain the sample at home, if a man is more comfortable doing so. However, all specimens must be protected from cold and transported under certain conditions to the laboratory within one hour.

According to Rav Moshe Feinstein, obtaining a semen sample using this method is forbidden. A man may obtain a sample by wearing a condom during regular intercourse or by *coitus interruptus*, which is withdrawing before ejaculation.[3] Most doctors prefer the use of a condom, for it provides the most accurate specimen collection. The halachic preference is for a condom over interruptus (for there is a chance that one would miss the test tube in pulling out, and that would be wasting seed). Moreover, it is simply less stressful for most couples to use a condom. On the other hand, if, for whatever reason, a couple may feel more stress in using a condom than the alternative method, then they may employ coitus interruptus. Anything that will reduce the couple's anxiety should be taken into consideration.

If a couple lives too far from the fertility clinic to bring the sample within an hour, they will need to make the proper arrangements such as using a nearby hotel room.[4]

The condom, provided by the laboratory, is a special type which is not made of latex and does not contain harmful chemicals which kill sperm. Additionally, some *poskim* rule that a small hole be made in the condom prior to its use.[5]

One report suggests that oligospermic males (men with a sperm count of less than 4 million in the ejaculate) have better

---

3. *Igros Moshe, Even haEzer,* vol. I, chaps. 70 and 71; vol. II, chap. 17; vol. III, chap. 14.

4. Ibid., vol. I, chap. 70; vol. III, chap. 14.

5. *Nishmas Avraham, Even haEzer* 1, in the name of Rav Shlomo Zalman Auerbach and Rav Yehoshua Neuwirth.

results while using the condom method of collection.[6]

Six sperm characteristics are tested in the sperm analysis:

◆ **Volume.** 1.5 to 5.0 milliliters is considered to be the normal amount. Too high a volume may be a sign of infection. Low-volume ejaculate may be associated with retrograde ejaculation or sexual dysfunction.

◆ **Viscosity.** Normally the semen coagulates (becomes thicker in consistency) immediately after ejaculation. If not, a structural abnormality of the seminal vesicles may be suspected. (The Gemara also tells us that semen that is not congealed but watery is a sign of male infertility.[7]) Within a half to one hour normal semen should liquefy. Agglutenization (sticking together) of sperm may point to the possibility of infection or the presence of sperm antibodies. If sperm antibodies are suspected, the sperm can be separated from the semen by means of spinning the test tube containing the sperm in a centrifuge, then washed and resuspended in a neutral fluid. The sample is then used for intrauterine insemination (IUI).

◆ **pH.** The pH (acid-base balance) should be between 7 and 8. Slight variations are generally not a cause of infertility. However, if the pH is very acidic, there could be urine contamination of the specimen and further investigation is warranted.

◆ **Sperm count** (*sperm concentration*). By using a microscope, the number of sperm per milliliter of fluid (semen) is counted. According to the World Health Organization (WHO), average sperm concentration is more than 60 million per milliliter (>60 million/cc). Counts of less than 20 million per milliliter are considered sub-fertile.

---

6. P.M. Zavos, "Seminal Parameters of Ejaculates," *Fertility and Sterility*, 44:517, 1985.

7. *Yevamos* 80b.

◆ **Motility.** Within two hours of the sample collection, more than 50 percent of the sperm should be motile (moving). Motility is measured by observing forward progression, which should be higher than 2 on a scale of 0 to 4. Abnormal sperm movement would also be noted at this time.

◆ **Morphology.** More than 30 percent of the sperm should have a normal shape.[8] Some abnormal shapes are always seen, but these are incapable of reaching an ovum and fertilizing it.

Kruger Morphology is a more detailed evaluation of sperm shapes. The sperm must meet stringent criteria which evaluate the sample and size of the head, midpiece, and tail in order to be considered normal. Normal results are when 14 percent or more of sperm have normal-shaped heads. Men with less than 4 percent normal-shaped sperm may have a significant fertility problem.

A man may be asked to give repeat semen samples if a problem is suspected either with the method of collection or with the sperm itself. Three separate semen analyses are often requested for greater accuracy, as there are variations from sample to sample.

In order to direct a plan of medical care, additional parameters in the sperm sample are often tested to complete the evaluation of the husband, as technology has brought us even more specialized testing of sperm beyond that which a standard sperm analysis can supply. Some additional parameters are:

◆ **Fructose.** Contributed by the seminal vesicles, fructose provides nourishment for the sperm, and its absence may point to the existence of an ejaculatory duct obstruction or the absence of seminal vesicles.

◆ **Cervical mucus migration studies.** Although the PCT

---

8. World Health Organization, *Semen Analysis Reference Values*, 2001.

remains the easiest and most widely used method of evaluating the qualitative interaction between sperm and cervical mucus, some laboratories perform this evaluation at the time of the sperm analysis, substituting bovine (cow) mucus. Cervical mucus migration studies test the sperm's motility and survival ability.

◆ **Sperm penetration assay (SPA).** SPA is an examination of sperm function which tests the sperm's ability to penetrate a hamster ovum from which the outer layer (*zona pellucida*) has been removed. The zona must be removed in order to allow for the penetration of a number of (human) sperm into one ovum. This is referred to as the zona-free hamster ova penetration test. Performing an SPA is helpful in predicting, with 88 percent accuracy, whether IVF alone or IVF with ICSI (intracytoplasmic sperm injection — see chapter 17) would be successful in that particular case of male-factor infertility. An SPA of greater than 20 percent is considered normal.[9]

◆ **Hypo-osmotic swelling test (HOS).** This tests the viability of ejaculated or testicular immotile spermatozoa for use in ICSI (see above paragraph). A single spermatozoon is placed into a small droplet containing a hypo-osmotic solution. If the sperm tail swells, the sperm cell is considered viable. The tail is then crushed, which is believed to stimulate the fertilization process.

◆ **Spect-Mar test.** This tests for anti-sperm antibodies.

◆ **Computer-Aided Sperm Analysis (CASA).** This test gives quantitative data by use of a video-microscope as opposed to a standard microscope, where the technician is personally involved in the quantitative manual assessment of sperm cells. Besides examining sperm cells for motility, num-

---

9. M. Freeman, A. Archibong, "Male Partner Screening before In Vitro Fertilization," *Fertility and Sterility* 76:1113–1118, 2001.

ber, and concentration, CASA examines the speed and the straightness of the sperm's path.

Endocrine Evaluation If blood hormone levels were not tested during the first fertility evaluation, they should be performed if a man has an abnormally low sperm concentration — especially less than 10 million per ml; impaired sexual function; or other signs suggestive of hormonal deficiencies. Endocrine disorders are uncommon in men with normal semen variables.

Postejaculatory Urinalysis In men with ejaculate volumes of less than 1 ml, a urine sample taken immediately following ejaculation may show the presence of sperm. This would suggest retrograde ejaculation. Further evaluation will be necessary to find out whether this is due to chronic health problems or current medications.

Genetic Screening Azoospermia (lack of sperm in the ejaculate) or severely reduced numbers of sperm may be associated with genetic abnormalities. Cystic fibrosis, gene mutations associated with congenital absence of the vas deferens (CAVD), or Y-chromosome aberrations are associated with impaired sperm production. Chromosomal abnormalities have been found in 10 to 15 percent of men with little or no sperm in the ejaculate.[10]

Transrectal Ultrasound *Transrectal Ultrasound* (TRUS) offers a noninvasive means of studying and diagnosing problems of the prostate, seminal vesicles, and ejaculatory duct. An ultrasonic probe is introduced rectally and structures within the testes are displayed on the ultrasound screen. Dilated seminal vesicles, dilated ejaculatory ducts, or

---

10. J.L. Pryor, M. Kent-First, "Microdeletions in the Y-chromosome of Infertile Men," *New England Journal of Medicine* 336:534–539, 1997.

the presence of cysts are suggestive of complete or partial ejaculatory duct obstruction. Some experts recommend performing TRUS in men with reduced sperm counts and low-volume ejaculates.

Testicular Ultrasonography

Ultrasound examination of the scrotum is recommended in men when the physical examination of the scrotum is abnormal. Suspected varicoceles or any other testicular pathology should be evaluated by ultrasound and with doppler scanning to measure blood flow within the spermatic veins. Scrotal ultrasound is also indicated if a testicular mass is suspected. Most scrotal abnormalities, including varicoceles, spermatoceles, absence of the vas deferens, or testicular masses are palpable upon physical examination.

Testicular Biopsy

Testicular biopsy is an important diagnostic tool in differentiating obstruction from testicular pathology (i.e. a blockage or malformation, or a missing component). A biopsy can help guide future medical therapy. The testicular biopsy is performed primarily on men with little or no sperm encountered in the semen analysis. For the halachah on testicular biopsy, see page 374.

Local anesthesia is administered and a small incision is made through the scrotum to take a tissue sample from one or both of the testes. If obstruction is suspected, a larger incision will be done in order to facilitate microsurgical repair. (See chapter 17 for information regarding microsurgery of the testes.)

Vasography

In addition to performing a testes biopsy if little or no sperm are found in the sperm sample, a *vasograph* or *vasogram* will be done to identify obstruction of the vas deferens or ejaculatory duct. Sterile saline, carmine, or methylene blue dye is injected into the vas deferens while

X-ray films are taken. Following the course of the injected fluid, your doctor can see if there is any obstruction. Prior to injecting the dye, your doctor may aspirate a small amount of fluid from the vas deferens to examine microscopically for the presence of sperm. Vasography will be performed during advanced diagnostic testing, or at the time of microsurgical repair (*vasoepididymostomy*) to ensure that no other sites of obstruction are present within the genitourinary tract.

All of the diagnostic tests discussed in this chapter are necessary tools for identifying the existence of fertility problems. A definitive diagnosis for one or both of you will result in any number of treatments, discussed in chapter 17 — hopefully bringing you closer to your goal of parenthood.

In Summary

A man's initial fertility evaluation follows these basic steps:

Level I evaluation:

- Interview and general examination
- Urinalysis
- Blood test

Level II evaluation:

- PCT
- Sperm analysis
- Endocrine evaluation
- Postejaculatory Urinalysis (retrograde ejaculation)
- Genetic screening
- Ultrasound, biopsy, or specialized X ray of the testes

Goals:

- Definitive diagnosis
- Plan of care

14. Why Us? Coming to Terms with Infertility

"God picks up all those who fall" — These are the
barren women [whose spirits have fallen].
"And He straightens all those who are bent over" —
And when God grants them a child they stand proud.
(*Bereishis Rabbah* 71:2)

MAZAL AND MITZVOS

Introduction

While experiencing the emotional anguish of infertility, most couples will ask the question, "Why us?" Why are we so unfortunate to have such difficulty having children — maybe even to be barren forever? Are we cursed? Are we being punished for anything we did wrong or is it just "bad luck"? Would we be such terrible parents that we would be better off not having children, or is it a test of our faith? Does God have a plan for us, or is this just arbitrary?

All of these questions point to the ultimate one: Why do good people suffer in this world? This same question is asked when children develop fatal illnesses. Much has been written on this topic, but we still don't understand it. We never will. Moreover, no one can answer these questions: no rabbi, no scholar, no philosopher; nobody. In this world, we only see a limited bit of reality; we are incapable of seeing the many layers that make up God's universe, both physical and metaphysical.

Instead of asking the ultimate question and expecting an answer, a person must rather ask, if this is the situation, what can I do about it? What can I learn from it? How can I serve God, given the present situation?[1] In life we are put into situations, and it is our job to learn how to serve God under these conditions. You need to ask, "How do I make the best of it?" Instead of asking why this is happening to you, ask how you should respond.

Nature and God's Intervention

There is confusion about the relationship between God's orchestration of world events, and what appears to be simply the laws of nature or "chance." Why does the world appear to be "unfair"? Why is one person born attractive, while another uncomely? Why is one person born blind, and another with perfect vision? Why are some people born intelligent, others with a low IQ? Why is this woman born with a defective womb and this particular man with a low sperm count? Is it God's plan? Is it an accident? Is it nature? And if it is nature, can one change it by praying or doing good deeds?

The *Tiferes Yisrael* wrote an important essay on this topic, and the following is a summary.[2]

The Recipe for Success

What procures success in a man? Is it his natural character? Is it hard work? Is it his good deeds? Is it a little bit of everything?

We are all born with certain characteristics. As the Talmud says, when a person is conceived, an angel responsible for pregnancy asks, "Master of the universe, what shall be the fate of this drop? Shall it produce a strong man or a weak man, a wise man or a fool, a rich man or a poor man?"[3] There are a

---

1. HaRav Yosef Dov Soloveitchik, *Kol Dodi Dofek*, section on *Tzaddik veRa Lo* (Jerusalem: Mosad haRav Kook, 5741).

2. Rabbi Yisrael Lipshitz, end of tractate *Kiddushin*. Most of the rest of this section is based on his essay.

3. *Niddah* 16b.

number of factors that contribute to our overall makeup.

Success certainly starts with natural talents or character traits. To attain a winning sports team, you must start with strong, natural athletes. Rigorous practices and a strong will are not enough. A person with a low IQ will not become a nuclear physicist. Someone with a weak back will not be a good laborer.

However, natural inclination will not be enough either. Without commitment to hard work, the goal will not be reached. So many students who don't study never realize their potential. Yet toil and talent are no guarantees either. So many people begin businesses with optimism and devotion, putting in long hard hours, but just don't make it. Yet others, who aren't any smarter, see success.

Mitzvah observance and good deeds do not guarantee worldly success either. We all know observant people who are unsuccessful and suffer, as well as nonobservant people who prosper and enjoy. Perhaps one answer is that there is no reward and punishment in this world, and all of our reward and punishment will be in the Next World.[4] If God would reward only the righteous and punish only the wicked this would contradict nature and free choice.

God runs the world *b'derech ha-teva,* through natural means. The Hebrew word for nature, *teva,* is related to the word *matbea,* which means stamp. Nature is the stamp of the King of kings. The King would only revoke His own stamp under great necessity. Therefore, if God gave one person a strong *natural* capacity in a particular area, but made him unsuccessful in that area because of his sins, and made a less talented individual successful because of his merits, it would conflict with the flow of nature that God Himself laid down for the world. God usually doesn't alter the pattern of natural order based on good or bad deeds. The Talmud gives an ex-

---

4. See *Kiddushin* 39b; *Chullin* 142a.

ample of this with the story of Rabbi Elazar ben Pedas.[5]

Rabbi Elazar was very poor. One day he had a blood-letting (an ancient health remedy) and couldn't afford to buy food to replenish his strength after the procedure. His son took a clove of garlic and put it in his father's mouth. He became weak and fell asleep.

The Rabbis came to visit him and saw that while he was asleep, he laughed and cried, and a ray of light radiated from his forehead. When he awoke, they asked him why he had laughed and cried. He answered: "I was sitting with the Almighty, and I asked Him, 'How long am I going to have to suffer in this world?' He answered: 'Elazar My son, would you be happy if I would turn the world back to the beginning of time, so that *maybe* you would be born at a time that is favorable for livelihood?' I responded, 'So much [i.e. turning the whole world back to the beginning of time] and [all I get is] *maybe* [I won't be a pauper]?' Then I asked Him, 'Have I lived most of my life already, or is most of my life still before me?' God answered: 'You have lived most of your life already.' So I said, 'If so, let it be. I don't want You to change the world for me.'"

It was Rabbi Elazar ben Pedas's *mazal* to be direly poor. It wasn't because he "deserved it," it was just his *mazal*. The word *mazal* does not mean luck. *Mazal* is a combination of all the causes that make us who we are. The word *mazal* is related to the Hebrew root *n-z-l*, which denotes flowing liquid. Like a river that flows and cannot be stopped, so too our *mazal* cannot change drastically. Just as a river is composed of drops of water, so too our *mazal* is comprised of different factors that make us who we are and guide us to where we are probably going to go. There is a certain flow of nature which cannot be excessively disturbed; but it can be altered a little.

---

5. *Ta'anis* 25a.

Understanding "Mazal"

What is *mazal*? The Tiferes Yisrael explains that there are two types of *mazal*, the visible and the concealed. The visible *mazal* encompasses numerous factors which are the field of anthropologists, biologists, scientists, and psychologists. We are what we are in every aspect — physically, mentally, emotionally, intellectually, and in our inclination to succeed — due to what was destined for us at birth and due to our environment. The genes we receive from our parents are the first component in our overall makeup. As the Mishnah says, "A father bequeaths to his son his beauty, his strength, his ability to accumulate wealth, his wisdom, and his longevity."[6] With recent research into the mysteries of DNA, the depths of this truth are only beginning to be discovered.

Another factor in a person's *mazal* is the place where he was born or at least descended from. Each country has a different culture. A person's diet has a great influence on his *mazal* also, as a person with a healthy diet will be more solid in mind and body and might even live longer than a person with an unhealthy diet. A person's upbringing affects his *mazal* as well. His neighborhood, home life, friends, family, type of school, interests, and hobbies will all influence his personality, his ambitions, and everything else about him. In *Mishlei* it says: "He who walks with wise men will become wise."[7] The profession that one chooses will also shape an individual's *mazal*. Some professions develop a person's mind, some strengthen his body, and some advance his social skills.

All this makes up who we are, and that is our visible *mazal*. But still the question can be asked, why was so-and-so born from such parents, from that particular country, in that particular city, with that inclination? This question can never be an-

---

6. *Eduyos* 2:9.

7. 13:20.

swered. We cannot ask, why was so-and-so born Jewish, while his neighbor was born a Christian? Why is he a man and she a woman? Why did this person grow up wealthy in California, while this person lived in starvation in Southeast Asia? Why was this animal born a giraffe, and this one a zebra? The human mind can never understand this. This is God's wisdom. It is a wisdom that no man can ever know. This is what we previously referred to as concealed *mazal*.

Mazal and Children

Now that we have established that *mazal* encompasses everything that makes us who we are and determines our capabilities, we need to see if or how religious observance can play a role in spite of it. The Gemara says there are three things which are not dependent upon good deeds, but upon our *mazal*: longevity, having children, and livelihood.[8] Most people consider these to be the most important things in life. How could it be, then, that they are dependent on our *mazal*? Furthermore, this *gemara* seems to contradict another *gemara* in tractate *Shabbos* that says there is no *mazal* for Israel (i.e. that our lives' circumstances are not determined according to *mazal*).[9]

Rashi and Tosafos, commenting on the latter *gemara,*[10] explain that our lives really are dependent upon our *mazal;* however, we can change our *mazal* by doing good deeds or through prayer. Today, it is in the general nature of the world for people to live well into their seventies and eighties — although sometimes an individual's personal *mazal* is to have a short life, *r"l*, or an exceptionally long one. It is also in the general nature of the world for people to have children, whether

---

8. *Mo'ed Katan* 28a.

9. *Shabbos* 156a.

10. *Tosafos* on *Mo'ed Katan* 28a, *d.h. Ela be-mazla;* Tosafos *on Shabbos* 156a, *d.h. Ein mazal l'Yisrael.* See also Rashi on *Shabbos* 156a, *d.h. Ein mazal l'Yisrael.*

naturally or through medical assistance. Yet there are people whose personal *mazal* is to have a structural abnormality or a low sperm count. Other people's *mazal* is to have children through assisted reproduction. And, *r"l,* some people's *mazal* is not to have children at all. Yet whatever your particular *mazal* is, you do all that you can — both spiritually and medically — to be worthy of the blessing of children.

The *Tiferes Yisrael* elaborates further. He says that basically you have a certain *mazal,* and it cannot be changed drastically. However, it can be changed a little, within reason, due to your merits. So doing mitzvos may help, but they cannot help everything all the time, for this would contradict the forces of nature that God put into the world to make it run. A person's individual *mazal* is part of the nature of the world. God will not change nature too much. But He will change it a little based on good deeds and prayer.[11] Our attitude needs to be that our prayers and mitzvos will be beneficial in helping us attain what we need, for they are certainly effective in strengthening our connection with our Father in Heaven. And that is the purpose of life.

A famous case in Jewish tradition is the story of the birth of Rashi. Rashi's pious parents were childless. Rashi's father was a merchant of precious jewels. One day he acquired a remarkably valuable gem. The ruler of the province heard of this, and sent a messenger to buy the jewel for a statue that he was designing. Rashi's father didn't want his jewel being used in an "idol," and therefore didn't want to sell it, but to refuse the potentate would have been fatal. So he said he would deliver the gem in person. As he journeyed on the boat, he dropped the gem into the ocean, making it look like an accident. We are taught that because he sacrificed his gem for God in order that

11. This is also the view of Tosafos, *Shabbos* ibid. See also Tosafos on *Niddah* 16b, *d.h. Hakol,* where this idea is expressed.

the jewel would not be used in an idol, God gave him a jewel of a son who will fill the world with gems of Torah.

Rachel's ultimately conceiving seems to be due to her good deeds as well as to her prayers, as it says, "And God remembered Rachel, and God heard her, and opened her womb."[12] Rashi says that "And God remembered" refers to her giving the signs to Leah at Leah's wedding to Yaakov,[13] and the Netziv says that "God heard her" refers to her prayers.[14]

Leah's prayer was answered as well. Although she was experiencing secondary infertility, she gave away her flowers (thought to be a fertility drug) to Rachel so she herself could be with Yaakov that night. Rashi says that God helped Leah conceive.[15] The next verse says that God heard Leah and she gave birth. What did He hear? He heard her prayers.[16] So sometimes prayer and/or good deeds can change our *mazal* of being childless to a *mazal* of having children, and sometimes we cannot change our *mazal* even with good deeds and prayer, as in the case of Elazar ben Pedas.[17]

PERCEIVING HARDSHIPS

A Common Misconception

It is common for many religious people to view hardships that befall them as punishments from God. This is particularly true for childless couples. God-fearing people believe that God is involved in their lives, so it stands to reason that suffering something as distressing as infertility must be a punishment

12. *Bereishis* 30:22.

13. See Rashi, *Bereishis* 29:25.

14. *Ha'amek Davar, Bereishis* 30:22.

15. Rashi, *Bereishis* 30:17.

16. *Ha'amek Davar, Bereishis* 30:17.

17. This is also what Tosafos says on *Shabbos* 156a, *d.h. Ein mazal*, and on *Mo'ed Katan* 28a, *d.h. Ela*.

from God. Many times, people who were less committed to mitzvos in the past will attribute their infertility to previous compromising experiences such as premarital sex, abortions or unsanctioned birth control, or some other sexual mistake.[18] Dr. Alice Domar writes: "Infertility can lead to an intense spiritual crisis. A lot of my patients find infertility to be the first time their prayers are not answered by God, and they lose faith. They think that God is punishing them or angry with them, or that God feels they would be poor parents."[19]

Yes, unpleasant experiences are the will of God, but the will of God does not have to mean a punishment. The infertility of Chanah and the mother of Shimshon, or of the matriarchs, for example, was not a punishment, but a stimulus leading to something else (as we will explore in chapter 15). You shouldn't automatically assume that your infertility is in retribution for "past sins" of any kind, and you should never think that God doesn't love you. God loves all His children. Too many people feel that their infertility is a punishment. This only magnifies their depression, for now they feel like bad people in addition to being childless. It is more productive to see your infertility as a stimulus for spiritual or personal development.

According to the Alshich, Rachel thought that her infertility was a punishment for tricking Yaakov on their wedding night by allowing Lavan to substitute Leah for her. Thinking she wasn't worthy of God's blessing, she ran to Yaakov to pray for her. Yaakov became angry with her, for he knew that her infertility was certainly not a punishment.[20]

Another expression of this erroneous conclusion by Rachel can be seen through *Chazal*'s comment that she was envi-

---

18. *Men, Women, and Infertility,* pp. 45 – 47.
19. *Conquering Infertility,* p. 18.
20. Alshich, *Bereishis* 30:1.

ous of Leah's good deeds.[21] She thought, Leah must be a *tzadekes*, therefore she merited to be a mother, but I must be lacking something so I am being punished. Rachel even named her son Dan, born to her maidservant Bilhah (from the word for judgment), as if to say, "God judged me and found me guilty (so I was barren), and now God judged me and found me meritorious (and gave me a child).[22]

Most people see their own suffering as a punishment from God, as Rachel did, but like Yaakov they don't see other people's suffering as retribution — just as he didn't see Rachel's infertility as a punishment. They see other people who suffer merely as unfortunate individuals, but they see themselves as being "out of favor" with God. We must stop being so critical of ourselves. We must stop thinking that our misfortunes are punishments. Negative thoughts are only "the advice of the *yetzer ha-ra*," self-destructive thinking. Thinking that God is punishing us will only leave us depressed. It will distance us from God and make us lose any hope of getting closer to Him. And that would be the last thing that God wants.

Even though the Torah does name childlessness as the punishment for some sins,[23] one should not automatically assume that he or she too is childless as a punishment. There are so many variables to put into the equation of reward and punishment that it is impossible to know. Only God can make the final accounting.

Similarly, rewards are promised in the Torah for the performance of certain mitzvos, but sometimes when we do those mitzvos we don't see their rewards being actualized in this world. So leave the reward and punishment accounting to the Lord. Don't think that being childless is a punishment. Like-

---

21. Rashi, *Bereishis* 30:1.

22. *Bereishis Rabbah* 71:7.

23. See, for example, *Vayikra* 20:20–21.

wise, if you merit to have a child, don't assume that it is a reward for some mitzvah that you did, even if you have fulfilled a mitzvah that promises the reward of children.[24] Just thank God for giving you undeserved kindness, as we explained in chapter 7. Generally, when the Torah or *Chazal* discuss reward or punishment, they are dealing with it on a theoretical, general level, not on a practical and personal level (as will be explained later).[25]

If you see your own infertility as a punishment, then what about other people who are childless, such as friends and family? Many great *tzaddikim* have been childless, such as the Chazon Ish and the Lubavitcher Rebbe. Would you claim that these righteous leaders or their wives were being punished? There was a Divine reason for their — and your — infertility, and it is known only in Heaven.[26]

Some people find it helpful to consult with a rabbi known

---

24. As Hagar thought that she was more righteous than Sarah when she became pregnant so quickly. *Bereishis Rabbah* 45:4.

25. See the Maharsha on Tosafos, *Shabbos* 156a.

26. There is a case in the Tanach (*II Shemuel* 6:23) where infertility does seem to strike as a punishment, at least at first glance. *Chazal* say that Michal was punished for rebuking her husband, King David, for showing too much joy in front of the multitudes as he danced with the Ark of the Lord. Her punishment was infertility. This was not really a punishment but more of a necessity for the future kingdom. The main halachah for a king is to write a *sefer Torah* and carry it with him at all times. This is to remind him that he is under God, and that he is obligated to the Torah. Since Michal's mistaken attitude was that a king shouldn't belittle himself before the nation even for the sake of the Torah, there was a danger that her offspring would inherit this attitude. If one of her children would become king then the whole Torah would be in jeopardy, for they would carry her personality trait of honoring oneself more than the Torah. Therefore she couldn't have any more children.

If one looks at our sources, a superficial case can be made that infertility is a punishment and having children is a reward. (Most people, though, naturally think that infertility is a punishment, without for his depth of learning and sensitivity. A rabbinic mentor of this caliber may be able to give you spiritual guidance — especially if you think that your infertility is a punishment. With something as personal as this, he will address your individual needs, and provide perspective on your suffering.

The Patriarchs' and Matriarchs' Infertility

The Gemara asks the question, Why were the patriarchs childless? It answers that God desires the prayers of the righteous.[27] *Chazal* knew that the infertility of our patriarchs and matriarchs was not a punishment, so they searched for an explanation for it. The fact that specifically those women who were to be the mothers of God's holy nation were all infertile implies the existence of a Divine plan. Their infer-

---

even being aware of any sources.) Based on Scriptural sources, one may think that if God blessed man to "Be fruitful and multiply," certainly it is good to have children and bad not to have them. This is the meaning of the verse in *Tehillim* (127:3), "The Eternal's heritage is children, a reward of the fruit of the womb." This doesn't mean that children are a reward for our good deeds, however; it means that children are a good thing, a treasure if you will (this is clear from the context of the entire passage).

In two places in the Torah, fertility is considered a reward: "There will be no woman who miscarries or is childless in your land. I will grant you your full number of years" (*Shemos* 23:26), and "There will be no infertile male or female among you" (*Devarim* 7:14). Again, these verses are general promises and blessings for the people. They are not necessarily meant to imply that if a person doesn't merit to have a child, he or she is being punished. The verses are trying to say that if the whole Jewish People is doing God's will, there will not be a situation of barrenness. Just like if the whole Jewish People do God's will, there will be peace in the Land of Israel. Conversely, if the people collectively do not fulfill God's will, there may be some who will suffer from infertility, the good people and the not so good people. When all the Jewish People fulfill God's will, then no one will suffer from infertility — as neither will there be anyone who suffers from poverty or illness, both promises of which are also stated in this same passage in *Devarim* (7:12–16).

27. *Yevamos* 64a.

tility was needed in order to create the atmosphere essential for beginning the Jewish nation. The nation needed to be built on a foundation of prayer.

Arising as a nation on the pillars of prayer implants in us a dependency on the Almighty. It also gives us hope, for children symbolize the future. The patriarchs' and matriarchs' praying for children symbolized the hope for God's future nation.

However, there are other parallel reasons for the matriarchs' infertility. In *Bereishis Rabbah* the Rabbis suggest that infertility could be a means of enhancing marriage.[28] Concerning Rivkah, *Chazal* say that she was infertile because God did not want the world to think that she was fruitful as a result of the blessing that her brother Lavan gave her, that she become a great nation![29] God didn't want the wicked Lavan to take credit for the growth of the Chosen People.[30] It was only because of the prayers of the righteous Yitzchak that Rivkah merited to have children. This could be the reason that Yitzchak and Rivkah's act of praying was recorded in the Torah. (Of all the patriarchs and matriarchs, the Torah only tells us explicitly that Yitzchak and Rivkah prayed.[31])

We can learn an important lesson from the Gemara in trac-

---

28. *Bereishis Rabbah* 45:4. See chapter 15 for more discussion on this.

29. *Bereishis* 24:60.

30. *Peninei haMidrash* on *Shir haShirim* 2:14, p. 88. *Midrash haGadol* extends this idea to all the mothers. The Midrash says, The elders were asked, why were the matriarchs barren? They answered that the matriarchs were the daughters of idol-worshipers.... God said, if I give them children, their fathers will praise their idols" (*Midrash haGadol, Bereishis* 25:21).

31. This of course poses a difficulty to *Chazal*'s answer to the question of why the patriarchs were barren. *Chazal* tell us that God craves the prayers of the righteous, yet we find that only Yitzchak's (and Rivkah's) prayers are explicitly mentioned in the Torah. In *Targum Unkelos* we see that also Rachel and Leah prayed (*Targum Unkelos* on

tate *Yevamos* that quotes Rabbi Yitzchak. Rabbi Yitzchak does not say that the patriarchs prayed. He says that God *craves the prayers of the righteous*. Who are the "righteous?" According to Rabbi Yitzchak, perhaps they are all those who are afflicted with infertility.[32]

A person going through such a difficult spiritual crisis might feel he is being punished, and therefore he might distance himself from God. But let's do some "cognitive therapy" on ourselves. Let us look at the patriarchs — the pillars of our nation — and understand that if they were not afflicted with infertility as a punishment, then perhaps neither are we.[33]

This is exactly what *Seder Eliyahu Rabbah* is telling us.

Bereishis 30:17, 22). Yaakov didn't. Sarah and Avraham didn't. (See, however, *Seder Eliyahu Rabbah* 18. See also chapter 24, footnote 26.)

If we see in the Scriptures that most of the patriarchs and matriarchs did not pray for children, then we must try to understand what *Chazal* meant when they said that God made them barren because He craves the prayers of the righteous. Of course we could conjecture that *Chazal* simply assumed that they all prayed. Could it be that such great people didn't pray for children? We could also explain that *Chazal* were talking in general terms, and didn't mean that each one of the patriarchs (and matriarchs) prayed, but that most of them did. Or perhaps *Chazal* were relying on other *midrashim*. For example, in *Midrash Tanchuma* on *Parashas Vayera*, and in *Shir haShirim Rabbah* 2:14, when the Midrash asks the same question about the matriarchs, it does say that the mothers prayed.

32. According to the *midrash* based on the verse in *Shir haShirim* 2:14, "My dove is in the clefts of the rock" (*Shir haShirim Rabbah* 2:14), the righteous are both us and our matriarchs.

33. The objective of this *gemara*, therefore, is to teach the importance of prayer. The *gemara* starts: "Rabbi Yitzchak says, Our patriarch Yitzchak was infertile.... Rabbi Yitzchak says, Why were the patriarchs infertile? Because God craves the prayers of the righteous. And Rabbi Yitzchak says, Why are the prayers of the righteous compared to a pitchfork? As a pitchfork turns the sheaves of grain from one position to another, so does the prayer of the righteous turn the dispensations of the Lord from the Attribute of Anger to the Attribute of Mercy." The *gemara* starts with the patriarch Yitzchak and tells us that he was infertile.

There it is written:

> One time I was walking from place to place and a *zaken*[34] aproached me and said, "Tell me Rabbi, why are people childless?" I said to him, "My son, because God loves them with a complete love and is happy with them, He wants them to increase their request for mercy from Him." He said to me, "No, [they are infertile] because they have resentment in their hearts (*tinah ba-lev*) and marry women without fulfilling the mitzvah to be fruitful and multiply [in other words, they are guilty of sexual sins]." I said to him, "My son, many ordinary people have only one wife and are childless. You should know that this is the truth, for we can learn from our patriarch Avraham who was infertile for seventy-five years, and prayed a lot until Yitzchak was born. Learn from Rivkah... learn from Rachel...learn from Chanah. Realize that what I told you is the truth. [They are infertile] because God loves them with a complete love, and afflicts them in order that they should increase their requests for mercy from Him."[35]

The main message of this *midrash*, then — and of the *gemara* in *Yevamos* — is that good people are afflicted with infertility because God loves them and wants them to pray to Him.

The infertility of the matriarchs teaches us something else as well. It guides us in how to deal with our own infertility. We can look at the matriarchs as role models. It gives us comfort, for we see that they struggled with the same difficulties

---

Then it talks about infertility and the importance of prayer, and then only about prayer itself. Yitzchak — infertility — prayer. It is clear that this Talmudic passage wants to teach us about prayer.

34. Either a wise man or an old man. Here, it probably refers to a wise man.

35. *Seder Eliyahu Rabbah* 18. See also *Bereishis Rabbah* 71:1 and *Pesikta d'Rav Kahana* 20.

as we do. It also teaches us that although there was a Divine reason why they were childless, they were unaware of the reason. Only *Chazal*, many years later, pointed the reason out to us.

There is also a Divine reason why you are presently childless. Maybe it's because you are righteous and God craves your prayers as He craved those of the matriarchs. Maybe it's for another reason, as it was concerning Rivkah.

Sarah was a prophetess, and she didn't know why she was barren. Rivkah possessed *ruach ha-kodesh* and yet didn't know why she couldn't have a child. We certainly will never know in this world the Divine reason why we are experiencing infertility, but that doesn't mean that the experience should not be significant to our life. We should learn from it. Why someone has to be afflicted with infertility is a mystery, but one thing is for sure: the sources point to infertility as visiting the righteous particularly. So instead of thinking that you are a sinner, why not think that you are righteous? Based on the sources, this is probably closer to the truth.

The bottom line, though, is that infertility afflicts the righteous, the wicked, and everybody in between. It is like sickness, war, terror, poverty, and every other unpleasant and even tragic possibility that we all want to avoid. When the collective Jewish People is doing God's will, all of these misfortunes will vanish — infertility among them. Until that time, however, collectively we will have to endure these harsh realities.

Remember the verse in *Shir haShirim*: "My dove in the clefts of the rock, in the secret places of the terrace, show Me your appearance, and let Me hear your voice; for your voice is sweet, and your appearance is beautiful."[36] *Chazal* explain that this is talking about the infertility of our matriarchs. Why did I

---

36. *Shir haShirim* 2:14.

make you barren? In order to see your appearance and to hear your voice.[37] The dove is in the clefts of the rock, which does not bear fruit. But God craves to see the dove's appearance and hear her voice in prayer. The dove is in the secret places of the terrace. It is all a secret; the reason the dove is in the "clefts of the rock" is unknown except to God. God nevertheless craves a relationship with the dove, for its voice is sweet and its appearance is beautiful.

Personal Growth Through Suffering

What makes us strong and insightful is not good fortune but life's hard knocks. Many couples who have suffered from infertility affirm that the ordeal made them stronger. It also made them look at life differently. If you ever read biographies of successful people, you will notice that they have one thing in common: they all overcame difficult obstacles. It was those obstacles that made them who they are. Had they not had to overcome those obstacles, they would not have achieved greatness. Of course, nobody would ever choose to suffer, but looking back, we recognize how suffering helped us develop our strengths, enhanced our wisdom, and built our character.

"My Back but Not My Face"

When Moshe Rabbeinu went up Mount Sinai to receive the Torah, he assumed that everything would continue in a natural progression: We were redeemed from slavery. We elevated ourselves to the pinnacle event of standing at Mount Sinai. Now we were ready for the next step, the actual Torah, written by "the finger of the Almighty." But then everything went wrong. As Moshe descended, he saw the Jewish People celebrating around their new "god," the Golden Calf. He threw down the tablets and was forced to start all over again.

---

37. *Bereishis Rabbah* 45:5.

Moshe didn't understand how this could have happened. What was the Divine plan? He therefore said to God, Show me Your ways. But the only answer he received from God was, "You cannot see My Face...and live, [only My Back]."[38] What does this mean? We cannot see God at all; God doesn't have a form.

Our only way of knowing God is through the way He reveals Himself in this world. Moshe wanted to understand God's plan. God told him, "Behold, there is a place here with Me; you will stand on the rock. When My Glory passes, I will place you in a **cleft of the rock**; I shall spread My [Protection] over you until I pass. I will then move My Glory and you will see My Back, but you will not see My Face."[39]

What was God telling Moshe? He was essentially telling him, You cannot understand My plan as it is happening. You can only see My Back; you can only understand the plan *after* it has happened. Sometimes you will see it in this life; sometimes you may not be able to see it until the World to Come. "You cannot see My Face...and live."

The ordeal of infertility doesn't seem fair. The **dove** is in the **cleft of the rock**, as was Moshe when he wanted to understand God's plan. The cleft in the rock where Moshe stood protected him from a Divine truth that no mortal would be able to withstand. The dove in the cleft of the rock is being kept away from a secret that it can never comprehend. Moshe and the dove are seeking the answer to the same question, the foremost theological question for humanity, but they can never grasp the answer.

We can only hope that when the infertility or any other suffering is over, we will be able to appreciate what we went through — but it probably won't happen fully in this lifetime.

---

38. *Shemos* 33:20.

39. Ibid., verses 21–23.

"You cannot see My Face [the Divine plan] and live." The Glory of God, the Divine plan, will only be seen in completion, on that day when "God will be One and His Name will be One."[40]

---

40. *Zechariah* 14:9. See *Pesachim* 50a.

15. Marriage and Infertility

Marriage implies the uniting of two people, two personalities, two minds, two wills, two talents — not just for now, but for always. Marriage means much more than two people sharing a home. It means two people who share their lives and enjoy a relationship so successful, that in thinking and acting as one, they are prepared to unite to bring children into the world. Marriage is so significant that it is the point of origin of all mankind. It is the one human institution which can bring to fruition man's greatest hopes and dreams.

(From Rabbi Aryeh Kaplan, *Made in Heaven*[1])

INTRODUCTION

WHEN SOMETHING SO ELEMENTARY, yet so important, as conceiving and having a child, becomes such a hardship, it is only natural that it will affect your relationship as a couple. For some couples, the challenge strengthens their marriage. For others, dealing with infertility adds tension to the relationship. Several factors can cause tension.

- **The infertility itself.** Not having something that is the expression of a natural progression in the relationship is a life stress.
- **The medical procedures.** They are painful, expensive,

1. Jerusalem/NY: Moznayim Publishing, 1983.

time-consuming, and not guaranteed to produce a baby.

- **Disruptions in the couple's intimate life.** Relations are usually damaged or altered because of the fertility treatments.
- **Differences in coping methods.** Husband and wife display "Mars and Venus" coping, respectively.
- **Blame.** Blaming each other, blaming oneself (guilt) — even if it's nonverbal.

In this chapter we will analyze the relationships of three Biblical couples: Manoach and his wife, Yaakov and Rachel, and Elkanah and Chanah. From their stories we can see the tension, the responses, and the competition; but also the love, the understanding, and the sympathy. We will be able to learn from their stories. After that we will discuss the topic from the practical day-to-day viewpoint.

If you feel that your marriage has been negatively affected by the infertility experience, then this is something you surely want to improve. Although you may be coping with other difficult aspects of infertility at the same time, such as the feeling of alienation from society and pressure from parents, your marriage comes first. "When there is peace between a couple, God dwells among them."[2]

TROUBLE IN PARADISE

Divine Reason for Infertility

Many times infertility introduces major anxiety into the relationship, so that even a loving couple will come to experience powerful feelings of anger and frustration toward each other. Since we believe that there is a Divine reason for everything that happens to us, each couple, especially religious couples, will wonder why, from a theological point of view, their mar-

---

2. *Sotah* 17a.

riage was afflicted with infertility.

In addition to what we discussed in previous chapters as to why a couple would be afflicted with infertility, *midrashim* in *Bereishis Rabbah* and *Shir haShirim Rabbah* say that the Divine reason for infertility could actually be to strengthen the couple's relationship.[3] They assert this as the reason for the matriarchs' infertility. In other words, being childless is a tool, so to speak, to strengthen a marriage. From a religious point of view, we see that a strong loving connection between husband and wife is important enough that God is willing to bring about something as painful as infertility in order to invigorate the couple's love for each other.

Concerning the matriarchs, one explanation for their infertility given in the above *midrashim* is in order that they "Could have many years without servitude." Having children takes away a mother's free time. Spending years together without the constant interruptions caused by fulfilling children's needs will make a couple very close.

Another answer offered is, "So that [the matriarchs] should stay beautiful and not spoil their looks by the pregnancy." Today, some women may find this answer offensive, but the beauty of women is God-given, as is the nature of a man to love his wife even more if he thinks she is beautiful. So in order to keep the matriarchs beautiful, God prevented them from having children. Another, similar answer is, "So that they will lean on, or cling to their spouses because of their beauty."

According to these *midrashim*, having children would have somehow marred the relationships of the patriarchs and matriarchs. In building what was to be the foundation of His Chosen Nation, God felt it was so important to establish the

---

3. All of the different aspects of this can be found in *Bereishis Rabbah* 45:4 . See also *Shir haShirim Rabbah* 2:14 for some minor alternative readings.

mothers and fathers as strong couples that He sent them barrenness in order that they develop a strong, loving relationship. It is therefore an ironic tragedy when infertility has the opposite effect and damages the relationship.

Silence of the Scripture Speaks Louder than Words

The story of Manoach and his wife, the parents of Shimshon (*Shofetim* 13), leaves the reader with many questions. To summarize the story: a man named Manoach had a wife who was barren. One day, an angel appears to her and says that she will have a child who will lead the Jewish People. He will be a Nazirite, and the angel tells Manoach's wife what to do in order to prepare him for his exalted status. She tells her husband. She speaks to the angel again, and so does Manoach. She gives birth.

We don't know anything about Manoach and his wife prior to this story, and are offered no clues as to why they were chosen to parent the man who saved the Jewish People from the strong arm of the Philistines. More germane to our topic, we are not privy to any dialogue concerning their infertility. The absence of dialogue between Manoach and his wife concerning their infertility is complete. Let us compare this with the dialogues recorded in the Scripture regarding the other Biblical infertile couples.

- **Yaakov and Rachel:** Much dialogue, tension — "And (Rachel) said to Yaakov, 'Give me children, for if not, I am [as good as] dead.' Yaakov became angry with Rachel and said [to her], 'Am I a substitute for God, Who has deprived you of offspring?'"[4]
- **Elkanah and Chanah:** Dialogue, compassion — "And her husband, Elkanah, then said to her, 'Chanah, why do you weep, and why do you not eat, and why is your

---

4. *Bereishis* 30:1–2.

heart troubled? Do I not hold you dearer than [the] ten children [whom Peninah bore to me]?'"[5]

- **Avraham and Sarah:** Dialogue: only a matter of stating the facts and finding a solution — "Sarai said to Avram, 'Look now. The Eternal has kept me from bearing children. Marry now my maidservant; maybe because of her I shall be established [with children].' Avram heeded Sarai's [word]."[6]
- **Yitzchak and Rivkah:** No dialogue, but a proactive attempt to improve the situation through prayer. Even though we are not told of any words spoken between them, there was a definite sense of working together, and a mutual caring about their barrenness — "Yitzchak pleaded with the Eternal, opposite his wife, because she was infertile."[7]
- **Manoach and his wife:** No dialogue whatsoever.

Without any reason to assume otherwise, the simple way of understanding Manoach and his wife's lack of communication is that it was just not important to notify the reader about their relationship, since the only important thing was that they were to have a special son. However, the Midrash sheds a completely different light on the subject.

Scripture introduces Manoach's wife to the reader with the verse:

> "His wife was infertile and had never given birth."[8]

The Midrash says:

> This teaches us that there was an argument between Manoach and his wife. He said to her, "You are infertile

5. *I Shemuel* 1:8.
6. *Bereishis* 16:2.
7. *Bereishis* 25:21.
8. *Shofetim* 13:2.

and that is why you have never given birth." She said to him, "You are infertile, and that is why I have never given birth."[9]

The Midrash is teaching us that the couple had a dispute over who was the cause of the infertility. Manoach blames her. She blames him. What compelled the Midrash to attribute a strained relationship to Manoach and his wife? Apparently it is the redundancy in the words, "Infertile and had never given birth." Why did *Chazal* think that there was a quarrel? There does not seem to be anything in the text to suggest one. There is no discussion between them, except for their dialogue regarding the tidings and instructions of the angel.

Chazal selected not only this particular verse to inform us about Manoach and his wife's contention. This theme runs throughout the whole section. When the angel informs Manoach's wife that she will give birth, this messenger of God starts by saying:

> Right now you are infertile and have never given birth.[10]

The Midrash says:

> [The angel] informed her that it was she who was infertile (and not her husband), in order to bring peace between [them]. For she complained about (blamed) Manoach that she had never given birth.[11]

The Midrash understands the redundancy in the verse to mean that it was Manoach's wife who was infertile. In the text, the angel stresses that "*you*" are infertile, not Manoach. Yet the Midrash also emphasizes the marital conflict.

The Midrash continues to find hints in the text that con-

---

9. *Bemidbar Rabbah* 10:14.

10. *Shofetim* 13:3.

11. *Bemidbar Rabbah* 10:15.

tribute to this notion that a conflict existed between Manoach and his wife. When interpreting the wife's report of her encounter with the angel, the Midrash points out her omission of the fact that the angel told her she was infertile. Rather, she merely told her husband that the angel said:

> You are going to become pregnant and will bear a son.[12]

The Midrash says:

> She did not reveal to him that he [the angel] told her that she was infertile, for she didn't want to disclose that it was her failure.[13]

One can postulate that there really wasn't anything in the Scripture to imply a conflict between Manoach and his wife.[14] Yet because of their lack of communication regarding the infertility, plus the wife's omissions when reporting to her husband what the angel said, *Chazal* use the vignette to teach us that couples who go through infertility experience much tension. The missing information in the story enables *Chazal* to teach us about the reality of the infertile couple's situation. The real motive is not to teach that just Manoach and his wife had difficulties, but that many couples experiencing infertility feel tension in their relationship. As Ellen S. Glazer sums it up, "Infertility is extraordinarily challenging, and for most couples there are times when they wonder if they will survive it."[15]

Many times blame plays a big role in the childless couple's relationship. One common theme is that one of the spouses

---

12. *Shofetim* 13:7.

13. *Bemidbar Rabbah* 10:17.

14. It is common for *Chazal* to use verses as a springboard for imparting morals and principles. See, for example, the commentary of Rabbi Baruch haLevi Epstein in *Torah Temimah, Bemidbar* 21:19.

15. Ellen S. Glazer, *Experiencing Infertility* (San Francisco: Jossey–Bass Publishers, 1998), p. 40.

"messed up" by putting off or delaying going for treatment. In other words, that spouse is blamed for the infertility itself. Another common theme is that a spouse "messed up" in the way he or she handled a specific situation regarding the treatments. Here, the spouse is blamed for causing pain and stress.

Dr. Aline P. Zoldbord describes the first theme:

> Sometimes one partner, usually the wife, believes the infertility to be the direct fault of the other. Such a belief adds immeasurably to the resentment, hurt, and even hate that she is harboring. It dramatically raises the tension level, implying that one partner has consciously set out to do something to deny the other a child...[the wife] is already behind in her own internal schedule of childrearing. That is, she is already angry with him....
>
> The wife deems it the husband's fault that "time is running out." She becomes panicked that her fertility has been impaired with every passed-up month, or that they should have pursued adoption...or some other alternative earlier in their lives, when their "chances were better." Occasionally, one runs across couples in which the husband and wife appear to be so full of hatred and in such poor communication that one wonders how they ever thought they loved each other enough to want to produce a child together. However, on exploration, it turns out that one of them is harboring this kind of grudge.
>
> This negative situation is maintained as follows: ...Each time that [the husband] is less than perfect in the relationship or lets [his wife] down in some way during the infertility process, she repeats this idea to herself: "And it's all his fault, anyway. If it hadn't been for him, we'd have a child already!"... She begins to think of the infertility as something her husband did to her, on purpose.[16]

Dr. Orit Luria expresses the second theme of blame

16. *Men, Women and Infertility*, p. 52.

through the testimonial of one husband:

> On the day that my wife was supposed to undergo the follicle retrieval procedure, I had an important meeting in [another city], so she went to the hospital with her mother. From the morning she was [hostile toward] me, even though we agreed that I would attend my meeting and [then] would pick her up from the hospital. As I traveled to [the other city], her teary-eyed face escorted me the whole way. Obviously I felt like a creep, and my head was [miles] away from the meeting. I flew back like a madman, and arrived before they released her. She seemed okay. A long time after this, she told everybody how I had abandoned her in her most difficult moments.[17]

Bemidbar Rabbah expounds on the story of Manoach and his wife to teach us that couples often blame each other for their infertility. In the case of Manoach and his wife, the mutual blame was apparently over the biological problem. However, as we see from the above two excerpts, "blame" is not limited to just the biological problem. Blaming the spouse accompanies the entire infertility process: for biological faults, spiritual inadequacy, and differences in dealing with the distress. Although today the biological "fault" can be determined in the laboratory, delaying pregnancy or fertility treatments may be an indirect cause of the infertility, so one spouse may blame the other for indirect causes. Once the "fault" is determined, thoughts of "Had I married someone else, I would be a parent by now" may be common. But love will cure those thoughts, as we will see below.

Chazal's insight regarding the parents of Shimshon is important for infertile couples. It shows them that even though they may quarrel, it is not a stain on their personalities. They may still be considered righteous in the eyes of God, as were

---

17. *Children of Love*, p. 108.

Manoach and his wife.[18] If a couple who were to be the parents of a Divine messenger felt tension in their marriage, then it is perfectly normal for every infertile couple to feel anxiety in their relationship.

Yaakov and Rachel

There is no need for Midrash to illustrate Yaakov and Rachel's relationship during their infertility. The Torah itself provides an illustration. The mutual blame for the infertility is seen clearly in Yaakov and Rachel's dialogue. The Torah clearly shows us that there was hostility. Although the hostility is explicitly stated in the Scripture, the grounds of the contention are left to interpretation, and here too, *Chazal* play an important role in providing some of the missing information.

> Rachel realized that she had not borne Yaakov children, and Rachel became jealous of her sister. She said to Yaakov, "Give me children, for if not, I am [as good as] dead." Yaakov became angry with Rachel and said [to her], "Am I a substitute for God, Who has deprived you of offspring?"[19]

Rachel threw the responsibility of conceiving on her husband: "Give me children." Rashi explains that she insinuated that the reason she didn't have children was because Yaakov didn't pray hard enough for her, the way Yitzchak had prayed for Rivkah.[20] In other words, she blamed him.

The Malbim also subscribes to the notion that Rachel blamed Yaakov. He says, "Rachel thought that the reason she didn't give birth was not because of her, but rather because of Yaakov. That is why the Scripture emphasizes, 'She had not borne *Yaakov* children.' She thought that the fact that he loved

---

18. See *Bemidbar Rabbah* 10:5.
19. *Bereishis* 30:1–2.
20. Rashi, *Bereishis* 30:1.

her so much caused the infertility, apparently an ancient medical myth."[21]

The commentators are filling in the backdrop for Rachel's confrontation with Yaakov — *blame*. According to Rashi, Rachel blamed Yaakov for his lack of cooperation and caring; she blamed him for the way he dealt with the situation. According to the Malbim, Rachel blamed Yaakov for the infertility itself.

Yaakov responds without compassion, and scolds her in anger. In doing so, he throws the blame back on Rachel: "Am I a substitute for God, Who has deprived you of offspring?" In other words, I have children; it is your fault.[22] Whether he meant that it was her fault spiritually, because of her lack of merit, or biologically, is irrelevant to our discussion. Simply, he blamed her.

Tension over dealing with infertility is common. As Dr. Luria writes:

> Even before it is even clear that there is a problem, already differences in the way the couple relate to the topic begin to emerge. Usually the wife will be the first to suspect that there is a difficulty, and she will begin to worry and gather information. In the beginning, most husbands sincerely feel that their wives are exaggerating.[23]

Elkanah and Chanah

We have now seen two cases of righteous couples who felt tension during the infertility crisis. In the book of *I Shemuel*, we have a glimpse of a completely different spousal relationship.

The book begins with the story of Elkanah and his two wives, Chanah and Peninah. Peninah had children, Chanah was barren. They would go to Shilo (the site of the Tabernacle

---

21. Malbim, ibid.
22. See Rashi, ibid.
23. *Children of Love*, p. 21.

in those days) on every Festival, as there was not yet a Temple in Jerusalem. Peninah would make Chanah feel bad that she didn't have children. Chanah was sad and would not eat.

> Her husband, Elkanah, then said to her, "Chanah, why do you weep, and why do you not eat, and why is your heart troubled? Do I not hold you dearer than [the] ten children [whom Peninah bore to me]?[24]

Elkanah sees Chanah's sadness and tries to comfort her as best he can. It is interesting to note that the verse says, "Her husband, Elkanah." The ostensibly extra emphasis of "her husband" may be coming to teach us that Elkanah acted the way a husband should act. A husband should give emotional support to his wife when she is feeling depressed. When he does so, he is acting like a true husband. Therefore, Elkanah merited to be called by Scripture, "her husband."

In Conclusion

These three Biblical stories teach us that every infertile couple's relationship will be affected differently by the challenge. Of course the relationship of Chanah and Elkanah is the one to be emulated. But even if a couple fights due to an infertility problem, they should take comfort in the knowledge that even the greatest *tzaddikim* — Yaakov and Rachel, Manoach and his wife — were not insulated from the fierce tension of infertility. And although they sincerely continued to love each other, they too fell victim to one of its side effects. But as the *midrashim* in *Bereishis Rabbah* and *Shir haShirim Rabbah* teach us, marriages grow stronger from the challenge.

Ellen S. Glazer says:

> Although there are some marriages that suffer severe and even irreparable damage as a result of infertility, this is un-

---

24. *I Shemuel* 1:8.

> usual. Far more often couples pull together in the face of infertility and discover that they have remarkable resources for coping with this problem. Many emerge from the experience with increased respect for themselves, their partners and their marital unit.[25]

Dr. Alice Domar also concludes that most couples emerge with a stronger relationship after the infertility ordeal.[26] They become even closer after they experienced the hardship, dealt with the difficulties, and overcame them. If people would not have obstacles to overcome, they would never become stronger. This is true for the individual; it is true for couples.

Misfortune and strength do not contradict each other. Rather, misfortune and difficulty in marriage can make a marriage strong.

PRACTICAL ADVICE

"Mars and Venus" We mentioned earlier that part of the tension that infertility causes is because of gender-based differences in coping. It is crucial to realize that because of the dissimilar psychological and emotional makeup of men and women there will usually be disparity in the way husband and wife react to infertility and the way they plan the strategy to defeat the problem. You can't get through the ordeal if you don't understand this. The way a man thinks is different from the way a woman thinks. Priorities of a man are not the priorities of a woman. Reactions of a man are not the reactions of a woman. Men and women are "north and south poles," says psychologist Eric Fromm. They are "different planets," says John Gray. The beauty of a relationship is making those two poles/planets work together.

---

25. *Experiencing Infertility*, p. 40.
26. *Conquering Infertility*, p. 16, 99.

Gender-Based Words

The Hebrew Biblical words for infertility are different for man and woman. Each word expresses the tragedy unique to each gender. The word the Torah uses to describe the childless man is *ariri* (ערירי). As Avraham said to God: "My Lord, Eternal God! What is [the benefit of] what You will give me [if] I am going to be obliterated (childless; *ariri* – ערירי)?" Rashi comments that the word *ariri* denotes inheritance. Avraham was saying that there was no one to inherit him. The Seforno says that Avraham was saying that there was no one to take his place.[27] According to both interpretations, the tragedy for Avraham vis-à-vis his infertility was that there was no continuation of his line.

Although the general word for infertility in the Torah is *akarus* (עקרות), it is generally used only for women,[28] as it says, "Sarai was infertile — *akarah* (עקרה)."[29] The word is from the root *akar* (עקר), which denotes being uprooted, eradicated. The barren woman feels uprooted from society. She is alienated. Rachel was called the *akeres ha-bayis* (עקרת הבית).[30] As the barren wife, she was pushed aside, "removed" from the other wives in Yaakov's house. She was alienated from the rest of the world.

A man feels the loss of continuity when he doesn't have any children. A woman, however, feels alienated. From the

---

27. See Rashi and the Seforno on *Bereishis* 15:2. Both commentators bring proof for their interpretations.

28. The word עקר, which means an infertile man, is used much later in the Torah (*Devarim* 7:14), but there it is used as a general term and not to describe a specific individual. See p. 432 for further explanation of the word עקר.

29. *Bereishis* 11:30.

30. *Akeres ha-bayis* was originally a sad term for a barren woman at home. Already in the time of *Chazal*, however, the meaning of *akeres ha-bayis* changed to housewife, the "foundation of the home," reflecting a different meaning of the same root word (see *Bereishis Rabbah* 71:1).

very beginning there is a huge difference in the way men and women interpret the problem of infertility. One is concerned for the future; the other has to cope with the present. Right away there will be differences of opinion as to when and how they should seek assistance. One spouse (usually the wife) will take a more aggressive role in pursuing medical intervention, while the other will be less inclined to seek assistance.

Usually the man will be more reluctant to go to an initial infertility consultation. He doesn't even want to admit to himself that there is a problem. The wife, on the other hand, is more in tune with her body and realizes the problem early. And as we learned, she is thinking of the present; she wants to have a baby now. Her husband is thinking of the future — there's time. She is less inhibited about asking for help; he is embarrassed talking about it. She will drag her husband to the doctor and take the lead in their pursuit of a solution. He still might not think there is a problem. And even when treatments begin there may be differences of opinion as to when and how to proceed.

Male and Female Coping

The concept of "Mars and Venus coping" will come up when the couple encounters obstacles. Your spouse will respond to the challenge of infertility differently from you. If you can accept your spouse's particular response to the ordeal as being both legitimate and natural for him or her, then it will be easier to meet the challenge together in harmony. Many times, a man will think his wife is being somewhat hysterical with her sense of urgency over every single aspect of the treatments. But she may think that he is uncaring: "How could you forget to call about the blood test results?" [By the way, she will often want *him* to make the call, creating a buffer between herself and the "verdict."] "How could you forget that we have a doctor's appointment today?"

In general, men tend to bury the issue. They apply the only coping strategy they know, which is to repress the pain of infertility or to express it in seemingly unrelated anger. They feel it is their duty as good husbands to be strong and calm. The social situations they face tend to lend themselves to this technique, since conversation often revolves around current events, job talk, and the *Daf Yomi* class rather than parenting and family matters. Women usually deal with the infertility experience on a much more emotional level. This is due in part to hormonal influences, especially when fertility medications are involved. They also usually care about it more.

Although most Orthodox couples still claim that even they have different ways of responding to their predicament, there is usually an equalizer, and that is the mitzvah to be fruitful and multiply. This, together with the social pressure within the community in general, forces the husband to be as concerned with fertility problems as his wife. He sees the men in his row at shul with their kids; he hears his peers at yeshiva talking about educating children. He too wants to fulfill the mitzvah of "You shall teach your children".[31]

Nevertheless, according to psychologist Sarah Barris, Orthodox couples in her counseling practice deal with the same dichotomy as secular couples do. In other words, the equal yearning for a child that both the Orthodox man and the Orthodox woman have, has no practical advantage at all when it comes to handling and understanding gender differences in relating to infertility.

Understanding the differences in the way that men and women relate to infertility should let you at least be capable of seeing your spouse's viewpoint, even if you don't agree with it. You will certainly have to find a course of action that will

---

31. *Devarim* 6:6.

not cause conflict. Most of this chapter deals with this topic on the theoretical level. Although love and teamwork are lofty, beautiful ideas, you may need some more practical advice how to achieve it. Perhaps you will want to seek counseling or read a book that deals with this issue. You will certainly need to discuss with each other your feelings about communication, treatments, coping, and the infertility itself.

Stress in Intimacy

The intimate life of the barren couple is usually impaired by several different factors. Spontaneity is affected. Part of the joy of intimacy is just being together, loving and enjoying each other. With infertility, however, the motivation of intimacy is defined. Instead of being a normal part of a loving relationship, intimacy becomes another fertility procedure. Marital relations become technical, and the desire for a positive outcome dominates all feelings.

During fertility treatments, the doctor's instructions and the wife's cycle prescribe the times the couple can have marital relations. It can sometimes be physically painful for the wife and difficult to perform for the husband. There are psychological factors as well. When a man has a low sperm count, he may begin to have doubts about his masculinity. This may have a negative effect on his performance. The same thoughts of inadequacy may haunt the wife as well. She may feel less feminine as a result of possessing a "defective womb." These thoughts will certainly affect her desire and her satisfaction. Of course a damaged intimate life will have a negative impact on the relationship in general. It is a vicious cycle.

What can be done? Take positive steps to make your intimate life more enjoyable and less stressful. Even during treatment periods, when your physician is dictating times for intimacy, try to turn these mandatory times into positive and pleasant ones. Go out on a "date," enjoy yourselves. Wear something attractive to your husband (as the wives of the Hebrew slaves in Egypt did. It was in their merit that the Jews were freed from bondage.[32]) Try to have the attitude that the relations in and of themselves are the purpose and not pregnancy. Conception either will or won't take place, so try not to worry about the outcome and concentrate on the moment. Husbands, compliment your wife. Prepare dinner with her, or do something to show more understanding of her.

Sometimes taking small vacations can relieve the stress. Get away, change the scenery, go to a resort or a hotel. If you find that the anxiety inherent in the situation is causing serious problems in your intimate life, don't hesitate to seek professional help.

Conflict and Empathy

How does one take conflict and tension and turn them into empathy and compassion? Receiving empathy and compassion from your spouse depends on how you respond to each other. This we will discuss now.

One can imagine Rachel's distress after her conflict with Yaakov. Not only was she barren and in competition with her sister Leah, who was the mother of four; she now had stress in her marriage as well. Going to her husband for comfort only made things worse.

Perhaps if Rachel had initiated the discussion in a different way, the tension between her and Yaakov might not have erupted. According to *Chazal*, Yaakov was punished for responding to Rachel in such a harsh manner.[33] Rachel was not punished for her remarks, however; she was not speaking with a rational voice. Still, it is not hard to understand Yaakov's reaction; people who feel attacked, attack back.

---

32. See Rashi, *Shemos* 38:8.

33. See *Bereishis Rabbah* 71:7.

Compare this to Elkanah and Chanah. Elkanah was not spoken to the way Yaakov was and he was able to be empathetic. Chanah didn't say a word to her husband; she directed her sadness inward. Elkanah, seeing her sadness, approached her: "Why do you weep, and why do you not eat?"

Before she gave birth, Rachel lashed out at and was confrontational with her husband. Chanah, on the other hand, was withdrawn. After they gave birth, however, we see that they switched approaches. Rachel says, "God has hidden away my disgrace."[34] She doesn't lash out anymore, she doesn't mention Leah or anyone else who caused her pain; she just refers to her great distress. But Chanah, who was so meek and uncommunicative before she gave birth, felt victorious over those who brought her sorrow: "My mouth has opened wide [to counter] my enemies, for I rejoiced in Your salvation.... While the barren woman bore seven, she who [had] many children is [now] desolate."[35] The disgrace and anguish of infertility victimized both women, and they both expressed their sorrow inwardly and outwardly, just at different times.

In most circumstances, when one expresses his or her pain in a way that it doesn't hurt others, he or she will receive the compassion of friends and loved ones. On the other hand, one who directs his or her anguish at others will cause strife and might even alienate the very people who can offer needed empathy.

If Rachel had approached Yaakov calmly, Yaakov might have responded differently. This does not exempt Yaakov from his responsibility to treat his wife with more compassion. Although Rachel "attacked" Yaakov, only he was punished. But the reality is that conflict at home is brought on when one verbally strikes the other, or when one blames the other for

---

34. *Bereishis* 30:23.

35. *I Shemuel* 2:1, 5.

problems. Yaakov should have understood his wife's anguish. He should have fathomed the deep pain that caused such a *tzadekes* as Rachel to lash out as she did. But her distress was obfuscated by her excessive demand and by her insinuation that Yaakov was to blame. Had Rachel expressed her pain differently, it stands to reason that she would have elicited Yaakov's compassion, in the same way Chanah did from Elkanah.

The Husband's Role

Many times a man feels as if he is somewhere "between a rock and a hard place." On one hand, as a man, he is supposed to be Mr. Fix-it, with the solution to every problem. But in reality, he feels helpless. There is nothing he can do. He needs to remain stoic in the face of his wife's fragile emotional state — yet if he is too calm, she perceives him as insensitive. And it is not as if he himself is not affected emotionally over this. He wants to be a father, and he wants his wife to be a happy mother. He cries too.

Yet a man also needs to concentrate on his work or his studies. How much time can he put into this? His wife needs to realize that not only is she going through stressful times, but he is too, even if he is keeping it inside. A man usually feels uncomfortable talking about pain. Part of being "masculine" is to act as if nothing hurts, neither physically nor emotionally. But men feel hurt.

Husbands, sharing your feelings with your wife about your own pain will probably help you become closer. The way to be a support to your wife isn't by showing her how tough you are, but by sharing the pain together. Being optimistic is also important, for if your wife loses faith in the treatments, or feels downhearted because of disappointing results, you will be the one she will look to for encouragement and reassurance.

Some men understand and feel their wives' pain easily. Others have difficulty in understanding why their wives get so upset over the various procedures, over glitches in the plans, or even over other events related directly or indirectly to the infertility experience. If you find that your wife seems to get unreasonably upset over anything related to the infertility experience, you should understand that her reactions are completely appropriate to her feminine nature.

Wanting a child is part of a woman's essence. When she doesn't have a child, it is as if she is uprooted from her fundamental nature. The Talmud says, "A woman is for beauty and children."[36] This is not a "man's view" of women; this is how women think of themselves. Even die-hard feminists are devastated by infertility. And every woman wants her beauty acknowledged.

Therefore, husbands, if your wife is having trouble becoming pregnant, know that she is suffering the pain of being denied the most important thing in her life as a woman. Men feel that way about their jobs. A man out of work is a man who feels he has lost everything. The Talmud says that a man without land is not a man.[37] (In those days agriculture was a person's livelihood.) A man without livelihood is a man who feels he is worthless. The same is true for a woman who cannot have a baby, in her case it is even worse, for the desire for children is actually part of her physical makeup. And so, while you may not be able to feel your wife's pain, but you should at least understand it.

It is important for the husband to take an active role in assisting his wife during the medical ordeals that she must go through. Although producing sperm for analysis and IVF is not pleasant, that is almost all the man needs to do in treat-

---

36. *Kesubos* 59b.

37. *Yevamos* 63a.

ment. The wife has to undergo "too many" procedures both in the clinic and at home. Even if he is sincerely with her in spirit, if the husband does not accompany her physically when she goes to the clinic and is not with her at home, at least some of the time, this will lead to his wife's feeling resentful. The fertility problem may even be her husband's, but she is the one suffering physically from all the treatments. If he does not even escort her, then this will lead to tension in the marriage. It is imperative to find the time to be with your wife for a good many of her treatments, even though there is nothing you can do except be with her and support her.

Husbands generally think, "I can't do anything helpful except be with her. Since there is nothing practical I can offer, I might as well stay at work or yeshiva, so I won't jeopardize my business or job or learning arrangements." This is a masculine way of thinking. Your wife does not want you to *do* anything for her. She just wants you to *be* with her so that she feels that both of you are going through this. She is helping you fulfill your mitzvah to be fruitful and multiply, yet she has all the work. So be considerate and be with her both physically and emotionally. Make sure you find time to drive her to the clinic, or to escort her on the bus, or to be with her whenever she has some major procedure or consultation.

Your presence is more important to her than you may think. Realize your position during this special and challenging time that you are going through. Your attitude and actions can make all the difference.

Teamwork

In order to get through infertility you will need to work as a team. Your wife will take the lead, as we have already pointed out, but you will have to be a good team player. Infertility is a couple's problem and you must tackle it as a couple, not as two separate individuals. It does not matter whose "fault" the infertility is. Unlike children, livelihood, and longevity, which is determined by our *mazal* and not by our merits,[38] our partner in marriage was either decreed by God before we were even born, or determined according to our merits.[39] Therefore, even if the "fault" of the infertility is your partner's, you must recognize that you were meant to be with that particular person. It is irrelevant whose body is malfunctioning, or who is overreacting. The problem belongs to both of you, for you were meant to be together.

If you are feeling guilty that you are causing your spouse to be childless, stop thinking that way. Marriage is determined by God. *Ishto kegufo*, a husband and wife are one body. If one of your bodies malfunctioned, it is as if both of your bodies malfunctioned. So, no feeling guilty allowed, only feelings of getting ready to win this war as a team.

Let the relationship of Adam and Eve be a lesson. An interesting phrase is used twice during the story of Adam and Eve's eating the forbidden fruit. The verse says, "The woman saw that the tree was good to eat… so she took some of its fruit and ate [it]. She also gave [some] to her husband, *with her*, and he ate."[40] Why does the verse say, "with her?"

Later on, when God asks Adam if he ate from the forbidden tree, Adam answers, "The woman whom You gave *with me*, gave me from the tree and I ate."[41] Why does Adam say "with me" and not "to me"? What does "with me" mean?

God gave Eve to Adam in order to give Adam a partner forever, someone to share his life. They were meant to be together, for good and for bad. Eve also understood this. She knew that Adam had to be with a woman, and it was meant to be her. Therefore, she involved Adam in the sin as well. This

---

38. *Mo'ed Katan* 28a. See chapter 14.

39. *Sotah* 2a.

40. *Bereishis* 3:6.

41. *Bereishis* 3:12.

way, God couldn't punish her alone. If Adam ate, she wouldn't die. So she gave the fruit "to her husband, *with her*" — with her for good and for bad, with her for life.

Adam immediately understood this, and therefore ate the fruit, knowing that this would save Eve's life and prevent their separation. And although he spoke ungratefully to God when he put the blame on Eve, he still didn't say, "the woman whom You gave to me." Rather he said, "the woman whom You gave *with me.*" In other words, I knew that it was wrong to eat the fruit, but I did it to be with her. That was Your plan, that we should be with each other, even if she made a mistake. So I ate the fruit, in order that we should always be with each other.

When Adam and Eve left the Garden of Eden, they left hand in hand.[42] Even when they tried to hide from God, they hid together, not separately. They understood the importance of staying together, even during hard times.

A strong couple is a couple that not only accepts each other's mistakes, but embraces the consequences of each other's errors and deficiencies as well. A strong couple knows that in the end, they will get through this and they will be even stronger in their love for and devotion to each other.

Yitzchak and Rivkah teach us all about teamwork in a relationship as well. The verse says that Yitzchak prayed across from his wife. They both prayed for fertility. But the beautiful message is how they prayed. Rivkah said to the Almighty, if You want to grant me a child, give me a child only from this *tzaddik*. And Yitzchak said, Master of the Universe, if You want to grant me a child, grant me a child only from this *tzadekes*.[43]

---

42. Heard from my friend and teacher, Rabbi Eliezer Pe'er.

43. See *Yalkut Shimoni, Shemuel* 88.

THE POWER OF LOVE

The Angel as Marriage Counselor

Let us return to the story of Manoach and his wife. The Midrash says that the reason the angel told Manoach's wife that she was barren was in order that they should stop arguing and live in peace with each other (see pages 227–233).

Chazal use the story of Manoach and his wife to teach us two realities of infertility. The first is the possibility of stress in the marriage. The second is the urgency of *shalom bayis* — peace between the couple. There comes a time when the infertility becomes such an obsession that even though the relationship is suffering, it doesn't matter anymore. Only a baby matters. The couple stops caring about the beauty of their relationship and only cares about having a child. The *midrash* concerning Manoach and his wife teaches that although it is a blessing to have a child, there still needs to be a loving relationship within the marriage. This is important for two reasons. If there will be a child, he or she should be brought up in a loving environment. Secondly, even if there will not be a child, for the sake of the couple, there needs to be love between them. This is consistent with the Talmudic saying, "If there is love between husband and wife, God's Presence dwells among them."[44]

The angel appeared to Manoach's wife and not to him in order to improve their relationship and lessen the anger and blame. Had the angel appeared to Manoach and not to his wife, he would have thought that he was the righteous one. So the angel made a beautiful compromise. He appeared to *her*, proving that she was a righteous woman, and trusting that this would make Manoach appreciate her in her righteousness. Yet the angel told her that the infertility problem

---

44. *Sotah* 17a.

was hers and not her husband's. This enabled her to stop blaming him (see pages 229–230).

As a polished diplomat, the angel appeared to Manoach's wife, implying that she was righteous and holy; yet he left it up to her to tell Manoach that the infertility was her "fault." (Interestingly, she didn't tell him this, because she wanted to protect her own pride. This is such a normal response.) Furthermore, when Manoach asked the angel about the pregnancy, the angel said to him, "About everything I told your wife she shall be careful."[45] The Midrash explains that the angel said this in order to inspire Manoach to see his wife in a more positive light, so that he should love her more.[46] The importance of *shalom bayis* in the midst of infertility is so great that God Himself intervened through the angel.

Flower Power

You must see your marriage as the bottom line, the foundation upon which everything else in your life is built. If you act loving toward each other and don't see each other as merely a means to fulfill your own needs and desires, then you should be able to weather and overcome the hardship of infertility together as a couple. It is essential to love each other. At difficult times you may need to work a little harder to sustain that love. Don't let the infertility treatments become more important than your relationship; your relationship is more important. If you see that the relationship is hurting because of the pressure of the treatments, then it might be time to take a break, to come back to yourselves, to strengthen yourselves as a couple — and then to consider again the right times and conditions for continuing treatments.

The Mishnah says that a couple who was married for ten

---

45. *Shofetim* 13:13.

46. *Bemidbar Rabbah* 10:5.

years without a child should divorce.[47] The Rema says that today we don't force couples to divorce.[48] There are different halachic reasons for this.[49] The bottom line, however, is that if the couple has a good relationship and if they do the mitzvos, and certainly if they raise an orphan in their home, then they could stay together. Most childless *gedolei Yisrael* did not divorce their wives after ten years of infertility. A beautiful relationship is a beautiful thing.

From another incident concerning Rachel we learn this important rule that the relationship comes before the fertility treatment. The Torah says that Reuven brought some flowers called *duda'im* to his mother Leah after she began to experience secondary infertility, for *duda'im* were considered a fertility aid.[50] Rachel saw the flowers and said, "Please give me some of your son's *duda'im*." Leah responded, "It isn't enough that you have taken my husband away [from me], and [now you wish] to take away my son's *duda'im* as well?" So Rachel said, "He will therefore lie with you tonight, in exchange for your son's *duda'im*."[51] Leah then had relations with Yaakov that night and became pregnant with Yissachar, without even the help of her fertility "wonder drug."

Rashi says that Rachel did not merit to be buried with Yaakov because she forefeited an opportunity to lie with a *tzaddik*.[52] This Rashi is hard to understand. What was Rachel's sin? She was with Yaakov all the time, but couldn't get pregnant. She finally had a chance to take a fertility drug, which only "cost" her one night less with Yaakov. After this "fertility

47. *Yevamos* 64a; see the Mishnah ad loc.

48. Rema, *Shulchan Aruch* 154:10.

49. See the *Pischei Teshuvah* on *Even haEzer* 154:27.

50. See Ibn Ezra, *Bereishis* 30:14.

51. *Bereishis* 30:14–15.

52. Rashi, *Bereishis* 30:15.

treatment," she would again be with the *tzaddik* and possibly be able to enjoy the birth of a child. Rachel's barren state was a major cause of shame and depression for her.[53] Wouldn't any woman have acted in a like manner? What mistake did Rachel make?

Whenever a personality in the Torah says or does something, its significance goes beyond the individual statement or deed that was brought down in the Torah. The statement or action reflects their whole outlook, attitude, and life. When Rachel traded her husband for the *duda'im,* she was making the statement that her "fertility treatments" were more important to her than her relationship with Yaakov.

At first Yaakov erred in being insensitive to Rachel's anguish, thus harming their beautiful marriage. Later, Rachel opted for fertility treatments over her chance to strengthen her marriage. Leah, who was anyway more concerned with having a better relationship with Yaakov, traded the treatments for the chance to strengthen her marriage.[54] Sensitivity and a strong marriage are more cherished by God than anything else. If there is love between husband and wife, God's Presence dwells between them.

Rachel saw the "fertility treatments" as more important than her relationship with Yaakov. That is also why she said to Yaakov in the first place, "Give me children, for if not, I am [as good as] dead." She was essentially saying: My marriage to you isn't worth anything if I don't have children. Elkanah and Chanah, however, put their relationship before having children. Elkanah says, "Do I not hold you dearer than [the] ten

---

53. Ramban, *Bereishis* 30:1; Rashi, *Bereishis* 30:23.

54. See *Bereishis Rabbah* 71:1 and *Pesikta d'Rav Kahana* 20. See also all the verses that explain the reason for the names Leah gave her children (*Bereishis* 30). They all mention the fact that the children would make her closer to her husband.

children [whom Peninah bore to me]?" He was saying, our relationship is more important than having children. Elkanah did not succeed in making Chanah happy.[55] Chanah was still sad about being barren, but their relationship as a couple was strong.

(As a parenthetical note, we see that in the eternal realm, God granted Leah and Rachel their deepest desires. Leah, who wanted more than anything to be close to Yaakov, was buried with him in the Cave of Machpelah in Hebron.[56] Rachel, who wanted children more than anything, not only had children, but will one day merit to see all of her children return to Eretz Yisrael, as the prophet says, "Thus says the Lord: keep your voice from weeping and your eyes from tears, for your work will be rewarded, says the Lord, and they shall come back again from the land of the enemy. And there is hope for your future, says the Lord, and your children will come back again to their own border."[57] In the end, both Leah and Rachel received what they wanted most in life. Leah ended up with Yaakov for eternity, and Rachel became the mother of the Jewish People for eternity.)

A LOVING RELATIONSHIP IS THE BOTTOM LINE

We will end this chapter with a story from the Midrash that beautifully expresses the motif of this chapter.

---

55. The Netziv says that Elkanah did not succeed in making Chanah happy because a woman has both a biological and an emotional need to have children. He was only able to meet Chanah's emotional need, but he could not satisfy her biological need. *Ha'amek Davar, Bereishis* 30:1.

56. See also the Zohar 1:223, which expresses a similar idea.

57. *Yirmeyahu* 31:15 –16. The Midrash says that Yaakov prophesied that his children would return to Eretz Yisrael. Therefore, he buried Rachel close to the road, so she would request from God to have mercy on them (*Bereishis Rabbah* 82:10).

> There was once a couple who was married for ten years and did not have any children. They came before Rabbi Shimon Bar Yochai and asked him if they should divorce. He told them that they should, but just as they married with food and drink so should they divorce with a feast. So they made a big party with a lot of wine, and the husband became drunk. In his drunkenness he said to his wife, "Take whatever you want from our house and bring it to your father's house [where she would be living]." What did she do? After he fell asleep, she told the servants to carry him to her father's house. Later on that night, he woke up. "How did I get here?" he asked. His wife replied, "You told me to take whatever I wanted from our house and bring it to my father's house. The only thing I want is you." With that, they went back to Rabbi Shimon Bar Yochai, who then blessed them to have a child.[58]

Why didn't Rabbi Shimon Bar Yochai bless the couple the first time they went to him? Why did he make them go through this "divorce party"?

Rabbi Shimon Bar Yochai wanted to teach the husband and wife a lesson about the power of love: You wanted to separate in order to fulfill a mitzvah, but you love each other so much that you must be together. Maybe you didn't realize until now how much you love each other. But with a resurgence of your love, now you can start over again, and with this rekindled love you will surely see the blessing in your love for each other.

---

58. *Shir haShirim Rabbah* 1:31.

16. "The Third Pillar": Adoption

These are the signs of the Jewish nation: They are merciful, bashful, and performers of kindness.

(*Yevamos* 79a)

INTRODUCTION

IN CHAPTER 2 OF this book, we raised the question: Why do we want children? The answer was that the desire to have children is something innate in all human beings. We inherently want to emulate God. God creates; we procreate. God bestows unlimited kindness on His world; we can bestow unlimited kindness on our children. The desire to raise children is a natural tendency. However, in order to accomplish this, we don't need biological children. We can feel fulfilled as parents by adopting a child and raising him or her as if he or she were our biological child. It says in *Tehillim*,[1] "Happy are those who preserve justice, who perform *tzedakah* at all times." The Talmud asks, How can someone perform *tzedakah* at all times? It answers, By raising an orphan in his home.[2]

AN ACT OF CHESED

The world rests on three pillars, Torah, prayer and *chesed* —

1. 106:3.
2. *Kesubos* 50a.

kindness.[3] The highest level of bestowing kindness is by adopting a child. The mitzvah of adopting a child is so great that it is a wonder why more couples, including couples with biological children, don't adopt.

It is praiseworthy to work for the community; however, most volunteer work has limits: When you finish you come home. You rest. You don't go when you are ill or excessively tired. You have a life outside of your volunteer life, and usually you only do it when it is convenient for you. But when you adopt a child you give up your freedom, your time and your money, and you become completely dedicated to insuring a good life for him or her. The child's life will take precedence over your own.

As mentioned in chapter 2, there are two innate reasons for wanting children: one is that it is part of a woman's essence to want to be pregnant and have children, and the other is a need we all have to give without limits. Although the biological need for pregnancy may not be satisfied by adopting, the second need, the need to give, definitely will. The receiver does not have to be your blood relative for you to experience that feeling of giving. It is for this reason *Chazal* say, "Whoever raises an orphan in his home is considered as if he gave birth to him."[4]

When Rachel realized that she was barren, she then offered her maidservant Bilhah to Yaakov. She didn't do it so that Yaakov could have yet another child, but so that she could feel fulfilled by raising this child as her own. She said, "Here is my maidservant, Bilhah — marry her. She will bear children and I will raise them, and thus I, as well, will have

---

3. *Pirkei Avos* 1:2.

4. *Megillah* 13a; *Sanhedrin* 19b.

children through her."[5]

DEVOTION VERSUS BLOOD

One does not have to have a biological child in order to love him or her. In fact, we do not automatically love blood relations. We love family, not blood. Esav and Yaakov are proof that blood does not guarantee love. Less extreme examples can be seen in everyday life, with family members not getting along and sometimes even hating each other. On the other hand, people love their spouses, although there is no blood relation. We love our good friends sometimes even more than we do our families.

If blood does not bring about love, what does? One answer is a shared value system. When we have values that we consider to be of prime importance, and we see them in other people, we not only admire those people, but we even love them. That is why we often love *tzaddikim* even though they are not family and we might not even know them very well or at all. Very often we choose and love our friends because they share our values.

Dedication to and labor on another person's behalf also engenders love. This is why we love our children so much. It is because of the ceaseless labor we devote to them every day of the year. It is precisely those chores and responsibilities that many parents complain about, that bring the parents to love their child. As Rabbi Eliyahu E. Dessler writes: "We usually

---

5. *Bereishis* 30:3. This is in contrast to Sarah, who offered her maidservant Hagar to Avraham so that Avraham would have a child. Sarah did not say, "So that she will bear children and I will raise them"; she only said, "Maybe because of her I shall be established [with children]," i.e. maybe she would have children in the merit of offering Hagar to Avraham. She never meant to raise Hagar's child. (Netziv, *Bereishis* 16:2.)

think it is love which causes giving because we observe that a person showers gifts and favors on the one he loves. But there is another side to the argument. Giving may bring about love for the same reason that a person loves what he himself has created or nurtured; he recognizes in it part of himself."[6]

There is a subtle message of how to love in the mitzvah, "You shall love your fellowman as [you love] yourself."[7] The question is asked, how can the Torah command us to love someone? The Torah can command us to do or not to do an action, such as put on *tefillin* or not work on Shabbos. But how can the Torah command us to feel an emotion toward someone, such as love? The Hebrew for "You shall love your fellowman" is *ve'ahavta **le**rai'echa,* which literally means, You shall love *to* your fellowman. Why did the Torah add the word "to"? The answer is because God knew that He couldn't demand of us to feel an emotion if we didn't really feel it. Yet at the same time He wasn't willing to relinquish, so to speak, the noble emotion of love, so He hinted to us how to achieve this exalted state. Do things that create love. Do things *to* your fellowman as if you love him, for that will bring genuine love. *Ve'ahavta **le**rai'echa.*

The same is true when it comes to loving our children. We love them the same, whether they are our biological children or our adopted children. It is the caring for them that brings us to love them, not their biological origins.

IMUTZ IS OMETZ

Bringing a child into the world as a result of your love for each other is a relatively easy decision. Psychologically you feel

---

6. Rabbi Eliyahu E. Dessler, *Strive for Truth!,* vol. I (Jerusalem: Feldheim Publishers, 1988), p. 127.
7. *Vayikra* 19:18.

that this baby is "ours." You may even feel it is an extension of yourself. You are more than happy to take on the responsibilities of caring for and raising your son or daughter. But accepting the responsibility of raising another human being who is not biologically yours is a major life decision. Binding yourself to the never-ending needs of this person is a step that will require much consideration. Even though adoption is a great mitzvah of *chesed*, you must be ready for it.

The halachic concerns (mentioned below) only complicate the matter. Adopting a Jewish child today is almost impossible. So do you adopt a non-Jewish child and convert him or her? Judaism is not a religion of missionaries. We are more than happy to accept converts when the initiative is their own, but not when they unwillingly or unknowingly convert. Is it God's will to convert small children in order to raise them to Torah and mitzvos?[8]

Is the only reason you want to adopt because of outside pressure, perhaps from your parents? Are you doing it more for them? Are you merely willing to adopt because you know it would make your spouse happy, but you yourself would rather not adopt? Are you doing it only for the sake of the mitzvah of *chesed*, but don't feel emotionally connected to the mitzvah? If you and your spouse are not equally committed to adopting, how will that affect the parent-child relationship in the future? How will it alter your relationship as a couple? If

---

8. See *Igros Moshe, Yoreh De'ah*, vol. I, at the end of 162: "If my advice will be listened to, there is no need to bring in the seed of gentiles, for this is without any purpose; only when they come on their own to convert for the sake of Heaven, must we accept them." This is how Rav Moshe Feinstein ended one of his responsa. However, we know of a family, presently living in Israel, who adopted a few babies, and Rav Moshe himself was the head of the *beis din* that converted them. He was with them at the *mikveh*, and according to the parents, he didn't hesitate for a moment and seemed to be very happy to be part of the occasion.

you already have a child, how will he or she feel about you adopting?

Do you only want a newborn, an infant, a toddler, or a school-age child? Would you be willing to accept the even greater mitzvah of caring for a physically impaired or mentally challenged child? Are you strong enough for that? Do you only want a baby who more or less looks like you, whose ethnicity is not obviously different from yours? Perhaps it doesn't matter to you, but are you and your spouse in agreement on that issue?

When you have children naturally, you don't get to choose the sex of the baby, the health status, IQ, or any other natural trait (although with genetic engineering that may change). When you are already adopting, it is common to have a "wish list." We want a girl; we want a boy. We want the biological parents to be intelligent, and only from a certain country, and so on. Couples are sometimes apprehensive about adopting because they aren't guaranteed a healthy, smart or good-looking child — although there are no guarantees with biological children either.

It may take time to come to terms with all these issues. Some couples are sure from the outset that they want to adopt. Some couples need time to get used to the idea. And some are sure that they don't want to adopt. You and your spouse need to be in total agreement before you take on the responsibility of raising a child. You will need to be confident that you are ready for this undertaking.

Logic doesn't always guide your decision. Sometimes feelings that you may have trouble explaining even to yourself are the decisive factor determining your final judgment, both in your resolution to adopt in general and whom are you willing to adopt in particular.

Once you decide to adopt, however, please be prepared.

Adoption, like infertility, can be a long, drawn-out ordeal. It can be an emotional roller-coaster ride filled with great hopes one day and disappointments the next. You will need a lawyer who specializes in adoption, and you will need to be careful not to fall prey to people who will take advantage of your emotionally sensitive situation by making you pay extremely high prices for a baby. You should contact support groups and organizations that can help you make suitable choices and direct you concerning the practical side of adoption.

After you adopt, there may be special considerations in raising your child that are beyond the scope of this book. You may need special counseling when the child is older, or you may just want to read one of the many books on the subject. Or maybe everything will go smoothly, and you will not need any extra guidance.

After you have emotionally accepted the notion of adoption, you should feel proud of your decision. Adoption should not be viewed as a secondary option for having children. It should be viewed as an opportunity and a privilege. The modern Hebrew word for adoption, *imutz,* has the same root as the word *amatz,* which means to gather one's strength. This implies that through adoption both you and your family will become stronger. Many people are apprehensive to adopt due to all the dilemmas mentioned above, but the extra effort will be well worth it.

The word *imutz* is also related to the words *amitz* and *ometz,* which mean bravery. Adopting a child requires extra courage and faith. You will need to be confident in your decision, educated about your options, tenacious in your efforts, and patient about the outcome. "[God] will give your heart courage; and hope to the Eternal."[9]

There are many couples who have been blessed with bio-

---

9. *Tehillim* 27:14.

logical children after adopting. Perhaps this is because adopting lowered their anxiety about having children, which removed some psychogenic obstacles that were preventing pregnancy. Some people even view it as a reward for the *chesed* the couple performed by adopting a child, although as we stated in chapter 14, one shouldn't think that having a child is a reward for a particular mitzvah he did but rather an "undeserved kindness." The bottom line is, adoption should be viewed as the goal itself, not as a means for attaining biological children. If you merit to both adopt and have biological children afterwards, be assured that you will love them both with the same parental love.

REAL CHILDREN — REAL PARENTS

You will love your adopted children. You will consider them your children, and you will be their parents. Parents who adopt are not "fill-ins"; they are the real parents.

Chazal knew this too. That is why Scripture established Michal as the mother of her sister Merav's children. The verse says, "The king (David) took... the five sons of Michal...."[10] The Gemara conjectures, "But Michal didn't give birth!" The resolution is that athough Merav gave birth to the five sons, Michal raised them. That is why they were called Michal's children. They were considered hers.[11]

Being a mother or a father, even if the child does not carry your generic line, is a beautiful and meaningful experience. In the eyes of everybody — God, *Chazal*, yourself, and your child — adopting a child earns the status of "as if you gave birth to

---

10. *II Shemuel* 21:8.
11. *Sanhedrin* 19b.

him/her,"[12] and you will be, in the true sense of the word, the real mother and father.

HALACHIC CONSIDERATIONS

There are many halachic considerations concerning adoption. Although they should not restrain you from embracing this wonderful mitzvah, you do need to be aware of them. There are many *halachos* that are either directly or indirectly related to adoption, and circumstances for each family may vary; therefore, only the most relevant ones will be mentioned. For further halachic guidance, you should consult a Rav.

The adopted child is part and parcel of your family in all practical and emotional aspects, but is not blood-related. Since there is no biological relationship, if the adoptive father is a Kohen or a Levi, the child does not have that status. If the child was born a Kohen or Levi and the adoptive father is a Yisrael, the child keeps his original status. If the child was born a non-Jew and then converted, he or she will always have the status of a convert.

Adopting a Jewish Child

If you adopt a Jewish boy he obviously needs a *bris milah* on the eighth day after his birth. If the baby becomes yours after the eighth day, you should circumcise him as soon as possible. Because the ceremony differs slightly from the *bris* of a biological son,[13] your *mohel* needs to be aware of the situation.

Whether your son needs a *pidyon ha-ben* or not depends on many factors. As with all Jewish-born boys, the child must be the firstborn of his biological mother. If the child is the biologi-

---

12. Ibid.

13. For halachic guidance for the ceremony, see Yehoshua Ze'ev Zand, *Birkas haBanim* (Jerusalem: Halachah and Refuah Institute, 1994), chap. 14, pp. 331–334.

cal son of a Kohen or Levi, or of a *bas Kohen* or *bas Levi*, then a *pidyon ha-ben* is not performed. If the birth was a cesarean section, then there is also no *pidyon ha-ben*. If the biological mother had a previous miscarriage, depending on what stage of pregnancy it occurred, there may or may not be a *pidyon ha-ben*. In light of all these issues, it is certainly wise to consult a Rav as to whether your adopted child needs a *pidyon ha-ben* or not.

You also need to know the halachic status of the child,[14] for instance whether he or she is halachically considered a *mamzer* or not. A *mamzer* is the result of either an adulterous or an incestuous relationship. A *mamzer* can certainly be a fine human being and even a great scholar; however, he or she cannot marry into the "congregation of Israel." Obviously the adopting parents need to know this. Someone who was born out of wedlock, merely from a single mother, is not a *mamzer*.

If the identity of the birth mother is known, and she is Jewish, but the identity of the biological father is not known, then the halachic status of the child is that of a *shetuki*.[15] This term is derived from the word *shetok*, which means "quiet," for when we ask the mother who the father is, she keeps quiet.

There is another term for a child whose birth parents are unknown, and that is *asufi*.[16] The word *asufi* is derived from the word *le'esof*, which means to gather, for he or she was gathered from the street, so to speak. An *asufi* does not know who either of his parents are. Both the *shetuki* and the *asufi* are considered *safek mamzer*, questionably illegitimate. They would not ever be allowed to marry.[17] However, many considerations may lead to lenient rulings in this matter. For in-

---

14. *Igros Moshe, Yoreh De'ah* vol. I, 162.
15. Mishnah *Kiddushin* 4:1.
16. Ibid.
17. See *Kiddushin* 73a.

stance, in the case of an *asufi,* if the baby came from any country other than Israel, and there is no clue as to who the parents are, it may be assumed that the child was born a non-Jew and the problem of *asufi* doesn't apply.[18] Even in Israel, where the assumption is that the baby is Jewish because the majority of people in Israel are Jewish, there may be circumstances that would suggest that the child was born of a legitimate relationship.[19] So not knowing who the birth parents are does not automatically mean the child will be branded as either a *shetuki* or an *asufi.* Obviously, you may not determine on your own that the child is neither a *shetuki* nor an *asufi.* On the other hand, you don't have to assume that just because you don't know the child's background, he or she is automatically a *shetuki* or an *asufi.* If the child's origins are in doubt, you need to be in touch with a halachic authority in order to determine the halachic status of the baby.

If the adoption agency tells you that the baby is Jewish, or even if they specifically tell you that the mother is Jewish, you will still need the involvement of a Rav in the case, so he can determine if the agency's definition of "Jewish" meets halachic criteria. Although adoption agencies' intentions are nothing less than noble, it needs to be said that the credibility of the agency, or of the individual social worker, could be questionable. There is no doubt that they are doing God's holy work and should be praised for that. Yet the adoption professionals may think you want to hear that the baby is Jewish, so they may tell you that even though it may not be true; or their "proof" may not be satisfactory evidence for Jewish le-

---

18. See *Shulchan Aruch, Even haEzer* 4, *Pischei Teshuvah* 41; see also *Chazon Ish, Even haEzer* 7:6. See also *Noda beYehudah, Even haEzer* 141:7.

19. *Shulchan Aruch, Even haEzer* 4:31, and see *Pischei Teshuvah* 41. See also *Noda beYehudah,* vol. 1, *Even haEzer,* chap. 7. See also *Otzar haPoskim* 4:31b, in the name of the *Even Yikarah.*

gal purposes.[20] There is no doubt that the agencies are trying to do only what is good for both the baby and the couple, but nevertheless an inquiry into the birth status will be required. Even if you would prefer to adopt a non-Jewish child to avoid the background problem, the agency or social worker may think that you want a Jewish child and then tell you that the child is Jewish. You may not have to believe them. [21]

Adopting a Non-Jewish Child

If you adopt a non-Jewish child, you will have to convert him or her. A girl needs to be immersed in the *mikveh;* a boy needs circumcision and immersion in the *mikveh*. The circumcision does not have to be on the eighth day of the child's life, and in fact if the eighth day falls on Shabbos or *Yom Tov*, it is forbidden to perform the *bris* then. It is important to realize that the circumcision is a conversion ceremony, not a regular *bris*, and hence there are procedural differences.

Rav Moshe Feinstein outlined the procedure regarding how the *bris* for converting a baby should be done, how the prayers should be read, and so on.[22] One should make sure

---

20. The fertility clinic needs checks and balances, too, to make sure that the sperm of the husband is indeed the sperm that will inseminate his wife's egg. We may not rely merely on the word of the doctor. This does not mean that you should be suspicious of all social workers and doctors. It means that on very important issues, when the information and evidence are not openly revealed, the burden of proof must be put on the shoulders of objective experts, and on them we may rely. This will ultimately give us a more secure feeling in the present and, more important, in the future.

21. See *Igros Moshe, Even haEzer*, vol. I, chaps. 10, 70, 71, where he states that even when the doctor says that the sperm from the sperm bank is from a Jew, we don't believe him, for he probably said that because he thinks that the client wants the sperm to be from a Jew.

22. See *Igros Moshe, Yoreh De'ah*, vol. I, 162. For instance, the blessing is *lamol es ha-gerim*. The blessing *Lehachniso* is not said. See the responsum for more details.

that the *mohel* is educated in this ceremony. It is better to formally name the child after he was immersed in the *mikveh,* not at the *bris.* However, if you really want to name him at the *bris,* you may do so. A girl should also be formally named at the *mikveh.*[23]

You may convert a baby even though he or she does not understand the process that he or she is going through. Since it is considered beneficial for the convert, we may benefit someone even though they are not aware of it. Before the age of twelve for a girl and thirteen for a boy, the child must be made aware that he or she was not born Jewish, for at these ages they may protest their conversion. If they do not protest their conversion at this point, they may not protest anymore and must stay committed to mitzvos forever. They must confirm their commitment to Judaism and mitzvah observance. However, if they were not told at bar or bas mitzvah age, they may protest or confirm at any age whenever they become aware.

For the precise procedure as to how the confirmation or protest needs to be expressed, consult your Rav.[24]

Halachos That Apply to Adopted Children

Halachically, an adopted child does not automatically inherit the estate of his adoptive parents. Since you probably want your adopted child to inherit your estate, the safest thing to do is to make a will right away, for a person may bequeath his possessions to anyone he desires. If you also have biological children, or if you may beget biological children, the writing of a will may solve future sibling disputes. The biological children halachically may be able to keep the adopted children out of an inheritance. Therefore, a will is

23. *Igros Moshe, Yoreh De'ah,* vol. I, 161.

24. *Kesubos* 11a; see also Tosafos, *d.h. Lechi,* and *Shitah Mekubetzes* ad loc.

necessary to empower the adopted child. The adopted child can still inherit from his biological parents.

The consensus of the Rabbis is that the adopted child should be notified that he or she is adopted.[25] The child's best interests should always be kept in mind, so the point at which the child is informed of the adoption will have to be determined accordingly. Some families will choose to tell the child from the beginning and some only later on, when the child is more mature. It is permissible to withhold the information about the child's birth status, as long as you intend to divulge the truth when the child is older.[26] Today, most people let the children know from an early age.

A Jewish-born child may not marry his close biological relatives. If his birth parents are unknown, he or she may not marry another adopted child whose background is unknown, for there is a possibility, albeit remote, that he or she is a biological close relative.[27] An adopted daughter who was converted would be forbidden to marry a Kohen like any female convert.[28]

According to Rav Moshe Feinstein, it is permissible for a father to show affection to his adopted daughter, and for a mother to show affection to her adopted son. Thus it is permissible to hug and kiss your adopted child as you would hug and kiss your biological child. Although hugging and kissing

---

25. The reason the child must know that he or she is adopted is based on the *gemara* in *Yevamos* 37b (see next footnote). Also, since an adopted girl who was converted may not marry a Kohen, she obviously needs to be made aware of the fact.

26. *Igros Moshe, Even haEzer*, vol. IV, 66:2.

27. See *Yevamos* 37b: "A man should not marry women from different countries, for maybe the children of both marriages will eventually marry each other, unaware that they are brother and sister."

28. *Shulchan Aruch, Even haEzer* 6:8.

the opposite sex is prohibited in general,[29] it is not prohibited in the case of adopted children, as it is natural for a parent to express his love and affection toward an adopted child.[30] Rav Feinstein likewise allows the parent to be in a situation of *yichud* (seclusion) with his or her adopted child for short periods.[31]

One should consult a Rav concerning the issues of physical affection and *yichud* in particular, because different factors can change the halachah. There is also a difference between physical affection and *yichud*. According to Rav Feinstein, based on the halachic sources, it is clear that one can be even more lenient with physical affection than with *yichud*. Additionally, one cannot assume that the halachah is the same for a child who was adopted as an infant and for a child who was adopted at a more mature age. The presence of biological chil-

---

29. *Igros Moshe*, 64:2., in the name of the Shach, *Yoreh De'ah*, vol. I, 157:1. See the Shach, note #10, in the opinion of the Rambam.

30. This dispensation is reserved for the parents of adopted or stepchildren, and should not be used for other relatives such as aunts and uncles.

31. *Igros Moshe,* ibid. Although he doesn't say how long a "short period" is, it seems reasonable from his next chapter concerning *yichud* of a brother and sister that as long as it is not over a long period of days, it would be permissible. Nevertheless, one should consult a halachic authority for guidance on this matter. It is important to note that in the responsum of Rabbi Feinstein he does not limit this leniency to *sha'as ha-dechak* (an urgent situation), as some Rabbis who wrote on this subject have claimed in his name.

For other opinions on this subject, some of which are lenient and some of which are strict, see: *Shevet haLevi*, vol. 6, *Even haEzer* 196; *Otzar haPoskim*, vol. 9, p. 130 — the letter of Rabbi M.M. Schneerson, the Lubavitcher Rebbe; and p. 132 — the letter of Rabbi Aharon Yakubovitch. See also the responsa of Rabbi Eliezer Waldenberg in *Tzitz Eliezer*, vol. 6, chap. 40:21, and vol. 7, chaps. 44 and 45. And see *Halachah and Contemporary Society*, essay by Melech Schacter, "Various Aspects of Adoption," who quotes Rabbi Yosef Dov Soloveitchik. See also essay by Rabbi Y. E. Henkin, *Bedavar Imutz Yeladim*, in *HaPardes*, Tishrei 5726 (1965), p. 7.

dren in the house may influence halachic rulings as well. Therefore, it is recommended to get halachic guidance concerning all aspects of living with your adopted child.

When your adopted son is called up to the Torah, he may be called by "his name" the son of his "adoptive father"; there is no need to call him by "his name" the son of Avraham Avinu, even if he converted. There is also no need to add the word "*hamegadlo*" (the one who is raising him) after the adoptive father's name. Also, when the adopted child is given a Hebrew name, the adoptive father's name may be used in the ceremony.[32] As far as what name your adopted son or daughter will use in their *kesubah* (or, *r"l*, *get*), consult a Rav when the time comes; don't worry about it now.

When the adoptive parent dies, then the adopted child should mourn and say *Kaddish* for the parent.[33] However, the adopted child is not required to mourn in all the minute details.[34] There are obviously many particulars to these laws and they should be studied when it becomes relevant.

A WHOLE WORLD, A WHOLE FAMILY

In the Gemara, there is no recorded custom of childless couples adopting children. Rather, adoption was done to take care of orphaned children. The benefit of the children was the objective, not the benefit of the couple. Therefore, some people feel that because now most adoption is done for the sake of the couple, *Chazal*'s words that through adoption one can perform *tzedakah* at all times[35] are not relevant today.

However, it is interesting to note that Philo says that the

32. *Igros Moshe, Yoreh De'ah*, vol. I, 161. According to Rav Feinstein, one does not have to add the word "*hamegadlo*" after the father's name.

33. *Magen Avraham, Orach Chaim* 132:2.

34. *Pischei Teshuvah, Yoreh De'ah* 7.

35. See footnote 2.

daughter of Pharaoh adopted Moshe because she was barren. If someone writing over two thousand years ago thought that Pharaoh's daughter adopted a baby because she was childless, it tells us that the desire to overcome the sense of loss caused by barrenness has always existed,[36] and adoption was viewed as a solution.

Secondly, the custom of giving one's handmaid to one's husband, as our matriarchs did, was common practice in the ancient world.[37] The purpose was mainly to raise the child. This was an ancient form of adoption.

Thirdly, and more important, when it comes to *chesed,* as long as the needy person receives that which he is lacking, the mitzvah is fulfilled. So if you are providing a warm home and a Torah life to a child, you're still allowed to get a little *nachas* from that as well. Furthermore, the fact that people want to adopt to fulfill their need to be parents is not a deficiency in the mitzvah of *chesed;* rather, it is an expression of a deep desire to bestow unconditional love on another human being. It is embracing the mitzvah of *chesed* with all of our soul. It is not merely an act of obeying God, it is emulating Him. Just as God cares for His world, we will care for a soul, which is like a whole world. God embraces His world, we embrace our children. God showers His world with love, we shower our children with love. Wanting to be a parent isn't selfish. It is the opposite. It is the manifestation of the mitzvah of *chesed* in its deepest and most complete fashion.

In the end, whether you adopt a Jewish child or a non-Jewish child, you will be performing unlimited kindness

---

36. *Aggada und Exegese bei Flavius Josephus*, pp. 27, 115.

37. J. Van Seters, "The Problem of Childlessness in Near Eastern Law and the Patriarchs of Israel," *JBL* 87 (1968), pp. 401 – 408. He writes that in Mesopotamia there was a law that if a woman was barren, she could give her maidservant to her husband to bear a child, who would then be adopted by the wife.

day after day, hour after hour, for a soul for whom you accepted complete responsibility. You will love this child with all your heart and the child will love you. You will give this child the best life you possibly can, and this child will make you proud. You will brag about his or her accomplishments in the same way any parent takes pride in his child's accomplishments. You will get used to being called Ima and Abba, or Mommy and Daddy, or Mamme and Tatty. You will feel anguish over his or her sorrows and you will feel happiness for his or her joys. You will be the one who knows all the answers, does everything the best, and is always there for him. You will go from one childrearing stage to the next, and like every parent, you will never be sure if you made the right decisions. You will grow to see your child build a family of his or her own, and you will love the sound of Savta and Saba, or Grandma and Grandpa, or Bubby and Zeidy. You will be a family.

May God give you *nachas*.

17.
Treatment of Infertility

FEMALE-FACTOR INFERTILITY: SPECIFIC TREATMENT OPTIONS

WHEN A WOMAN is found to have a fertility problem related to a hormonal imbalance then the first step in treatment will be a non-invasive attempt to chemically bring her body to its maximum fertility potential. Just as the first and second stage of the fertility investigation consisted of one step leading to another, so too will each hormonal therapy, if unsuccessful, advance to another level, and — only if necessary — lead to invasive, surgical intervention or assisted reproduction.

Treatment of PCO

As discussed previously, *polycystic ovarian syndrome* (PCO), is a state where anovulation (lack of ovulation) persists for any length of time, and unruptured follicles are "trapped" inside the ovary. Cyclic hormones remain at a constant level without surges or dips in their amounts; thus follicles develop only up to a certain point. The endometrial lining of the uterus is built up but never shed because a woman does not get her period.

A common treatment, given to a woman who does not ovulate and who does not get her period, is the induction of menstrual bleeding with the administration of progesterone for five to ten days a month. This is called the *progesterone challenge treatment*. The administration of progesterone is not only therapeutic, it is also a test of menstrual function, i.e. whether the uterine lining is responding normally to monthly hormonal fluctuations.

The progesterone challenge treatment consists of administering 10 mg of *medroxyprogesterone acetate* daily for five days. Uterine bleeding (menstruation) should be seen. If there is no bleeding, the medical investigation must be directed toward the possibility of hypothalamic and pituitary dysfunction or perhaps an estrogen deficiency. PCO can be accompanied by other hormonal disturbances. However, with true PCO there should be no estrogen deficiency.

Even while other hormonal disturbances are being ruled out, a woman diagnosed with PCO will be a candidate for medical induction of ovulation (to be discussed in the next section).

PCO is often associated with insulin resistance or hyperinsulinism (an excessive amount of insulin in the blood). In this case, an oral diabetic medication called *metformin* has attained very positive results in correcting the insulin-glucose imbalance. Besides reducing hyperinsulinism, metformin treatment lowers LH levels, testosterone concentrations, and in combination with moderate weight loss, induces ovulation, thereby enabling women with PCO to achieve pregnancy.[1]

The effect of moderate weight loss of even 10 percent in obese women has been proven to be instrumental in enhancing the treatment of PCO with metformin. Lean women suffering from PCO can also benefit from metformin, which when coupled with the ovulatory drug clomiphene, results in ovulatory cycles.

Side effects of metformin include stomach upset, nausea and vomiting, diarrhea, and loss of appetite.

If drug therapy fails to end the PCO-anovulation cycle (no ovulation and no period), then surgical intervention is an op-

---

1. E. Diamonti-Kandarakis, C. Kouli, "Therapeutic Effects of Metformin on Insulin Resistance and Hyperandrogenism in Polycystic Ovary Syndrome," *European Journal of Endocrinology* 138:269, 1998.

tion. During laparoscopy, a procedure called *ovarian drilling* is done where the surgeon uses a laser or a specialized instrument to puncture the tiny cysts. This may result in the reduction of a significant amount of hormone-producing tissue, specifically a sustained reduction in testosterone levels.

Treatment of Hyperprolactinemia

As mentioned earlier, prolactin, a hormone secreted by the pituitary gland, stimulates milk production after childbirth. Prolactin inhibits ovulation for a period of time in nursing mothers as well. However, elevated prolactin levels in a woman who is not breastfeeding can contribute to infertility. Elevated prolactin can be caused by pituitary tumors, certain medications, or hypothyroidism (an under-active thyroid gland). Thirty-three percent of these women will have symptomatic secretion of milk from the breasts (*glactorrhea*). Any woman who is not pregnant or nursing, and has any type of secretions from her breasts, should seek medical attention.

Once a *pituitary tumor (macroadenoma)* is ruled out, hyperprolactinemia can be simply treated with *bromocriptine* (Parlodel), which suppresses pituitary secretion of prolactin. In twenty-two case studies, 80 percent of women with hyperprolactinemia due to hormonal imbalances had menstruation restored, many within six to eight weeks, with bromocriptine therapy.[2]

Once a woman becomes pregnant, she stops taking the drug. There has been no evidence that bromocriptine usage during early pregnancy is harmful to the fetus.[3]

Bromocriptine is available in a once or twice-daily tablet

---

2. F. G. Cuellar, "Bromocriptine in the Management of Amenorrhea/Glactorrhea associated with Hyperprolactinemia," *Obstetrics and Gynecology* 55:278, 1980.
3. C. Weil, "The Safety of Bromocriptine in Long-term Use; A Review of the Literature," *Current Medical Research Opinion* 10:25, 1986.

taken orally or administered vaginally. Side effects include: nausea, diarrhea, dizziness, headache, and fatigue. Many women report less side effects when bromocriptine is administered vaginally at bedtime.

Lisuride hydrogen maleate (Dopergin) is another medical treatment available to reduce prolactin levels. Tablets come in 0.2 mg amounts and should be taken with meals. Side effects include nausea, headaches, tiredness, dizziness, drowsiness, and sweating. As with bromocriptine, this medication is stopped once pregnancy is achieved.

Cabergoline (Dostinex) was approved by the U.S. Food and Drug Administration in 1997. It is given in a twice-weekly dose of 0.5 mg. The most common side effect is nausea.

Treatment of Adrenal Hyperactivity

When the adrenal glands secrete an overabundance of male hormones, ovulatory disturbances will result. This imbalance is common in women with PCO. In women with elevated blood levels of DHEAS, treatment with *Dexamethasone* (an oral steroid preparation) can lower these levels. Dexamethasone treatment can be given concurrently with both medical intervention of PCO and ovulation induction.

NOTE: It is permissible for a man or a woman to take pills, syrup, or suppositories for fertility treatments on Shabbos.[4]

Ovulation Induction

For over fifty years, the ability to induce ovulation has been one of the crowning achievements of reproductive endocrinology. Continuing advancements in this field have given hope to women with even the most severe ovarian dysfunction. However, as promising as these new technologies are, the disparity between successful ovulation and pregnancy is still wide. In

---

4. Rabbi Yigal Shafran, "*Tipul Poriut baShabbat*," *Techumin*, vol. XVII, pp. 335–340; *Birkas Banim*, pp. 249–252.

other words, we might be able to make the ovaries function, but this does not ensure that there will be a healthy pregnancy as a result.

According to the World Health Organization, ovulatory deficiencies are classified into three groups:

- **Group I:** Hypothalamic-Pituitary Failure

  Patients diagnosed with stress-related amenorrhea, anorexia nervosa, Kallman's Syndrome (poorly developed reproductive organs), and isolated hormonal deficiency. *Gonadotropin* (FSH & LH) and estrogen levels are low and there is a failure to bleed after the administration of the progesterone challenge test.

- **Group II:** Hypothalamic-Pituitary Dysfunction

  Women who have normal gonadotropin and estrogen levels, but are anovulatory (do not ovulate), and/or are *oligomenorrhagic* (have infrequent or irregular periods). This classification includes those women with anovulatory polycystic ovarian syndrome (PCO).

- **Group III:** Ovarian Failure

  This category includes all variants of women with non-functioning ovaries or with ovaries that are unresponsive to treatment.

Prior to Induction of Ovulation

- **Diagnostic tests** are given to confirm that there are no structural problems within the hypothalamic-pituitary-ovary axis.
- **Suspected hyperinsulinism** — which can cause obesity, thyroid abnormalities, elevated levels of androgens, DHEAS, or prolactin in the bloodstream — is treated.
- **A semen analysis** is preformed in order to rule out the

possibility of untreatable sperm defects.

Medications for Induction of Ovulation

◆ **Clomiphene citrate:** Also known as *Clomid* or *Ikaclomin*, clomiphene citrate is the initial drug of choice when there is absent or infrequent ovulation. Clomiphene therapy does not directly stimulate ovulation, but intensifies the sequence of events that are already occurring in a regular cycle. Clomiphene exerts a weak estrogenic effect that raises FSH and LH (gonadotropin) levels. As a result, more than one egg may be released, which accounts for the increased incidence of twins or multiple births. In order for clomiphene to be effective, a woman must exhibit estrogen and gonadotropin production. This is evidenced either by spontaneous monthly menstrual bleeding or by withdrawal menstrual bleeding as a result of a 5-day course of progesterone.

Dosage: Clomiphene citrate, 50 mg in pill form, is usually given on day 5 of the menstrual cycle, for five days. Clomiphene delays ovulation, which is helpful in cases of prolonged menstrual flow or a shortened follicular phase (the phase before ovulation). The dosage of clomiphene can be started as early as day 3 or 4 of a woman's cycle and continued for seven days in cases where ovulation is thought to occur before the day the woman goes to the *mikveh*.

Ovulation can be expected five to ten days after the last day of medication. Once it occurs, the couple is advised to have relations every other day for a week beginning five days after the last day of medication. Because there is no benefit to continuing a woman on the same dosage if ovulation is not achieved, every effort should be made to document ovulation on the first cycle and in any subsequent cycle in which the dosage has been changed. For a more sophisticated prediction of ovulation than measuring basal body temperature, commercially available urinary dipsticks that identify the luteinizing hormone (LH) surge can be used at home. Your doctor may choose to take serum LH measurements (a blood test) or to perform an ultrasound to pinpoint the timing of ovulation. A midluteal phase serum progesterone level (a blood test around day 21 of the cycle) can also help to confirm ovulation.

Overall, the pregnancy rate with clomiphene therapy is 40 percent. Dosage can be increased in a staircase fashion by 50 mg increments to a maximum of 200 to 250 mg daily. In addition to clomiphene therapy, administration of *human chorionic gonadotropin* (HCG) can be used to trigger ovulation. If the highest dose is pursued for three to four months without success, prognosis with clomiphene therapy is poor.[5] (Hint: time to move on.)

Side effects: The most common side effects of clomiphene are headache and blurred vision. They can also include hot flashes, abdominal bloating, breast discomfort, and the mixed blessing of a multiple pregnancy rate of 10 percent. Approximately 15 to 20 percent of women will develop a problem with the quality of their cervical mucus, which interferes with with the ability of the sperm to migrate through the cervix. A postcoital test (PCT) will determine if this side effect exists. In these cases, a couple would turn to *intrauterine insemination* (IUI) to overcome less than optimum cervical mucus. (See page 292 ff.)

Clomiphene may also hinder the build-up of the uterine lining (endometrium), which in turn can interfere with implantation. Low-dose estrogen can sometimes prevent this.

In women with elevated blood levels of DHEAS, a combi-

---

5. E. Kousta, D.M. White, S. Franks, "Modern Use of Clomiphene Citrate in Induction of Ovulation," *Human Reproduction Update* 3:359, 1997.

nation of clomiphene and Dexamethasone can improve ovulation rates and lower the dose of clomiphene required to achieve ovulation.[6] The recommended Dexamethasone dosage is 0.5 mg at bedtime beginning two weeks before menstruation and taken throughout the clomiphene cycle.

Human Gonadotropins

Women who fail to respond to clomiphene administration, but demonstrate functioning ovaries, unobstructed fallopian tubes, and no uterine pathologies, may be candidates for the next stage of treatment with gonadotropins (FSH and LH). Gonadotropin therapy only works on women with functioning ovaries. FSH inducts follicular growth (i.e. causes the egg to grow), while LH aids in follicular maturation (i.e. helps the egg to mature) and causes ovulation.

There are different forms of human gonadotropins:

- **Human menopausal gonadotropins (HMG):** A preparation extracted from the urine of postmenopausal women, each ampule consists of 75 units of FSH and 75 units of LH. HMG is known commercially as *Pergonal, Humegon, Menogon, Menopur*, and *Repronex*. It is administered by intramuscular or subcutaneous injection.
- **Purified urinary FSH:** Some women may be given a preparation of *purified FSH* where most of the LH has been removed. Its trade names are *Metrodin, Normegon, Orgafol*, and *Urofollitropin*. It is also administered intramuscularly.
- **Highly purified urinary FSH:** Also known as *Fertinex* or *Metrodin HP*, it can be administered by a simple subcu-

---

6. R.A. Lobo, W. Paul, C.M. March, "Clomiphene and Dexamethasone in Women Unresponsive to Clomiphene Alone," *Obstetrics and Gynecology* 60:497, 1982.

taneous injection (a shot with a smaller needle, under the skin).

- **Recombinant FSH:** This form, produced in Chinese hamster ovary cells, is known commercially as *Puregon, Gonal-F,* or *Follistim.* It is also administered subcutaneously.
- **Human chorionic gonadotropin (HCG):** Prepared from human pregnancy urine and placental tissue, HCG is used to stimulate the midcycle LH ovulatory surge and subsequently, ovulation. HCG, also known as *Pregnyl, Profasi, A.P.L.,* and *Chorigon,* is administered by intramuscular injection.
- **Recombinant HCG (Ovidrel) and Recombinant LH (Lhadi):** These fairly new preparations allow self-administration by subcutaneous injections.

Instruction and counseling before initiating treatment is essential. You need to know that there may be frequent visits to the fertility clinic for blood tests and ultrasounds. There will be daily injections (husbands can be taught to administer them), and many treatments, not covered by insurance, are expensive. There will be daily recordings of basal body temperature and body weight, and intercourse will be scheduled.

One ampule of Pergonal or Metrodin is given by intramuscular (IM) injection starting on day 2 to 3 of the menstrual cycle for seven to fourteen days. From the seventh day (or the fourth day in a woman with polycystic ovaries) there will be daily assessments of blood estrogen levels (estradiol) and vaginal ultrasonic measurement of follicle numbers and size. The gonadotropin dosage is adjusted daily at this point to achieve the delicate therapeutic balance that will be effective, yet not overstimulate the ovaries.

The usual clinical routine: Once daily assessments for follicular development preceding ovulation begin, your early mornings will be occupied with hormonal blood tests and ultrasounds. This involves going from one area in the doctor's office or clinic to give blood and then to the ultrasound testing area. Chances are there will be some waiting at both stations, although the staff makes great efforts to streamline this process so you can get on with your day.

During the next four hours or so, you try to go about your business with work, family, or friends as normally as possible while you are awaiting word about the continuation of your treatment.

Your doctors, meanwhile, are evaluating the results of your estrogen levels and the size of the ovarian follicles as seen by ultrasound. The amount of gonadotropin medication to be given that evening, and when the next morning's blood and ultrasound check-up needs to be done, are decided at this point.

The couple, or more often the woman, phones the clinic at a designated time and speaks to one of the nurses to receive instructions regarding that evening's dosage of medication and whether to come back in the morning for another blood test and ultrasound scan.

Once the estrogen levels and follicular size reach a certain point (see below), a one-time dose of 10,000 units of human HCG will be given to trigger the release of the ovum from the maturing follicle. The couple is advised to have intercourse the day of the HCG injection and for the next two days. By the fourteenth day, after the injection, a B-subunit assay of HCG in the blood is the most reliable test of pregnancy.

A blood test should not be done on Shabbos unless the woman is under an incredible amount of stress to have it done. In a case of great necessity a non-Jew should perform it.[7] The couple should consult a Rav.

Hormone injections should not be given on Shabbos. It is

7. Rabbi Yigal Shafran, *Techumin*, vol. XVII; *Birkas Banim*, pp. 254–255.

preferable to time every injection prior to sunset; therefore, Friday evening's injection would be at the regular time and Saturday's would be given right after Shabbos. If the woman is in a very stressful state, however, it would be permissible for a non-Jew to give the injection on Shabbos.[8]

Side effects: Gonadotropin therapy can cause mood swings and irritability (husbands, don't take this personally). There exist slightly higher rates of miscarriage (25 percent) and higher risk of ectopic pregnancy (implantation in the fallopian tube). The multiple gestation rate is approximately 20 percent (15 percent twins, 5 percent high-order multiple gestations [triplets or more]).[9]

The most serious side effect: *Ovarian hyperstimulation* (OHSS) is a serious and possibly life-threatening side effect of a medicated cycle to produce more follicles. Although "*superovulation*" is essential in preparing more follicles for IVF or other assisted reproduction techniques to increase chances of fertilization, sometimes the ovaries are inadvertently overdosed which causes them to produce too many follicles. In mild cases, symptoms include ovarian enlargement, abdominal distention, and weight gain. In severe cases (1 to 2 percent), hospitalization is required to deal with fluid accumulation in the abdomen and in the lungs, along with electrolyte imbalance, which can cause symptoms of pain, excessive weight gain, difficulty in breathing, and the possibility of ovarian rupture and hemorrhage.[10]

---

8. Ibid.

9. J. Dor, I. Ben-Shlomo, D. Levran, "The Relative Success of ...Gonadotropin in 1099 Cycles of In Vitro Fertilization," *Fertility and Sterility* 58 : 986 – 990, 1992.

10. R.S. Morris, R. J. Paulson, M.V. Sauer, "Predictive Value of Serum Estradiol Concentrations and Oocyte Number in Severe OHSS," *Human Reproduction* 10:811, 1995.

If you develop any of the following signs or symptoms while taking ovarian stimulation medications, then you must contact your doctor immediately:

- Abdominal pain
- Vomiting
- Significant swelling
- Bloating
- Weight gain of more than one pound a day
- Shortness of breath
- Decreased urine output

Sometimes OHSS cannot be avoided even with the diligent ultrasonic monitoring of the ovaries and measurement of blood estrogen levels that are routine in ovulation stimulation cycles.

In order to prevent ovarian hyperstimulation, estrogen measurement in the blood and ultrasonic monitoring of the ovaries are an integral part of gonadotropin therapy. In addition to preventing hyperstimulation, close monitoring is necessary to choose the correct moment for administering HCG. If estrogen levels are more than 1,500 pg/ml for an ovulation induction cycle or more than 3,500 pg/ml for an IVF cycle, and when follicle number is greater than 10, hyperstimulation is likely to develop and the following measures should be taken to prevent the occurrence of OHSS:

- Reduce HCG dose
- *Coasting* — where stimulating drugs are withheld for one to three days and then HCG is given
- Administration of GnRH analogues instead of HCG
- Albumin IV to reduce to severity of OHSS symptoms
- Cancellation of the cycle

Alternatively, high responders to gonadotropins can be "converted" mid-cycle to IVF. Mature eggs would be retrieved, fertilized, and the embryos frozen for transfer in a future cycle.

Hyperstimulation syndrome will undergo gradual resolution with time, in about seven days. Pregnancy compounds symptoms of OHSS, which will resolve during the first two to four weeks of pregnancy.

There are two tools used to monitor the woman's situation and to hopefully prevent hyperstimulation:

- **Estrogen monitoring.** Testing estrogen levels in the bloodstream is referred to as *estradiol assay*. On day 7 of gonadotropin therapy, daily blood estradiol levels are checked and the results recorded in a graph-like fashion. The therapy schedule during these days usually consists of administering the gonadotropin injections in the early evening based on the estradiol levels from the blood samples obtained earlier that morning. Optimally a linear rise in estradiol is established with the maximum estradiol level reaching no more than 1500 pg/ml. The risk of hyperstimulation is significant from 1500 to 2000 pg/ml. If the estradiol level rises over 2000 pg/ml, HCG should not be given, and the ovarian follicles should be allowed to regress.
- **Ultrasound monitoring.** Ultrasound assessment of the growth and development of ovarian follicles enables the physician to have first-hand evidence of successful ovarian stimulation. During normal cycles, growing follicles can first be identified by ultrasound on days 5 to 7 as small cysts in the ovary. One follicle will grow faster than the others (dominant follicle) and occasionally two dominant follicles will develop. Employing the vaginal ultrasound technique, the maximal follicular diameter to be reached is 15 to 18 mm, following gonadotropin therapy, and 22 to 24 mm diameter with clomiphene induction. When follicles reach this size, HCG will be given. Ovulation will occur approximately 40 hours af-

ter HCG is administered. Determining the exact time to administer HCG can be quite elusive (like the blink of an eye), as ultrasonic observation has shown that ovulation is associated with complete emptying of the follicular contents in only 1 to 45 minutes!

In order to protect against multiple gestation and hyperstimulation, it is common practice to withhold HCG if there are more than three to five follicles 13 mm or greater in diameter. A large number (eleven or more) of smaller follicles will also preclude HCG administration.[11]

In addition to monitoring follicular size, the lining of the uterus is measured to assess hormonal influence on the development of the endometrium. At the same time that the ultrasound technician inspects the ovaries, he or she examines and calculates endometrial thickness. The chance of pregnancy is greatest if endometrial thickness is 9 to 10 mm or more. Implantation cannot occur when the endometrial thickness is measured at less than 6 mm.[12]

A Review of Steps toward Induction of Ovulation

- A five-day program of clomiphene therapy is begun. Ovulation is confirmed with basal body temperature charting, urinary LH predictor sticks, or ultrasonography.
- After increasing the clomiphene dosage to the maximum level, 10,000 IU of HCG can be given as a single intramuscular dose around seven days after beginning clomiphene to trigger the release of matured eggs. This is when follicular maturation is at its peak.

---

11. J. Blankstein, J. Shalev, T. Sasdon, E. E. Kukia, "Ovarian Hyperstimulation Syndrome: Prediction by Number and Size of Preovulatory Follicles," *Fertility and Sterility* 47:597, 1987.

12. J. Isaacs and C.S. Wells, "Endometrial Thickness as a Valid Monitoring Parameter," *Fertility and Sterility* 65:262, 1999.

- If three or four months of ovulatory cycles, induced by clomiphene (where ovulation is confirmed), do not result in pregnancy, reevaluation of abnormal hormone levels is recommended.
- Bromocriptine, Dexamethasone, or metformin (drug treatment for obese, hyperinsulinemic women) can be added to the clomiphene regime.
- If there is no pregnancy after three to six cycles, with ovulation — proceed to induction of ovulation with human gonadotropins. Therapeutic cycles of ovulation induction may be alternated with non-therapeutic cycles. In other words, taking a break from extra hormones can be beneficial to the body and is common practice in fertility treatment.

More Is Not Better

You may mistakenly think that the more developed follicles, the more eggs released, the more ova fertilized, the better. However, maternal complications and fetal loss caused by prematurity in multiple gestations continue to be serious obstetrical problems. Multiple pregnancy rates can range from 10 to 30 percent for twin gestations and 5 percent for triplets or greater.[13]

Maternal morbidity (illness or injury) and maternal mortality (death) is increased in multiple gestation. Mothers carrying *high order pregnancies* (three or more fetuses) are at higher risk for developing anemia, hemorrhage, severe infection, high blood pressure, and liver disease.

The risk of multiple pregnancy for babies is premature delivery. Since premature labor and delivery is common, even

---

13. J.J. Kurinczuk, R.J. Pemberton, S.C. Binns, D.E. Parsons, F.J. Stanley, "Singleton and Twin Confinements Associated with Infertility Treatments," *Australian – New Zealand Journal of Obstetrics and Gynecology* 35:27, 1995.

with bed-rest at home or in the hospital, most twins are born before week 35 and triplets before week 33. As a result, children born pre-term and of low birth weight are at an increased risk of both physical disabilities and learning difficulties. The rate of cerebral palsy is greatly increased in twins and triplets.[14]

Fetal Reduction Some medical professionals prefer selective reduction of fetuses in pregnancies of triplets or greater to reduce the number of fetuses early in the pregnancy — thus hoping to increase the chances of a successful outcome. Many members of the medical profession are of the opinion that a woman carrying twins or a single baby will have a better chance of reaching her due date and having a healthy child.

Pregnancy reduction is done under ultrasound guidance. The gestational sac can be aspirated or a toxic drug can be injected into or next to the fetal heart. This would induce a miscarriage of that fetus. Selection of which fetus or gestational sac is based solely on technical considerations. The procedure is performed transvaginally between the eighth and ninth weeks of gestation and transabdominally between the eleventh and twelfth weeks.

The subsequent overall risk of losing one or more of the remaining fetuses is 4 to 9 percent, and of losing the entire pregnancy is 10 percent. There are reported total pregnancy losses of 4.5 to 7.6 percent for triplet-to-twin reduction.[15] There is also research that points to lower birth weights for twins re-

---

14. For articles on the dangers of high-order pregnancies, see the website of the National Library of Medicine, http://ncbi.nl.nih.gov/entrez/query.fcgi?CMD=Display&DB=pubmed.

15. M.I. Evans, R.L. Berkowitz, "Improvements in Outcomes of Multifetal Pregnancy Reduction with Increased Experience," *American Journal of Obstetrics and Gynecology* 184:97–103, 2001.

duced from triplets.[16] These risks will be weighed against the dangers of multiple (high order) birth and the chances for a successful delivery. It is an extremely difficult decision to reach, especially when a couple has traversed such a difficult path toward conception.

Just as there are inherent risks of carrying more than one child, there are also many dangers involved in the procedure of fetal reduction. The difficult decisions faced by medical professionals and couples alike are not without potential consequences. Yet conventional medical wisdom holds that there are two options in cases of multifetal pregnancies:

- Continue the pregnancy (all the fetuses)
- Perform multifetal pregnancy reduction on one or more of the fetuses.[17]

It should be made clear that fetal reduction means destroying one or more of the fetuses. Abortion is forbidden in Jewish law unless there is a danger to the mother.[18] According to some halachic authorities, including Rav Moshe Feinstein, abortion is considered murder.[19] Therefore, there is a problem when the doctor recommends implanting multiple fetuses: Paradoxically, he is hoping that at least one will implant, however if they all successfully but undesirably implant, the

---

16. B.T. Helfand and R.K. Silver, "Multifetal Reduction Increases the Risk of Preterm Delivery and Fetal Growth Restriction in Twins," *Fertility and Sterility* 67:30-3, 1997.

17. *Multifetal Pregnancy Reduction: Committee Opinion 215*, American College of Obstetricians and Gynecologists, April 1999.

18. According to Rabbi Moshe Feinstein (*Igros Moshe, Choshen Mishpat*, vol. II, chap. 69), for an abortion to be permitted there needs to be a strong possibility that the fetus endangers the mother. See also *Nishmas Avraham, Choshen Mishpat*, chap. 425, in the name of Rav S. Z. Auerbach, for another approach.

19. *Igros Moshe*, ibid. See also *Tzitz Eliezer*, vol. IX, chap. 51:3, for a different opinon.

only solution will be to abort one or two or sometimes even three. It is sadly ironic that a couple going through fertility treatments might be faced with the prospect of abortion at the same time that they are about to realize their greatest hope of having children.[20] The decisionmaking process can be traumatic. Some individuals may feel guilty about one fetus being chosen over another, and the guilt may haunt them for years.[21]

Not all the research on the benefits of fetal reduction, or the number of fetuses that pose a danger to the mother, is conclusive, and some of it is contradictory.[22] Some studies show that fetal reduction will help insure a healthy pregnancy, yet

---

20. See the lengthy article by Stacy Pinchuk, "A Difficult Choice in a Different Voice: Multiple Births, Selective Reduction and Abortion," *Duke Journal of Gender Law and Policy,* Spring 2000, pp. 29–56: "The thought of injecting potassium chloride into the heart of one or several fetuses, and then having the woman carry around a dead fetus or several dead fetuses for weeks to months is not a pleasant one. Neither is the thought of a one-year-old septuplet being fed formula through her belly, and facing an uncertain medical future. The decision to selectively reduce or carry multiple fetuses to term is not simple, and neither are its consequences...." The article is also available online at http://www.law.duke.edu/journals/djglp/gentoc7nl.t\htm.

21. Ibid. Pinchuk discribes the psychological trauma that follows the decision to undergo legal abortion. Citing Thomas Eller, "Informed Consent Actions for Post-Abortion Psychological Trauma," *Notre Dame Law Review* 71:668, 1996, she identifies depression, a sense of loss, guilt, sleeping disorders, reactions on the anniversary of the abortion, and other more severe reactions. She also claims that the same negative feelings are manifest even when one or more healthy babies have resulted from the pregnancy.

22. See N.J. Sebire, "Preterm Delivery and Growth Restriction in Multifetal Pregnancies Reduced to Twins," *Human Reproduction* 12:173–175, 1997/January. This article can also be found at http://www.Ivf-et.comtlc/redux.html. Also noted are the contradictory conclusions from different studies.

others indicate the contrary.[23]

In order to avoid all potential problems associated with fetal reduction, couples should insist that the doctor implant no more than three or even just two embryos.[24] In Israel and in many European countries, this is standard protocol,[25] and the trend is to lower the implantation to two or even one. The idea of implanting more embryos, hoping that at least one will successfully implant while at the same time knowing that any "excess" embryos can be aborted, creates an ethical dilemma. Even though the chance of successful implantation is greater with a larger number of embryos, this must be weighed against the problems and pitfalls this procedure engenders.

According to the British Fertilisation and Embryology Authority in its HEFA Code of Practice, women under the age of 40 at the time of transfer should receive no more than two embryos in any one cycle. Women age 40 or over at the time of transfer should receive no more than three embryos in any one cycle. For women using fresh or frozen donated eggs, no more than two embryos may be placed in a woman regardless of her age, as egg donors are fertile women under the age of 36. The French National Consultative Ethics Committee is of

23. For more information on this subject, see: American College of Obstetricians and Gynecologists Committee on Ethics, "Multifetal Pregnancy Reduction and Selective Fetal Termination," April 1991; I. Tadin, D. Roje, I. Banovic, D. Karelovic, and M. Mimica, "Fetal Reduction in Multifetal Pregnancy — Ethical Dilemmas," *Yonsi Medical Journal* 43:2, pp. 252–258, 2002; N. G. Valko, "Fetal Reduction: Good Medicne or Atrocity?" Lifeissues.net:/writers/val/val/02fetalreduction; American College of Obstetricians and Gynecologists Committee on Ethics, "Ethics in Obstetrics and Gynecology," 2004:41–45; R.L. Berkowitz and L. Lynch, "Selective Reduction: An Unfortunate Misnomer, *Obstetrics and Gynecology* 1990:75–87.

24. This suggestion is sanctioned by Prof. Ehud Margalioth, director of the IVF unit at Shaare Zedek Medical Center in Jerusalem.

25. Under normal circumstances.

the opinion that "Unless a case is exceptional and duly justified by impressive and solely medical reasons compatible with the state of the art, no more than three embryos should be transferred."[26]

As fertility treatments improve, the need for fetal reduction will diminish because there will be better success with the implantations.[27]

If couples convey to doctors that they don't want to have multiple embryos implanted and that aborting is out of the question, doctors will seek solutions other than multiple implantations. Consequently, this ethically dubious practice will be used more sparingly,[28] if at all.[29]

If there are extenuating circumstances[30] such as the woman has already had a few unsuccessful IVF treatments, the woman is significantly older, there are serious health issues, or the medical staff suggests performing fetal reduction after telling the couple that multiple embryos were already

---

26. http://ccne-ethique.fr/english/avis/a_024.htm.

27. See Pinchuk, "A Different Choice," p. 55: "Recent advances now allow doctors to transfer on the fifth day of growing fertilized embryos outside of the womb, instead of on the third day. This allows for implantation of the two or three embryos that appear most likely to thrive in the womb. Obviously as reproductive technology continues to evolve, so too will the possible medical solutions to the problems exposed herein."

28. See Sebire, "Preterm Delivery and Growth Restriction," who in his summary comment expresses the same sentiment.

29. It is our pleasure thank Rabbi Yisroel Belsky for opening our eyes to the magnitude of this issue, and for his tenacious stand against the common practice of fetal reduction in America. We would also like to thank R' Yaakov Feldheim for taking an especial and active interest in this part of our book.

30. See http://ccne-ethique.fr/english/avis/a_024.htm: "The National Consultative Ethics Committee advocates that fetal reduction should not be undertaken unless there is no other possible course of action and the motive is of exceptional gravity."

transferred, then the couple should be in consultation with a competent Rabbi before proceeding.[31]

Intrauterine Insemination

Intrauterine insemination (IUI) is a couple's option for overcoming female fertility problems. Insemination with sperm from the husband is used to treat infertility from a variety of causes. IUI is the direct introduction of sperm into the uterus, bypassing the cervix and hostile cervical mucus. The goal is that this will bring the sperm closer to the egg and facilitate successful fertilization in the fallopian tube.

A semen sample is collected from the husband and transferred to the laboratory. As we pointed out in chapter 13, Rav Moshe Feinstein forbids obtaining a semen sample by self-stimulation. A man should obtain a sample by wearing a condom during regular intercourse.[32] If a couple lives too far from the fertility clinic to bring the sample within the hour,

---

31. Rabbi Yisroel Belsky holds that the halachah does not sanction reduction from quadruplets, unless there are extenuating circumstances that justify it. For additional Rabbinic literature on this topic, see Dr. Fred Rosner and Rabbi Moshe Tendler, *Practical Medical Halachah* (Hoboken, NJ: Ktav, 1990), pp. 35-37; Rabbi Yitzchak Zilberstein, "Induced Abortion for Multiple Fetuses," *Assiah,* vol. VIII, 1995; Rabbi Chaim David HaLevi, "Induced Abortion of Multiple Fetuses and the Status of Test Tube Babies," *Assiah,* vol. VIII, 1995, pp. 3-6; Rabbi Mordecai Eliyahu, *Techumin,* vol. XI, pp. 272-274; Rabbi Nachum Rabinowits, *Techumin,* vol. XVII, 1997, p. 340; Rabbi Yehoshua Ze'ev Zand, *Birkas haBanim,* chap. 12, sec. 41; "Pregnancy Reduction," in Rabbi J. David Bleich, *Bioethical Dilemmas* (Hoboken, NJ: Ktav, 1998), pp. 269-278; Prof. Avraham Steinberg, *Encyclopedia of Jewish Medical Ethics,* vol. II, pp. 92-99 (Hebrew) and vol. I, pp. 2-3 and vol. II, pp. 580-581 (English); Richard Grazi and Joel Wolowelsky, "Multiple Pregnancy Reduction and Disposal of Untransplanted Embryos in Contemporary Jewish Law and Ethics," *American Journal of Obstetrics and Gynecology* 65:5, Nov. 1991; Daniel Eisenberg, "Multifetal Pregnancy Reduction," http://www.aish.com/societyWork/sciencenature/Multifetal.

32. *Igros Moshe, Even haEzer,* vol. I, chaps. 70 and 71; vol. II, chap. 17; vol. III, chap. 14. See page 198 of this book for more discussion on the mat-

they would need to make other arrangements such as using a nearby hotel room.[33]

The condom, provided by the laboratory, is a special type for semen analysis which does not contain harmful chemicals that kill sperm and which is not made from latex. Some *poskim* rule that a small hole should be made in the condom prior to its use.[34]

If acquiring sperm though this method is impossible or not feasible, or if your doctor does not agree with this method, then consult your Rav.[35]

According to many Rabbis, insemination from the husband is only permitted if there is supervision to prevent the husband's sperm from being replaced or mixed with another man's sperm. (See page 374 ff.)

The two most common methods used to separate the best quality sperm are the swim-up and resuspension of sperm. The goal is to isolate live, healthy sperm (normal form and motility) from the semen. This creates a specimen that is free of all the extra components of semen such as hormones, prostaglandins, and certain kinds of proteins that are harmful to the uterus, causing it to contract. The seminal fluid can be toxic to the sperm, and once removed this increases fertility potential. Optimally, the woman should be inseminated with at least 5 million motile sperm, because lower numbers are sel-

---

ter. Another alternative is coitus interruptus, which is pulling out before ejaculation and depositing the sperm in a receptacle.

33. Ibid., vol. I, chap. 70; vol. III, chap. 14.

34. *Nishmas Avraham*, in the name of Rav S. Z. Auerbach and Rav Y.Y. Neuwirth, *Even haEzer* 1.

35. See *Achiezer*, vol. III, chap. 24:4. Rabbi David Cohen holds that if there is no other choice, a Rav may rely on this Achiezer for purposes of *Pru Urvu*.

dom associated with success.[36]

Inseminating 10 to 15 million sperm combined with ovulation induction resulted in the highest IUI pregnancy rates.[37] Combining two ejaculates obtained a few hours apart can increase the numbers of sperm available from men with low sperm counts.

Sperm washing and preparation for insemination should not be done on Shabbos. If it is anticipated that ovulation will

INTRAUTERINE INSEMINATION (IUI)

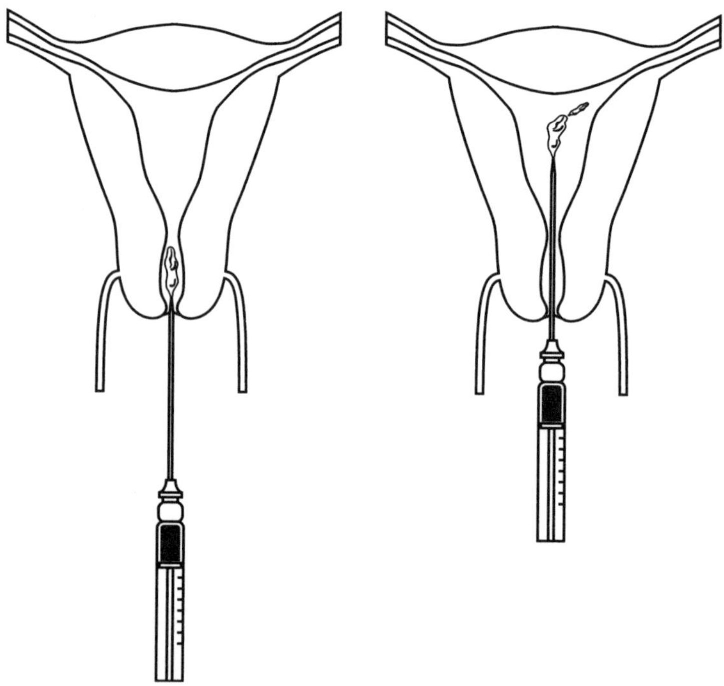

36. J.C. Nulsen, S. Walsh, S. Dumez, D.A. Metzger, "A Randomized Study of Intrauterine Insemination in the Treatment of Infertility," *Obstetrics and Gynecology* 82:780, 1993.

37. L.M. Chaffkin, J.C. Nulsen, A.A. Lucian, D.A. Metzger, "A Comparative Analysis of IUI Versus either HMG or IUI Alone," *Fertility and Sterility* 55:252, 1991.

occur on Shabbos, the sperm should not be inseminated on Shabbos, but on Friday (even twice) and if possible again on Saturday night. The sperm will stay active throughout Shabbos. Do not feel stress or pressure if a procedure cannot be done on Shabbos. Most procedures can be put off a day or manipulated to overcome this issue. In the United States and Europe most laboratories and clinics are closed on Sundays and in Israel on Saturdays.

The IUI procedure is performed in the doctor's office or clinic. A woman lies down on the examination bed and a speculum is inserted into the vagina. A slender, flexible, plastic catheter is inserted through the cervix and semen is released into the uterus. Insemination does not hurt, but can cause some minor cramping similar to taking a Pap Smear. The entire procedure takes only minutes and afterwards, the woman is asked to remain lying down for another twenty minutes. She does not become a *niddah* following this procedure.

IUI is most commonly timed for the day following the LH surge, measured in the urine, or at approximately thirty-six hours after an HCG injection. Some studies have shown increased pregnancy rates by doing two IUIs in a cycle, the morning after the HCG injection and then two mornings later. Some couples prefer the option of having one IUI on the day of the HCG injection followed by natural intercourse the next day.

If a woman ovulates before she completes her seven clean days prior to going to the *mikveh*, it is permissible to perform IUI. A child conceived at this time will not be considered as if he or she was conceived in impurity (*pagum/ben niddah*).[38] According to Rabbi Moshe Feinstein, she should not go to the

---

38. *Igros Moshe, Even haEzer*, vol. II, chap. 18; *Har Tzvi*, notes on the *Tur, Even haEzer*, chap. 1; haRav Minzburg, *Noam*, vol. I, 5718, pp. 145 –166;

mikveh before her regular time.[39]

Rabbi David Cohen reminds us that if a woman is inseminated during the seven clean days, she obviously needs to continue counting her seven clean days after the insemination; however, the insemination and the following 72 hours are considered an interruption (of *poletes shichvas zera*), and she can continue the counting only after the 72 hours and the remainder of that day.[40] For instance, if she was inseminated at noon on Sunday, which was the sixth day of her seven clean days, she would wait three full days (until Wednesday at noon), plus until sunset on Wednesday, to continue her counting. Thursday would then be her new sixth day (as the

---

Minchas Yitzchak, vol. I, chap. 50; *Tzitz Eliezer*, vol. IX, chap. 51, gate 4:66. See also *Divrei Malchiel*, vol. IV, chap. 107; Rav Y. Teitelbaum, the Satmar Rebbe, *haMaor* 16, Av-Elul 5724, for the opposite opinion. See also Prof. Avraham Steinberg, *Encyclopedia of Jewish Medical Ethics*, vol. I, pp. 152–153 (Hebrew) or vol. I, p. 72 (English); and *Assiah*, vol. V, 5746, pp. 112–124, for summaries of the different opinions.

39. *Igros Moshe*, ibid. See *Encyclopedia of Jewish Medical Ethics*, ibid., and notes ad loc., for a list of other opinions.

Rav Feinstein's view is a minority opinion. It is consistent with his stand that only illicit intercourse and not insemination causes a change in status to either the woman or the child (adultery, *mamzerus* or *ben niddah*). Therefore, the *mikveh* is not necessary, as the insemination will not result in the child being a *ben niddah*. He is even against a woman going to the *mikveh* prior to insemination, before the end of the seven clean days, for fear that the couple will have relations — mistakenly thinking that it is already permitted. Most *poskim* hold that she should go to the *mikveh* before the insemination, for at least she will not be *niddah d'Oraisa* (according to the Torah). According to Rabbis Y. Y. Neuwirth and David Cohen, many women want to go to the *mikveh* before the insemination, because they would rather be inseminated when they are not considered *niddah d'Oraisa*. It gives a woman a better feeling. Therefore, if a woman does go to the *mikveh* before the insemination, she and her husband need to be careful to follow all the laws of *niddah* and certainly not to have relations until after she goes to the *mikveh* the second time, at the end of her seven clean days.

40. *Shulchan Aruch, Yoreh De'ah* 196:11.

insemination invalidated her original sixth day), Friday would be her seventh day, and she would go to the *mikveh* on Friday night. Only from that point on would she be permitted to her husband.

For a woman with a short menstrual cycle who ovulates before her *mikveh* date, see pages 59–60 and the relevant footnotes.

One study of couples with unexplained infertility demonstrated a pregnancy rate per cycle of 2.7 percent with IUI alone and 6.1 percent with human gonadotropin therapy alone, but 26.4 percent when gonadotropin/IUI was used.[41]

Because sperm must find their own way into the fallopian tubes with IUI, this technique is not used if the woman has severe tubal damage or if the man has very poor sperm quality. Treatment would shift to assisted reproductive techniques (ART). The insemination procedure is usually tried for at least six cycles before attempting something new.

Artificial Insemination with Donor Sperm

Some couples may choose to receive sperm from an anonymous donor due to the husband's lack of sperm or some other intractable fertility problem. This is called *therapeutic donor insemination* (TDI) or *artificial insemination by donor* (AID). Frozen sperm is usually used, as it has been rigorously tested for HIV and other communicable and hereditary diseases. The American Society for Reproductive Medicine (ASRM) recommends that:

- The donor test negative for HIV before the sample is taken
- The sample be frozen for six months

---

41. P.F. Serhal, M. Katz , V. Little, H. Woronowski, "Unexplained Infertility — The Value of Pergonal Superovulation Combined with IUI," *Fertility and Sterility* 49:602, 1988.

- The donor retest negative for HIV before the sample is used

Most couples prefer to investigate the origins of the donor concerning age, ethnicity, religion, general health status, physical characteristics, and educational background. The woman is prepared for insemination by monitoring LH surges with or without the use of ovulation drugs, and IUI will be attempted once or twice per cycle.

Obviously, this procedure cannot be done without consultation with and a ruling from a Rav. See chapter 22 for a better understanding of the halachic and ethical implications of artificial insemination with donor sperm.

In Summary

Below are the treatment options for the following causes of female-factor infertility.

PCO:

- Lifestyle — weight loss
- Medical — progesterone challenge treatment
- Surgical — ovarian drilling

Hyperprolactinemia (elevated protein):

- Rule out pituitary tumor
- Rule out hypothyroidism
- Proceed to medical treatment i.e., Parlodel, Dopergin, Dostinex

Adrenal hyperactivity (common in women with PCO, elevated DHEAS):

- Medical treatment — Dexamethasone

Thyroid abnormalities:

- Eltroxin to raise thyroid levels
- Radioactive iodine to lower thyroid levels

In addition, ovulation induction is used to treat ovulatory deficiencies:

- Clomiphene citrate
  - — 50 to 250 mg for 5 to 7 days
  - — Diagnosis of ovulation (confirm LH surge)
  - — PCT, IUI, and estrogen for better quality cervical mucus and uterine lining
- Gonadotropin therapy
  - — Day 2 or 3 for 7 to 14 days
  - — Includes E2 (estradiol) blood assays and frequent ultrasounds
- Human gonadotropins
  - — HMG (75 IU FSH / 75 IU LH) (Pergonal, Humegon, Menogon, Menopur, Repronex)
  - — Purified FSH (75 IU) (Metrodin, Normegon, Orgafol, Fertinex, Metrodin HP)
  - — r-FSH (Purgeon, Gonal-F, Follistim)
  - — r-LH (Lhadi)
  - — HCG (Pregnyal, Profasi, A.P.L., Chorigon) (one shot to stimulate LH surge — 5000 or 10,000 IU)
  - — r-HCG (Ovidrel)

Goals of Care:

- Ovulation
- Fertilization
- Prevention of Ovarian Hyperstimulation Syndrome (OHSS)

MALE-FACTOR INFERTILITY: SPECIFIC TREATMENT OPTIONS

Medical and Surgical Intervention

In recent years there has been a great deal of progress in the treatment of male infertility. The range of treatment options currently available includes drug therapy, surgery, and assisted reproduction techniques (ART).

Nonsurgical treatment is often considered the least effective therapy for male infertility. In a few instances, after diagnosis of a particular cause of infertility, drug therapy may help. Infections of the male reproductive tract are diagnosed through cultures of semen, urine, and prostatic secretions (from the prostate). After processing the cultures in the laboratory, a man with positive results will be further tested for sensitivity to a particular antibiotic. Based on these results, antibiotics will be prescribed for three to six weeks for both husband and wife. The culture will be repeated several days after completion of the medication.

Hormone therapy is effective in fewer than 5 percent of infertile men. After ruling out pituitary tumors and performing a full range of blood tests, the following hormones can be given to supplement low levels of testosterone for the development of secondary sexual characteristics (lower voice, increase in body hair, broader shoulders), maintenance of libido (sex drive), and the promotion of sperm production (spermatogenesis). Treatment needs to continue for several months, with repeated blood tests and sperm analyses.

- **Depo-testosterone** induces the development of masculine physical traits and the strengthening of the sexual drive.
- **Gonadotropins FSH or HMG and HCG** by injection, or pulsatile administration of GnRH by pump encourages sperm production.[42] In another course of treatment, HCG was given for six months to bring serum testosterone to normal levels, then r-FSH was added for another eighteen months of treatment, which caused men who

---

42. C. Foresta, A. Bettella, "Use of Recombinant Human Follicle-Stimulating Hormone in the Treatment of Male-factor Sterility," *Fertility and Sterility* 77:2, 2002.

had no sperm due to hormonal deficiencies to produce sperm cells to the range of fertility in 63 percent of these men.[43]

- **Clomiphene citrate** 25 mg daily has also proven successful in elevating testosterone blood (serum) levels and increasing the amount of sperm in the semen, but it is doubtful whether this changes the fertility potential in these men.
- **Bromocriptine (Parlodel)** has been useful in treating hyperprolactinemia (too much prolactin hormone in the blood), which impairs sperm production and occasionally causes impotence.

Ejaculation disorders can be treated by changing the causative medication or with psychological counseling. Viagra has helped many men suffering from erectile dysfunction, and can be given under medical supervision. Retrograde ejaculation, where the sperm is directed into the bladder, can be treated in 25 percent of men with Sudafed 120 mg, three times daily.[44] Alternatively, sperm cells can be retrieved from the urine for IUI.

There are two approaches to treating men with *obstructive azoospermia* (no sperm in the ejaculate due to an anatomical obstruction). One is surgical correction of the obstruction, which may produce pregnancy spontaneously by intercourse. Alternatively, doctors can bypass surgical correction and proceed directly to assisted reproductive technology (ART). It is often preferable to intervene surgically, if possible, as restoration of natural fertility is still advantageous over ARTs. Some-

---

43. P. Bouloux, D. Warne, "Efficacy and Safety of Recombinant Human Follicle-Stimulating Hormone in Men with Isolated Hypogonadotropic Hypogonadism," *Fertility and Sterility* 76:6, 2001.

44. Cornell Institute for Reproductive Medicine, Specific Medical Treatments, 1997.

times, in choosing the "quick fix" we forget the downside of jumping prematurely to ARTs, as they:

- Bypass natural sperm selection in the woman's reproductive tract
- Have a lower overall pregnancy rate
- Have a high early pregnancy loss rate
- Increase perinatal mortality (due to prematurity, multiple gestation)
- Are very invasive, labor-intensive, and costly

According to the Male Infertility Best Practice Policy Committee commissioned by the American Urological Association, Inc., in 1998, assisted reproductive techniques are preferred to surgical treatment when:

- The female partner is advanced in age
- Female infertility factors requiring IVF are present
- The chance for success of sperm retrieval with IVF/ICSI exceeds the chance for success with surgical treatment
- The couple prefers sperm retrieval with IVF/ICSI[45] for financial reasons

Surgical therapy for male infertility aims at overcoming anatomical barriers impeding sperm production, maturation (in the testes and the epididymis), or ejaculation. Before microsurgery is performed on the man, his wife should be evaluated for female infertility factors. Microsurgical reconstruction of the reproductive tract is often successful in men with obstructive azoospermia. Vasectomy reversal (reconnecting the severed vas deferens) is effective in 70 to 95 percent of patients.[46] Using microsurgical techniques to treat obstruction of the epididymis caused by infection, trauma, or congenital fac-

---

45. See pp. 307 ff.

46. A.M.Belker, A.J. Thomas, "Results of 1,469 Microsurgical Vasectomy Reversals," *Journal of Urology* 145:505–11, 1991.

tors achieves pregnancies with intercourse in 20 to 40 percent of couples.[47]

How Is Surgery Performed?

Depending on the location of the obstruction, surgery will be performed through the scrotum or through the urethral opening of the penis. Microsurgical reconstruction of the vas deferens or the epididymis will be approached from a point slightly above the scrotum. Each testis is lifted through the surgical opening (in the scrotum) to ascertain the exact location of the obstruction. Your surgeon may also perform sperm retrieval for cryopreservation (freezing sperm for storage) at the time of microsurgery in order to avoid a second procedure in the event that the surgery is unsuccessful in restoring a normal sperm count.

This surgery is performed under general anesthesia or with an epidural, with a one or two-day hospital stay. Minor discomfort after surgery is to be expected and can be relieved with mild pain relievers. The success of microsurgery is fully assessed after one year. However, your doctor may want a sperm analysis two months postoperative.

Ejaculatory duct obstruction will be treated by performing a transurethral resection (TUR). The ejaculatory duct is reached through the penis (urethral opening). The procedure is done under general anesthesia. Often a foley catheter (tube to drain urine from the bladder) will be left in place for a few days to prevent retention of urine. Postoperative pregnancy rate with TUR is about 25 percent.[48]

Varicoceles are common, and are considered a major contributing factor to male infertility. Varicocele affects up to 15

---

47. Ibid.

48. *Best Practice Policies for Male Infertility*, American Urological Association, 1998.

percent of the male population, 35 percent of men with primary infertility, and up to 80 percent of men with secondary infertility. Only those varicoceles manually palpated are thought to require surgical intervention. Although some controversy continues to surround surgical treatment of varicoceles, a great deal of evidence exists to support this form of therapy.[49]

Repairing varicoceles (varicocelectomy) can be performed in three different ways:

- Open surgery — incision above the scrotum (either above or below the groin) or through the abdomen (retroperitoneal)
- Laparoscopy
- Percutaneous embolization (Sclerotherapy)

Open surgery is performed under general anesthesia using an operating microscope. This approach is favored by many surgeons because it enhances visualization of the veins, arteries, and lymph vessels, thereby protecting and preserving normal scrotal circulation. This reduces the risk of recurrence of varicocele. Surgery takes about one hour and can be performed as an ambulatory (outpatient) procedure with no overnight stay.

Laparoscopy is also performed under general anesthesia as an ambulatory procedure. Operative laparoscopes are passed through three 5 to10 mm incisions above the scrotum. One scope is used for visualization and the other two cut and close the effected vessels. Laparoscopy carries an increased risk of damage to the bowel, bladder, and major blood vessels.

Percutaneous Sclerotherapy requires a highly trained and experienced radiologist. Under local anesthesia, a long thin catheter is inserted through the spermatic vein by way of a

---

49. J.I. Gorelic, M. Goldstein, "Loss of Fertility in Men with Varicocele," *Fertility and Sterility* 59:613, 1993.

small incision on either side of the groin. Constant fluroscopic (X-ray) guidance is used to guide the catheter as it is threaded toward the effected vessel. A sclerosing agent (a type of permanent adhesive) is injected into the vein to occlude the varicocele. The catheter is then removed and a pressure dressing is applied to the groin, with discharge from the hospital possible after two hours.

In place of a sclerosing agent, occlusion of a varicocele can be accomplished by inserting a spring-coil through the catheter into the enlarged vein. This technique is also done on an outpatient basis, with rapid recovery at home.

The most common complications of varicocele surgery are the formation of a hydrocele (a fluid-filled, sac-like cavity) and the recurrence of the varicocele. Hydrocele occurs as the result of obstruction of the lymphatic vein in 5 percent to 7 percent of the time.[50] Fluid becomes trapped in the obstructed vein, making additional surgery necessary. However, the use of microscopic techniques has tremendously reduced the risk of hydrocele formation after varicocelectomy.[51]

The rate of recurrence of varicocele is the same in all three methods, but proportional to varicocele size.[52] The choice of which method of repair to use is based upon the severity and the location of the varicoceles.

The Specific Role of IUI in Male-Factor Fertility Treatment

Intrauterine insemination and assisted reproductive techniques will be considered for couples in whom infertility persists after medical or sur-

50. R. Szabo, R. Kessler, "Hydrocele Following Internal Spermatic Vein Ligation," *Journal of Urology* 132:924, 1984.

51. M.Goldstein, B.C. Gilbert, "Microsurgical Inguinal Varicocelectomy," *Journal of Urology* 148:1808, 1992.

52. M. Abdulmaaboud, A. Shokier, "Treatment of Varicocele: A Comparative Study," *Urology* 52:294–300, 1998.

gical intervention. IUI will be attempted with men whose sperm count or other parameters of sperm quality (mobility, morphology, or density) is subnormal. IUI in cases of male-factor infertility, with additional hormonal support for the woman to improve her fertility, is credited with a delivery rate of almost 35 percent.[53] (see page 292 ff for more details about IUI.)

If a man's sperm is not restored to the ejaculate after reconstructive surgery, or if repeated attempts at IUI have failed, the next step is in vitro fertilizaton (IVF) with micromanipulation (microscopic insertion of sperm into the egg). In chapter 20, we will discuss the woman's involvement in and preparation for IVF.

Moving On to Assisted Reproductive Techniques

In vitro fertilization promotes the meeting of sperm and egg when the usual process of fertilization is disrupted due to interference in the female or male reproductive tract. Women experiencing structural problems of the uterus, fallopian tubes, or cervix are suitable candidates for IVF. Additionally, those with intractable hormonal imbalances are also helped with all methods of ART (IVF is but one assisted reproductive technique).

The ISCI Hope for Male Infertility

Male-factor infertility was initially considered a contraindication to IVF because abnormal sperm are less likely to fertilize eggs than normal sperm. However, subsequent experience starting just a decade ago indicated that fertilization followed by live births were possible despite impaired sperm quality. Although IVF alone has had some success in cases of male-fac-

---

53. E. Rammer, F. Friedrich, "The Effectiveness of Intrauterine Insemination in Couples with Sterility Due to Male Infertility," *Fertility and Sterility* 69:31–35, 1998.

tor infertility, still even normal concentrations of sperm from oligospermic men (those with low sperm counts), placed directly alongside the eggs in the culture dish, do not fertilize at the same rates as sperm from men with normal sperm counts. Fortunately, the addition of ICSI to IVF has revolutionized fertility treatments for these couples.

Intracytoplasmic sperm injection (ICSI) is a *micromanipulation technique* in which fertilization is brought about by the injection of a single spermatozoon (sperm cell) into an unfertilized oocyte (egg). ICSI is performed with eggs obtained after ovarian stimulation (as in standard IVF) and has greatly improved the treatment of male infertility as a result of severe oligozoospermia (abnormally low sperm count). In men with azoospermia (no sperm in the ejaculate), sperm cells can often be located in the testicular tissue or the epididymis, and surgically retrieved for use in IVF/ICSI.

ISCI

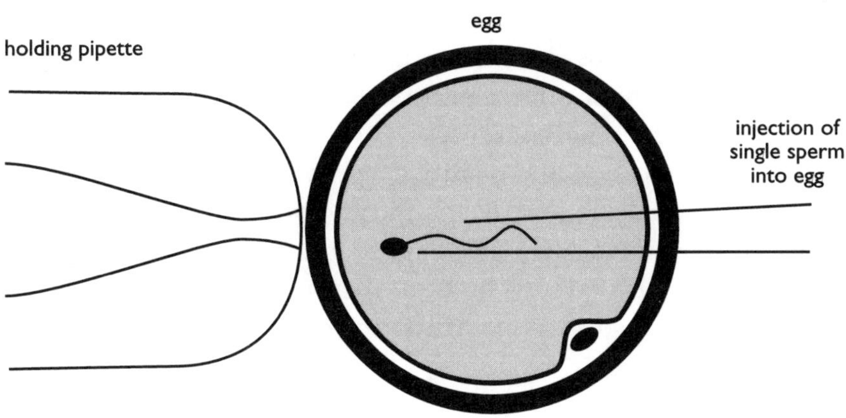

Sperm Retrieval

Micromanipulation technology has enabled the reproductive biologist to circumvent inefficient steps in the fertilization process. We will now discuss the various sperm retrieval techniques and their implications in treatment.

There exists a technique where the eggs themselves can be manipulated to facilitate easier penetration of the sperm into the oocyte by drilling an opening in the outer layer of the egg (*zona drilling* or *partial zona dissection* [PZD]) or by placing the sperm under the outer layer of the egg (*subzonal insertion of sperm* [SuZI]). The most successful form of microsurgical fertilization, however, is the microinjection of a single sperm into the oocyte. Intracytoplasmic sperm injection (ICSI) has superseded PZD and SuZI as the technique of choice because of the higher fertilization and pregnancy rates.

Men who have non-viable or no sperm in the ejaculate require their sperm to be located, withdrawn, and manipulated manually before fertilization can take place. Now that we have the technology of ICSI, fertilization can take place anywhere from 55 to 80 percent of the time, depending on the male-factor problem and the method of sperm retrieval.[54]

Surgical sperm retrieval is needed only in azoospermia. If there are even a few sperm cells in the semen, ICSI can be done without sperm retrieval.

The location and quality of spermatozoa must be tested by sperm analysis and testes biopsy prior to any attempts at sperm retrieval. The site of sperm retrieval affects sperm quality, and the quality of that sperm in turn may affect the chances for successful fertilization and cryopreservation of retrieved sperm.

---

54. G.D. Palermo, P.N. Schlegel, "Aggressive Sperm Immobilization Prior to ICSI," *Human Reproduction* 11:1023–1029, 1996.

The goals of surgical sperm retrieval are:

- To obtain the best quality sperm possible
- To retrieve an adequate number of sperm for both immediate use (fresh) and for cryopreservation (frozen)
- To minimize damage to the testicles so as not to jeopardize testicular function, future attempts at sperm retrieval, or surgical reconstruction.

Sperm Retrieval Techniques

◆ **Testicular fine needle aspiration (TEFNA).** This procedure is similar to other fine needle aspiration samples (FNA) where a tissue sample is taken from various parts of the body for diagnostic testing of cysts or tumors. Sperm retrieval is routinely possible with TEFNA for men with obstructive azoospermia. Using local anesthesia, this procedure can be performed in the doctor's office. There is little postoperative discomfort. This method is not an optimal diagnostic tool and can result in occasional hematoceles and hematomas (blood blisters and blood clots), requiring further medical attention.

◆ **Percutaneous epididymal sperm aspiration (PESA).** This is a non-microsurgical technique that can be performed under local or general anesthesia, and is considered a relatively easy and low-cost procedure for extracting sperm from the epididymis in men with obstructive azoospermia. A small needle attached to a syringe is inserted by the surgeon through the scrotum and into the epididymis. This is repeated until adequate numbers of sperm are retrieved.

The downside of PESA is that only small amounts of sperm are usually recovered and they are often contaminated with blood cells, which impair sperm function. Sperm are washed, rinsed, and processed using special biological medium. Upon successful retrieval, a pregnancy rate of 24 to 28 percent has been achieved using PESA with IVF/ICSI.[55] For the 10 to 20 percent of attempts where sperm are not retrieved with PESA, percutaneous testicular aspiration is possible (see below).

◆ **Percutaneous biopsy of the testis (PercBiopsy).** A step further than PESA, percutaneous sperm aspiration from the testis yields a higher amount of sperm in a man with obstructive azoospermia. Under local anesthesia, a small amount of testicular tissue is removed from which sperm can be retrieved and used in ICSI/IVF. Though the postoperative discomfort and expense is less in this procedure than in microsurgical techniques, more damage can be caused to the testicular tissue and relatively poor quality and low numbers of sperm are retrieved per aspiration when compared to microsurgical aspiration.[56]

◆ **Testicular sperm extraction (TESE).** Testicular sperm extraction is an effective method for sperm retrieval for ICSI from men with non-obstructive azoospermia. The safest way to perform TESE is by using an operative microscope in order to avoid both harming blood vessels of the testes and the need to excise larger amounts of testicular tissue, which can cause permanent damage to the testes.

Under local or general anesthesia, an incision is made in the scrotum and the testis is exposed. Avoiding any blood vessels, testicular tissue is viewed under the microscope and 2 to 3 mm patches of tissue are removed. The sample is usually evaluated for the number and quality of sperm in the operating room. Additional samples are taken if necessary. Further

---

55. G.J. Matthews, M. Goldstein, "Amplified Methods of Epididymal Sperm Aspiration," *Urology* 47: 123–125, 1996.

56. S. Fiedler, A. Raziel, "Testicular Sperm Extraction by Percutaneous Fine Needle Aspiration Compared with Testicular Sperm Extraction by Open Biopsy," *Human Reproduction* 12:1488–1493, 1997.

processing of testicular tissue and sperm is performed in the IVF laboratory. The scrotal incisions are then sutured with dissolvable sutures and a sterile dressing. Oral pain relief (acetominophen or acetominophen with codeine) can be prescribed.

Repeat TESE procedures must be delayed for at least six months. Sperm is found in 58 percent of men attempting retrieval cycles with testicular sperm. Subsequently, for all couples attempting sperm retrieval, including cases where no sperm were available for injection, the overall ongoing delivery rate was 23 percent.[57]

◆ **Microsurgical epididymal sperm aspiration [MESA]** (microsurgical retrieval of epididymal sperm). Using MESA with IVF/ICSI appears to maximize the chances of pregnancy for infertile couples whose male partner has unreconstructable reproductive tract obstruction.[58] This means that both men who have obstructive azoospermia that cannot be successfully resolved with surgery and men who have non-obstructive azoospermia can equally benefit from MESA. Sperm retrieval with MESA necessitates only a single retrieval procedure and typically results in retrieval of over 100 million motile sperm to reliably freeze five to ten samples of sperm or more.

With local or general anesthesia, an incision is made in the scrotum and the testes are opened to expose the epididymis. Using an operating microscope, the epididymis is inspected and delicately punctured. Epididymal fluid is gently aspirated by the surgeon and is immediately examined by the IVF team

57. P.N. Schlegel, "Testicular Sperm Extraction: Microdissection Improves Sperm Yield with Minimal Tissue Excision," *Human Reproduction* 14:131–135, 1999.

58. W. Watkins, F. Nieto, "Testicular and Epididymal Sperm in a Microinjection Program: Methods of Retrieval and Results," *Fertility and Sterility* 67:527, 1997.

in the operating room. Sequential punctures can be made, if necessary, until optimal sperm quality is obtained.

Because sperm in the epidiymal fluid are highly concentrated, only microliters of epididymal fluid are needed to be retrieved. In this way, MESA provides adequate numbers of sperm for immediate use with ICSI, as well as for cryopreservation for future use.

The puncture sites are sutured closed and a sterile dressing is applied. Analgesics are given for discomfort. Pregnancy rates for MESA with IVF/ICSI are as high as 52 percent.[59]

Every effort is made to time sperm retrieval with ovulation induction and egg retrieval in the woman. Fresh sperm is preferred for use in IVF/ICSI. However, successful sperm cryopreservation (storage in subfreezing temperatures) allows the opportunity for multiple ICSI cycles without the need for additional sperm retrieval procedures. Forty to fifty percent of spermatozoa remain viable after cryopreservation. This is true for ejaculated spermatozoa as well as for testicular and epididymal spermatozoa after freeze-thaw. Since ICSI enables even severely impaired sperm to fertilize, as long as sperm are viable, cryopreserved sperm can achieve rates of fertilization and pregnancy similar to fresh sperm.[60]

In Summary

The following are the male-factor infertility treatment options:

- Medical: antibiotics, hormones, Viagra
- Surgical: microsurgical reconstruction, repair of varicoceles

---

59. Ibid.

60. N.E. Bachtell, J. Conaghan, "The Relative Viability of Human Spermatozoa from the Vas Deferens, Epididymis and Testis before and after Cryopreservation," *Human Reproduction* 14:3048 –3051, 1999.

- IUI
- Biopsy and sperm retrieval for use with Assisted Reproductive Technologies: ICSI / IVF

Goals of Care:

- Treat existing infections
- Supplement low hormone level
- Treat physical symptoms of sexual dysfunction
- Surgically repair structural problems
- Supply sperm for IVF / ICSI

18.
They Mean Well: Dealing with Your Social Circles

In You, O Lord, have I taken refuge, let me never be ashamed; in Your righteousness rescue me. Incline to me Your ear, speedily deliver me; be to me a stronghold rock, a fortress to save me. For my rock and my stronghold are You, and for the sake of Your Name guide me and lead me.

(*Tehillim* 31:1–4)

INTRODUCTION

LIVING UP TO SOCIETY'S expectations can always cause anxiety, and feeling the pressure to fulfill the hopes of one's family can be even more stressful. Our whole lives are plagued with that burden. From a very young age, children want to "fit in." As schoolchildren, they want to be an accepted part of the class, their small society. For a boy, this might mean being good in sports or funny in class. For girl, this might mean dressing fashionably and being popular. At the same time, children try to please their parents by doing well academically and in their religious duties. As they mature, they look at what their society values, whether it's diligence in Torah studies, a nice family, monetary success, or social standing. Failing in one of these areas generates a feeling of inadequacy and humiliation.

Some women may feel an element of shame because they are childless. In fact, when our matriarch Rachel finally gave birth to Yosef, the Torah says, "She became pregnant and gave birth to a son. She said, 'God has hidden away my disgrace.'"[1] Is that the most significant blessing that her new son brought? Did she view God's gift as mainly taking away her disgrace? Apparently, for some women, the shame of being barren is so great that it becomes the overwhelming sentiment.

Chanah responded in an even stronger way. In the prayer that she says after giving birth to Shemuel, Chanah uses some extreme images: "And Chanah then prayed and said, 'My mouth is opened wide over my enemies, for I rejoiced in Your salvation.... Do not speak excessively [with] high [and] haughty words; do not let harsh words leave your mouths.... The bows of the mighty are crushed, but those who stumbled were strengthened. Those who were satiated are [now] hired out [for their bread]; and those who [were] hungry have ceased [to toil]. While the barren woman bore seven, she who [had] many children is [now] desolate. The Lord causes death and creates life; He lowers to the grave and raises up.'"[2]

Chanah's prayer sounds like the victory song of an army after a bitter war. Yet this is the prayer of the woman who taught the Jewish People how to pray.[3] There is barely mention of her own happiness in becoming a mother. It seems that her hostility toward her rival Peninah outweighed her happiness in becoming a mother. This attitude of Chanah doesn't sound virtuous. We would think that a righteous woman would just be happy with her own success and blessings, and wouldn't compare herself to others. She wouldn't see her blessing as retaliation. Was Chanah so humiliated by her childless state that victory was the overwhelming sentiment she felt when she finally had a child?

---

1. *Bereishis* 30:23.
2. *I Shemuel* 2:1–6.
3. *Shabbos* 31a.

This attitude is normal, and is representative of many barren women. If you feel humiliation in being childless, if you feel that having a child will contain an aspect of victory over your enemies, then realize that so did the righteous Chanah.[4] The Midrash also testifies that barren women are "prisoners in their homes," for they are too ashamed to go out.[5] Therapist Alice Domar tells of a scenario where hearing of a friend's pregnancy may cause a barren woman to not want to walk outside.[6] Even Sarah's response after Yitzchak was born related to how the birth would be viewed by society: "And Sarah said, 'God has caused me happiness; whoever hears [about it] will rejoice for me.'"[7] So to ignore the effect that society has on the childless couple would be to ignore a major element of the sorrow of infertility.

It is difficult to live in a society that expects you to have children, especially when you yourself also sincerely desire to be a parent. Many childless couples have trouble fitting in. All their social groups seem to be involved in activities that revolve around children. Pregnancies and childbirth experiences dominate women's conversations during the childbearing years. To the childless woman, every other woman seems to be pregnant, about to be pregnant, or immediately postpartum. If you live in a religious community, this is not just perception but might very well be the reality. Becoming pregnant and starting a family is a natural progression. It's like going up a grade in school. If you don't have children after a certain stage in life, it feels like you "stayed back."

The Talmud has a statement about an unmarried woman which is applicable to the barren woman as well. It says that

---

4. See *I Shemuel* 2:1–10.
5. *Bereishis Rabbah* 71:1.
6. *Conquering Infertility*, p. 12.
7. *Bereishis* 21:6.

an unmarried woman feels inadequate among other women, but if she marries even a pauper, she can sit among the aristocrats.[8] The same thing can be said about an infertile woman. Until she has a child, she doesn't feel comfortable among other women. Men also feel uncomfortable in many social and family settings, including the synagogue. It is difficult for a man to see the men in his *minyan* sitting and teaching their children every Shabbos. Men are luckier, though, because they can more easily hide behind Torah learning, work, sports, and other activities. It is much more difficult for women.

REMARKS ABOUT YOUR INFERTILITY

If remarks about your infertility hurt you, you are not alone. Common causes of burning anger and hurt are the verbally expressed observations about our barrenness from family, friends, and neighbors. From our own parents and siblings to strangers we meet in the grocery store, we are exposed to offensive, insensitive remarks. The Midrash tells us of the insensitivity that Sarah endured from other women who used to mock her, calling her "the barren one."[9] Although most people probably don't come into contact with too many malicious remarks such as that, they still are hurt by people's pointless, senseless comments.

Childless couples will agree that the inquiries and unsolicited advice from others concerning their infertility problem

---

8. "Abaye said: '[Even] if a woman has a husband as short as an ant, she places her seat among the great.' Rav Papa said: 'Though her husband be a flax-beater [i.e. in a very humble occupation], she calls him to the threshold and sits down at his side [i.e. she is proud of him despite his lowly social status].' Rav Ashi said: 'If her husband is only a cabbage head [i.e. dull or ugly], she requires no lentils for her pot [i.e. she doesn't need anything else, as she has a husband]'" (*Yevamos* 118b).

9. *Bereishis Rabbah* 47:2; see also *Midrash Tanchuma, Vayera* 17.

make an immense hardship much, much worse.

Acrimonious remarks emerge in an array of onslaughts. Whether direct coercion, such as "Make me a grandparent already," or inappropriate references to your intimate life, or the well-meaning "Soon by you" blessing, all such statements hurt. Indirect assaults on our already fragile spirit can injure just the same. Hearing someone brag about her baby's first steps, or her child's winning a prize, or her toddler's wonderfully cute pearls of wisdom, can be like having salt poured on an open wound. Most people don't mean anything by innocent remarks such as, "I've got to go home and check on my kids," or "My kids are such a handful," but they can still send you off crying. Sometimes you will be confronted with remarks from strangers who might say things like, "How many children do you have?" or, "Who is watching your kids?"

In this section we will discuss how to judge these people favorably and how to respond to both direct attacks and innocent statements that remind us of our infertility. Most of the suggestions included in this chapter were compiled from what childless couples told us. Some were taken from other books on infertility.

JUDGING OTHERS FAVORABLY

According to *Chazal*, the verse, "With justice you should judge your friend,"[10] means that we should judge others favorably.[11] The accomplishment of fulfilling this mitzvah reaps benefits for us in both this world and the World to Come. The word "accomplishment" is used here, because judging others favorably is often a very difficult mitzvah to fulfill. When one judges others favorably it is indeed an accomplishment. Judg-

---

10. *Vayikra* 19:15.
11. *Shevuos* 30a.

ing the insensitive, fertile world favorably is a triumph that will bring you reward in the World to Come and make living in this world more tolerable and even pleasant.

By judging others favorably you will see the world more positively. This will give you a better feeling about your surroundings and, more important, about yourself.

Earning God's Favor

How does one earn God's favor? The Chafetz Chaim assures us that the way for us to be judged favorably by God is by judging others favorably.[12] This can be the most effective method to awaken God's mercy for us and to grant us our deepest wishes.

There is nothing we want more than to be seen favorably by God. Nobody is perfect. Just as we have shortcomings and hope that God will, as it were, overlook our faults and focus on our good qualities, so too we should excuse the faults of others and concentrate on their positive side. Hopfully, this will cause God to look at us auspiciously. Most of us are very good at explaining away the downsides of our personalities and our negative behavioral patterns. If we can be as generous with rationalizing the dispositions and conduct of others, we would be happier people, and it would be a better world.

Of course, this is easier said than done. How can we start looking at the fertile world with good will?

We Are All Insensitive Sometimes

When judging others favorably, first of all think about yourself. Have you ever hurt someone unintentionally with a comment you said without thinking? There are many people who are sensitive about aspects of their appearance or situation that may seem trivial to you. For instance, many redheaded children hate being associated with the color of their hair. They hate being called "red," or "carrot top," or "jinji." They detest

---

12. *Shemiras HaLashon, Sha'ar haTevunah,* chap. 4.

hearing about someone's uncle having the same color hair as theirs. They endure insensitive comments from people who are basically nice but just want to be cute or make conversation. Have we fallen into the trap of making someone's hair color, freckles, or other external quality a topic of an innocent little remark? Did we ever "kid" anyone about something they would like to ignore? If we did, we surely found a way to forgive ourselves. We told ourselves that we didn't realize that it was inappropriate, or that we were just joking, or he should be proud, etc.

Singles in their late 20's and up generally detest hearing the same, "So *nuuuuuu*," or "When are we going to hear good news?" or the eternally popular knife in the heart, "Soon by you." Think: Have we ever made comments of this type to someone? If we have, then we should think that just as we do not hold ourselves in contempt, we should not discredit someone else for committing the same "crime."

At his nephew's bar mitzvah, Howard, who is almost forty, good-looking, and with a successful business, was harassed about his non-marital status by practically everyone who said hello to him. Why do people do this? He knows he isn't married. He realizes that he has been out with half the unmarried women in the Tri-state area and is still single. What is another remark about it going to help? People need to realize that their comments are not going to get Howard married faster. But everyone who said something to him surely didn't think they were saying anything wrong. They were just careless in their thoughts, careless in their speech.

Creative Positive Thoughts

In order to successfully judge others favorably, you must accept that all people have character flaws. You should spend some time thinking of how you can excuse the slights of family members and acquaintances. You may want to sit with your spouse and come up with some creative good thoughts about those who are insensitive to your condition. It might be fun. Here are two, just to get you started.

> "This person is basically a nice person, but just doesn't realize how much these statements hurt. I am sure that if someone pointed out to him that making such statements is hurtful, he wouldn't do it. He is simply unaware."

> "This person unfortunately doesn't understand basic *derech eretz*. I feel sorry for him. He is lacking tact and good sense, *nebbach*. I pray that one day he will realize this."

By thinking in this manner we will not see people who hurt us in such a negative light. We must realize that most people don't understand the delicate nature of being childless. The good feeling that you will get by knowing that you accomplished the difficult mitzvah of judging people favorably may partially compensate for the hurt. Furthermore, when you minimize your expectations of others, you will not feel so disappointed when they don't act as you would like them to.

VERBAL RESPONSES

When confronted with insensitivity, how should you respond? There are times when you will want to be silent and ignore the remark. There are times when you will want to give a half-smile and pretend that you appreciate the remark. There are times you will probably want to speak with your fists rather than respond verbally. Or sometimes you may want to say something that cuts like a knife as well. And yet there are times you may want to actually discuss the issue.

The Gemara says, "One should always be the insulted and not the insulter."[13] This doesn't mean that you should look for

---

13. *Shabbos* 84b and *Yoma* 23a.

people to insult you. It means that it is much better to be insulted, or to be oppressed, than to be either the insulter or the oppressor. It is preferable to hold back your sting. This isn't always easy.

Take care of yourself. You cannot teach the whole world ethics or about the tender condition of childless couples. You must be concerned primarily about protecting yourself from hurt. Don't begin a crusade to teach the world what childless couples go through, by responding when someone says something insensitive. If you do decide to respond, say something that will make you feel better, as long as you don't hurt anyone else or make matters worse. On the verse, "You shall rebuke your neighbor, and you shall not bear sin because of him,"[14] Rashi teaches us that "You shall not bear sin because of him" means that you should not sin by embarrassing him.[15] So when someone does something wrong, you can rebuke him as long as you don't embarrass him. There are three conditions for rebuking someone, as we learn from the Rambam: (1) Do not embarrass him, so speak in private; (2) speak in a soft voice; and (3) make sure he is aware that you are rebuking him for his benefit.[16]

When it is appropriate to say something, what should be said? It depends. If it is a person close to you, such as family, or a person whom you see on a regular basis, such as at work, you should probably just be straight with him or her and say something like, "It hurts me when you talk about my infertility. It is a sensitive subject and my spouse and I are dealing with it."

---

14. *Vayikra* 19:17.

15. Rashi, ibid.

16. Yehudah Morial, *Bederech Tovim,* in the name of the Rambam (Jerusalem: Education Department of the World Zionist Organization, 1985), p. 135.

Another option is to write the offending party a letter. One couple we know wrote to the husband's parents explaining how they felt when they came for a family Shabbos and were surrounded by all their nieces and nephews. The parents were totally unaware of how devastating that was to the couple, and have since became much more sensitive to the childless couple's needs. They also thanked them for explaining their situation in such a calm and respectful manner.

If the relationship with the person is more casual, then you may want to just forget it, and refer to your own personal "judge your friend favorably" manual. If you feel that you should say something, then you will need to be straightforward. Let them understand that it is a painful subject and you don't want them to refer to it.

Responding to Indirect Reminders

It is difficult to respond to indirect reminders of infertility. What can you say when someone brags about their child's charm, intelligence, etc., or tells you all about the activities they do with their children? They probably aren't even thinking about the fact that you don't have children.

There probably isn't much you can say. If it isn't too uncomfortable, and the person is an open-minded, sensitive, understanding type, then maybe you can open up and explain that it is painful for you to hear constant references to their children when you are trying so hard to have children yourself. Some people, even the open-minded ones, may find this hard to understand, but others will endeavor to be more sensitive in the future.

Responding to Complaints about Kids

Hearing people complain about their children can be annoying. "That kid doesn't give me a night of sleep." "This kid is such a handful." "These kids always want something."

You will surely think: "What a lack of appreciation! God

gave these people such a blessing, and they complain about trivial problems like being up with them all night!" You could say something like, "I would be so happy to have your problems." Perhaps it will make them realize how they sound. But again, you don't have to be their mentor, so you don't have to say anything.

In general, you may want to discuss with your other childless friends what responses they found to be helpful, although most of the time you will just not want to respond. What you mostly need is common sense. The only rule is not to embarrass or hurt others. The rest is up to you. What is most important is to judge others favorably and to protect yourself from being hurt.

THE WORK PLACE

Should a woman inform her employer about her fertility treatments? On one hand, maybe she should because otherwise her boss won't understand why she needs to take so much time off from work. On the other hand, perhaps exposing the problem may make her boss nervous about her taking off too much time, and therefore he or she might want a more "reliable" employee. Or maybe a woman simply doesn't want other people, including her employer, to know her personal business.

Only the woman herself can answer the question of whether to tell her boss, but perhaps there is at least a little bit of comfort knowing that most women going through fertility treatments face this dilemma.

LIVING IN A RELIGIOUS ENVIRONMENT

Is being religious an added hardship to infertility? In a way, it can be, for there is added stress in living in a society which values large families.

Not only religious society, but secular society as well, expects couples to start families. They just expect smaller ones! But there is pressure to have children. Even non-Jewish, career-oriented women claim that there is powerful pressure to start a family. However, in a non-religious society there are shields that one can hide behind for a few years. Career, education, financial considerations, or lack of readiness are common reasons for delaying starting a family in the secular world. They protect a woman from everyone's pity and probing for a few years.

In a non-religious society, if a woman does not have a baby right away, people assume that it's her choice. She can wear the mask of the career woman and nobody will suspect a problem. In the religious world this luxury does not exist. Because of the mitzvah to "be fruitful and multiply," one is expected to be pregnant within the first year of marriage.

Other factors that add strain are the constant little "reminders" running around you all the time. In a religious neighborhood there are children wherever you go. They are your next-door neighbors, they are playing on the street, they are being pushed in baby strollers at the supermarket, they are sitting in your row in shul. You cannot get away from other people's children.

We opened this chapter with the theory that the shame of infertility is a major cause of the suffering. It is obvious, therefore, that in a society where the "shame" is so self-evident, the over-stress will be that much greater.

VESAMACHTA B'CHAGECHA: DEALING WITH STRESSFUL TIMES

Special Events and Occasions

There are times when being childless is more difficult than others, such as your nieces' and nephews' birthday parties or

Semachos such as piano recitals, and kindergarten graduations. A *bris* especially can bring on relentless stress. Some people take it in stride and don't mind it, but others suffer great pain, for being in the presence of something that you want so badly and cannot have, only reinforces your hurt. What should you do? There is no universal answer. There are some "*simchah* events" that you will want to attend, some that you will feel obligated to attend even though you would rather not be there, and others that will cause so much pain that you may simply decide to miss them for your own peace of mind.

You are faced with a dilemma: if you go to these events, then you might be doing yourself a disservice. However, if you don't attend, then you may find it unpleasant making up excuses or — if you tell the truth — exposing your inner feelings. You might not want to do this. You also run the risk of your family or friends thinking you are jealous. Or they may begin to pity you, something you don't want either. They may not be able to understand the pain a childless couple goes through. If you refrain from attending these affairs too many times, then your reclusive lifestyle may possibly intensify your isolation.

Uncomfortable feelings toward these events are perfectly normal and reasonable. Don't give yourself added stress by feeling guilty for having these feelings. Don't torture youself with thoughts of, "Maybe I am not a good person; maybe I am too jealous. Why can't I be happy for someone else? (See chapter 23 for more information on envy.)

Nobody can give you advice as to which affairs you should attend and which ones you should miss; you will have to find the balance that is right for you. You will attend some and stay away from others. Single adults go through similar uncomfortable situations. They may find it unpleasant to visit friends who have already established families. Don't feel bad for missing some affairs, and don't feel bad for attending others while hating to be there.

Holidays

Holidays can be a time of sadness instead of *zeman simchaseinu,* "the time of our rejoicing." Almost every holiday revolves around children, and therefore holidays can be painful reminders of what you don't have but yearn for.

- **Pesach:** *Vehigadeta le-vincha.* Everything at the Pesach Seder is done in order to encourage the kids to ask questions. It is hard reading about the four sons, when you don't even have one. It can be especially hard if you are invited to your brother's house for Seder, and everyone, including your parents, is charmed with your nephews' and nieces' recital of the Four Questions.
- **Chanukah** is a joyful holiday for children. You may feel very lonely lighting your Chanukah lights all alone, with no children to give presents or "Chanukah gelt" to.
- **Purim:** We do not need to elaborate on the pain that seeing other people's children frolicking in their costumes brings to the childless couple.
- **Simchas Torah** can be the most stressful holiday of all. There are men who just aren't able to bear the sight of their peers dancing with their children on their shoulders, waving flags and holding little Torah scrolls. Men have admitted going home from *hakafos* crying, not being able to go back to shul.

  If you find Simchas Torah uncomfortable, then the best thing may be to attend only a limited part of the services. The *hakafos* are an important tradition, but their purpose is to bring happiness, not discomfort or sorrow. If you quietly walk out of shul during the *hakafos*, no one will notice. You don't have to withstand that pain.

Social and Religious Functions

Sometimes just going to shul can be distressing, as all the men are sitting next to their children, learning with them, showing them the place in the *siddur*, and bringing them over to kiss the Torah. You can't stop attending shul, but the difficulty you experience is understandable. Maybe you can find a shul with fewer children if that will make it easier for you.

You can't stop participating in everything, but you can minimize the pain by being selective about which functions, religious or social, that you attend. Don't try to be extra pious by attending everything as if there is no hurt, telling yourself that you must put those feelings aside and pretend that they aren't there. Just like someone on a diet shouldn't fill his kitchen with appetizing temptations, so too the childless couple shouldn't surround themselves with children at all times.

If it is financially feasible for you, you may even want to go away for the holidays. Go to a place where kids are not the main attraction. Even if this will not be viewed positively by the rest of your family, you must think of yourselves first. The best way to serve God on the holidays is to be happy and to make others happy. You must put yourself in the right circumstances to achieve this.

There are of course couples who may not be negatively affected by the holidays and the presence of so many children. They may enjoy being around their nieces and nephews on the holidays without suffering pain.

It could also happen that one year you may enjoy family gatherings and one year you may not. It is important that you and your spouse discuss this matter before each holiday, and be sensitive to each other's needs and feelings. With family relationships it can get complicated, as "family politics" come into play. You will have to weigh this constantly. Sometimes you will conclude that it will be more uncomfortable not attending certain family gatherings.

Chazal tell us that one who gives charity will become rich. The reason he will become rich is because if he has enough to give others, then he won't feel like he needs more. So make yourself happy by making others happy. Make your holidays special by inviting others, less fortunate than you, to your table. Invite people without any family — the elderly, singles, students, etc. If you bring others, who need to be in a nice home environment, into your home, then you will feel good about your holiday, for you will be making others happy.

FRIENDS

There is a famous Talmudic adage, *O-chavrusa, o-misusa,* which means "If I don't have a friend, I'd rather die."[17] This describes everybody's situation: If you don't have people to whom you can relate, it is too difficult to get through life. We all need people who understand us and our perspective. We need people to whom we don't have to explain the ABCs of how we are feeling and what is going through our mind. For instance, senior citizens need to be around people their age. This is many times more important to them than being constantly around their children and grandchildren. People going through infertility need the same kind of support.

You will need a sympathetic and understanding person to whom you can speak about your infertility — a parent, a sibling, or a good friend. She can be a mother or a childless woman. She should be patient, and sensitive to your situation.

Most men don't want this kind of support — at least they

---

17. *Ta'anis* 23a.

don't admit that they do. But a man too can benefit greatly from having a good friend with whom he can share his feelings about being childless.

Support groups comprised of other infertile couples can be of great benefit as well. It is important to share experiences and feelings, the type that only others who are experiencing them will be able to understand. This will help you realize that you are not alone, and help make it easier for you to clarify and accept your feelings. Another benefit of an infertility support group is that participants share ideas, recommend doctors, and apprise others of new treatments.

There is a certain "danger" for a woman in becoming very close to another childless woman, because one of you might become pregnant before the other. This can cause pain to the one left behind. And the other will feel guilty for leaving her good friend.

You will have to find the right support group for you and the right friendships that will be comfortable in every situation. A supportive environment is crucial for everyone going through the infertility experience.

19.

Sensitivity Advice for Family, Friends, and Neighbors

And she provoked her to make her cry out.
(*I Shemuel* 1:6)

If you care about the good of your friend,
learn about what is good for him.
(*Pirkei Avos d'Rabbi Eliezer* 1)

INTRODUCTION

THIS CHAPTER IS MEANT, not for the childless couple, but for those who are close to the couple — parents, parents-in-law, siblings, neighbors, relatives, friends, and co-workers. By being in contact with a childless couple you are in a sensitive situation. The way you act and the comments you make can have an immense effect on the couple. Being totally unaware of it, you may say something that will send them off crying the whole night long. Our Sages teach that the effect our words and deeds have on our fellowman is something for which we will all be held accountable.

Even if you didn't mean to hurt anybody, but someone felt bad because of something you said or did, you will be held responsible. The Gemara says that if a person spits on the floor and someone else is disgusted by that action, the spitter will have to give an accounting.[1] Even though when the person spit on the floor he wasn't even thinking about the repercus-

1. *Chagigah* 5a.

sions of his act, he will still have account for it, as he should have been more sensitive to his surroundings.

There are people who "spit" insensitive remarks in the presence of a childless couple, not necessarily to be hurtful, but without thought behind their words. Sometimes they are the people who care the most about them, such as their parents. During one family get-together, an unmarried daughter told her father she didn't want to get married yet. In the presence of his childless son and daughter-in-law he replied, "You have to get married soon! I want grandchildren!" The son and daughter-in-law felt like their whole lives were just one big disappointment to their parents.[2]

The pressure of weighing all your words and deeds might make you feel as if you are "walking on eggs." And it's hard to be close to someone with whom you can't be spontaneous. So how do you act? It really isn't so hard. Just treat the childless couple normally, and use your common sense. This chapter will give you some guidelines.

When you come into contact with childless couples, don't constantly talk about your own pride and joy, your children. Don't carry on about their cute remarks, don't brag about their accomplishments, and certainly don't stick your nose into the childless couple's business by inquiring about the progress of their family. First of all, it is none of your business. Second, you must realize that there is probably nothing you can say that will help. They are aware of their predicament. Think about it. When you say something like, "So *nuuuuu*," what do you expect? Do you think that you are waking them up? Don't tell them that you are praying for them, and don't say anything that will imply that you feel sorry for them. They don't want to be pitied.

---

2. From Karen Bradstreet, *Overcoming Infertility Naturally* (Utah: Woodland Books, 1995), p. 84.

YAAKOV AND PENINAH

In the two principal stories in the Tanach about infertility, Rachel's and Chanah's, *Chazal* point out the punishment of those who hurt the childless woman with their remarks. When Rachel complained to Yaakov about being barren, he snapped at her, "Am I a substitute for God, Who has deprived you of offspring?"[3] *Chazal* take issue with Yaakov. "Is that the way to speak to the suffering?" they ask. "Therefore, your children will bow down to her children."[4]

Rachel came to Yaakov with an irrational charge by saying, "Give me children." So although Yaakov's response might have been correct from a logical perspective, what he said was still hurtful. That is why he was punished. Even Yaakov — who loved Rachel, who was provoked by Rachel, and who merely answered her with a rhetorical question — was punished; imagine how severe the punishment would be for making even more hurtful comments.

Hurtful remarks of this kind are hinted at in the Prophets as well, as an even more serious crime was committed against Chanah by her co-wife (*tzarah*) Peninah. The verse says, "Her *tzarah* [Peninah] repeatedly provoked her [Chanah] to make her cry out [feel bad], because the Lord had closed up her womb. And...every year, when [Chanah] went up to the house of the Lord, so [Peninah] provoked her, therefore she wept."[5] Rashi tells us that Peninah used to goad Chanah, saying things such as, "Did you buy a coat for your elder son today, or a garment for your younger son?" The Sages tell us that she was severely punished for her cruel remarks.

Concerning Peninah, there is some dispute as to her inten-

---

3. *Bereishis* 30:2.

4. *Bereishis Rabbah* 71:6.

5. *I Shemuel* 1:6–7.

tions. Some say that she had pure intentions and deliberately made Chanah feel bad so that she would take a more active role in her "fertility treatments," which meant to pray more and with more feeling.[6] Others say that her intentions were dishonorable, and she just wanted to make Chanah feel bad, since they were rivals for the same husband. Some even say that her intentions were so bad that she wanted Chanah to be angry at God, hoping that God would be angry back at Chanah.[7]

By analyzing the verse, it seems likely that both opinions can be correct. The verse says, *Vechiasatah tzarasah, gam ka'as*, which literally means, "And her rival provoked her, and also provoked her to cry out." In other words, Peninah provoked her once in order to push her to pray more, but she also provoked her again for no other reason than to make her feel bad. This is typical of the way all people behave. We all have mixed emotions; we don't only think or feel one way about something or someone. We can do things with the intention of both hurting and helping somebody at the same time. Nevertheless, if we hurt someone's feelings we will pay a bitter price.[8]

"THOU SHALL NOT OPPRESS"

The Torah prohibits hurtful comments (*ona'as devarim*), as it says, "And no man [among] you may [verbally] abuse his fellowman, and you shall be afraid of your God."[9] *Chazal* tell us that hurting another's feelings is worse than defrauding

6. *Bava Basra* 17a.

7. See Rabbi Yehudah Leib Ginzberg, *Mussar haNevi'im*, ad. loc.

8. See *Tzidkas haTzaddik*, #175 (Melamed edition, p. 84), who warns against causing anybody any pain, even if that person has good intentions.

9. *Vayikra* 25:17.

him of his money.[10] Many times a person may rationalize his hurtful comments as innocent statements not meant to harm anybody. That is why the Torah says, "You shall be afraid of your God," to remind us that God always knows our true intentions. One must be extra careful not to hurt anybody's feelings.

Overly Sensitive? Many times you may just want to make a harmless comment about the couple not having children, or offer some helpful advice. It seems unreasonable that they should be offended or hurt. Certainly it is ridiculous not to be able to talk about your children with them. "My sister should love to hear about her nephews and nieces," one of our friends exclaimed. "If she can't bear to hear about them, then maybe she is just jealous. Doesn't she love them?"

People cannot understand the depth of the pain that is felt by the childless couple. They think that if someone's sister cannot bring herself to appear at her nephew's birthday party, then she is envious and there is a serious flaw in her personality. Of course she loves her nephews and nieces, but hearing too much about them just reminds her of her own misfortune.

The childless couple may love your children, but discussing them may cause unbearable grief. To some couples, it may only cause minimal discomfort. To some it may cause great discomfort but only at certain times, such as if the couple is currently undergoing treatment. You may not be able to know, because everybody is different. What you should always be aware of is that the childless couple is under great stress to have children. Anything you say will only add salt to their wounds. You must be sensitive.

---

10. *Bava Metzia* 58b.

Being sensitive does not mean holding their hand and saying, "You poor things, I feel your pain." Being sensitive means being extra careful about what you say, and about which topics of conversation you choose. Most women would never discuss all the intimate details of their pregnancy with a male friend or acquaintance; they would choose to speak about something else entirely. Similarly, when you are with a childless woman, find something to talk about other than pregnancy and children.

A Few Suggestions

Here is some advice about what not to say to childless couples, and what to refrain from — or at least minimize — talking about.

- Don't be nosy. Don't ask why they don't have children. Certainly don't toss out some comment like, "So when are we going to hear good news?"
- Don't offer advice, unless you really know what you are talking about. Chances are they know a lot more about the topic than you do. It is probably better not to offer advice unless they ask you for it.
- Don't complain about the difficulties of childrearing in the presence of a childless couple. Don't complain about pregnancy.
- Don't brag about your children.
- Don't remind them of the fact that they don't have children, even indirectly, such as by honoring them with *kvatter* at a *bris*. Being *kvatter* exposes them to everybody's pity. They don't want that. (If it's a young couple in their first or second year of marriage, it's probably all right. Use your common sense.)
- Be careful with innocent remarks about your children, such as: "I have to go home to check on the kids" or "I have to call the babysitter." Just say, "I have to go home."

- Don't say things that make them feel that you are pitying them, like, "I pray for you all the time."
- Don't tell them to relax.

What Can You Say?

So far this chapter has dealt with all the things that you shouldn't say to a childless couple. But what should you say? The answer to that depends upon the nature of your relationship with them. If you are a casual acquaintance, then don't say anything — that's right, nothing at all. If you are casual friends, or were friends when you were younger, then you probably shouldn't say anything either.

If you are a close friend or a family member, the best thing to do is to wait until they open up to you about it. However, if you feel you can initiate a dialogue, you may want to. They may in fact want to talk to you about their feelings, so let them know tactfully that if they want to speak to you, you have an open ear and, more important, an open heart for them. Of course, everybody reacts differently: Some people may have no problem discussing the distress of being childless, and others cannot mention it. But it is preferable to err on the side of caution than to assume that they won't mind your involvement.

Your conversation with a childless couple in general should focus on other aspects of life — Torah, work, politics, sports, anything but having kids. Still, the couple wants to be treated like everyone else. Invite them for a Shabbos meal, even if you have a table full of children; just don't speak about your kids all the time. You might want to have a little less *divrei Torah* from the children, even if your custom is to have the kids say something. Let the adults deal with the *divrei Torah* instead. You don't have to hide your kids, but don't constantly put the spotlight on them either. Some couples will want to get extra close to your children, and others won't want to be involved with them at all. You will have to evaluate each situation individually. Just be aware, and think before you act.

If your sister is childless, you can invite her to your child's piano recital or school play or birthday party, but don't be surprised or insulted if she doesn't come. Although your kids are an integral part of your life, you don't have to make them the *center* of your life when you are around people who want nothing more than to have their own children. On the other hand, you cannot and should not hide your children. Your sister may want to come to an event one time, and perhaps not the next. Be understanding, without showing pity.

A WORD TO THE PARENTS OF A CHILDLESS COUPLE

The parents of the infertile couple feel tremendous pressure to become grandparents — and they too are in pain. It is human nature for a person to have children, and to hope that their children will have children. The halachah tells us that a person only fulfills the mitzvah of *Pru Urvu* if he has children who can have children.[11] This seems consistent with our natural desire for both *kiyum olam* and the perpetuation of our line. As mentioned in the previous chapter, having a child at the "right" age is like "going up a grade" in society; likewise, having a grandchild is also a natural progression — "going up a grade" for the parents of grown children.

Even if they already have grandchildren, older parents still desire more grandchildren. They also want their children to experience the beauty and joy of having a child. What makes their anguish even greater is seeing their own children's grief. It is the worst feeling to see your child suffering

---

11. *Shulchan Aruch, Even haEzer* 1:4–5.

and to know that you are helpless. You would rather suffer the pain yourself twofold.

As parents of the childless couple, you are suffering both because you are not becoming grandparents and, even more, because you know that your children are unhappy. However, you need to be even more careful in dealing with the issue than anyone else. You must be especially careful not to confuse your natural desire to become grandparents with your children's best interests. You also need to know what to say — and especially what not to say. Be a source of support, not pressure. The wisdom that a parent needs does not end under the child's *chuppah*. Being a parent of married children brings new challenges to parenthood.

If parental advice is motivated by the parents' own craving to be grandparents, this ultimately will only put more pressure on the childless couple. Parents need to make sure that when they discuss the topic of infertility with their children they have only their children's best interests in mind. Parents also need to be careful not to show favoritism to those of their children who have given them grandchildren.

Of course, not every parent of a childless couple says hurtful things. Unfortunately, however, we have heard many stories about how parents meddled in the wrong way, even though they "meant well." You should be the one with whom your daughter or daughter-in-law can be completely honest, the one whom she takes along to the doctor's office, the first one whom she calls crying after another failed cycle — and the first one to share good news, God willing. Try to see yourself in that role — be the shoulder to lean on. Everybody needs someone with whom they can feel comfortable; it is best for everyone if it can be you. Parents who understand this can make a difficult situation much more manageable.

If you have not been in that role until now, it may not be

too late. Every child wants to be able to confide in his or her parents and parents-in-law. If you feel you do not know exactly how to respond, ask your kids. Let them take the lead in establishing the style of relationship you will have throughout this trying experience.

* * *

When hardships befall one member of a family, the whole family feels the pain. Everybody has a role within the family structure in dealing with any problem that may arise. Your daughter has her role; your son has his role; you have your role. Extended families have the power to ease hardships. That is the beauty of a family. They are always there for each other. Whether right or wrong, misfortune or mistake, a family always stands by each other. Be there for them in a positive, helpful way, and may the Almighty be there for all of you.

20. Assisted Reproductive Technology (ART)

His greatness is that He makes
the barren give birth.
(*Shochar Tov* 112)

THE FIELD OF INFERTILITY has undergone and continues to undergo rapid changes. In the 1950's, 1960's, and 1970's, management of the infertile couple focused on the female. The 1980's witnessed an awareness of the frequency of male-factor infertility, leading to increased emphasis on the evaluation of the husband. At the same time, the development of Assisted Reproductive Technology (ART) has led to an explosive rise in its use for the treatment of both male- and female-factor infertility. This has resulted in a shift in the emphasis from treatment designed to improve fertility toward an approach designed to achieve conception by bypassing fertility problems. The *poskim* have investigated the various procedures. Whether they are permissible or not may depend on a number of factors. See chapters 21 and 22 for a presentation of the halachic opinions on this topic.

Assisted Reproductive Technology[1] (in laymen's terms,

---

1. Very often, the term IVF (in vitro fertilization) is used interchangeably with ART, as it is the most common of the ART techniques. We have tried to differentiate between the two terms, but don't be surprised if the term IVF is used instead of ART in your specific clinic.

"test-tube babies") refers to all techniques involving direct retrieval of oocytes from the ovary. We will first list several different types of ARTs, and then describe each one in greater detail later in the chapter.

- **IVF — In vitro fertilization:** Extraction of oocytes, fertilization in the laboratory, transcervical transfer of embryos into the uterus.
- **GIFT — Gamete intrafallopian transfer:** The placement of oocytes and sperm together into the fallopian tubes.
- **ZIFT — Zygote intrafallopian transfer / TET — Tubal embryo transfer:** The placement of fertilized oocytes into the fallopian tubes.
- **POST — Peritoneal oocyte and sperm transfer:** The placement of oocytes and sperm together into the pelvic cavity.

IN VITRO FERTILIZATION (IVF)

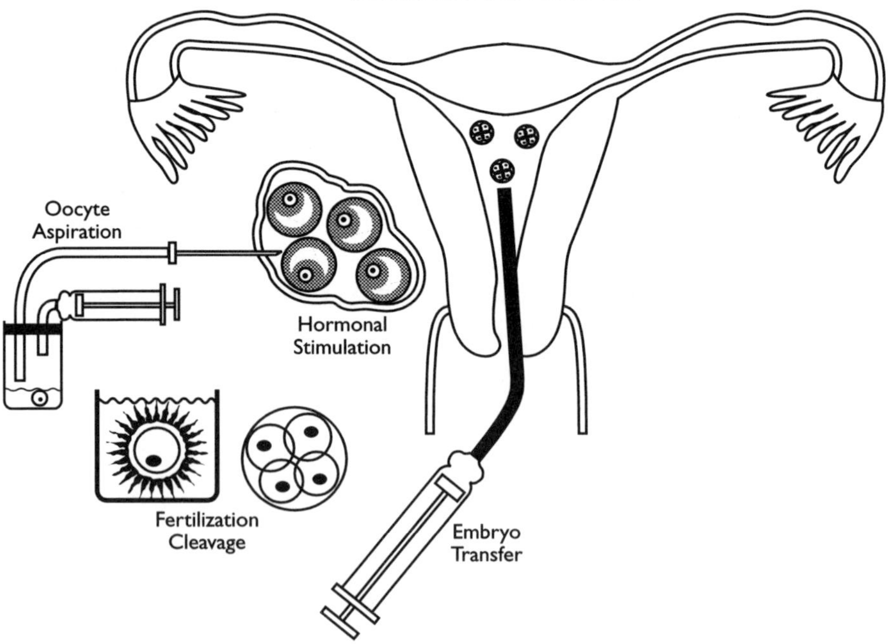

For those of you who are unfamiliar with some of the terms mentioned above, we will define them briefly here.

Oocytes are the female gametes located in the *follicles* (fluid-filled pockets) of the ovaries. (A *gamete* is one sperm cell or one egg [ovum].) A gamete has 23 chromosomes. The female gamete is 23X, whereas the male gamete is either 23X or 23Y. The two gametes combine during fertilization to form a *zygote,* which carries the genetic qualities of the parents. A zygote is one cell, and is either 46XX (female) or 46XY (male).

Twelve to twenty-four hours after fertilization, the zygote starts to divide. The group of cells, *blastocyst,* develops into an *embryo,* which it remains from the second until the eighth week after fertilization. The embryo is then referred to as a *fetus* until birth. (In order to simplify things, we will use the term "embryo" throughout this chapter when referring to a fertilized egg at any stage until the eighth week of pregnancy.)

It has been over twenty years since the first "test-tube baby" was conceived by in vitro fertilization. In vitro is a Latin phrase meaning "occurring in a laboratory." The idea of bringing sperm and eggs together outside the human body can be viewed as the ultimate act of medical intervention in a supposedly "natural process." However, we see how bypassing otherwise seemingly insurmountable obstacles to the "old-fashioned" way of fertilization offers hope to thousands of couples who would not otherwise be able to conceive. In this chapter, we will deal only with the technical aspects of assisted reproduction techniques. Chapters 21 and 22 cover the halachic, psychological, and philosophical implications.

Just as this chapter on ART is toward the end of the book, so too is the use of ART a final step in fertility treatments. It is considered standard and conservative medical practice to try other fertility options before resorting to the costly and invasive treatments that ART entails. And as in all fertility treatments, success is not guaranteed on the first, second, or even the third attempt. Since ARTs are so complicated, time-consuming, and expensive, and often the only option left to some couples, it is a pressure-packed period for everyone to endure.

WHO WOULD BE CANDIDATES FOR ART?

People who are considered for Assisted Reproductive Technology include the following:

- Women with obstructed fallopian tubes
- Women with endometriosis
- Women with premature ovarian failure
- Couples with immunologic causes for infertility
- Men who have been diagnosed with male-factor infertility
- Couples with unexplained infertility (infertility without a known cause)

HOW DO ARTs HELP?

Assisted reproduction techniques bypass "trouble spots" that prevent normal fertilization. When the fallopian tubes are blocked because of structural damage, placing fertilized ova inside the uterus overrides the non-functioning tubes. Although it is reasonable to recommend tubal surgery in young women with mild tubal disease, IVF is the treatment of choice for patients with more severe disease or six months to two years after tubal surgery without resulting pregnancy. An older woman with tubal disease would proceed directly to IVF.

Endometriosis, for instance, interferes with normal fertility in a largely unknown way. ARTs can overcome this as well. Although medical or surgical management of endometriosis is usually the first line of treatment, if not successful, IVF is recommended.

Although IVF can overcome a number of the barriers to fertility, it suffers the same limitations as in vivo fertilization (normal conception) when it comes to ovarian aging and age-related failure. Women start losing their fertility potential at the age of 34. It decreases gradually up to the age of 40 and rapidly thereafter. At 40 years of age, only 50 percent of women are fertile, and at the age of 45, less than 5 percent are fertile. IVF cannot overcome age-related infertility, and the only solution is oocyte donation.[2]

Beyond the simple effect of age on oocyte quality, there is also a negative influence on IVF success from decreased ovarian response to hormonal stimulation.[3]

In successful IVF programs, where the delivery rate per oocyte retrieval can be over 30 percent in women age 35 or younger, the figure is 10 percent or less in women age 40 and over.[4]

Assisted reproduction techniques can successfully bypass other natural barriers which may be interfering with natural fertility. For instance, anti-sperm antibodies found in a man's sperm or in hostile cervical mucus are overcome using IVF in combination with ICSI. The zona pellucida, a thick, transparent membrane surrounding each oocyte preventing fertilization by more than one sperm at a time, is also resistant to penetration by antibody-laden sperm. With ICSI, a single sperm cell is injected into a retrieved oocyte, which is then im-

---

2. Professor Ehud Margalioth, IVF department head, Shaare Zedek hospital, Jerusalem.

3. R.T. Scott, J.P. Toner, S.J. Muasher, "Follicle-Stimulating Hormone Levels Predictive of In Vivo Fertilization Outcome," *Fertility and Sterility* 51:651, 1989.

4. M.V. Sauer, R.J. Paulson, R.A. Lobo, "Pregnancy in Women Fifty or More Years of Age," *Fertility and Sterility* 64:11, 1995.

planted in the woman's uterus.

With certain male-factor infertility problems, ART with sperm retrieval techniques allows a man with no sperm in the ejaculate to father children. Sperm is retrieved microsurgically or aspirated from the testes either by the TESE or MESA technique, followed by ICSI (see chapter 17). These new technologies of ART enable men who are absolutely infertile (sterile) to father a child.

For the 10 to 15 percent of couples suffering from unexplained infertility, ARTs are the last hope that modern medicine can offer. As with any medical intervention, there are many factors that enter into its success or failure. No one can assure the success of any medical treatment. Why one thing works and another doesn't is an unanswerable question. Researchers may try to explain why for some couples IVF works on the first or second try and for others only after six attempts. Unfortunately for some, no medical treatment will be successful. We can also never explain why some couples conceive spontaneously after taking a break from fertility treatments. There are a lot of "whys" in medicine — and in life, for that matter.

Success rates for ART are increasing nearly every year. While in 1980 the success was only 1 percent, in the late 1980's it rose to 10 percent. We have seen a steady increase from 10 to 20 percent in the early 1990's to 30 to 50 percent in 2003.

Many couples feel that ARTs are their last chance at having biological children. It is emotionally painful to be placed in this category of having "severe" infertility problems — the way most couples define themselves when they reach this point in the fertility treatment process. This is it — or give up.

Up until now you may not have told anyone except a few of your closest family and friends that you have been going through fertility treatments. With ARTs, however, life gets a little more complicated: there are missed days of work, periods of mandatory bed-rest for days at a time, uncomfortable side effects, and, rarely, hospitalizations. Your loving relationship is put to the ultimate test, as your lives are dictated by telephone calls informing you to take this test, to get these shots, and to have or not to have intimate relations.

PREPARATION FOR ASSISTED REPRODUCTION

Setting the groundwork for in vitro fertilization or any of the other ARTs is an invasive and involved clinical process. ART is a "couple's" treatment. However, unless the man is taking some sort of medication or undergoing another kind of treatment for fertility, preparation for the ART cycle begins with the woman, and only immediately before retrieval of oocytes (removing the eggs from the body) is scheduled, will the husband be physically involved.

Before any preparation begins, we are assuming that the woman has been thoroughly evaluated in order to provide the optimum treatment plan. Each course of ART is referred to as a "cycle." It can be very frustrating for a couple if everything seems to be going smoothly and on schedule, and then have a cycle canceled due to overstimulation of the ovaries, missed ovulation, an inadequate sperm sample, or a host of other interferences. Costly and agonizing cancellations of ART cycles can be kept at a minimum with thorough explanations of the treatments and with effective communication between the couple and the medical staff. Every couple has their own special situation and needs, but we hope the following general information will clear up any misconceptions and prevent any misunderstandings.

Medically preparing the body for a cycle of ART can begin up to two weeks before menstruation (from the luteal phase of the preceding monthly cycle), and then continue into the days following menstruation of the next month. This preparation entails medical regulation of a woman's cycle, which can be achieved using a number of different chemical recipes.

Down-Regulation of the Cycle

Down-regulating a woman's cycle entails literally "canceling out" the body's hormonal control over her cycle (endogenous hormones) and substituting hormones produced in the laboratory (exogenous hormones). *Gonadotropin-releasing hormone agonists* (GnRHa) are used to suppress a woman's own production of hormones, giving her fertility specialist more control over her cycle — thus preventing untimely LH surges, premature ovulation, and other hormonal imbalances which could lead to a costly and distressful cancellation of a fertility cycle in progress.

One of three treatment regimens will be chosen if GnRHa down-regulation is to precede induction of ovulation. Depending on how a woman's system is to be regulated, preparation protocols will be started either before the onset of menstruation or a few days afterward.

- **Long protocols** — Suppression is started in the midluteal phase of the previous month's cycle (around day 21).
- **Short or flare-up protocols** — GnRHa is initiated in the early follicular phase of the present cycle (days 3 to 5).
- **Ultrashort protocols** — GnRHa is used only during the beginning of the cycle (days 1 through 3).

GnRHa suppression is given in conjunction with human menopausal gonadotropins (HMG), followed by regular intercourse, and either IUI (see chapter 17) or IVF. Research has shown that combining a GnRH agonist with gonadotropin treatment prevents the risk of premature ovulation and cycle cancellation. Pregnancy rates are higher and miscarriage rates are lower.[5] A review of GnRHa treatment cycle outcomes concluded that the clinical pregnancy rate per cycle was significantly improved after GnRHa use for IVF.[6]

The GnRH agonist is administered twice daily, 0.5 mg by subcutaneous injection. Common side effects include menopausal-like symptoms, especially hot flashes. These reactions are temporary and resolve with cessation of the medication. In order to help support a developing pregnancy, progesterone supplementation is initiated after oocyte retrieval for about two weeks.

Not all women or all cycles of IVF require down-regulation of the menstrual cycle. Only if it is feared that a woman's hormones may interfere with the proper hormonal manipulation and that greater control of hormonal input would result in a higher probability of conception will a GnRH agonist be used.

Whether or not GnRHa is introduced into the protocol, the process of ovulation induction for ART is similar to gonadotropin therapy followed by IUI or intercourse (see chapter 17). This includes daily injections of gonadotropins, followed by clinic visits every other day (estradiol assays and ultrasounds) as ovulation approaches. The goal of stimulating ovulation is to achieve a lead follicle (the largest developed follicle in that cycle) of at least 18 mm in diameter. There should be at least three or four other follicles with diameters of 14 mm or greater. Estradiol levels should correspond to 200 pg/ml per 14 mm or greater size follicle. Cancellation of a cycle — i.e. withholding HCG — due to the threat of overstimulation of the ovaries will be considered if there are more than twenty-five

5. P. Devroey, B. Mannarets, J. Smitz, "Clinical Outcome of a Pilot Efficacy Study," *Human Reproduction* 9:1064, 1994.

6. E.G. Hughes, D.M. Fedorkow, S. Daya, "A Meta-Analysis of Randomized Controlled Trials," *Fertility and Sterility* 58:888–896, 1992.

follicles or a total estradiol greater than 4000 pg/ml.

Though laboratory values vary from clinic to clinic and ultrasound is subject to human interpretation, once the appropriate level of stimulation is achieved, a single injection of 5000 or 10,000 IU of HCG is given to induce final follicular maturation. Before ovulation is permitted to occur spontaneously, the woman will undergo oocyte retrieval within thirty-four to thirty-nine hours after administration of HCG.

OOCYTE RETRIEVAL

This next step in the IVF protocol is invasive and complicated. Oocyte retrieval (removing the eggs from the ovaries to be combined with the sperm; also called Ovarian Pick-Up or OPU) is carried out in a high-tech setting in a hospital operating room, next to a fully equipped embryology laboratory.

When a woman steps from the waiting area into the operating room, especially for the first time, it is like entering another universe. Doctors, nurses, and technical staff wear baggy gowns, caps, booties covering their shoes, and masks. All you can see are their eyes. The patient walking into the operating suite will also be wearing a gown and have booties on her feet. This, along with a much cooler room temperature, creates a very impersonal atmosphere. In reality, it is only to promote a germ-free environment. But it is scary and pretty startling, especially the first time.

Minutes after a woman lies down on the narrow operating bed, the anesthesiologist will begin an intravenous and attach a pulse monitor and blood pressure cuff to make sure all is well during the short procedure. Before the procedure begins, the woman is given either an epidural or general anesthesia. Some women receive an intravenous sedative as well. Which form of anesthesia is used is decided with the doctor before this time.

OOCYTE RETRIEVAL

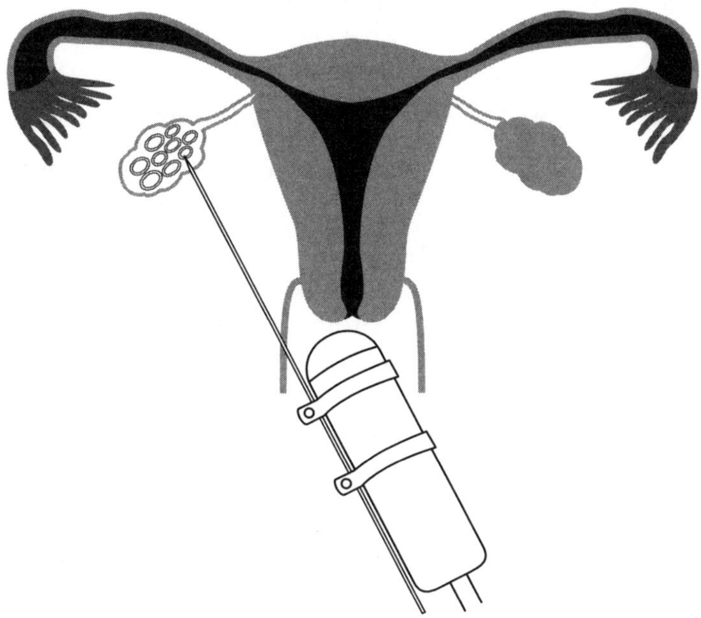

Once a woman is comfortable, her doctor will insert a high-frequency ultrasound transducer into her vagina. Guided by the ultrasound picture, which is provided on a monitor screen, the doctor directs a needle attached to the transducer through the upper vaginal wall toward one of the ovaries. With one puncture, the needle is then advanced into each mature follicle and the follicular fluid is aspirated. Once the follicles from both ovaries are aspirated, the fluid is delivered immediately to the embryology laboratory. The retrieval procedure usually takes about thirty minutes, and as the woman is wheeled out of the operating room on a gurney, she will already be awake and/or aware enough to know how many follicles were aspirated and delivered to the lab. Blood loss and risk of infection is minimal, although a woman may be given antibiotics as a precaution. After resting for a couple of hours, most women are sent home to rest. Some women go right back to their daily routine, while others take the opportunity to rest up before the next stage of treatment.

Oocyte retrieval would not render a woman a *niddah*, as any bleeding would be from the vagina, not the uterus.

In the Laboratory

While the oocyte retrieval is taking place, arrangements for obtaining the semen specimen are undertaken. The husband's sperm is either obtained at the hospital or transported to the lab within an hour of collection. Some IVF programs prefer to have a sperm specimen cryopreserved (frozen) ahead of time in case of situational anxiety or difficulty with collection. The semen is washed of seminal fluid and placed in a centrifugation apparatus in which a pellet of sperm is formed. Fresh medium (a protein-based substance) is added and the healthiest sperm are allowed to "swim-up" from the pellet to the medium. The sperm remains in the medium for about four to six hours. After this, an optimum number of approximately 100,000 motile sperm are placed in the petri dish alongside each egg.

Following an 18-hour incubation period, the oocytes are examined microscopically to determine the presence of two pronuclei (ensuring that the chromosomes of the sperm have been incorporated into the egg). This is an early sign of fertilization. Extra embryos that will not be implanted during this cycle can be cryopreserved at the pronuclear stage. As of this writing, the life expectancy of frozen embryos is about seven years, although one third will not survive the thawing process. Unfortunately, medical technology has not yet reached the point of being able to successfully freeze the ovum before fertilization. If egg cryopreservation proved clinically successful, it could be used to store younger women's eggs for pregnancy at a later time, or for women prior to exposure to chemotherapy or other cancer treatments.

Most fertilized oocytes will then go on to cleave (divide) into two- to four-cell embryos after twenty-four hours in the laboratory. Another twenty-four hours will result in an eight-cell embryo. The amount of time allowed for cell division after fertilization depends upon the type of embryo transfer procedure to be done.

There has been a growing trend to allow the embryo to advance from the early cleavage stage of two days to a more developed blastocystic stage of five or six days. It is thought that prolonging the duration of culture (laboratory incubation) to day 5 may allow the selection of the highest quality embryos, which will result in higher implantation rate and eventually lower the risk of multiple pregnancy.[7]

Deciding which egg or eggs to transfer is a major decision for the embryologist. Tests are being perfected to assess early cleaving in the lab at the two-cell stage before transfer to ensure the most successful outcome. A more rigorous and efficient method of embryo selection will also reduce the need to transfer more than one embryo per cycle.[8]

The number of embryos to be transferred continues to incur worldwide debate. The guidelines provided by the American Society for Reproductive Medicine are influenced by the age of the woman:

- **Women 35 years or younger** — No more than 3 embryos
- **Women 35 to 40 years** — No more than 4 embryos
- **Women age 40 and older** — No more than 5 embryos

(In many European countries there are laws preventing

7. G.M. Jones, A.O. Trounson, "Factors Affecting the Success of Human Blastocyst Development," *Fertility and Sterility* 70:1022–1029, 1998.

8. G. Percival, D. Sakkas, "Assessment of Early Cleaving in In Vitro Fertilized Embryos at Two-cell Stage Before Transfer Improves Embryo Selection," *Fertility and Sterility* 76:6, 2001.

the transfer of more than two or three embryos as part of a worldwide trend to reduce the consequences of multiple pregnancy.)

Transfer of more than one embryo increases the chances for pregnancy, but the multiple pregnancy rate with IVF is approximately 35 percent.[9] Reproductive specialists are constantly working to perfect the ART procedures so that eventually only one embryo will need to be transferred to ensure success.

Successful embryo transfer (ET) and implantation are no simple feats. Much research has been conducted into improving implantation rates after IVF. It is widely believed that improving embryo quality holds the greatest chance for increasing IVF success rates. Therefore, the competency of the embryologist and the quality of the laboratory are the major factors for increasing pregnancy rates. It is common practice for the embryologist to grade the quality of the embryos, and on the basis of the score, to choose the highest quality embryo for implantation. Any additional embryos of suitable quality are then set aside for cryopreservation.

In another big test of *shalom bayis*, the couple finds themselves waiting for the telephone to ring, hoping to receive instructions to come back to the hospital to "receive their embryos." While praying to hear that all the eggs retrieved were fertilized, there are a few relaxation techniques that can help. Aromatherapy, massage, or even acupuncture can relieve a lot of tension and make the wait pass more easily. According to one study, acupuncture twenty-five minutes before and twenty-five minutes after IVF can boost chances of pregnancy by increasing the blood flow and energy to the

---

9. S. Senoz, A. Ben-Chetrit, R.F. Casper, "An IVF Fallacy: Multiple Pregnancy Rate Is Lower for Older Women," *Journal of Reproductive Genetics* 14:192, 1997.

uterus by 26.3 to 42.5 percent.[10]

To rule out possible genetic disorders, *pre-embryonic genetic diagnosis* (PGD) may be done. This entails removal of a single cell from the embryo three days after the egg has been fertilized. Remaining cells continue to grow. The removed cell is examined for genetic defects such as cystic fibrosis, Tay-Sachs, hemophilia, or chromosomal defects that cause Down's syndrome. The sex of the embryo can also be determined. Following this examination, the healthy embryo will be transferred back to the mother.

(In a highly publicized case in 2002, an Israeli couple with a son suffering from a usually fatal genetic disease was able to literally infuse him with a new life by transferring stem cells from his baby sister's umbilical cord. She was conceived through IVF and as an embryo was specifically chosen through PGD, as she was genetically matched to her ill brother.)

EMBRYO TRANSFER

Embryo transfer (ET) is most commonly performed at the eight-cell stage, approximately seventy-two to eighty hours after retrieval. This procedure is quick and painless, with no anesthesia necessary. ET is low-tech compared to the oocyte retrieval. Done in a clinic setting, the woman lies in the standard gynecological position (i.e. feet in stirrups), as a speculum is inserted into her vagina. The cervix is gently rinsed. An ultra-thin plastic catheter is inserted through the cervix into the uterine cavity. The embryo(s) are gently propelled through the catheter into the uterus where implantation of at least one embryo will hopefully take place. Embryo transfer does not render a woman a *niddah* as any bleeding

---

10. P. Wofgang, "Acupuncture and IVF," *Fertility and Sterility* 4:87, 2002.

would be a result of trauma to the cervix.

Successful embryo transfer requires the joint efforts of the reproductive biologist (part of the laboratory personnel) and the doctor. Without healthy embryos that are able to implant, ET is sure to fail. Research has shown that the transfer technique and expertise of the physician is also a factor in the procedure's success. Problematic embryo transfer with complications of difficult introduction of the catheter into the cervix, bleeding, retained embryos in the catheter, uterine contractions and expelled embryos immediately following ET, have all been associated with unsuccessful embryo transfers.[11]

Post-Transfer Care

Immediately after the transfer, the woman rests lying down for about thirty minutes before going home. The luteal phase, the development of the uterine lining, will be supported with supplemental progesterone. Supplementation can be given by injection, by vaginal suppositories, or orally. Progesterone supplementation may continue for up to four to six weeks after pregnancy is established. According to some studies, however, progesterone supplementation can be withdrawn at the time of a positive pregnancy test, but the common practice is to continue progesterone supplementation until the tenth week of pregnancy.[12]

Between embryo transfer and the first diagnostic pregnancy test are twelve long, long days! Beforehand you were both so busy with the appointments and the treatments, and now it's like you rushed just to hurry up and wait. A woman's mind can play powerful tricks. One minute she feels devastated that she's getting her period, and the next she feels

---

11. W. Schoolcraft, E. Surrey, "Embryo Transfer: Techniques and Variables Affecting Success," *Fertility and Sterility* 76:863–870, 2001.

12. A. Andersen, B. Todorovic, "Progesterone Supplementation during Early Gestation," *Human Reproduction* 17:2, pp. 357–361, 2002.

symptoms of pregnancy.

Both husband and wife handle this tense time differently, often having difficulty in relating to the other's "coping mechanisms":

"How dare he act like nothing's happening!"

"Why is she in such a bad mood, either yelling or crying?"

It's not easy for either of you. Remember that your love for one another as well as your strong desire for children brought you to undergo such heroic measures to conceive a child. That same love will help you survive this difficult time as well.

After this lifetime of waiting, HCG is measured in the blood to confirm pregnancy. If positive, a follow-up HCG is obtained three days later. This establishes a trend of the HCG elevations and provides prognostic information. Five to six weeks after the transfer, an ultrasound should show a fetal heartbeat.

The procedure described above is representative of IVF. The following procedures are variations of IVF, specifically the timing of embryo transfer, and where sperm and oocytes are combined.

GAMETE INTRAFALLOPIAN TRANSFER

In the Gamete Intrafallopian Transfer (GIFT) procedure, oocytes are aspirated following hyperstimulation of the ovaries. Aspiration is performed through a small opening in the abdominal wall (laparotomy — abdominal incision, or laparoscopy — navel incision), or more easily through the vaginal wall. After the oocytes are identified in the laboratory, they are drawn into a transfer catheter that contains 100,000 sperm isolated by the swim-up technique. The transfer catheter is then guided by laparoscopy into the fallopian tube and the contents gently discharged. A woman does not become a *niddah* after this procedure.

The goal of GIFT is for fertilization to take place in the fallopian tubes and for the embryo to implant safely in the uterus. Success with GIFT (i.e. deliveries) in one study of the collected statistics from the United States and Canada (1999) was as high as 28.2 percent per transfer.[13]

Two oocytes along with thousands of sperm can be placed in each fallopian tube, although placement in one tube is more common and equally successful. Extra eggs obtained at retrieval can be fertilized and cryopreserved for future use.

ZYGOTE INTRAFALLOPIAN TRANSFER / TUBAL EMBRYO TRANSFER

In the Zygote Intrafallopian Transfer (ZIFT) procedure, oocytes are obtained by vaginal aspiration (which would not render a woman a *niddah*) and then fertilized in vitro (in the laboratory, as with IVF). One day later, after the initial stage of fertilization (pronuclear stage), the zygotes are placed in the fallopian tubes by laparoscopy. This is called Tubal Embryo Transfer, or TET. In contrast to standard IVF-ET, ZIFT allows early embryonal growth in the natural (fallopian) tubal environment and transport of the embryos into the uterine cavity under natural physiological regulation. However, because of the complexity (necessity for the operating room and general anesthesia with both laparoscopies for retrieval and transfer) and higher cost of ZIFT over IVF-ET, ZIFT has been discontinued in many IVF units. Reports in a 1999 study showed results of 32.3 percent deliveries per transfer.[14]

The choice of method — IVF, GIFT, or ZIFT/TET — can be

---

13. "The American Society for Reproductive Medicine, Assisted Reproductive Technology in the US and Canada: 1999 Results," *Fertility and Sterility* 78:918, 2002.
14. Ibid.

made on the basis of infertility factors, cost, and risk. If there is tubal damage, GIFT or ZIFT is not a good choice. In rare instances where there is severe scarring of the cervix, one of the intratubal techniques is preferable. The comfort level of the procedure with each of the techniques and the program's experience in terms of pregnancy results are important considerations. Use of GIFT or ZIFT can incur greater costs, depending on the setting for the surgery and the anesthesia used.

PERITONEAL OOCYTE AND SPERM TRANSFER

One other technique which has not gained wide acceptance and use is the Peritoneal Oocyte and Sperm Transfer (POST). This is the placement of oocytes and sperm together into the pelvic cavity (the space between the uterus, the ovaries, and the fallopian tubes). This technique is based on the premise that the oocytes and sperm will be swept from the pelvic cavity into the fallopian tube by the fringed appendages at the end of the fallopian tubes; fertilized; and then implanted in the uterus.

Embryologists are constantly attempting to successfully mature oocytes in vitro and then to freeze them. However, as of this writing (2004), the survival of and fertilization rates for oocytes after cryopreservation are so low as to make this process an impractical option at this time. Embryologists continue to achieve excellent survival and fertilization rates with cryopreserved embryos.

In conclusion, we see that ARTs present ever-improving chances of pregnancy and hope for so many couples. But it is not that simple, as all fertility treatments are emotionally trying and can be very discouraging if success is not met within a short time. All assisted reproduction techniques together have a less than 30 percent success rate per retrieval. Psychological counseling services associated with ART programs and support groups are very helpful to almost every couple.

RECOMMENDATIONS

No two couples are the same. Your fertility issues are as individual as you are. Treatment decisions are based on many different factors, and no two couples will be managed alike. However, the American Society for Reproductive Medicine has reached some conclusions about which treatments are best suited to which types of infertility:

- **Inoperable tubal damage.** IVF is often appropriate for women with blocked fallopian tubes from surgical sterilization that cannot be reversed, from severe endometriosis, or from scarring and adhesions that have resulted from tubal infection. Many IVF programs recommend the removal of severely damaged tubes before IVF is performed, in order to increase the chances of pregnancy and decrease the risks of infection after the procedure.
- **Unexplained infertility.** Ovulation induction with IUI (see chapter 17), IVF, GIFT, or donor oocytes may be suitable for couples who remain infertile despite normal fertility evaluations.
- **Ovulatory disorders.** Donor oocytes are appropriate for women with premature ovarian failure and for any woman past the age of 43, even if she still has regular periods. (See chapter 22 for the halachic and ethical aspects of donor insemination.)
- **Male infertility.** Ovulation induction with IUI, GIFT, or IVF, with or without ICSI, may be used if treatment of male infertility is unsuccessful.

In Summary

Assisted Reproductive Technology (ART) includes:

- IVF
- GIFT
- ZIFT / TET
- POST

IVF can be the answer for:

- Obstructed fallopian tubes / structural infertility in the woman
- Age-related infertility with donor oocytes
- Male-factor infertility problems (ICSI)
- Unexplained infertility

Woman's preparation and procedure for IVF:

- Hormonal regulation
- Estradiol (E2) and ultrasound monitoring
- Oocyte retrieval 34 to 39 hours after HCG
- Embryologist – which to transfer / which to freeze
- Guidelines on number of embryos to transfer
- PGD
- Embryo transfer
- Post-transfer care
- GIFT, ZIFT / TET, POST

Man's preparation and procedure for IVF:

- Provide sperm sample for day of egg retrieval (ovarian pick-up [OPU]) or make sure there is a frozen-thawed sample available

21.
Understanding the Halachic Ruling for AIH (Artificial Insemination by Husband) and IVF (In Vitro Fertilization)

The precepts of the Eternal are upright, gladdening the heart; the commandment of the Eternal is illuminating, enlightening the eyes. The fear of the Eternal is pure, enduring forever; the judgments of the Eternal are true, righteous altogether.

(*Tehillim* 19:9–10)

INTRODUCTION

MEDICALLY ASSISTED REPRODUCTION is one of the major topics in bioethics today. Not only is the Torah world concerned about this issue, but it is of great concern to society at large. Does mankind have the right to manipulate the creation of new life? Can man "play God"? These are questions of astronomical proportions, questions that can change the course of history and redefine the mission of mankind.

Ineresting1y, the above questions, which seem to be the fundamental issues of medically assisted reproduction, are barely touched upon by Torah authorities. Judaism does not see these issues as problems, as the Torah gave human beings the mandate to dominate the physical world and to manipulate it for the development of civilization: "God blessed them and God said to them, 'Be fruitful and multiply, populate the earth and take control of it.'"[1] With mankind's commandment, "Take control of it," man became partners with God, so to speak, in building up the world that He created.

Scientific exploration and medical research, even in fields that will change conventional conceptions, is not only permissible but is man's charge.[2] Of course, governments have to be careful to limit the use of scientific advances in fertility, for otherwise we could eventually end up in a cold, futuristic "Brave New World" reality. However, that concern is not particularly Jewish; it is a concern for all of mankind.[3]

What then becomes the issue for Jews? Why is medically assisted reproduction considered "bioethics?"

When any new technique is developed, we need to see if it in any way is at odds with halachah. It could even be a tangential issue, or a small procedure within a greater process — but this is what concerns us. In other words, bioethics for us is not asking the obvious question, may man assist reproduction in the laboratory? but rather, is this an infraction of our code of conduct?

Whenever an action is deemed prohibited by Jewish law, there must be some Torah edict or Rabbinic directive that it is transgressing. The violation of Rabbinic law is equally as grave as violating a Torah law, for our Sages gave their laws in order to safeguard the Torah. When our Rabbis made decrees, they did it with the intention of strengthening the spirit of God's laws. It follows, then, that any violation of a Rabbinic decree is in essence a violation of Torah law.

---

1. *Bereishis* 1:28.

2. See Ramban, *Bereishis* 1:28. See also Rabbi Dr. Chaim Zimmerman, *Torah and Reason* (Jerusalem: Hed Press, Ltd., 1979), pp. 29 – 49 and pp. 134 –171.

3. See by Rabbi J. David Bleich, "Test Tube Babies," in Fred Rosner and J. David Bleich, *Jewish Bioethics* (Hoboken, NJ: Ktav Publishing, 1979), p. 81.

Although personal opinions and world outlook influence the way in which a *posek* perceives an issue and views the sources, still he will always have to find some technical halachic violation in order to prohibit an act or technique.

THE HALACHIC ISSUES

If the Jews don't have a problem with the scientific breakthroughs of artificial insemination and IVF from an ethical point of view, what then are the issues that concern us? In a case where a man other than the husband contributes the sperm, there are obviously manifold problems, which we will discuss in chapter 22. When the sperm is from the husband of the woman, however, what are the issues?

The main problem with medically assisted fertility from the husband (AIH) is procuring the sperm, either as a sample for testing or for the insemination itself. There are tangential issues that come up, such as whether the husband thereby fulfills the mitzvah of *Pru Urvu*. There are also Shabbos-related and *niddah*-related questions. But the main question is, how does the husband procure the sperm?

The halachic problem is that it is forbidden to "waste seed." Normal intimate relations are not considered wasting seed, even when it is certain that the relations will not result in a pregnancy. But is producing semen for the purpose of artificial insemination considered wasting seed? Does it matter how the sperm is acquired? Is there a preferable way?

TORAH LAW OR RABBINIC LAW?

There isn't an explicit Biblical source for the prohibition of wasting seed. Because of this, there is a discussion of whether the prohibition is of Torah or Rabbinic origin.

Possible Torah references can be derived from:

- **The Ten Commandments:** *"Lo sin'af."*[4] This is translated in English as, "You must not commit adultery." *Chazal* added, however, "Do not have *ni'uf* (from the same Hebrew root as *tin'af*) either by hand or foot"[5] — in other words, self-stimulation.
- **The book of Devarim:** "You shall be careful of all evil things."[6] *Chazal* said that this means you should not have sexual thoughts by day so that you won't have impurities at night.[7]
- **The generation of the Flood:** "[The earth] was corrupted, for all flesh had perverted its nature upon the earth."[8]
- **The sin of Er and Onan:** The sons of Yehudah who practiced coitus interruptus with Tamar.[9]

The Gemara cites the opinion of various Rabbis who say that wasting seed is a transgression that can be compared to the most grave of sins.[10] Because of the seriousness that the Gemara attributed to this act, both the Rambam and the *Shulchan Aruch* codified the prohibition of masturbation (and coitus interruptus) in very harsh language.[11]

The Levush's interpretation of this prohibition is that since man's seed was created to settle the world — for God created the world to be settled — then whoever destroys his seed is destroying the world. This, he explains, was the sin of the generation of the Flood, which was punished by hot

---

4. *Shemos* 20:13.
5. *Niddah* 13a.
6. *Devarim* 23:10.
7. *Kesubos* 46a.
8. *Bereishis* 6:12.
9. *Bereishis* 38:7,10, and Rashi on 38:7.
10. See *Niddah* 13a.
11. Rambam, *Hilchos Isurei Bi'ah* 21:18. *Shulchan Aruch, Even haEzer* 23:1.

floodwaters. They sinned with hot liquid; therefore, they were punished with hot liquid.[12]

The *Aruch haShulchan*'s explanation for the prohibition of wasting seed is: "Sexual attraction was only created in man in order to populate the world, but sexual passion for the sake of mere pleasure is considered repulsive. Therefore it is a sacred obligation for a man to preserve his seed, for seed is considered holy.... If it is wasted, it is like spilling blood."[13]

The following is an overview of some of the *poskim*'s opinions regarding the prohibition of spilling seed.

Some *poskim* hold that spilling seed is a Torah transgression,[14] for he who is commanded in the mitzvah of *Pru Urvu* is commanded not to waste his seed.[15] However, the Tzitz Eliezer cites the book *Meshivas Nefesh,* which says that spilling seed is not a Torah transgression, because the Torah didn't prohibit the act directly. Only indirect references prohibit it.[16] Rabbi Yaakov Etlinger, in his book, *Aruch laNer,* also says that all Biblical references to spilling seed in the Gemara are only hints (*asmachta*). He suggests that if there is a Biblical transgression, it is the prohibition of wasting in general (*bal tashchis*).[17] In his responsa, *Binyan Tzion,* Rabbi Etlinger repeats this position, and suggests that perhaps the prohibition was handed down through tradition — *halachah leMoshe miSinai.*[18]

According to the Pnei Yehoshua, comparing the spilling of

---

12. Levush, *Even haEzer* 23:1.

13. *Aruch haShulchan, Even haEzer* 23:1.

14. *Responsa Maharash Engel,* vol. VI, chap. 18. The *Semak* counted it as one of the 613 mitzvos of the Torah.

15. *Tochachos Chaim, Seder Shemos,* chap. 12, *daf* 16, brought down in *Otzar haPoskim* 23:1.

16. HaRav Aryeh Lev miPlusk, *Meshivas Nefesh,* chap. 18.

17. *Aruch laNer, Niddah* 13a.

18. *Binyan Tzion,* 137.

seed to the capital sins of murder and idol worship is only an exaggeration or embellishment, in the same way that the sin of *lashon ha-ra* is compared to the three capital crimes. Just as it doesn't make practical sense to say that someone who speaks *lashon ha-ra* is as bad as someone who murders, the same is true with one who wastes his seed.[19] The Tzitz Eliezer says that in light of all this, the Rambam and the *Shulchan Aruch* must have written about spilling seed in such a strong manner specifically in order to over-emphasize the seriousness of the act.[20]

The Mabit proposes that the prohibition of wasting seed might indeed be a Torah transgression.[21] The Toras Chesed points out that there is a dispute among the *Rishonim*.[22] Rav Moshe Feinstein holds that it is a Torah transgression.[23] Although he also maintains that to say that it is more severe than the other laws of the Torah is an overstatement, he does say that if it were only a Rabbinic transgression the Gemara wouldn't have made such an exaggerated statement about it.[24]

According to the Zohar, wasting seed is one of the gravest sins and one cannot repent for it. The Beis Shemuel says that this is an exaggeration and is not to be taken literally.[25] The Yaavetz wonders about this statement from the Zohar, saying that we know that there is repentance for everything. If there is repentance for the three capital sins, then there is certainly

---

19. *Responsa Pnei Yehoshua, Even haEzer* 44.

20. *Tzitz Eliezer,* vol. IX, chap. 51, section 1, 3.

21. *Kiryas Sefer* of the Mabit, *Hilchos Isurei Bi'ah.*

22. *Toras Chesed* (Lublin), *Even haEzer,* chap. 43:1-2. Some say that the prohibition of wasting seed is connected to mitzvah of *Pru Urvu.* See *BeOhelah shel Torah, Even haEzer,* chap. 69, for a discussion of the implications of this connection. For a survey of the opinions concerning the issue of wasting seed, see *Otzar haPoskim* 23.

23. *Igros Moshe, Even haEzer,* vol. III, chap. 14.

24. Ibid.

25. *Beis Shemuel, Even haEzer* 23:1.

repentance for this sin, he says.[26]

The Tzitz Eliezer cites a few opinions that explain the Zohar's statement. The Zohar means that it is difficult to repent, but repentance is possible. (Any time the Zohar means that something is difficult, it says that it isn't possible.[27]) The reason is clear. Anybody addicted to certain activities will find it very difficult to stop their destructive behavior, be it drugs, gambling, or sexual misbehavior. Rehabilitation is always theoretically possible, but true recovery, complete repentance, is so difficult that it is as if it's impossible.

According to the Beis Yitzchak, the prohibition not to spill seed is only Rabbinic and not Biblical for a man who already fulfilled his mitzvah of *Pru Urvu.*[28] Even then, the reason for the Rabbinic prohibition is because of the verse in *Koheles*, "In the evening do not rest,"[29] from which *Chazal* extrapolate that one should continue to have children even after he has fulfilled his mitzvah of *Pru Urvu.*[30] From here we see that the prohibition of spilling seed is connected to the mitzvah of *Pru Urvu*. Although the Rabbeinu Tam that is cited in both the Tosafos and the Rosh[31] holds this opinion, the Ramban maintains that spilling seed is a Torah prohibition even after the fulfillment of *Pru Urvu.*[32]

There is discussion whether the commandment not to spill seed applies to a man who doesn't have sperm that can produce a child. Perhaps the prohibition is only on seed that

---

26. *Mitpachas Sefarim*, vol. I, 20, cited in the *Tzitz Eliezer*, vol. IX, chap. 51, section 1, 3.

27. *Tzitz Eliezer*, ibid.

28. Rav Y.Y. Shemelkish, *Beis Yitzchak*, vol. I, chap. 91, 2, cites in *Otzar haPoskim* 23:2.

29. *Koheles* 11:6.

30. *Yevamos* 62b.

31. Tosafos and Rosh, *Niddah* 13a.

32. Ramban and *Chiddushei haRan, Niddah* 13a.

can fertilize, and seed that can't fertilize can be wasted. Or is the prohibition independent of the mitzvah of *Pru Urvu*? If so, even if the sperm cannot fertilize, there is still a commandment not to waste it. In *Binyan Tzion*, Rabbi Etlinger holds that it is independent, so therefore even if someone cannot have children he is still commanded not to spill his seed.[33]

In any event, whatever the level of seriousness the act of wasting seed is, it is forbidden. And even if the strong statements against spilling seed aren't to be taken literally, the fact that they were said about this matter in particular tells us that the prohibition cannot be taken lightly. When the issue of acquiring seed for semen analysis or insemination comes up, we must ask, is it allowed, and if so — how?

FOR THE SAKE OF HAVING A CHILD

Is procuring sperm for the purpose of artificial insemination permitted? Although the Divrei Malkiel,[34] a major *posek* from the late nineteenth century, prohibits procuring sperm in any way other than by regular marital relations (without a condom),[35] most *poskim* allow it, including the Yaavetz,[36] the Achiezer,[37] Rav Tzvi Pesach Frank,[38] Rav Ovadiah Yosef,[39] Rav

---

33. *Binyan Tzion* 137.

34. Rabbi Malkiel Tzvi haLevi Tannenbaum, *Divrei Malkiel*, vol. I, chap. 70; vol. III, chap. 91; vol. V, chap. 157. But see *Divrei Malkiel*, vol. IV, chap. 107, where he allows it if the sperm was extracted from the woman after regular intercourse.

35. Other *poskim* who prohibited the procurement of sperm for artificial insemination: *Mishpetei Uziel*, vol. II, chap. 19, Rav A.D. Rubenstein in *Tel Talpios* 5691, R. Ovadiah Hodiyah, *Yaskil Avdi*, vol. V, chap. 10.

36. *Responsa Yaavetz*, vol. I, chap. 43.

37. Rav Chaim Ozer Grodzinski, *Achiezer*, vol. III, chap. 24:4.

38. *Har Tzvi* on the Tur, *Even haEzer* chap. 1.

39. *Yabia Omer*, vol. II, *Even haEzer* chap. 1.

Moshe Feinstein,[40] and Rav Shlomo Zalman Auerbach.[41]

The reasons for prohibiting the procurement of sperm for artificial insemination are:

- Since the semen isn't going into the natural place it is supposed to go, it could be considered wasting seed.[42]
- The medical staff cannot be trusted to ensure that sperm used for insemination is the sperm of the husband.[43]

The main reason for allowing the procurement of sperm for artificial insemination is that since the sperm will be used for a purpose, it is not considered wasting. The person producing the sperm is doing it for the purpose of having a child, so it is not wasting.[44]

THE TALMUDIC SOURCE

The tractate *Yevamos*[45] provides us with the backdrop for all responsa literature that confronts this topic. The Gemara here is dealing with the law of a man who is not qualified to marry, i.e. a neutered, castrated, or mutilated man.

The Gemara brings the problem of a man who had a puncture on the tip of his reproductive organ and later the puncture was closed. The Gemara says that the man is disqualified

---

40. *Igros Moshe, Even haEzer,* vol. I, chap. 70, vol. II, chap. 16.

41. *Noam* (Jerusalem: Machon Torah Sheleimah, 1958), vol. I.

42. *Yaskil Avdi,* vol. V, chap. 10. *Mishpetei Uziel,* vol. II, chap. 19.

43. See, for example, Rav S. Z. Auerbach in *Noam,* vol. I. For a survey of opinions, see *Birkas Banim,* pp. 166–169.

44. In addition to the *poskim* mentioned above, see also the *Avnei Nezer,* chap. 83. The *Mitzpeh Aryeh Tanina,* chap. 6 (*Otzar haPoskim* 23:10) learns from the Rambam concerning the law of wasting in general (cutting down trees) that it is forbidden only when it is for no reason — but not in a case where it is for a purpose. See the *Pri Sadeh,* vol. III, chap. 53, for the same line of reasoning.

45. 76a.

to marry if the puncture hole reopens when semen is emitted, but if it doesn't reopen the man is deemed fit to marry. The problem, then, is that he needs to emit semen when he is still single in order to determine whether he is fit to marry or not. How will he do so? The Gemara, as we will see, deals with this.

Rava the son of Rabbah asks Rav Yosef, "How can we test him to see if he will be able to marry or not?" Rabbi Yosef says, "The test is to put warm barley bread on the man's anus; thereby the flow of semen sets in, and the effect can be observed. [Nowadays a similar procedure is done with an electronic device.] Abaye objects, "Is everybody like our father Yaakov, concerning whom it is written, 'My strength and the first of my virility,'[46] because he never experienced the emission of semen?!" "No," says Abaye, "[Instead], colored garments [of a woman] are dangled before him [which will cause him to have erotic thoughts and then have an emission]." Says Rava [this is another Rava, not Rava the son of Rabbah], "Is everybody then like Barzilai the Gileadite [who was known for being able to discharge semen merely by looking at a woman's garments]?! In fact, it is obvious that the original answer is to be maintained."

The Gemara here is ambiguous. It seems that supplying semen is permissible in a case of necessity, but it doesn't state clearly which is the best method for obtaining semen.

THE POSKIM

The Yaavetz holds that from this *gemara* we learn that procuring seed for a good reason is permitted.[47] The Achiezer holds that according to the Yaavetz even masturbation would be al-

46. *Bereishis* 49:3.

47. *Responsa Yaavetz*, vol. I, chap. 43. See also *Beis Shemuel, Even haEzer* 23:2. See also *Achiezer*, vol. III, chap. 24; *Tzitz Eliezer*, vol. IX, chap. 51:2, 3; and *Otzar haPoskim* 23:10, quoting the *Avnei Nezer*.

lowed if there were no other ways of attaining the semen.[48] The main message from this *gemara* is that in a case of need, it is permissible to produce semen. The Achiezer holds that since masturbation in this case would be for the mitzvah of *Pru Urvu*, there is no reason for concern. However, he also says that it is better to procure the semen by normal intercourse with a condom, since there are opinions that masturbation, even in this case, is forbidden. The Achiezer concludes that if there is no way of procuring the semen by way of indirect action (*grama*), it would be permissible by masturbation. He says that according to all opinions, intercourse with a condom with one's wife is permissible.

According to Rav Moshe Feinstein we learn a number of things from this *gemara*. He agrees with the Yaavetz and the Achiezer that a man can supply semen if it is needed. Rav Feinstein holds that if procuring semen for the sake of merely seeing whether a man can marry is allowed, then it is certainly allowed for the sake of having children. However, unlike the Achiezer, he prohibits masturbation, because the Gemara doesn't offer it as a solution. The reason it is forbidden is because the Torah says, *Lo sin'af*,[49] which according to *Chazal* means "Do not have *ni'uf* either by hand or foot."[50]

We can deduce that according to Rav Feinstein there are two problems regarding procuring seed. One is wasting the seed if it will serve no constructive purpose. The second is a technical problem of how the semen comes out. Producing semen by using one's hand or any other object is prohibited, even if the purpose is for reproduction. In the case where the semen is needed for either analysis or insemination, the purpose is valid but the method is not.

---

48. *Achiezer*, vol. III, chap. 24:4.

49. *Shemos* 20:13.

50. *Niddah* 13a.

In the case of a man producing semen for fertility there is an acceptable option, and that is procuring the sperm by intercourse with his wife. In the case of the *gemara* cited above, the man wasn't married, so that option didn't exist. But a married man can produce the sperm either by having intercourse and then pulling out (coitus interruptus) to empty the sample into a receptacle,[51] or by wearing a special condom made for this purpose.

Rav Moshe Feinstein says that wearing a condom is preferable, so by use of a condom one may procure sperm, either for analysis or for insemination.[52]

Rav A. Wolkin gives a practical reason to prefer a condom over coitus interruptus, and that is because it will not be so easy to get all the semen into the receptacle.[53] If for whatever

---

51. Coitus interruptus is permissible because it is performed in the course of normal relations (permissible method), and even though the semen will not enter his wife, the seed is not going to waste because it will be used for having children (permissible purpose). In the case of using a condom, according to the Achiezer, the method and purpose are anyway valid, and according to Rav Feinstein condom use is no different from coitus interruptus. See *Tzitz Eliezer*, vol. IX, chap. 51, who holds that coitus interruptus is preferable.

52. *Igros Moshe, Even haEzer*, vol. I, chap. 70 and vol. II, chap. 18. See also *Achiezer*, vol. III, chap. 24, who prefers this method since there are those who don't allow masturbation. The *Minchas Yitzchak*, vol. III, chap. 108, allowed the use of a condom for this purpose. For more opinion, see *Otzar haPoskim* 23:11.

See also *Tzitz Eliezer*, vol. IX, chap. 51, who says that the best way is by having normal intercourse without a condom, and having the doctor extract the sperm from the woman with a needle. However, if because of the mixtrue with other fluids the analysis would be less accurate, then one should use one of the other methods mentioned in the text above. We did not include this opinion in the text because practically, to the best of our knowledge, it isn't an option. However, this is the only way the *Divrei Malkiel* allows artificial insemination. See *Divrei Malkiel*, vol. IV, chap. 107.

53. *Zaken Aharon*, chap. 97, cited in *Otzar haPoskim* 23:17 (p. 178).

reason these two options are impossible, you must speak to your Rav.[54]

Testicular biopsy, extracting the sperm directly from the testicles, is also permitted. Some authorites prefer that it be done on the left testicle. Others don't express any preference.[55]

SUPERVISION

There are some Rabbis who although they allow artificial insemination, demand that there be a *mashgiach* (supervisor) to make sure that the woman is inseminated with her husband's sperm and not someone else's.[56] Fertility clinics have been known to switch sperm, usually by mistake. But sometimes it is done on purpose because chances for success are better with strong sperm, and a clinic wants to keep its numbers up. Imagine how many times switching sperm happens — either mistakenly or purposely — without the mishap being revealed.

Lately, insemination with supervision has become the preferred way in the religious community in Israel. Machon Puah, a Jerusalem-based fertility resource center run according to halachah, can help you with this. According to Rav Yaakov Ariel, since it is almost impossible to watch over all the steps involved in artificial insemination, it is permissible to rely on a God-fearing lab technician.[57] If getting a *mashgiach* (supervisor) is an impossibility for you, there may be enough

---

54. See *Achiezer*, vol. III, chap. 24.

55. *Zaken Aharon*, vol. I, chap. 66; *Minchas Yitzchak*, vol. III, chap. 108:6; *Igros Moshe, Even haEzer* vol. II, chap. 3:2; *Tzitz Eliezer*, vol. IX, chap. 51, 1:2, vol. XVI, chap. 42, vol. XX, chap. 48.

56. *Yabia Omer*, vol. II, chap. 1; Rav S. Z. Auerbach, *Noam*, vol. I, cited in *Otzar haPoskim* 23:17; *Tzitz Eliezer*, vol. IX, chap. 51, (summary). HaRav Waldenberg in *Tzitz Eliezer*, vol. XV, chap. 45, wrote against relying on the health professionals in very strong language.

57. *BeOhelah shel Torah, Even haEzer*, chap. 72; *Tzitz Eliezer*, vol. IX, chap. 51, 6:9.

to rely on to allow insemination without it. Rav Moshe Feinstein did not write that supervision is a requirement. Years ago it wasn't done. Of course it is better to have the process watched, but if you cannot have it watched by a trained professional, you may still be allowed to have artificial insemination performed. However, you must consult your Rav.

Each fertility clinic is different; some are more reliable than others. It is possible that since the parents can now have the child checked by DNA testing, clinics may fear legal action against them and therefore be more careful. On the other hand, perhaps some clinics are banking on the fact that most people would never risk spoiling their happiness at finally having a baby by having him or her tested. Rabbi David Cohen recommends that in a case where you cannot arrange supervision, drop a casual line to the doctor, something like: "My Rabbi wants to arrange DNA testing; how do I go about that?" or "By the way, my Rabbi requires that we have DNA testing after the birth." This will be enough to insure that the medical staff will take every precaution to use the semen of the husband.

There is no doubt that having the artificial insemination procedure watched is not only best halachically, but it will give you peace of mind as well. So try to get a trustworthy person, who is also trained to watch over the process. If supervision is impossible, then you should consult your Rav to see if you can have the process done without it.

THE STARTING POINT

At what point may someone consider going for fertility assistance? A book called *Chai Nefesh*[58] cites the Chazon Ish as hav-

---

58. *Chai Nefesh,* vol. I chap. 84, cited in *Otzar haPoskim* 23:13 and *Tzitz Eliezer,* vol. IX, chap. 51:14.

ing allowed a couple to go for assistance after only two years. The *Tzitz Eliezer* says there is no set time; it all depends on the circumstances.[59]

We stated in the beginning of this book that if after a year of normal marital relations the wife does not get pregnant, there is reason for concern. At that point you may go to the doctor to see what the problem is. If he suggests that the husband go through a semen analysis or any other procedure you should ask your Rav. The wife may go through tests at any point.

One cannot of course compare a couple in their early twenties to a couple who only married in their late twenties or thirties. Older couples will have to be more aggressive about seeking treatment sooner in their marriage. They won't have the luxury of waiting as long as a very young couple. But even young couples may not want to wait too long, for the longer you wait, the harder it will be emotionally, and consequently it will be harder to become pregnant. Why go through years of emotional pain when you have the possibility of correcting the problem?

Waiting even a couple of years may be an unnecessary stringency that may complicate things — and may keep people from serving God with joy. Because today doctors can identify problems quite accurately, your Rav might allow a fertility workup even earlier than this. And as already mentioned, Rav Woldenberg in the *Tzitz Eliezer* holds that you don't have to wait any amount of time. Once you have reason to suspect a problem, you can seek medical assistance. You should speak with your Rav concerning this issue.

---

59. *Tzitz Eliezer*, vol. IX, chap. 51 (in his summary). See also *Igros Moshe, Even haEzer*, vol. II, chap. 16, and *Maharsham*, vol. III, chap. 268. See also *Otzar haPoskim* 23:13, for more opinions.

IVF

The *Tzitz Eliezer* makes an interesting distinction between artificial insemination and in vitro fertilization, and therefore allows artificial insemination but forbids IVF.[60] However, most *poskim* make no distinction between AIH and IVF.[61]

* * *

The halachos that were touched upon in this chapter are the most central to the purpose of this book. We live in a great day and age, and we need to be thankful to God for the wealth of possibilities offered us in this modern generation. Halachic limitations should not be perceived as an obstacle to our goals but rather as a guide to lead us to our goals appropriately. Together with the "third Partner" in the creation of every child — the Almighty — and through the use of modern technology, we will fight for our "mandate to parenthood." As we give thanks to God for all that He has given us up until now, may it be His will that we shall be successful in fulfilling the most inherent desire in us all, that we may have children.

---

60. *Tzitz Eliezer*, vol. XV, chap. 45. In AIH, the husband's sperm is transferred directly into the uterus (by way of the cervix). Whether there is successful fertilization or not, the husband did not waste his seed because the seed ended up in the natural place. He holds that it isn't any different than if the couple had regular relations without a pregnancy. With IVF, however, the sperm meets the egg in a test tube. If it fails, then the husband retroactively spilled his seed in vain. Additionally, with IVF, not all the sperm is used, so it is possible that it will be saved for use for someone else. See the responsum for other reasons. See also Rav Moshe Sternbach, *BeShivlei haRefuah*, 5747, pp. 29 –36.

61. Rav Ovadiah Yosef, cited in the essay of M. Drori in *Techumin*, vol. I, p. 287, and in *Nishmas Avraham*, *Even haEzer* 1. See also HaRav Avigdor Nebenzahl in *Assiah*, vol. V, 5786.

22. Third-Party Reproduction: Halachic and Ethical Aspects

Whoever heeds the advice of the wise men will not fail.

(*Bereishis Rabbah* 71:1)

PREFACE

We have chosen this chapter to discuss the general topic of asking for halachic guidance. We chose to speak about this topic here specifically, for the halachic considerations in this chapter are the most consequential. Most fertility problems have solutions, and the question is basically, Which is the best way to do it? and not, Is it permitted? Here, the answer can be "yes" or "no" — and the "yes" usually has many conditions to it. Asking the Rav for a ruling about third-party reproduction is a big step. The ruling could allow you to go after your dreams... or not.

You will not go to your Rav with a question of such magnitude, that carries with it such emotional weight, with an attitude of neutrality vis-à-vis the answer. You will already know which answer you want to hear. Asking about options for third-party fertility is not like asking about using your oven on Passover. The question — and the ruling — could be life-changing.

INTRODUCTION: ASKING THE RAV

The use of sperm from a donor is a medical option that offers the infertile couple, or more correctly the wife, a chance at having a baby. Few couples would opt for such an alternative if they felt they had a chance at achieving fertility through the sperm of the husband. There is no doubt that using another man's sperm to impregnate a woman is a last-resort solution.

Third-party fertilization raises many ethical and halachic questions. Is it an ethical alternative? Is it good for the couple but bad for society? Is it a choice that may seem beneficial for the couple now, but may be harmful for the couple in the future? If having children is supposed to be the extension of a couple's love for each other, then why would they even think of third-party reproduction? Is adoption preferable to third-party reproduction?

There are many answers to the question of why a woman would even think of opting for third-party reproduction. First of all, there is a psychological and to some extent a biological need for a woman to be pregnant. It is the key expression of her femininity. Adoption does not answer that need, although it answers other needs. If a woman can become pregnant even by an anonymous sperm donor, she will fulfill that aspect of her femininity. Third-party reproduction, or AID — artificial insemination by donor — as it's usually called, allows a woman the opportunity to experience a pregnancy together with her husband. Furthermore, the child may resemble the mother, a possibility that does not exist with adoption. There is also the knowledge that the child is hers — something she may not feel with an adopted baby, whose biological parent may reappear a few years later. Also, the couple may be afraid of possible genetic problems of an adopted baby. Through third-party reproduction, at least they are 50 percent sure of the genetic background.[1]

It is difficult for a couple to ask for halachic permission for third-party fertility. They are thinking, "We need a positive ruling from the Rabbi, even though we ourselves admit that it's not the most desired way." Couples who turn to third-party reproduction aren't looking to throw away traditional family values. A traditional family is what they crave more than anything. The option of AID is in their opinion the best method, under the circumstances, for achieving that goal.

When the couple goes to the Rabbi for guidance they should realize that they are basically asking what God's will is in this case. Even though the Rabbi is not a prophet, and the written Torah does not relate to this problem directly, our tradition gives the leading Rabbis of every generation the right and the obligation to try and determine the halachah — which is in essence God's will. A God-fearing couple will have to be willing to accept the ruling of the Rabbi as what is ultimately for the best, even if they neither agree with nor are happy about it.

Imagine a sensitive issue such as fertility. One couple asks a Rabbi if they may undergo a certain procedure, and they receive an affirmative answer. Another couple asks a different Rabbi if the halachah permits them to undergo the same procedure, yet they receive a negative answer. Both couples are seeking the will of God. Yet each couple may be told something else.

This can be confusing. Many people have the erroneous assumption that the Rabbi who doesn't allow the procedure is not as sensitive to people's feelings as the Rabbi who does allow it, or that he is old fashioned. This is not at all the case.

The Rabbi who says "no" is not "more religious" or more

---

1. See Fred Rosner, "Artificial Insemination in Jewish Law," in *Jewish Bioethics*, p. 106.

God-fearing. Rabbis have different opinions, but they are all looking out for what is best for you, to the best of their ability according to what they understand to be the law of the Torah. In today's time, there is no "one answer."

Because of the complexity of this issue, not every Rabbi can answer the difficult questions that arise regarding fertility treatments. The majority of today's Rabbis rely on the views of those few halachic experts who do offer their opinions on the matter. You might go to a Rabbi who can render his own halachic decisions, or you might go to someone who studies the views of the *poskim* and reaches a decision for you based on his survey of the halachic opinions.

Being aware of some of the opinions and the reasons for them will give you a feeling of confidence when you go to your Rabbi for advice or a ruling. The halachic reasoning is presented here, not to empower you to determine the halachah, but rather to educate you. This will help you discuss the ruling with your Rabbi, as well as enable you to understand his point of view in whichever direction he decides. It won't seem like his decision is arbitrary. It is frustrating to come away "in the dark" from a halachic ruling, wondering, "Why did he say that?" A little knowledge of the halachic background will help you realize that the ruling you have received was not arbitrary.

If you receive an opinion from a Rabbi that is hard for you to accept, you may ask another Rabbi for his opinion on the condition that you tell the second Rabbi that you went to the first Rabbi, and tell him what he told you.[2] It will be up to the second Rabbi to decide whether he wants to give a different

---

2. See the Shach at the end of *Hilchos Kevod Rabo, Kitzur be-Hanhagos Hora'os Isur ve-Heter*. See also essay by Rabbi Moshe Tendler in *Techumin*, vol. IX, p. 191, and see *Encyclopedia Talmudit, d.h. Hora'ah achar hora'ah*.

opinion or whether he will honor the first opinion. For many reasons, it is best to have just one Rabbi to speak to about all your fertility issues. This way he will know you and be aware of your history. This will be beneficial for you in the long run. The Rabbi you choose should know the topic well, or should be open enough to consult Rabbis who are experts in this area.

UNDERSTANDING THE HALACHIC RULING FOR AID

Jewish Donor The halachah across the board concerning donor sperm from a Jew is that it is forbidden. The reason is based on the Tosefta in tractate *Kiddushin*: "Someone who was intimate with many women, and doesn't know whom he was with; or a woman who was with many men and doesn't know whom she was with, will cause (a scenario) that a father will marry a daughter, a brother will marry a sister, and the whole world will be filled with illegitimate children. On this (scenario) it was stated, "The land will become full of lewdness (*Vayikra* 19:29)."[3]

The Bach quotes Rabbeinu Peretz, who says that a woman is forbidden to lay on the sheets of another man lest she becomes pregnant, for we are afraid that the child will not know who his or her father is and may marry a sibling without knowing it.[4] The *Taz* quotes the Bach on the *Tur* in *Yoreh De'ah*:

> In the Bach it says, "I found in the glosses of *Semak Yashan* in the name of Rabbeinu Peretz that a woman in the *niddah*

---

3. Tosefta *Kiddushin* 1:2; Gemara *Yevamos* 37b.

4. *Hagahos Semak*, quoted in the *Taz* in *Yoreh De'ah* 195:7; *Beis Shemuel, Even haEzer* 1:10, which was copied from the Bach in *Yoreh De'ah* 195. [In the Machon Yerushalayim version there is a note on the *Hagahos Semak* which says, "I didn't find it."] See also *Shiltei Giborim* on the Rif in *Shevuos* 2a, who brings a different opinion from the Maharam of Rottenberg. The Maharam of Rottenberg and Rav Shlomo of London (one of the *Ba'alei Tosafos*) are the sources for those *poskim* who don't rely on Rabbeinu Peretz's opinion.

> state may sit on her husband's sheets, yet [women] are careful not to sit on the sheets of another man lest one become pregnant from the seed of the other man. Why doesn't she worry that she will get pregnant (from the seed of her husband) — and therefore she will have a child born from her *niddah* state? Rabbeinu Peretz answers that since there is no forbidden intercourse the child is perfectly kosher. Even if she gets pregnant from the seed of another man (the child would be kosher), for Ben Sira was kosher.[5] It is just that from the seed of another man we are careful that there should be *havchanah* (a separation period of three months, to distinguish between her husband's seed and this other man's seed) [and][6] it is a Rabbinic decree that maybe he (the child) will (eventually) marry his sister from his father's side (the man who left the seed on the sheets).

Based on this, sperm from a Jewish donor is forbidden lest the child marry a sibling without knowing it.

According to some opinions there is an additional and much more serious problem, and that is that the child would be a *mamzer*. Some Rabbis hold that the relationship between the mother and the donor is adulterous.[7] According to other opinions,[8] the child of AID is considered to be a *safek* (possible) *mamzer*. There is also an opinion that the wife is not consid-

---

5. See chapter 5. There are some *poskim* who don't rely on this legend about Ben Sira (Rav S. Z. Aurbach, *Noam*, vol. I, and others).

6. In the Bach itself the letter *vav* ("and") is not printed, but the *Taz*, who copied the Bach word for word, has the *vav* here. This may have major halachic consequences.

7. Rav Y. Teitelbaum, the Satmar Rebbe, *HaMaor*, Av–Elul 5724. See also *Tzitz Eliezer*, vol. XIII, chap. 97; *Shevet haLevi*, vol. III, chap. 175; *Yaskil Avdi*, vol. V, *Even haEzer*, chap. 86. See also Rav Yaakov Brisch, *Chelkas Yaakov*, who says she is *"overes al das Moshe."*

8. Rav S.Z. Auerbach, *Noam*, vol. I, 5718. Rav Auerbach leans more to the opinion that says the child would be considered a *mamzer*. See also *Tzitz Eliezer*, vol. XIII, chap. 97, 2. According to the *Seridei Eish*, vol. III, chap. 5, the child is considered a *shetuki*.

ered adulterous but the child is considered a *mamzer*.[9]

Action or Result?

The question of whether the child is considered a *mamzer* or not is based on how the child's status is determined — by an illicit sexual act, or by a forbidden outcome. According to the latter opinion it doesn't matter whether intercourse took place or not; the fact that there was a child born to a married woman, fathered by another man, especially with her consent, would render the child a *mamzer*.[10] According to the first opinion, only through the act of adultery would the offspring be illegitimate, but in a case where no sexual contact occurred there is no problem of adultery or of *mamzerus*.[11] In any event, because there is still the problem of a brother marrying a sister, a woman cannot receive sperm from a Jewish donor. However, if a woman did, then according to Rav Moshe Feinstein and other *poskim*, the child would not be a *mamzer* and the wife would not be considered adulterous.

The use of sperm banks in Israel, where the majority of the country's citizens are Jews, would therefore not be permissible.[12]

Non-Jewish Donor

Would AID be allowed if the donor is a non-Jew? There is no problem of *mamzerus*, because a *mamzer* can only be the offspring of two Jews.

---

9. See Rav S. Z. Auerbach, ibid.

10. Rav Y. Teitelbaum, the Satmar Rebbe, *HaMaor*, Av–Elul 5724; *Tzitz Eliezer*, vol. XIII, chap. 97, quoting the *Ma'arachei Lev*, chap. 73. See also Rav S. Z. Auerbach, *Noam*, vol. I.

The Ramban on *Vayikra* 18:20 is a strong source for those who consider the "outcome" to be the determining factor. See also *Sefer haChinuch*, mitzvah 35, for the same line of reasoning.

11. *Igros Moshe, Even haEzer*, vol. I, chaps. 10, 71; *Yabia Omer*, vol. II, chap. 1. See also *Tzitz Eliezer*, vol. III, chap. 27,1.

12. See *Encyclopedia of Jewish Medical Ethics*, vol. I, p. 159 (Hebrew), or vol. I, p. 67 (English).

There is also no problem of two siblings possibly marrying, for when the father is a non-Jew, the children are only halachically related to the mother. Even if the sperm donor's children would convert, they are considered as reborn. Therefore, they are not at all related to the offspring of the sperm donor and the Jewish mother. Because of this, Rav Moshe Feinstein allowed donor sperm of a non-Jew on a theoretical level,[13] but advised against it. In other words he held that it was allowed technically, but was not recommended.[14] We will get back to this idea later.

There are other *poskim* who hold the same opinion as Rav Moshe, i.e. that AID from a non-Jewish donor is technically allowed.[15] There are other opinions that hold that it is forbidden, as it is considered ugly and disgraceful.[16] According to these opinions, a husband would have the right to divorce his wife if she did AID from a non-Jewish donor, even if the procedure was unsuccessful.[17] Most contemporary Rabbis who allow AID with non-Jewish donor sperm are basing themselves on the *psak* of Rav Moshe Feinstein.

In an early volume of *Igros Moshe*, Rav Feinstein wrote that in a case of great need, when the couple is very sad that they don't have a child, it is permissible to inseminate the wife with the sperm of a non-Jew.[18] However, one must be very careful when using this ruling, and must read everything else that Rav Feinstein wrote on the subject. This is because in a later

---

13. *Igros Moshe, Even haEzer,* vol. I, chap. 71.

14. *Igros Moshe, Even haEzer,* vol. IV, chap. 32,5.

15. Rav S. Z. Auerbach, *Noam,* vol. I.

16. Rav Y.Y. Weinberg (the Seridei Eish), *HaPardes,* Tishrei 5711; Rav M. Meiri, *HaPardes,* Shevat 5716; Rav Y. Woltz, *Tel Talpios,* Tammuz 5691.

17. *Tzitz Eliezer,* vol. III, chap. 27, and vol. XIII, chap. 97; *Minchas Yitzchak,* vol. IV, chap. 5; *Seridei Eish,* vol. III, chap. 5; *Shevet haLevi,* vol. III, chap. 175.

18. *Igros Moshe,* vol. I, chap. 71.

volume of *Igros Moshe,* Rav Feinstein said that he recommends against it, for it will cause "jealousy in the family." Our interpretation of this is: It is possible that Rav Feinstein was concerned that in the future the husband may not view that child as his own, for unlike adoption, where the couple has equal status as parents of the child, AID is her biological baby, not his. And it is a constant, strong reminder that he could not produce a baby. Maybe now your husband is willing, but fifteen years from now problems may arise. If there is jealousy in the future, it will be the cause of tension in the home. Interestingly, professional psychologists articulate the same concern.[19]

A child should be a blessing to a couple. A child should build a family, not destroy it. Rav Feinstein apparently understood this possible scenario. Technically he allowed AID, but in practice he was against it, for his major concern was building the family.

More Concerns

Let us consider some other problems that may arise when a couple opts for donor sperm. Each individual problem may not be enough to persuade you against donor sperm, but all of them together might paint a picture fraught with more problems than solutions.

◆ **Fulfillment of the mitzvah.** From a halachic point of view the husband accomplishes nothing. He is commanded to be fruitful and multiply, and AID does not help him fulfill this mitzvah.[20] Perhaps by giving birth the wife fulfills *Lasheves,* the charge to populate the earth. In chapter 9, we said that a person should pray for a child for the sake of God. Is this considered for the sake of God, if no mitzvah is fulfilled?

---

19. *Men, Women, and Infertility,* pp. 107–109.

20. See *Igros Moshe, Even haEzer,* vol. IV, chap. 32, 5.

◆ **Fulfillment of your dreams.** The wife achieves pregnancy, but not by her husband. Is this what she intended? No, of course not, but at this stage she is at the very end of the fertility road. She is eager to be pregnant. Physically, emotionally, her whole essence demands it. How can she forfeit her only chance to conceive?

She must try to think objectively. She must put herself in her husband's shoes and then think, will this be better or worse for our marriage? It is easy to imagine cuddling a cute little baby wrapped in his baby blanket on a cold winter night, but it is hard to see how things will be twenty years down the road. Sometimes we have to extend our imagination that far when making life-changing decisions.

◆ **Monetary issues.** What if there would be a divorce down the road? Would the husband owe any child support? It isn't his baby. He can claim that he never adopted the child and therefore has no connection to the child whatsoever. He can say, let the sperm donor pay for child support, it is his child. On the other hand, perhaps his consent to AID is enough to obligate him to the child's well-being, just as if he adopted the baby. It could be a messy divorce.[21]

There could also be a problem of inheritance in the future. In a situation where no one is told that the child is the product of AID, if the couple were to have other children naturally in the future, the child born from AID would inherit his mother's husband, even though halachically he is not entitled, and he would be taking from the portion of the rightful heirs. If a couple adopts a child the same problem arises, but there the couple's other children will most likely be aware of it, and the arrangement would (hopefully) be accepted beforehand. But

21. See *Encyclopedia of Jewish Medical Ethics*, vol. I, p. 158, notes 86–87 (Hebrew), or vol. I, p. 66, notes 100–102, for source material for this case. See also Rav Shlomo Goren, *Toras haRefuah*, p. 189.

in the former case, since the child's lineage was kept secret, he will end up inheriting a portion that isn't his.[22]

◆ **Chalitzah.** For obvious reasons, most couples don't tell other people, including their close relatives, that the wife was impregnated from donor sperm. What would happen if, God forbid, her husband would die, leaving no biological children of his own? She would be obligated to perform the mitzvah of *chalitzah* with her husband's brother. But everyone thinks that her husband had a child and therefore *chalitzah* would not be necessary. She now faces a challenging dilemma. Does she tell the truth and perform *chalitzah* with the husband's brother, or does she stay quiet and let everyone think that the child is her deceased husband's?

If she tells the truth, she will be humiliating herself, her husband's family, and most of all the memory of her former husband. If she stays silent, she will remain an *agunah* for the rest of her life, for she is forbidden to remarry until she performs *chalitzah*. In addition to that, she may be doing a disservice to her brother-in-law, for he may want to fulfill the mitzvah of *chalitzah* if he would have the chance — but he may never know that he has the chance. If they are older, and she doesn't care to remarry, it may not matter, for according to most opinions if the widow and the brother-in-law both don't want to do *chalitzah*, they don't have to do it.[23] However, some *poskim* hold they still should do it, for it is a mitzvah that stands by itself regardless of setting her free for remarriage.[24] Putting a woman through this type of dilemma would be very

---

22. *Tzitz Eliezer,* vol. IX, chap. 51, 5.

23. See *Beis Yitzchak,* chap. 17. This also seems to be Rashi's opinion in *Sanhedrin* 19b.

24. See the Rashash on *Sanhedrin* 19b, and see the Netziv in *Emek Halachah* 154. See also Rav S. Z. Auerbach, *Noam,* vol. I.

difficult and challenging, to say the least.[25]

◆ **Separation.** Some Rabbis are of the opinion that the husband must separate from his wife for at least three months, and some say even during the whole pregnancy and nursing period, if his wife were to get pregnant from a sperm donor.[26]

◆ **A Kohen.** A Kohen would have a problem if his wife has a son from donor sperm, for everyone will assume that the child is a Kohen — while in reality he isn't. The son would not be able to bless the congregation, get the first *aliyah* to the Torah, or perform all the other duties and honors that a Kohen has.[27] One *posek* has suggested that the father should change his name, so no one will assume that his child is a Kohen. Another option is to have a daughter, for a daughter doesn't have the communal responsibilities that a son has.[28] This is possible through PGD (see chapter 20), as the sex of the child can be seen before implantation in the womb.

◆ **Your will or God's will?** Just because something is allowed doesn't mean that it is recommended. There are many actions that are allowed but the religious world refrains from them nonetheless because they do not contribute to the standards of behavior that Judaism as a whole, or a specific mitzvah in particular, is trying to reach.

---

25. Rav Y.Y. Weinberg in *HaPardes*, Tishrei 5711. *Tzitz Eliezer,* vol. III, chap. 27, section 2,10. Rav S. Z. Auerbach says that if the woman came and asked a Rav for halachic guidance concerning AID, we see that she is God-fearing and would not do anything against the halachah. Therefore, this concern that she may not do *chalitzah* shouldn't be a problem. Rav Moshe Feinstein was also not concerned with the *chalitzah* problem. See his responsum printed at the end of *Dibros Moshe, maseches Kesuvos.*

26. *Tzitz Eliezer,* vol. IX, chap. 51 (summary). See also Rav S. Z. Auerbach, *Noam,* vol. I.

27. See *Minchas Yitzchak,* vol. VI, chap. 140.

28. *BeOhelah shel Torah, Even haEzer* 70.

Even actions from the Torah that are permissible are not always recommended. For instance, taking a *yefas to'ar* (a female captive taken for the purpose of marriage) as a spoil of war is allowed but not recommended. Having more then one wife used to be allowed, but was not recommended. Marrying a girl before she was twelve years old was allowed but not recommended. Taking a slave used to be allowed but was not recommended, as was selling a daughter into slavery – allowed but not recommended. Donor sperm from a non-Jew may be allowed by some *poskim*, but it is not recommended.

◆ **The family.** Twice God commanded mankind to be fruitful and multiply — once to Adam and Eve, and once to Noach, his wife, his sons, and their wives when they left the Ark. Why did God command mankind a second time? What nuance did He add when commanding Noach and his family?

Rav Y. E. Henkin suggests that since God spoke to Noach's entire family, the nuance is that the blessing to be fruitful and multiply is only a blessing when it is within the framework of a family.[29] This was God's message to the new world: populate the world, but do it in the framework of families. The beauty of having a biological child is when a husband and wife who love each other bring that child into the world, be it naturally or with high-tech assistance — as long as the child is theirs. God was telling Noach, and essentially mankind: I know you can populate the world outside the family framework, but I bless you to have children as a family.

If you opt for non-Jewish donor sperm become pregnant, even if it is your last resort — and God knows how much you desperately want a baby — are you really achieving God's blessing as He stressed to Noach and his family? Is this what God wants, even if it is what He allows?

---

29. Rabbi Yosef Eliyahu Henkin, *"Yichus Mishpachah u'Pru Urvu," Hapardes*, Tammuz 5713 (1953), pp. 1–5.

Extenuating Circumstances

There may be extenuating circumstances that warrant the use of donor sperm. Since AID is technically allowed by some of the *poskim*, its potential use cannot be completely disregarded. You should speak to your Rav, and together you can determine if your particular case calls for the use of non-Jewish donor sperm to build your family. It goes without saying that any type of dispensation for such a procedure would be given only when it is medically determined that there is no possible way of getting any viable sperm from the husband, even by way of extraction.[30]

Here are examples of when some rabbis allowed AID:

- The husband could probably never conceive a child, and without the use of AID with non-Jewish sperm the couple would certainly get divorced
- Severe depression
- The infertile husband has cancer and the wife is in her mid-thirties, and without AID she might never have a child

Mutual Consent

It is forbidden for a woman to undergo AID without the consent of her husband. As mentioned earlier, according to some *poskim* going through an AID procedure without the consent of the husband is a grounds for divorce, even if no child resulted.[31] Even Rav Moshe Feinstein, who allowed AID in a case of great need and

---

30. *Tzitz Eliezer,* vol. IX, chap. 51 (summary).

31. *Chelkas Yaakov* 24; Rav Y.Y. Weinberg in *HaPardes,* Tishrei 5711; *Tzitz Eliezer,* vol. III, chap. 27. Rav Eliezer Waldenberg (author of the *Tzitz Eliezer*) is against AID, even though he holds that there is no problem of adultery or *mamzerus*. However, he holds that it is ethically wrong and prevents the *Shechinah* from resting on the Jewish People, for the *Shechinah* only rests on the families of identified lineage. Rav Ovadiah Yosef in *Yabia Omer,* vol. II, chap. 1, expressed the same thoughts as Rav Waldenberg.

if the couple was very depressed, only allowed it if the husband agreed (although he does not hold that carrying out the procedure is grounds for divorce).[32] On the other hand, a husband has no right to demand that his wife undergo AID if she doesn't want to do it.[33] There needs to be consent from both husband and wife to even entertain the option.

Even if you and your husband agree to AID in principle, under no circumstances may you opt for non-Jewish donor sperm without a specific ruling from your Rav.[34] If your Rav says that it is halachically permissible, he might hold that you must refrain from intimacy for three months after the insemination, in order not to confuse paternal identity.[35] According to Rav Moshe Feinstein, only if the doctors think there is a chance that the husband's sperm will improve within the next three months must the couple separate, but otherwise they don't have to.[36] (Practically, however, if that was the case, the couple most likely wouldn't decide on AID at that time; they would probably still try with the sperm of the husband.) As fertility treatments improve, the necessity for AID will diminish. Most of the time, AIH will be feasible.

---

32. *Igros Moshe, Even haEzer,* vol. I, chap. 71; *Tzitz Eliezer,* vol. XIII, chap. 97. See also *Yabia Omer,* vol. II, chap. 1.

33. *Shevet haLevi,* vol. III, chap. 175. See also Rav S. Z. Auerbach, *Noam,* vol. I.

34. See *Tzitz Eliezer,* vol. IX, chap. 51, section 5:4, who quotes a letter from Rav Moshe Feinstein to Rav Tzvi Hirsh Freedman. In that letter Rav Moshe said (my loose translation), "Only a *rav muvhak,* who is a well-known and competent *posek,* can answer these questions properly. God forbid that any Rav allow this based on my responsum. There was one time when a couple came to me and I prohibited it." (In *Igros Moshe, Even haEzer,* vol. IV, chap. 32, Rav Moshe wrote that he doesn't regret what he previously wrote, even though the *Tzitz Eliezer* claims that Rav Moshe regretted his earlier ruling.)

35. See *Otzar haPoskim* 20:8, last paragraph.

36. *Igros Moshe, Even haEzer,* vol. I, chap. 71.

If a woman has a daughter through artificial insemination from the seed of a non-Jew, according to Rav Moshe Feinstein, the daughter is permitted to marry a Kohen.[37] This is a minority opinion among the *poskim*.

Other Issues

The halachah clearly forbids mixing donor sperm with the sperm from the husband (booster). Doctors sometimes suggest this in order to give the husband a feeling that perhaps the child is his, even though chances are that the donor sperm fertilized the egg.[38] If you mix weak sperm with healthy sperm, the healthy sperm will most likely reach the egg first — as the Gemara says, only the best of the sperm can fertilize. The chance that one of the husband's sperm cells will fertilize the egg is too improbable. Therefore, the "booster" procedure is clearly forbidden. There is even the problem of the husband's wasting seed, because in this case his seed will almost for sure go to waste — unlike AIH, where there is the possibility that a pregnancy will result from it.

According to Rav Moshe Feinstein, if someone used sperm from a sperm bank outside of Israel, it can be assumed that the sperm is from a non-Jew. Even if the doctor tells you that the sperm came from a Jew, still this may not be the case. Perhaps he only told you that because he thought it would make you

---

37. Even though the *Shulchan Aruch* (*Even haEzer* 4:19) says that a daughter born to a Jewish mother and a non-Jewish father should not marry a Kohen, Rav Feinstein allows it in a case of artificial insemination. See *Igros Moshe, Even haEzer*, vol. I, chap. 10, for his reasoning. See also the three letters that Rav Feinstein wrote to Rabbi Yaakov Briesh, which were published at the end of *Dibros Moshe, Kesuvos* (1:8). In those letters, Rav Feinstein defended his controversial opinions regarding artificial insemination and responded to almost all the points of disagreement between him and the other *poskim*.

38. *Igros Moshe*, ibid., Rav Y. E. Henkin, *HaMaor*, Tishrei–Cheshvan 5725. *Tzitz Eliezer*, vol. VIII, end of chap. 97.

feel better.[39] In another responsum in the same volume of *Igros Moshe,* Rav Feinstein says it is good to find out for sure if the sperm came from a non-Jew, but if you can't or didn't know for sure you can assume that it was from a non-Jew.[40]

SURROGATE PREGNANCIES AND EGG DONATIONS

Determining the halachah for AID pales in comparison to the complexity of the halachic concerns that come with the procedures of surrogate pregnancies and egg donations. Before we discuss the halachic problems, we will give a brief description of the procedures.

Surrogate Pregnancy

Surrogacy is an arrangement in which a woman carries a pregnancy for an infertile woman. There are two types of surrogate pregnancies:

- The surrogate carries a pregnancy that was created from the sperm and egg of two other individuals (the husband and wife). This procedure is similar to IVF (induction of ovulation and retrieval), but after the retrieved eggs are fertilized in the laboratory they are transferred to the surrogate. Surrogacy may be considered when a woman has functioning ovaries but no uterus or cannot successfully carry a pregnancy to term.
- *Traditional surrogacy,* where IUI (see chapter 17) is used to impregnate the surrogate with sperm from the husband. (The wife has no biological connection to the pregnancy.) This may be considered when a woman does not produce viable eggs, or might even be an option for women with genetic disorders that could be passed on to her children.

---

39. *Igros Moshe, Even haEzer,* vol. I, chap. 10.
40. Ibid., chap. 71.

Donor Embryos

Embryo donation involves donor eggs that have been fertilized, through IVF, either by the woman's husband or by another man, and implanted in the woman.

Halachic Difficulties

Whether surrogate pregnancies and egg donations are allowed, and who is the "real" mother according to halachah, are questions that cannot be answered so easily. Regarding artificial insemination, there are a few sources in the Talmud that shed light on the topic (see page 382 ff). Even though there are different interpretations and conclusions from these sources, still there is a Talmudic source for the theoretical case of medically assisted insemination. With surrogacy and egg donation, however, although there are sources, they are not as direct. Much depth of knowledge and understanding is needed in order to develop halachic solutions.[41]

Secondly, the topic of medically assisted insemination has received much rabbinic attention, dating back to the mid-1800's. Halachic decisions were rendered back then (and even before that regarding the theoretical case of insemination in a bathtub). We have continuously had great rabbinic authorities concerning themselves with the question of artificial insemination. However, egg donations and surrogacy are relatively new phenomena that only recently

---

41. See, for example, Rav Ezra Bick (quoted by Rabbi J. David Bleich), who tries to learn the law of planting an egg into a womb from the agricultural laws, as it can be compared to planting a seed in the fertile ground (also quoted in Susan Martha Kahn, *Reproducing Jews* [Durham, NC: Duke University Press, 2000], pp. 129 –130.) See also *BeOhelah shel Torah, Even haEzer*, chap. 70, who brings models from the laws of *orlah*, *chadash*, and others, but then disregards them, saying that each topic has its own type of ruling (הלכות חדש לחוד והלכות יחוס לחוד).

are being discussed by modern scholars.[42]

With artificial insemination the Rabbis had clear opinions. With egg donations it seems that even after a halachic decision was rendered, they were still in doubt.[43]

As far as whether the procedure of surrogate gestation or egg donation should be considered or not, you must seek rabbinic guidance. You should not decide on your own if it should be done.[44]

Surrogate arrangements carry many legal and ethical dilemmas. The big question with egg donations and surrogate pregnancies is maternal identity — is it the egg donor, or the woman who carries the pregnancy? The *poskim* who wrestled with this dilemma found Talmudic and even Midrashic sources to prove the starting point of the maternal relationship. As with many halachic issues of this magnitude, there is no consensus among the major *poskim*. Identifying maternal relationship is crucial, however, for it carries many halachic concerns.

There are some authorities who hold that the carrier is the

---

42. See *Encyclopedia of Jewish Medical Ethics*, vol II, pp. 129ff (Hebrew), or vol. II, pp. 573–583 (English).

43. See, for example, the responsum printed in *Toras haRefuah*, pp. 184–185, and the conclusion of the essay, "In Vitro Fertilization: Maternal Identity and Conversion," in Rabbi J. David Bleich, *Contemporary Halachic Problems*, vol. IV (Hoboken, NJ: Ktav Publishing, 1976), p. 250. See also the conclusion of the essay by Rav Kelav in *Techumin*, vol. V, p. 260.

44. Rav Mordechi Eliyahu, addressing a convention on Medicine, Ethics, and Jewish Law at Shaare Zedek Hospital (1996), mentioned that he was against the practice of surrogacy. Rav Yosef Shalom Elyashiv and Rav Shlomo Zalman Auerbach have also condemned the practice. See *Nishmas Avraham, Even haEzer*. Published in "The Second Annual Conference on Medicine, Ethics, and Halachah," Tammuz 1990. See *Reproducing Jews,* chap. 5, note 8.

According to Rabbi David Cohen, if a Rav permits egg donations, he should only allow it if the egg donor is single and Jewish.

mother. We will call her the gestational mother. Some are of this opinion because they hold that there is Talmudic justification to say that the moment of motherhood starts at birth,[45] and others because they hold that motherhood begins at day 40 of pregnancy.[46] Other authorities hold that the egg donor (the genetic mother) determines parentage.[47] There are even those who hold that since there is a doubt, we must consider both the egg donor and the carrier as the mother.[48]

Concerning the religion of the child, some authorities hold that as far as maternal identity is concerned the gestational mother is the mother, but the egg donor determines the child's religion. According to that opinion the mother of the child could be the Jewish carrier, but the child will still need be converted if the egg donor was not Jewish.[49] Other authorities hold that the carrier is the mother in every aspect, so if the carrier is a non-Jew, then the child is a non-Jew.[50]

There seems to be a little more weight on the side that says that the carrier is the mother, but not yet enough to rule out the other possibility that the egg donor is the mother. If you are involved in surrogacy or egg donation, you will have to

---

45. Rav Z.N. Goldberg in *Techumin,* vol. V, p. 248; see also Rav A.Y. Kelav in *Techumin,* ibid., p. 260.

46. Rav Shaul Yisraeli in *Chavas Binyamin,* vol. II, chap. 68.

47. *Toras haRefuah,* p. 173; see also *BeOhelah shel Torah,* ibid., where the author claims in the conclusion that the *Nishmas Avraham* wrote in the name of Rav S.Z Auerbach that the child should have the *chumros* of both mothers. But then after speaking to Professor Ze'ev Lev, Rav Auerbach changed his mind and said that the egg donor is the one to determine parentage.

48. Rabbi J. David Bleich, "In Vitro Fertilization: Maternal Identity and Conversion," in *Contemporary Halakhic Problems,* p. 272. Also see the conclusion of Rav Ariel's essay in *"BeOhelah shel Torah," Even haEzer,* chap. 70.

49. See *BeOhelah shel Torah, Even haEzer,* chap. 70.

50. Rav Mordechai Eliyahu, quoted in *Reproducing Jews,* chap. 5, note 8.

get rabbinic advice.

Below are some of the halachic, legal, and ethical dilemmas that result from surrogate pregnancies and egg donations. Some of these dilemmas are applicable to IVF as well.

Halachic dilemmas:

- Whom is the child obligated to honor?
- Who are the baby's siblings? Are they the children of the egg donor or the carrier? Which siblings are forbidden to marry each other?
- Can both women be considered the halachic mother?
- If the egg donor is a non-Jew and the carrier is Jewish, is the child Jewish or does he or she need to convert?
- If the egg donor is a Jew and the carrier is a non-Jew, is the child Jewish or does he or she need to convert?[51]
- If the egg donor or the surrogate is a *bas Levi* or a *bas Kohen*, does the baby need a *pidyon ha-ben*?
- Is there even a *pidyon ha-ben* when the egg and womb are of different women?[52]
- If the egg donor is not allowed to marry into the Jewish nation (i.e. she is a *mamzeres*, for example), what is the status of the baby? If the carrier is a *mamzeres*, what is the status of the baby?
- Is it better to use the eggs of a married woman who went through infertility treatments herself and has some extracted eggs that were left over, or is it better to

---

51. See Rav Z.N. Goldberg in *Techumin*, vol. V, pp. 248–259, and Rav Kelav in the same volume, p. 260. See also Rav Y. Ben Meir in *Assiah*, vol. IX (book version), pp. 153–168, who proves that there are four different opinions concerning this issue.

52. See Rav Z.N. Goldberg in *Techumin* vol. V, pp. 248–259. See also essay of Rav Shlomo Goren in *HaTzofeh*, 14 Adar 5744.

extract an egg from a single woman?[53]

- Is it better to use a Jewish or a non-Jewish donor?
- If an egg was retrieved, fertilized, and frozen, and after that, another egg from the same woman was retrieved and fertilized and then implanted first, which one is considered the firstborn?[54]
- May one destroy a fertilized egg or is it considered like an abortion?[55]
- May one desecrate Shabbos to save a fertilized egg that has not yet been implanted?[56]

Legal dilemmas:

- Who is considered the legal mother of the child?
- If God forbid the child is born deformed, can the parents or the doctor be blamed?
- What happens if the surrogate decides to terminate her pregnancy?
- What if a fertilized egg was frozen and then the couple divorced? Can the woman go through pregnancy without her former husband's permission, or does he need to agree? (This is also a dilemma for IVF.) Can the former husband give the fertilized egg to a surrogate without his former wife's permission?
- How binding is the surrogate contract? What is done if one of the parties decides to break it?

Ethical dilemmas:

- Can and should you tell the child who the egg donor or the surrogate mother is?

---

53. See *Encyclopedia of Jewish Medical Ethics*, vol. II, pp. 115–150 (Hebrew), or vol. II, p. 580 (English).

54. See Rav Z.N. Goldberg, ibid.

55. See M. Hirshler, *Halachah and Refuah* 5740.

56. See *Shevet haLevi*, vol. V, chap. 47.

- What is done with a frozen fertilized egg if the parents died or divorced? Can one destroy fertilized eggs? Who owns them?[57]
- Is experimentation allowed on fertilized eggs?[58]
- Would the sale of fertilized eggs be ethical? What if it turned into a big business? What if poor people become exploited for their reproductive capabilities?
- Should this type of pregnancy be limited only to married women, or should it be available to single women as well? Should we fear the ultimate destruction of the family unit, or will that hypothetical danger never eventuate?[59]

For a summary on the topics of surrogates and egg donation see *Encyclopedia of Jewish Medical Ethics* by Professor Avraham Steinberg, vol. II, pp. 129–150 (Hebrew), or vol II, pp. 577–580 (English). For more information in English, see "Surrogate Motherhood," in *Bioethical Dilemmas*: A Jewish Perspective, by Rabbi J. David Bleich (Hoboken, NJ: Ktav Publishing, 1998). For an even more comprehensive examination, see the essay "In Vitro Fertilization: Maternal Identity and Conversion," in *Contemporary Halachic Problems*, vol. IV, also by Rabbi J. David Bleich (Hoboken, NJ: Ktav Publishing, 1976).

57. See Rav A. Nebenzahl, *Techumin*, vol. XVII. See also "Test Tube Babies," by Rabbi J. David Bleich, in *Jewish Bioethics*, p. 81.

58. See Rabbi J. David Bleich, "Fetal Tissue Research: Jewish Tradition and Public Policy," in *Contemporary Halachic Problems*, vol. IV, pp.171–202.

59. See Prof. Avraham Steinberg in *Assiah*, vol. I, p. 137. See also *Encyclopedia of Jewish Medical Ethics*, vol. I, p. 159 (Hebrew), or vol. I, p. 68 (English).

23. Dealing with Envy, Guilt, and Shame

And Rachel envied her sister.
(*Bereishis* 30:1)

A sound heart is the life of the flesh; but envy is the rottenness of the bones.
(*Mishlei* 14:30)

INTRODUCTION

"And you must not desire your fellowman's wife, nor may you crave your fellowman's house, field, servant, maidservant, ox or donkey, or anything [else] that belongs to your fellowman."[1] Does "anything that belongs to your fellowman" also mean your sister's adorable newborn, your next-door neighbor's fifth pregnancy, and any woman's "fruitful" womb? Is envy of the fertile world a sin?

Childless couples, especially the female partner, are plagued by terrible feelings of guilt because of their envy toward those whom God has blessed with children. They feel their soul decaying and their spirit weltering, as their once-cheery personality turns into a dark, acrimonious "justice seeker." Many women's envious thoughts are too horrifying to express out loud. They are ashamed of their thoughts and may only admit them, if at all, to a therapist, in the hope

1. *Devarim* 5:18.

that he or she can help rid her of them. The Biblical prohibition of envy is especially distressing to the religious childless woman, making her feel sinful for her inability to conquer her feelings. It's not enough to suffer the stabbing pains of envy; childless women have to endure the pangs of guilt and shame that arrive unexpectedly to assail their already fragile self-image.

"What does God want from me?" exclaims one woman, age 27 and married for six years without a child. "How much can I bear? Does God expect that when my entire family 'ooohs' and 'aaaahs' in harmony over my younger sister's charming baby girl with her pink berets and booties, that my stomach doesn't churn with envy? I'm not made of stone; it hurts."

UNDERSTANDING JEALOUSY

Shades of Envy

Envy comes in different shades and forms. It can besiege us suddenly like a bolt of lightning, or it can subtly creep up, as each tormenting blow we endure makes us a bit angrier, a little more bitter, and a trifle more spiteful. Like a whirlpool, envy can spin us into the depths of agony, furtively drowning us in our ocean of tears. Or it can erupt like a volcano, bursting the shackles that previously kept the lid on our misery. At times it makes us sarcastic, at times cruel. The sufferer can become self-destructive or abusive to others. Envy is always unfortunate and it prevents the individual from reaching perfect unity with both God and mankind.

Often, childless women are obsessed with becoming pregnant, certainly during the treatment stage and many times before and even after. A childless woman in the grip of uncontrollable envy can have irrational, cruel, destructive, and even murderous thoughts, such as: "If I see another pregnant woman on the street today, I won't be able to bear it"; "Sally is such an incompetent mother! If her child were mine, I'd be a better mother than she is"; "I hope she miscarries one of these years, then she'll know how it feels!"

If your friend calls you and tells you news of her pregnancy, you respond happily, but you may be insanely jealous. You can't get off the phone fast enough. The call is making you sick. And then you begin to feel guilty for not being able to be happy for her.[2]

The Torah gives an example of unsound responses to "fertility envy" through our matriarch Rachel. "And Rachel saw that she had not borne Yaakov children, and Rachel envied her sister. She said to Yaakov, 'Give me children, or else I am dead.'"[3] The Ramban comments that Rachel's jealousy prompted her to respond irrationally. "Or else I am dead" implies that Rachel threatened suicide, or at least that she would die of sorrow at not having children.[4]

According to Rabbeinu Tzadok haKohen,[5] Rachel did vent her envy at Leah. Rachel's envy was so strong that she caused Leah to stop bearing children through *ayin ha-ra*, the "evil eye." Leah's secondary infertility lasted until Rachel rid herself of jealousy, evidenced by her statement, "[Yaakov] will therefore lie with you tonight."[6]

---

2. *Conquering Infertility*, p. 11.

3. *Bereishis* 30:1.

4. Ramban, *Bereishis* 30:1. According to the Ramban this is the reason that Yaakov became angry at Rachel.

5. Rabbi Tzadok haKohen, *Tzidkas haTzaddik*, (Beit El, Israel: Beit Yesharim, 5748), p. 164.

6. *Bereishis* 30:15.

"Jealousy Drives a Person from the World"[7]

Chazal warn us of seven sins that result in *tzara'as* (a leprosy-like affliction). They are slander, spilling blood, a vain oath, incest, arrogance, robbery, and stinginess.[8] The afflicted person is sent outside the camp (i.e. society). This is because all of these transgressions separate a person from society. One who slanders someone else, or lies, or steals, or certainly kills, feels "above" his neighbor — he can hurt the other because the other is insignificant. He is therefore sent outside the camp, humiliated and grotesque-looking, to contemplate and appreciate his humble position in the community. Rabbeinu Tzadok haKohen says that the root of all seven causes of *tzara'as* is jealousy.[9]

Nowadays, *tzara'as* does not exist. But that doesn't mean that the same effect doesn't occur. Instead of our body being afflicted by *tzara'as*, the "disease" is transferred to our soul.[10] Isolation still remains; however, it is a psychological detachment. A person driven by envy feels different from others. He feels cheated, and in a desperate attempt to rectify "the wrong," he will slander, steal, or commit any or all of the other seven sins. His "elitist" feeling is really a response to a deeper feeling of inferiority (as we will discuss later). He feels a gap between himself and the rest of the community. In short, envy segregates us from society, and drives us from the world.

Worse than the feeling of isolation, however, is the intolerable pain of a crippled self-image. One can hide from society, but one can never hide from the self. Living with a battered self-image is devastating. A person must feel good about him-

---

7. *Pirkei Avos* 4:21.
8. *Arachin* 16a.
9. *Tzidkas haTzaddik,* p. 233.
10. *Shemiras haLashon, Sha'ar haZechirah,* chap. 6.

self. It is written, "Serve the Eternal with happiness,"[11] yet it is inconceivable to serve Him with happiness if you don't feel good about yourself — and it is impossible to feel good about yourself when vexed by envy. A person's own self-esteem is the primary victim of his envy.

Envy is a devastating attribute that thoroughly consumes us.[12] Although it is an innate human quality,[13] it is nevertheless harmful to society as well as to the individual who experiences these feelings. It afflicts our peace of mind, and clouds our facility to judge favorably and objectively. It is a barrier between us and others, and is the seed of unwarranted hatred. It compelled Kayin to kill Hevel, and the brothers to sell Yosef. It is the derivation of racism, and the root of anti-Semitism. It thrusts the meek and the mild into feeble isolation, and drives the assertive and forceful to belligerent aggression. It transforms the amiable into the iniquitous, and turns the gracious dreams of righteous women into the malicious thoughts of the unfortunate.

Defining Envy

"Envious tension is an excruciating awareness of disparity between oneself and something else, inevitably something desirable beyond one's reach. The envier desires an immediate release from his tensions, wishing to rid himself of the torment that is consuming him. This is often accomplished with the use of aggressive, destructive behavior."[14]

Feelings of inferiority are the essence of jealousy. Envy is only a symptom and not the cause. The real source of the

---

11. *Tehillim* 100:2.

12. *Midrash Shochar Tov, Tehillim* 94.

13. As the Midrash says, "If not for envy, the world could not exist" (ibid.).

14. J.H. Berke, "Shame and Envy," in D. Nathanson (ed.), *The Many Faces of Shame* (New York: Guilford, 1987), pp. 318–334.

problem is the envier's inability to deal with his own failure. Hence when his neighbor achieves his coveted goal he is reminded of his own inadequacy, resenting the person who causes him so much pain. Since he is, for whatever reason, unable to overcome his deficiency, he directs his energy (physical or mental) to taking away that which belongs to his neighbor. There is a certain pseudo-satisfaction in that too.

The Gemara says that "an intellectual is envious of an intellectual and a warrior is envious of a warrior."[15] A person is only envious of that which is important to him. An athlete will be envious of another athlete; he will not be envious of a writer who won the Pulitzer Prize for literature. A writer will not be jealous of an athlete who won an Olympic gold medal. The more that the desired article is needed to build one's self-esteem and to prove one's self-worth, the more distress he will experience when he is deprived of it, and the more hostile he will be toward those who have attained it.

It is no wonder, then, that childless women have such intense feelings of jealousy. Almost every woman, no matter how interested she may be in other facets of life such as career goals and so forth, wants first and foremost to be a mother. Lacking that basic human need is tragic. "The infertile woman, regardless of the cause of her infertility, is concerned about her bodily integrity and intactness. She experiences a profound depression over the loss of her reproductive function, and feels herself to be damaged or defective."[16] Add to that her feelings of incompatibility with a society that revolves around children and you have a woman who has a fierce daily battle to preserve her self-esteem. "This woman aims her men-

---

15. *Avodah Zarah* 55a.

16. M. Mazor, "The Problem of Infertility," in M. Notman and C. Nadelson (eds.), *The Woman Patient* (New York: Plenum, 1978), vol. I, pp. 157–160.

tal aggression and humiliation at pregnant women, mothers, and even children.... The woman compares herself [to other women] and is tortured by feelings of pervasive inferiority. These painful feelings cannot simply remain buried. The abhorrence of one's defectiveness is unbearable...."[17]

Jealousy does not only affect childless women, it can influence anyone — even *tzaddikim*, as we can see in the story of Yosef and his brothers. Using the two premises that people only get irrationally jealous over that which is meaningful to them, and that the essence of jealousy is a feeling of inferiority, we can better understand the deep emotions that the sons of Yaakov felt in their conflict with Yosef, and what compelled them to try to eliminate the cause of their anguish.

The Torah says: "Yosef reported evil gossip about [his brothers] to his father. Yisrael loved Yosef more than all his [other] sons, because he was a son of his old age, and [Yisrael] made him a coat of many colors. His brothers saw that their father loved him more than all his brothers and they hated him, [and] they could not speak with him in a friendly manner."[18]

What exactly did the brothers hate about Yosef? If it was only because he "reported evil gossip about [them] to his father," then the Torah should have stated that they hated him in that same verse. Why did the Torah wait to mention their hatred only after we are told that Yaakov loved Yosef the most?

The term "hatred" is mentioned two more times in this episode: "Yosef had a dream and told [this] to his brothers, and they hated him even more. He said to them.... 'There we were, binding sheaves in the middle of the field, when my sheaf straightened and even remained upright, while your sheaves surrounded my sheaf and bowed down to it.'.... And they

17. *Men, Women, and Infertility*, p.117.
18. *Bereishis* 37:2 –4.

hated him even more, [both] for his dreams and for his [evil] reports."[19]

The word "envy," however, is used only once, after the second dream: "He had another dream.... 'And there were the sun, the moon and eleven stars bowing down to me.'... And his father chided him.... And his brothers envied him...."[20]

Obviously, the second dream was of a more serious nature than either the first dream, the coat of many colors, or the evil report. One would think that the favoritism would cause envy and the second dream would generate hatred, for in the second dream Yosef rules over them. Further more, it was the dreams, not the favoritism, that made the brothers want to annihilate Yosef. This is evident from the statements they made when they plotted to kill him: "They said to each other, 'Look! Here comes the dreamer. Let us kill him.... And we shall see what will become of his dreams."[21] There is no mention of the favoritism, only the dreams. The dreams served exclusively as the motive for their scheme. Why, then, after hearing the second dream, does the Torah tell us that they felt envy, and not hatred? Surely hatred is a stronger emotion than envy and would be more of a motive for murder!

However, as we explained previously, envy becomes uncontrollable when the envier's obsession with being deprived of the desired object leaves him with unbearable feelings of rejection, failure, and inferiority. The "villain" who denies him this desired object, or simply reminds him of his deficiency, is causing him great harm. He is wounding him with the realization that he is insufficient and not as "good" as he wants to be. Hatred, on the other hand, could merely be a dislike of someone's attributes. You might not like him, maybe can't even

19. Ibid., verses 6–8.

20. Ibid., verses 9–11.

21. Ibid., verses 19–20.

stand to be in his presence, but you don't necessarily wish him any harm either.

Until the second dream the brothers disliked Yosef for his slander, his coat of many colors, the special relationship he had with their father, and his first dream. But none of these factors had the potency to arouse violent jealousy. The brothers hated Yosef, but he wasn't a threat to their self-worth. They couldn't speak with him peaceably but they didn't want to kill him either. Until the second dream, the only advantage that Yosef had over them was worldly success. Even the first dream was not portentous of the brothers themselves bowing down to Yosef; only their sheaves bowed down to his sheaf. This alluded to a materialistic dependency. The brothers could live with this.

But the second dream symbolized a spiritual advantage. Their bowing down to him symbolized that Yosef's approach in spiritual service would triumph. The conflict between Yosef and his brothers was not an ordinary dissension of siblings; it was on a much higher level. Their dispute was over the spiritual direction of the Jewish People. Whoever would prevail would determine the spiritual aspirations of God's Chosen Nation. This is all that the brothers lived for. Nothing else was meaningful to them. If they were defeated on the spiritual level, then their whole life's work and their self-respect would be shattered. It was therefore the second dream that caused such compelling jealousy that it provoked them to attempt the unmentionable.

The *Beis haLevi* illustrates this notion with a popular proverb that people say regarding their wealthier friends: "Let my vault be shamed by his vault. Let my pocket be disgraced by his pocket. But let me never feel humiliated before him."[22] The brothers could accept Yosef's dominance over worldly mat-

---

22. *Beis haLevi, Parashas Vayeishev.*

ters, but they couldn't tolerate his advantage over them in the spiritual realm, for that tormented their very essence.

State Envy/ Trait Envy

There are two types of envy: state envy and trait envy. State envy is envy caused by a certain situation (state). The individual is generally not an envious person, but because of his exceptionally difficult circumstances, he is overcome with jealousy. State envy is likely to disappear when the individual obtains what he wants. In the case of infertility, it will disappear when the woman gets pregnant, adopts, or resolves that she will live a child-free life. A woman with state envy wants to get back to her old self, to the way she used to be.

Trait envy, on the other hand, is deeply rooted. It won't go away so quickly or easily. The person feels swindled or cheated by life, and probably has felt this way for a good part of his or her life. Even after a problem is resolved, animosity still persists. The person feels that life isn't fair, that others have it easier than he. A childless woman with trait envy, even after she has a baby, will feel cheated by life. "Why can so-and-so get pregnant every year and I got pregnant only once? Why did I have to go through so much? Why is life always so hard for me and so simple for her? It's so unfair!" She was probably embittered before infertility, and doesn't have a happy model of herself with which to work when true problems come up.

A simple imagery exercise can help ascertain if you have "state envy" or "trait envy." Imagine that you know for certain that you will be pregnant in two years. While imagining that, you should simultaneously picture a pregnant woman. Do you still feel envious? Most women will say that they don't. This is because the envious feelings are transitory and consequently much easier to heal. This is state envy. Women with trait envy, however, desperately need to be soothed but have to combat a lifelong sense of being cheated. They will need to spend time and effort to conquer their resentful, caustic feelings.[23] Professional help is recommended.

The Prohibition Against Envy

Different types of envious feelings constitute different transgressions — or none at all. In order to restrain envy, it is essential that you first have a clear knowledge of each emotion's prohibition. In this way you can focus your energies in the right direction. Certain feelings, which you perceive as envy, may not be transgressions at all, while some thoughts might be defined as actual hatred. Secondly, you must understand the stimulus for your envy, in order to see that you aren't so "bad" after all, just human, with very human sentiments.

Although it is preferable not to compare oneself to anyone, doing so is not necessarily a violation of the tenth Commandment. The Torah says: *Lo sachmod* — You must not desire your fellowman's wife, and *Lo sisaveh* — You must not crave your fellowman's house.[24] Our Rabbis teach us that *Lo sachmod* doesn't mean that it is forbidden to desire that which is in the possession of your friend. There needs to be some attempt to relieve him of it and make it your own (such as harassing him to sell it to you) to transgress the prohibition of *Lo sachmod*.

Lo sisaveh means, don't even contemplate getting it from him. If you fantasize about acquiring it from him, even if you do not actually carry out your intentions, you have transgressed *Lo sisaveh*. The thought alone is sinful. Craving an object, however, without scheming to obtain it from your neighbor, is not forbidden.[25] This is not coveting. There must be two conditions to transgress this Biblical prohibition: you

---

23. *Men, Women, and Infertility*, pp. 119–120.
24. *Devarim* 5:18.
25. *Aruch haShulchan, Choshen Mishpat* 359:5.

must crave the object as well as attempt, or at least contemplate attempting, to acquire it.

The Rabbis further limit the prohibition to include only items which are purchasable. Possessions that are not normally obtained through monetary transactions do not fall under the classification of "Do not covet."[26] (Therefore, a woman's womb does not fall under this category; surrogacy probably doesn't count either.)

Therefore, a childless woman who, upon seeing her friend playing in the park with twin toddlers, says to herself, "Oh! I can't bear to see another child today," has not transgressed a Biblical commandment. In other words, if you already feel bad about not having a child, and upon coming into contact with a "reminder" of your misfortune, that is not envy. Even if it pains you so much to be in a certain mother's presence that you try to avoid contact with her, or if you can't stand hearing another word about her son, you are not transgressing anything. It is perfectly normal and to be expected. What you are feeling is not the envy that the Ten Commandments warns against.

CONTROLLING JEALOUSY

Ridding Yourself of Envy

As mentioned at the beginning of this chapter, some infertile women have dreadful thoughts often triggered by a devastated self-image. Taming these thoughts is crucial. Although understandable, a woman who upon seeing her pregnant neighbor wishes her bad, is transgressing the commandment, "You must not hate your brother in your heart."[27] A woman who falls victim to these feelings has to accept the

---

26. *Mechilta, Shemos* 20:14.
27. *Vayikra* 19:17.

challenge of trying to defeat them.

Sometimes negative thoughts seem to pop up uninvited. You aren't even aware of it, and suddenly you realize that you are thinking loathsome thoughts! There is no sin if these thoughts suddenly pop into your head; it is considered *ohness* (forced upon you).[28] Once they enter your head, however, you are obligated to eliminate them. You must turn your thoughts to something else. If you accomplish this, you transform the potential sin of "hating your brother in your heart" into the mitzvah of "loving your neighbor as yourself."

Another way to wipe out hatred from your heart is to realize exactly what it is you're hating. Stop and think: "Do I really hate *her*? Does she mean me any harm?" You will probably answer yourself: "No. I hate my infertility, that's all. She just reminds me of my problem. She doesn't do it intentionally. God gave her a baby. If I have any grievance, what does she have to do with it?"

It is vital to see the absurdity in our aversions. The Gemara says that a person only sins when a spirit of foolishness enters his mind.[29] This is true for iniquitous thoughts also. When we wish harm to befall others, we need to see that our thoughts are not as evil as they are senseless. Remember that what you are envying is someone's reproductive capacities. We must try to control our feelings instead of letting our feelings control us.

Learning *sifrei mussar* and *machshavah* (books on ethics and Jewish philosophy) on a regular basis can help you master your thoughts and emotions. However, these works must be reviewed again and again. Without review, the benefit in learning them will be limited. Reviewing keeps their ideas constantly in our mind. If we only learn them once, then al-

---

28. *Tzidkas haTzaddik*, p. 235.

29. *Sotah* 3a.

though we might know what we should be thinking, we won't be thinking it. In almost every yeshiva today, ethical and philosophical works have become an integral part of the curriculum. Every Jew should learn ethics, and certainly someone with a special situation, such as infertility, should make every effort to have regularly scheduled times to learn them.

As we said in chapter 10, saying *Tehillim* can help tremendously. King David incorporated every human emotion into these beautiful, poetic verses, which ascend straight to Heaven. *Tehillim* are praises and prayers which speak from — and to — the heart of every Jew. Whatever you are feeling, from sadness to joy, from frustration to accomplishment, you will find it expressed in *Tehillim*. This should give every Jew a wonderful feeling of inspiration and faith.

Different Planets

Sometimes a woman will think to herself, "It's not fair that my former high school classmate already has four children and I don't have any." Although that is not the envy of *Lo sachmod*, it is, however, the way of the righteous not to compare themselves with anyone in any area: not their bank account, not their job, not their house, not their social stature, not their success, not their family. Even natural spiritual attributes, character traits, and intelligence should not be compared. Thus we should not look at someone's ability to get pregnant and compare it to our inability.

Greed originates when we compare ourselves to others and we feel that we deserve more. Although we should be happy with what we have, this praiseworthy attribute is easier said than done. Many of us might have mastered it concerning material possessions, but when it comes to having a child it's another story. It is much harder. It is, however, an achievable goal.

When one compares herself to another, she is expressing a

lack of *bitachon* (faith) that everything is God's will — including someone's pregnancy and her infertility. Someone with *bitachon* will say, "My life is not her life. We are each two entirely different worlds. I should not compare myself with her because there is nothing to compare."

Most people are not jealous of the rich and famous. Their lives are so different from ours that there is nothing to relate to; it is as if they live on a different planet. But if our neighbor adds an extra room to his house, or our colleague gets a raise and promotion, we can feel the sharp blade of envy cutting into us. However, the commendable outlook is to feel as distant from those people's accomplishments — those of our friends and siblings, and those of other people whose lives parallel ours — as we do to those who really do "live on a different planet."

Envy is innate. In fact, it is the positive driving force that makes the world go round. *Chazal* say, "If it were not for envy, the world would cease to exist, as no one would marry a woman or build a house."[30] (We will discuss this later in more depth.) Moreover, society is getting more accomplishment-oriented. Our whole value system is intoxicated with competition and comparative results: Top 10 percent of the graduating class, medals, certificates and trophies for the winners. Even literature and the arts, two areas based on individual creative imagination, have been corrupted by awards ceremonies.

The Torah world has been affected by this too. Much of children's education is "enhanced" by contests and competition — under the doleful guise of "incentive." This type of "encouragement" might have fruitful short-term results, but the long-term echo is malignant. The student matures, subconsciously thinking that life is one big tournament. Even

30. *Midrash Shochar Tov, Tehillim* 37.

children's Purim parties are dampened by costume contests, which are great for the winner. But what about the losers? The loser gets a message that his amusing, creative costume, the one that he was so proud of and so happy about, apparently wasn't that good after all. For him, Purim became a little less fun.

We are conditioned to compete and compare. Although competition is the life force and characteristic of the male gender, the Gemara says that "A woman is only jealous of her girlfriend's thigh."[31] This means that even though a woman may not have the brutal competitive force of men, she nevertheless has an innate jealousy of other feminine attributes — be they another woman's beauty or another woman's ability to give birth.

Thus, due to the influence of a man's competitive environment, and owing to a woman's natural envy of her "girlfriend's thigh," it takes persistent determination to cure one's self-destructive envy of the fertile world. Just like studying a book on *mussar* once will not make someone a *tzaddik,* so it is with conquering envy: it needs a great deal of work. Trying is all we can do, but we must try.

Don't Feel Guilty

When envy strikes, there is no reason to feel guilty. First of all, you are not alone. Many, if not most, childless women have felt the same way. Not all women are plagued by vicious, spiteful envy, but many are, or have been during one stage or another of their infertility. If you are, you should not feel guilty or ashamed. You should work on ridding yourself of these feelings, but never feel guilty because of them.

Guilt is a foreign concept. Jews shouldn't feel guilty. We should correct mistakes and try to improve, but we don't con-

---

31. *Megillah* 13a.

demn ourselves. As stated previously, a person only sins when a spirit of foolishness enters his head. What happens when you do or say something foolish? You may feel embarrassed or ashamed, but you don't feel guilty. You say to yourself something like, "Boy! I'm not going to be that foolish again." The same attitude should be adopted when you find yourself thinking envious thoughts. You should say something like, "What nonsense! I have to stop having these ridiculous ideas." Envious thoughts are not wicked, they're just plain senseless.

Some women say to themselves, "Envy is the worst of all the negative *middos*, and I'm drenched in it. I guess this is the real me, I'm really evil deep down. I have a hateful heart. Maybe that's why I don't have any children, I'm too bad to have them. How can someone as wicked as I be a good mother? How can someone as sinful as I expect that God will grant her a baby?"

Abusive thoughts like these are an injustice to ourselves; moreover, they can turn us against God: since we're already so "bad," we think, it's futile to serve Him. But because God pardons our mistakes we have reason to correct our errors and failures. We must never condemn ourselves. The fact that we can always do *teshuvah* allows us to always have a relationship with God.

Rachel's Righteousness

To fully understand the magnitude of Rachel's righteousness, we must study the following *midrash*.[32]

> When the Jews were banished from the Land of Israel, Avraham (in Heaven) asked the Holy One, Blessed be He, "Creator of the Universe, why did You exile my children and deliver them to the nations, who killed them with all

32. *Pesichta d'Eichah Rabasi.*

kinds of horrible deaths, and destroyed the *Beis haMikdash*, the place where I brought Yitzchak as a sacrifice before You?"

God answered Avraham, "Your children sinned. They transgressed the Torah and the twenty-two letters in it."

...Avraham immediately retorted, "Creator of the Universe, at the age of 100, You gave me a son. When he grew, at the age of thirty-six, You told me to bind him before You. I became 'cruel' [i.e. I conquered my natural desire to spare him], and did not pity him. I myself bound him. Won't you remember that and have mercy on my children?" God did not accept his plea.

Yitzchak then spoke, saying, "Creator of the Universe, when my father said to me, 'God will provide the lamb for the burnt-offering, my son,' I didn't prevent it, I went with a willing heart, and stretched my neck out for the knife. Won't You remember that for me and have mercy on my children?" God did not accept his plea.

Yaakov and Moshe also tried to persuade God, but to no avail. "It is a decree before Me," said a *bas kol*. Moshe then attempted to produce arguments from the Torah. "Creator of the Universe, it is written in the Torah, 'An ox or a lamb and its offspring should not be slaughtered on the same day.' And here already many children and their mothers have been killed. How can You be silent?" God did not accept his plea.

Finally Rachel jumped in front of God and said, "Creator of the Universe! You know that Your servant Yaakov loved me immensely. He worked for my father for seven years for me. When the seven years were completed and it was time for me to marry him, my father schemed to swap me for my sister. This was mortifying to me. I gave Yaakov signs to recognize me.

"Then I changed my mind. I pitied my sister and conquered my passion so that she wouldn't be ashamed. On the wedding night, I handed over the signs to my sister, so that Yaakov would think that she was me. Not only that, I even hid under the bed, and whenever Yaakov spoke, my sister was silent and I answered, so that he would not recognize her voice. I acted kindly toward her. I was not jealous of her, and did not shame her. I am only flesh and blood, dust and ashes; yet I did not envy my rival wife. So why are You envious of insignificant idols?"

Immediately God became merciful and said, "For you, Rachel, I will bring the Jewish People back to their Land."

From this *midrash* we learn that conquering envy, and forfeiting that which is beloved to you for someone else's sake, is more praiseworthy than being willing to give up your life — for Avraham and Yitzchak's readiness to sacrifice to fulfill God's will could not match Rachel's overcoming her desire to marry Yaakov for the sake of her sister's honor. Conquering envy is so exalted that it is in this merit that the Jewish People will be redeemed.

Although in the book of *Bereishis* the Torah tells us that Rachel was envious of her sister, the above *midrash* tells us that she "conquered her passion" and was not jealous of Leah. There is an apparent contradiction. However, the answer is that when it came to getting married, Rachel defeated her passions, but when it came to having children, she couldn't conquer her envy. How could the same righteous Rachel, who was willing to give up everything — to relinquish her husband and forfeit her entire future — become defeated by envy when she couldn't conceive?

Two crucial lessons can be derived from this, which should be a source of strength and comfort to any childless woman who suffers from jealousy.

Imagine Rachel, the righteous matriarch who was willing to lose her husband in order to save her sister's honor, not being able to control her emotions when it came to her infertility.[33] There was no guarantee that Rachel would ever get married after she forfeited Yaakov to Leah. She had no way of knowing that Yaakov would ultimately marry her. She accepted the possibility of living the rest of her life as a lonely spinster.

But when Rachel failed to conceive, and watched as her rival gave birth to one child after another, she felt envy. The drive for a woman to have children is many times stronger than her will to live.

When Rachel gave Leah her husband, she was rewarded with the greatest reward in Jewish history. Yet, when she was envious of her sister's fertility, we don't find anywhere in *Chazal* that she was punished. She received no castigation, for she committed no sin.

If you find yourself being envious of the fertile world, please don't be hard on yourself. Work on yourself, but never condemn yourself. God knows how difficult your situation is. If Rachel felt envy, chances are we would all feel envy.

Second, remember that the nature of a human being is to be dynamic and, therefore, inconsistent. Hence, the apparent contradiction in Rachel's behavior — i.e. that one time she wasn't jealous and another time she was — is understandable. Not only do our feelings change from one moment to the next, but at any given time we have mixed emotions. People can feel fulfillment and worry, hope and despair, joy and grief in the same instant. The parents of a bride feel happy that she is getting married, sad that she is leaving their home, relieved that she found someone to love and take care of her, and worried lest things don't work out well for them. It is very human to vanquish negative thoughts one day and be inundated

---

33. Dr. Alice Domar also tells of women who never felt envy in their lives, but in the face of infertility couldn't control their envious feelings when someone else got pregnant (*Conquering Infertility*, p. 18).

with them the next; to be heroic during one particularly difficult time in our lives and to withdraw at another. So although Rachel conquered her envy once, but couldn't do it the second time, what is important here is that when Rachel conquered her envy, her merit was even greater than Avraham and Yitzchak's merit from the *Akeidah*.

When Rachel claimed that she overcame her passion and was not jealous of her rival, God didn't rebuke her saying that at a later date she *was* jealous of her sister. It didn't matter that she couldn't conquer her envy the second time. Defeating envious passions, even if it isn't consistent, is so extolled that it has repercussions for generations.

The Gemara even says, "Someone who is envious of his friend and holds his peace, God will espouse his cause."[34] A childless woman may not be able to avoid jealous feelings, but if even occasionally she is able to divert her thoughts to loving benevolence, then her reward will be immeasurable. If she has an earnest desire to rid herself of envious feelings forever and tries hard to do so, but sometimes is overwhelmed, then the times she does prevail will uplift all the other "failures." Together, her triumphs and failures will ascend to Heaven as a merit, to testify that there is a woman with a good heart, who also requests happiness for others.

Redirecting Envy

If envy is such a negative quality, then why did God make it a part of the human experience? Why is it inborn? The answer is that there are no good or bad traits. All characteristics are neutral. The way that we direct them determines their merit. The right envy can help us in our life's quests, whatever they may be.

Although jealousy signifies a lack of gratitude for all that God has given us, sometimes it is also the manifestation of jus-

---

34. *Gittin* 7a.

tice-seeking. People tend to get angrier at other people's "undeserved" good fortune. The aspect of envy that seeks justice is intrinsically healthy and respectable. Our task is to funnel that aspect of justice into seeking altruistic goals instead of satisfying selfish passions.

Another positive aspect of envy is expressed in the Talmud: "The envy of scholars enhances wisdom"[35] — or what is popularly called "healthy competition." Seeing somebody striving for something and acquiring it should encourage us to do the same — not because we want to be victorious over someone else, but because we want to improve. The scholar should be concerned with gaining wisdom, but not with "outsmarting" his colleague. This type of competition is the beneficial side of envy.

The Hebrew word for envy, *kin'ah,* can also be translated as zealousness. We can transform our self-destructive envy of another's good fortune into zealousness for self-improvement. If he can do it, I can do it. If he can get up every morning at five o'clock to learn Torah, so can I.

The childless couple can redirect their envy to serve their endeavors. Instead of comparing themselves to the fertile world, they can look at other infertile couples who worked hard at becoming parents. Perhaps they can re-vitalize their daily prayer regimen or take more aggressive steps for treatment. Maybe someone they know adopted a child and is happy with their choice, and perhaps they could be happy adopting too.

Transform your desire to be a parent into a mitzvah. All of your actions involving your treatment and your quest to be a parent should be directed toward the goal of fulfilling God's will. In this way you will be zealous for God, and will fulfill the words of *Chazal,* "Do not be envious of anything that is not

35. *Bava Basra* 21a.

everlasting, but rather covet the fear of God all day long."[36]

According to one *midrash*,[37] this is what Rachel did. The *midrash* asks: "How could Rachel have been jealous? Doesn't it say; 'Let not your heart envy sinners, but fear the Lord all the day long' (*Mishlei* 23:17)?" The *midrash* answers, "She was envious of [Leah's] good deeds." Here, *Chazal* ask how Rachel could have been jealous of Leah's maternal success, based on a verse that admonishes envy of sinners. Was Rachel envious of a sinner? Was our matriarch Leah a sinner? *Chazal* understood that Rachel was envious only of Leah's success. Yet through *Chazal*'s question we learn that coveting worldly attainment is comparable to envying iniquity. Victory, achievement, and prosperity are all vanity. That's not what we're here for. Even the ability to have children is considered worldly attainment. All that is important in this world is getting closer to God. Someone who envies worldly success lacks the realization that all of our possessions, including our children, are Heaven-sent.

Every human being is given a different life situation. It is our task to devote the bounty God has bestowed on us to meritorious endeavors. Envy of someone's fertility is equivalent to coveting his good fortune, which is like envying his sinfulness. Therefore someone like Rachel, who was devoted to good deeds and spiritual aspirations, could not have been jealous of Leah's maternal success. Rather, Rachel pondered, "If Leah is having babies, and I'm not, maybe she is more righteous than I. I have to improve." Rachel saw her infertility as an opportunity to look deep into herself in order to strengthen her connection to God.

The commentators, such as the Rambam and the Alshich, do not interpret Rachel's jealousy in light of this *midrash*. They

36. *Midrash Shochar Tov, Tehillim* 73.

37. *Bereishis Rabbah* 71:6.

explain it according to its simple meaning. By uniting the two concepts (the *midrash*'s understanding and the simple meaning), we can learn a most valuable lesson. When our matriarch Rachel saw that her rival wife was having babies, one after another, she was struck with the common unwholesome envy that would blight all of us under those circumstances — but instead of letting those thoughts linger, she worked on herself. She transformed her envy of Leah's fertility into jealousy of her good deeds. She channeled her harmful envy into healthy zeal.

May our matriarch Rachel be a symbol of strength and fortitude for all of us. May we turn our envy and resentfulness into determination and zeal, and our weltered spirit into animated vigor. In that merit, may we witness the fulfillment of the promise, "The covetousness that God will covet for Zion in the future will be great zealousness."[38] As it is written: "Thus says the Lord of Hosts, 'I coveted Zion a great deal, and I was zealous for her with a great fury.... I have returned to Zion, and will dwell in the midst of Jerusalem. And Jerusalem shall be called the city of truth.... And the streets of the city shall be full of boys and girls playing in the streets.'"[39]

May God bless us that they will be ours.

---

38. *Shir haShirim Rabbah* 8:6.
39. *Zechariah* 8:2–5.

24. Spiritual Life without Children

He has told you O man, what is good, and what God seeks from you; only the performance of justice, the love of kindness, and to walk humbly with your God.

(*Michah* 6:8)

IT IS VERY DIFFICULT TO end this book. For what is the ending? There are three possible endings to any couple's infertility saga. You may become pregnant either naturally or through medical intervention. If so, we hope you buy our book on pregnancy and childbirth, *B'sha'ah Tovah* (Jerusalem: Feldheim Publishers, 2001), and we wish you Mazal tov. You may adopt a child, and in that case — we also wish you Mazal tov! Or you may find fulfillment and meaning in life as a Jew without children, and in that case we wish you the blessing of joy and success in all your endeavors. It is to that aim that this chapter was written.

* * *

There will come a time when you will have had enough — when the treatments will become too tiresome, the disappointments too frequent, and the pain and stress too great.

When is the correct time to stop fertility treatments? Is there a point prescribed by halachic authorities, by your doctor, or by therapists, at which to cease pursuing medical assistance to become parents?

It would seem that halachically, one would never be able to stop fertility treatments. Since you need to fulfill the mitzvah of *Pru Urvu*, you must do your utmost to have children, even if it is difficult. You must do your *hishtadlus*. However, as mentioned in chapter 5, the halachah allows you to stop, because although you must do your *hishtadlus* to succeed at a mitzvah, you are only required to do "normal" *hishtadlus*. In other words, you are still required to have regular intimate relations, but you don't need to go beyond that. You don't have to resort to high-tech solutions.

Fertility treatments are a *reshus* (an option), not a requirement. A person never has to start fertility treatments in the first place. So if you feel you need to quit, you may do so, as long as you continue having intimate relations with your spouse. This is especially important for women to understand, since technically the mitzvah of *Pru Urvu* only applies to men. If you decide it is time to stop, you shouldn't feel any guilt from a religious perspective. It is your decision.

When to stop depends on a few factors. First of all, what does your doctor say? How does he or she evaluate your chances of success? How long have you been going through treatments? How many years have you been childless? How are your emotions holding up? How is your marriage? Has life become too stressful because of the treatments?

It may be time to quit if:

- You feel that you have been doing this for too long, or you feel that the treatment periods are so intense that you are not able to concentrate on other aspects of your life that give you enjoyment and fulfillment.
- The tension and anxiety are too intolerable to bear anymore (this is one of the reasons most frequently cited

for ending fertility treatments[1]).

- Your marriage has been suffering from the intensity of the treatments and their side effects. (As we said before, fertility should not take precedence over *shalom bayis*.)
- You feel that you need to regain control of your life, and the treatments are keeping you from doing so.
- You feel that you have been doing this for too long.

Only you will be able to determine when enough is enough. You must keep in mind that your marriage, your psychological health, your other goals, and your peace of mind remain your priorities.

What if one spouse wants to continue and the other does not? Of course every couple will have to work out this problem together, with mutual understanding of and concern for what is best for each partner. Logic and fairness would ascertain that the wife should have the determining opinion, since she is the one who is usually more affected physically and emotionally by the whole ordeal. As much as every husband wants to be a father, and as much as he anguishes greatly over not having a child, it is usually the wife who has to go through the treatments. You may want to seek Rabbinic guidance or counseling if there is a strong difference of opinion as to whether or not to stop the treatments.

There are many stories of people who stopped infertility treatments and then became parents naturally. Maybe that will happen to you as well. But put your faith in God and not in these stories. Perhaps you will see this blessing. Or perhaps you will merit to live a fulfilled life without children, as God wants for His very beautiful children who have no children of their own.

There is a process that people often go through before

---

1. See *Management of the Infertile Woman*, p. 304.

they stop treatments.[2] At first you may push off treatments, maybe check out new specialists, forget to call for appointments, and possibly look for alternative methods. You have become such experts in all aspects of fertility treatments, that when you hear a health professional recommend a new treatment, your reaction may be, "I've already tried that one!" At this stage you may not think you are terminating treatments; you are just taking a break, just being less aggressive.

After a while you realize that a few months have gone by and you have ignored treatments. You have been focusing on other aspects of your life. You begin to realize that you may not be able to go back to the fertility clinics anymore; you no longer have the strength. The longer you stay away, the harder it is to go back. You can't deal with the tests, the nurses' questions, the shots, the reports, the doctor's promises, the high hopes, and the tremendous letdowns. A certain feeling of failure takes over. After everything you went through, and still no child. It wasn't supposed to end like this. You thought that it would be a long, hard road but that in the end there would be a baby in your arms. So many other couples went through this and enjoyed a happy ending to their story.

Once the reality that you have ceased medical intervention sets in, you will react in different ways. At first you will feel shock, the same as you felt when you realized that you had a problem. You are now giving up something that for years you were fighting for so strongly. You were so sure you were going to win, you had so much *bitachon*.

After the shock comes anger. You are mad at the world. You feel cheated by life. You will be enraged with the doctors who failed, who you suspect didn't try hard enough for you. You may feel resentment toward your spouse, whom you

---

2. See *Children of Love*, pp. 195–199.

may still blame either for having the problem to begin with, or for not being understanding enough of your feelings throughout the process. You may feel hostility toward your parents, parents-in-law, siblings, and siblings-in-law for pressuring you, and animosity toward everyone pushing a baby carriage. You may even feel anger toward the Almighty, Who with all His might and compassion still didn't give you a child.

After the anger stage comes depression. A powerful feeling of heart-ripping sadness will consume you. The dream is over. Tears will flow like a river, in a way they haven't flowed in a long time. The old pain that you lived with for so many years, and thought that you had gotten used to, attacks ruthlessly. At least before, there was hope.

Finally comes the stage of acceptance. There will still be some pain, but there will be an element of peace and comfort. You will get on with your life and focus on your career, spiritual endeavors, *chesed*, travel, and anything else that seems important to you. But there will always remain a spark of hope in your heart. This is human nature. The Talmud also tells us, "Never give up the hope for salvation."[3] This hope may stay dormant inside of you; it may even be expressed now and again at unexpected moments. You may hear of someone who was successful with some non-conventional method and get the urge and the courage to try it. You may even decide to return to the fertility clinic. You may finally feel good around children or you may not. Everyone is different. So at this stage, there is a mixture of sadness, peace, and hope.

THE EGLAH ARUFAH AND NOACH

Many people think that if they do not have children, their life

---

3. *Berachos* 10a.

will be empty of meaning, fulfillment, and happiness.[4]

This does not have to be the case. As important as having children is, it is not the only purpose of life. When you are in your childbearing years and all your friends seem to be busy only with their children, and when all their plans seem to revolve around them, it is hard to imagine that this isn't the only purpose of life, that there are other things of great importance. In fact, the word "offspring" can mean something else entirely.

There is a Biblical law called the *eglah arufah*. If a man is found murdered outside a city's limits, and the murderer is not known, then the city that is nearest to the slain man sends out the elders of that city. They take a calf which has never been put to work nor worn a yoke, and bring it to a ravine which is neither plowed nor sown. There they break the calf's neck. Afterwards, they wash their hands over the calf and proclaim, "Our hands have not shed this [person's] blood, nor have our eyes seen [him]."[5]

Rashi says that a calf is brought to an untilled ravine because neither has borne fruit. This atones for the death of a person who can no longer bear fruit.[6] Thus the ritual of the *eglah arufah* symbolically expresses the irrevocable loss of the slain man's childbearing potential. That is the greatest tragedy of his death. So it would seem from this commentary that having children is man's prime function and reason for living, for losing the ability to have children is the tragedy of his untimely death.

The Sifsei Chachamim, however, comments that according to this interpretation, if a man who was unable to have children, or an elderly man, was found murdered, then the

---

4. See *Men, Women, and Infertility*, p. 46.

5. *Devarim* 21:1–9.

6. Rashi, *Devarim* 21:4.

details of the *eglah arufah* ceremony would be pointless, for the slain person was in any case incapable of "bearing fruit"! Yet the Torah does not distinguish between a fertile man and an infertile man. Therefore, the Sifsei Chachamim concludes, being unable to bear fruit does not refer to producing children, but rather to performing mitzvos,[7] for the fruits of a person are not his children but his good deeds.

Many times people will say things such as, "My children are all I have." This is an absurdity from a Jewish point of view. The Torah makes this point clear in the following two verses: "These are the generations of Noach: Noach was a righteous man, perfect in his generations, and Noach walked with God. Noach fathered three sons: Shem, Cham and Yefes."[8] Rashi asks, why did the Torah begin to tell us about Noach's generations, and then interrupt itself by telling us that he was a righteous man? The Torah should have said, "These are the generations of Noach: Noach fathered three sons: Shem, Cham and Yefes. Noach was a righteous man, perfect in his generations, and Noach walked with God." Why was his righteousness inserted before the names of his children?

Rashi answers that the primary "generations" of a man are his good deeds and not his children.[9] Our pride and joy shouldn't be merely our children, but our mitzvos. The good deeds that we do in this world will indeed stay with us through eternity.

Not only do our children give us immortality, but the Torah that we learn and the mitzvos that we do throughout our lives give us immortality as well. They, too, are our fruit, our offspring, our generations.

---

7. Sifsei Chachamim, ad loc., *os pei*. See also *Sotah* 46a.

8. *Bereishis* 6:9–10.

9. Rashi, ibid.

Parashas Ekev begins with Moshe encouraging the Jews to keep the mitzvos of the Torah. By doing so, he assures them, they will receive God's love and Divine blessing. They will merit material wealth and military dominance, and "there will be no infertile male or female among you": *Lo yihiyeh becha akar v'akarah.*[10] Interestingly, our Sages do not interpret this verse literally.[11] According to *Chazal,* "There will be no *akar* or *akarah* among you" means that your prayers will not be uprooted, but rather they shall all bear fruit.[12] Another interpretation is you shall not be uprooted from repentance.[13] Rabbi Moshe Sofer, citing this *Chazal,* explains, "You shall not be uprooted from learning Torah."[14] The Netziv broadens the explanation. He says, "You will not have anyone who is unproductive, who doesn't fulfill a purpose."[15] By combining the interpretations of *Chazal* and the broader interpretations of the later commentators, we can conclude that the Torah is telling us that the blessing of fruitfulness is the fulfillment of spiritual endeavors and contributing to society.

A NEW SPIRITUAL EXPRESSION

The Talmud says, "There are four types of people who are considered dead: a needy person, a person afflicted with

---

10. *Devarim* 7:14.

11. The obvious reason for altering the literal meaning is because just before this promise, Moshe guaranteed the people that God "will love you, bless you and make you numerous; He will bless your progeny" (ibid., 7:13). Our Sages saw the redundancy. If God already promised the blessing of children, why would He repeat Himself? Therefore the words *akar* and *akarah* have to mean something else.

12. *Devarim Rabbah* 3:6, in the name of Rabbi Chanina ben Levi.

13. Ibid., in the name of Rav Yonasan.

14. *Chasam Sofer,* ad loc.

15. Netziv, ad loc.

tzara'as, a blind person, and a childless person."[16] What can this possibly mean? Does this mean that the above-mentioned people have no purpose in life? Rav Chaim Shmuelevitz in his *Sichos Mussar* explains that these are all people who are not naturally inclined to do *chesed* in an unlimited way.[17]

Our task on earth is to emulate God. Just as God does *chesed*, kindness, without limits, so too we need to practice acts of *chesed* without limits. A poor person is incapable of doing *chesed* for others, for like the blind man he needs *chesed* done for him. A person afflicted with *tzara'as* cannot do *chesed* for others, for he is an outcast. A blind person is handicapped in his ability to do for others; it is hard for him to do *chesed* when he cannot see. Although a person without a child is capable of bestowing kindness on others, he is naturally handicapped in his ability to do limitless *chesed*. Only for our children do we usually do *chesed* without boundaries. So because of the natural tendency of these people to do less *chesed* in their lifetime, they are considered "dead," for they cannot emulate the Almighty to the fullest extent that is humanly possible.

The situation, of course, doesn't have to be this way; it is merely a natural human tendency. A poor person can do great kindness if he puts his mind to it. Many penniless people fill their lives with *chesed* and Torah learning. And it would be ludicrous to propose that the many righteous men and women who are known to be childless are unproductive, or that they are considered "dead."

In the Scriptures, there are very few direct spiritual descriptions of people, including the great *tzaddikim*. Women are usually described by their appearance, such as *yefas to'ar* and *yefas mar'eh*. One woman who merited to be called "great," however, is the Shunamite woman, who was childless. Imme-

---

16. *Nedarim* 64b.

17. *Sichos Mussar*, essay 31, *Badad Yeishev*, *Beha'alosecha* 5732.

diately after she is called "a woman of great note,"[18] the text describes the act of *chesed* she did by taking in guests. Therefore, it seems reasonable to say that she merited to be called a great woman because of her acts of *chesed*. Even while she was childless, the Shunamite woman was so exalted that Scripture was compelled to bear witness to her greatness. She achieved greatness without children. She put her infertility aside and made the most out of her life. She found her niche within her people.

In order to counterbalance the loss of raising children, one must find fulfillment in other spiritual pursuits. Being involved in *chesed* or learning more Torah can accomplish this. Finding a way to fulfill your obligation to emulate God might require extra creativity or further effort on your part. Of course this might be practical only after you have resigned yourself to the fact that you will never have children of your own. Once you have internalized that you may go through life without children you will be able to find fulfillment through a new and stronger spiritual expression. Nevertheless, as mentioned earlier, it would be beneficial to try and find a spiritually fulfilling activity even during the fertility treatments.

SARAH'S MISSION

Throughout this book, examples from the matriarchs showed us that these righteous women experienced the same emotional trauma during infertility as we endure. Most of the examples were regarding Rachel, whose suffering was the most dramatically expressed: "Give me children, for if not, I am dead." Rivkah's suffering was not mentioned in the Torah, because Yitzchak and Rivkah's story picks up only after she be-

---

18. See *II Melachim* 4:8.

comes pregnant. However, the story of Avraham and Sarah takes place during Sarah's years of infertility — yet we don't see that she suffered emotionally from her infertility as Rachel did.

Concerning Sarah's infertility, the Torah simply states, "Sarai, the wife of Avram, had not borne him a child, and she had an Egyptian maidservant whose name was Hagar."[19] Even through Sarah's words we don't find any reference to emotional anguish. She just says as a matter of fact to Avraham, "Look now. God has kept me from bearing children. Marry now my maidservant."[20] The Netziv points out that Sarah realized that she could never give birth, but since God promised Avraham that he would have a child, she acted without hesitation to make that promise a reality in the best way that she knew how. But why wasn't Sarah devastated by the thought of being barren forever?

When Avraham journeyed to the land of Canaan, he took his wife Sarah, his nephew Lot, all of his possessions, and "the souls they had made in Charan."[21] Who are the "souls they had made in Charan?" Rashi says that they were the ones whom Avraham and Sarah brought under the wings of the Divine Presence, those converts from paganism to monotheism.[22]

Sarah was busy. She had a mission in life. She was involved in teaching the truth of God to the world. Although she wanted children, she had other spiritual pursuits; she did not let her infertility stop her from working toward her goal. Sarah's dedication to "creating souls" was not merely a coping mechanism — it was her life's work. Since she was absorbed in

19. *Bereishis* 16:1.
20. *Bereishis* 16:2.
21. *Bereishis* 12:5.
22. Rashi, ibid.

teaching, she didn't allow the pain of infertility to take over her life. She lived her life and got close to God by bringing others close to God.

Chazal tell us that Sarah never lost hope that she would have a child. On the verse, "And God remembered Sarah, as He said..."[23] the Rabbis explain that God remembered Sarah after she said to herself: "What! Am I going to lose my hope? No! Rather I will be delighted with my God, and I will rejoice with the Lord, my Savior."[24]

Previously, we cited this *midrash* to show that Sarah never lost her faith in God that she would have a child. But by looking carefully at the *midrash*, we see that it doesn't say that she believed she would have a child. It says that she would still be delighted with her God and she would rejoice with Him. In other words, Sarah didn't let herself slump into depression over her infertility. She made a conscious decision to continue rejoicing in God. Infertility was not going to keep Sarah from living a fruitful life.

Sarah did not express her faith by saying that God would yet grant her a biological child. Rather, even though she might have gone through life childless, she would still be faithful to God. There are so many other aspects of life to be thankful for. There are so many other ways to make life spiritual and beautiful. Sarah found her spiritual expression. She found purpose and beauty in her life.[25]

We don't find that Sarah prayed for a child — nor do we find even a hint in any verse that would have enabled *Chazal*

---

23. *Bereishis* 21:1.

24. *Bereishis Rabbah* 53:3.

25. There is a *midrash* (*Yalkut Shimoni, I Shemuel* 77) that says that Elkanah said to Chanah, "Why do you cry? Sarah didn't cry. Rivkah didn't cry." Elkanah was saying to Chanah, there are other ways to react to infertility. There are other areas in life to find happiness.

to say that she prayed.[26] Perhaps the absence of her prayer in Scripture is not arbitrary. Perhaps Sarah didn't pray for a child. Like the Shunamite woman, she accepted this as a fact of life and didn't feel the need to ask God for fulfillment as a mother, since she found fulfillment in spreading the truth of God's existence, saying, "I will be delighted with my God."

Sarah taught the world about God. The Shunamite woman dedicated her life to kindness. Everyone needs to find that special activity that will give spiritual satisfaction, be it Torah education, *chesed, tzedakah,* prayer, honoring parents, counseling other childless couples, or whatever. You will have to choose your spiritual focus.

If you let pregnancy remain the focus of your life, then the rest of your life will pass you by. If you let the mitzvah of *Pru Urvu* be the focus of your spirituality, then the rest of the

---

26. There is, however, a *midrash* that says that the Satan came to Yitzchak on the way to the *Akeidah* and said to him, "Pathetic one, how many days did your mother fast and how many prayers did she pray for you, and this old man wants to slaughter you?!" See *Pesikta Rabbasi* 40:69. (Of course, this testimony that Sarah prayed came from the Satan, whose goal was to convince Yitzchak to retreat from the *Akeidah*.)

Concerning Avraham, to our knowledge, the Midrash does not explicitly state that Avraham prayed for Sarah to have a child. There is a *midrash* that seems to suggest that he prayed, but it could be understood to mean that he only helped Sarah by agreeing to take Hagar. See *Bereishis Rabbah* 71:7.

Another *midrash* says that Avraham would pray for barren women and they would get pregnant (*Bereishis Rabbah* 39:11). Accordingly, it is difficult to understand why he would pray for other childless women but not for Sarah. We can conclude that he also prayed for Sarah — unless there is a special reason why he wouldn't have prayed for her. Yet we could ask, if Avraham successfully prayed for others, why didn't God answer his prayers for Sarah?

According to the Zohar, Avraham did not pray for Sarah (see Zohar, *Toldos* 137b). There is a *midrash Eliyahu Rabbah* (18) that says that Avraham did pray for Sarah. However, this *midrash* is written in the third person, as someone telling this over to somebody else; it is not a direct teaching based on a Scriptural reference.

mitzvos will pass you by. If the joy of having a child will be the only focus of your happiness, then the rest of life's joys will pass you by.

A woman's exemption from the mitzvah to be fruitful and multiply teaches us that a woman in particular needn't see motherhood as her primary function in life. Fulfillment from your special spiritual activity will enable you to put your infertility aside and live a fruitful, productive life. You will be able to find joy in the rest of God's blessings, and you will be very proud of your "generations."

BITACHON: ACCEPTING REALITY AS THE WILL OF GOD

Even once you have accepted the fact that you may go through life without children, and once you are able to find some other spiritual expression — or even if you are ultimately blessed with children — you will still need to make sense out of your infertility. Why did it have to be this way? It will be difficult to truly feel close to God without understanding how He is still so close to you, and how you can still have faith through the tears.

Rabbi Moshe Chaim Luzzatto begins the first chapter of his famous work, *Mesillas Yesharim* (*The Path of the Just*)[27] with these words: "Our Sages of blessed memory have instructed us that man was created for [the sole purpose of] reveling in the Eternal and delighting in the splendor of the Divine Presence, this being the ultimate joy and the greatest of all pleasures in existence. And the true place for this pleasure is the World to Come, which was created with this purpose in mind." We establish a relationship with God through prayer and mitzvah observance. If God wanted you to establish that

---

27. Jerusalem: Feldheim Publishers, 2004.

relationship without children, then you must work on it without being able to harness that one mitzvah.

The Chazon Ish says that what ultimately is, is the will of God.[28] Even if a certain spiritual endeavor is stopped through no fault of your own, that is also the will of God. Apparently you didn't need that specific spiritual elevation which you thought you needed. Accepting this reality as the will of God, as something that is somehow for your ultimate good and for the good of humanity, is the supreme expression of *bitachon.*

But how do we accomplish this? The only way to attain this is by acquiring the attribute of *bitul,* which means nullification. We must nullify our personal desires for the sake of God's will. We do not nullify ourselves. Rather, we nullify our desires and goals for God's "desires and goals," as it were.

Rebbe Nachman of Breslav asks, "Why don't we experience God's goodness all the time? The reason is because our whole attention is focused on what we want — our own goals, projects and purposes. We want to control things and have them go our way. We get tense and fearful that things won't go the way we want them to go. And when they don't, we get frustrated, angry, and depressed."[29] If we can lift ourselves beyond our ego-bound desires, if we can live our life for the sake of God's will, then we will not be disappointed when our will is not fulfilled.

When a person takes on the attribute of nullifying his own self-centered desires for the desires of God, he will need to suppress his desires at the beginning. But *bitul* really isn't about suppression. It's about keeping the light of God in front of our eyes at all times. It's about seeing the truth of God all the time, not only on special days like Rosh Hashanah or

---

28. *Emunah U'vitachon,* chap. 2, p. 17 (Grinman version, Tel Aviv, 5739).

29. Avraham Greenbaum, trans. and ed., *Garden of Souls: Rebbe Nachman on Suffering* (Jerusalem: Breslav Research Institute, 1990), p. 19.

when our personal desires happened to be fulfilled. *Bitul* is about nullifying that which is transient, that which is of little or no importance.

You may be facing a huge and glorious mountain, but if you take a little coin and hold it in front of your eyes, you won't be able to see the mountain. So it is when we come into this world — we get sunk in its vanities and think there is nothing better, because this tiny mortal world prevents us from seeing the great light of God's will. The tiny coins of this world block out the view of Mount Sinai.[30]

The road to *bitul* can be long and exhausting. Putting the idea into practice may involve extensive reevaluation of your goals and priorities. There may be difficult adjustments, or major changes to make in your habits and lifestyle. You may pick yourself up, only to fall down again. But if you do fall down, you can always pick yourself up again and again. You can put down the coin and head for the mountain.

"EVERYTHING THAT GOD DOES"

Having *bitachon* when life seems so harsh is a difficult test. If eventually things work out to your satisfaction, then the "test" that you endured seems worth it: you toiled, you walked in the darkness holding on to the hand of God, and you emerged a winner. You feel stronger, now that there is a happy ending. You may even feel that now you understand the whole process. "Everything that the All-Merciful One does, He does for the best," said Rabbi Akiva.[31] Now you can say it too.

But what if you held on to God's hand through it all and ended up, in your viewpoint, lacking? You did everything

---

30. Ibid., p. 20.
31. *Berachos* 60b.

you should have done: You faithfully went through all the treatments and even some alternative ones. You spoke to rabbis, took advice from rebbetzins, and became a regular visitor at *kever Rachel*. You cried at the graves of the *tzaddikim*. You poured out your heart at the Kosel. You were extra careful in lighting Shabbos candles. You took on extra stringencies and enhancements in your mitzvah observance. You begged God, in the solitude of your home, and watched your tears soak the pages of your prayer book.

And your house is still empty. Your plans for naming the baby after your beloved grandfather will not be fulfilled. There wasn't a day you didn't fantasize about making challah with your daughter or watching your son go off to shul with his father. The hours spent contemplating which schools you would send the little ones to turned out to be all wasted time. Your dreams have dissipated, your prayers seem unheard, and your tears have dried on your cheeks.

You withstood the physical hardship and pain, the stress on your marriage, the tension with your in-laws. You continued even while bombarded with the psychological stress from your social circles. The tormenting comments from everybody who had something to say still echo in the empty rooms of your home and the corridors of your heart, and you are left without a jubilant reward for enduring them. As far as you can see, the spiritual exertion you mustered up to find Divine salvation, failed. Could Rabbi Akiva have been wrong, at least some of the time? At least this time?

Rabbi Akiva was known for his statement that everything God does is for the best. The story related in the Talmud in connection with this statement goes like this: Rabbi Akiva attempted to find a place to sleep in a village he was passing through, but he was refused. He said, "Whatever God does is for the best." He slept that night in the fields. He had with him a donkey, a rooster, and a lamp. That night a lion attacked the donkey, a wildcat devoured the rooster, and the wind came and blew out his lamp. Now he had nothing, yet he reiterated, "Whatever God does is for the best." Later that night the Roman army came and conquered the village. Had he found a place to sleep in the village, or had the donkey, rooster, and lamp not been destroyed, the Romans would have discovered him."[32] In this case the good was seen quickly. But such a happy ending doesn't always take place.

This story is a metaphor for all of life's circumstances. In telling us that everything that God does is for the best, Rabbi Akiva uses the Aramaic word *Rachmana* ("the Merciful One") for God, telling us that whatever is for the best, is merciful as well.

Rabbi Akiva goes to an inn to get some rest. This symbolizes mankind's yearning for peace and tranquility. But the inn was closed because there is no tranquility for the righteous in this world, as Rashi says concerning Yaakov.[33]

Rabbi Akiva had a donkey, a rooster, and a lamp with him. A donkey represents our animal instincts. It symbolizes pure materialism without spirituality. A rooster has the ability to distinguish between night and day. In fact, one word for rooster in Hebrew is *sechvi,* which also means insight, and consequently symbolizes our own intellectual capacities. Therefore the rooster in Rabbi Akiva's story is a metaphor for our intellectual yearning. We all strive for perfection in our understanding of the world. The lamp symbolizes our spiritual pursuits, as the Torah says, "The lamp is a mitzvah and the Torah is light."[34]

Mankind is always striving for the perfect balance be-

---

32. Ibid.

33. Rashi, *Bereishis* 37:2.

34. *Mishlei* 6:23.

tween our material needs and desires, our intellectual abilities and understanding, and our spiritual objectives. But we never find it. The lions and wildcats come and devour the product of our toil. The wind comes and blows out our hopes. But this is all for the best, for if it didn't happen, the army — the heavenly prosecutor who attacks in the ultimate "inn," the World to Come, will conquer. But if we experience some degree of suffering in this world, we escape the "army," so we can enjoy the best that God has in store for us.

Later, Rabbi Akiva went into dangerous circumstances with the same *emunah*. He was told that he could not teach Torah anymore, or he would be put to death by the Romans. Yet he didn't stop. He taught Torah publicly. He was captured and incarcerated. He was put to a painful death. Yet when he was being tortured, he began to recite the *Shema*: "Hear O Israel, the Lord is our God, the Lord is One." His students who were present marveled, "Rebbe, even here, now? Surely you are going too far." Rabbi Akiva replied, "This has been my dream all my life. All my life I recited in the *Shema* that I should love God with all my heart and all my soul. My whole life, I wondered when I would have the opportunity to fulfill this mitzvah in its entirety. Now finally I have the opportunity to love God with all my soul. Shouldn't I be happy about fulfilling this mitzvah?!" His soul departed as he said "One."[35]

The numerical value of the word "one" in Hebrew is thirteen. This symbolizes that God's Oneness is His thirteen attributes of *rachamim*, mercy.[36] Rabbi Akiva left this world with the ultimate message that "Everything that God — *Rachmana* — does is for the best."

This story of Rabbi Akiva didn't conclude the way the previous one did. In the first story, Rabbi Akiva saw the ultimate

35. *Berachos* 61b.

36. *Garden of the Souls: Rebbe Nachman on Suffering*, p. 9.

good, as he was saved. In the second story he was killed. If Rabbi Akiva had never been arrested, and if he had continued to teach Torah; or if he had taught Torah in jail to some special student, perhaps there would have been a happy ending to that story as well. But instead Rabbi Akiva was thrown into jail and put to an excruciating death. Yet he went to his execution with the same joy that he had when doing any other mitzvah. It was not only "for the best"; he died doing *kiddush Hashem.* Although this particular story doesn't have an objectively happy ending, Rabbi Akiva saw the opportunity to give it a happy ending as well. To Rabbi Akiva it was a matter of the right perspective. Perhaps he couldn't actually teach Torah anymore to his specific students, but through his death he taught all subsequent generations of the Jewish People the lesson of *kiddush Hashem*. The image of Rabbi Akiva's martyrdom is imprinted upon the heart and soul of every Jew.

* * *

There was once a man who came to the Maggid of Mezritch and said, "My wife and I didn't have children for many, many years. Finally, God answered our prayers and my wife gave birth to a son, a beautiful boy who was dedicated to Torah and good deeds. When he was only eighteen years old he passed away. My question is this: The Gemara says that with the same joy that we bless God for the good we should bless Him for the bad.[37] I can understand that even when bad things happen, we should bless God, but how can we do it 'with the same joy' as the good?"

"That is a very good question," replied the Maggid, "I am sorry I don't have an answer for you. But I know someone who does. His name is Zusha of Anipoli. Go to him and ask him your question." Reb Zusha was known for his faith in

---

37. *Berachos* 60b.

God even though he lived in constant poverty and suffering.

So the man went to Anipoli and came to the dwelling of Reb Zusha. It was a broken, tiny, overcrowded shack that testified to the life of misery that Reb Zusha lived. He met Reb Zusha and asked him the question. Reb Zusha looked at him pensively for a moment and then said, "That is a very good question. But I always had a different question on that Gemara. Where is there bad in the world?"

The man received his answer. It is all a matter of perspective.

Not every story of a childless couple will have a Cinderella ending. Some will live without the blessing of raising a Jewish child to Torah and mitzvos. Reb Zusha brought healing to the world through his acceptance of his dire straits. Rabbi Akiva elevated the world with his martyrdom. You withstood both physical and emotional torture. You survived through it all believing that it was for the best. Rabbi Akiva's acceptance of his suffering rebuilt the world. Your suffering has also mended the world.

You will never know why God decided it would be best for you to go through infertility. God knows your pain. He has been with you every step of this long, heart-wrenching journey. Your prayers, your tears, and your shattered dreams brought this world closer to perfection.

Through the pain that you endured and in the merit of your faith that it is all for the best, let us hope that the salvation of the world will come swiftly in our days. And may we then live to enjoy the fulfillment of God's promise, "There will be no infertile male or female among you." And we will all be the beneficiaries of God's blessing — the third key.

Appendix A
Index of Laboratory Values

The following are the most common blood tests performed during fertility testing. The values below reflect the normal range of test results. Laboratory values can vary with individual labs, and usually a normal-range scale will be provided when the printed results are given.

LABORATORY VALUES

Substance	**Conventional Units**	**SI Units**
Estradiol (E2)	20–400 pg/mL	70–500 pmol/L
FSH (reproductive years)	5–20 mIU/ml	5–20 IU/L
FSH (cycle day 3)	<10 mIU/ml	<10 IU/L
Glucose (fasting)	70–110 mg/dl	4.0–6.0 mmol/L
HCG (non-pregnant)	<5 IU/L	<5 mIU/mL
HCG (pregnancy)	>5 IU/L	>5 mIU/mL
[approximately doubling every 2 days until titer is greater than 10,000]		
Insulin (fasting)	5–20 uU/ml	35–145 pmol/L
LH (reproductive years)	5–20 mlU/mL	5–20 IU/L
Progesterone		
Follicular phase	<3ng/mL	<9.5 nmol/L
Secretory phase	5–30 ng/mL	16–95 nmol/L
Prolactin	1–20 ng/mL	44.4–888pmol/L
Testosterone (total)	20–80 ng/dL	0.7–2.8 nmol/L
Testosterone (free)	100–200 pg/dL	35–700 pmol/L
TSH	0.35–5.0 uU/mL	0.35–5.0 mU/L

Appendix B
Guide to Medications

CLOMIPHENE CITRATE

Trade names: Clomid, Ikaclomin

Supplied: 50 mg tablets

Administration: By mouth

Mechanism: Stimulates the release of pituitary gonadotropins (FSH & LH) which results in the maturations of the ovarian follicle, ovulation, and development of the corpus luteum.

Dosage: 50 to 250 mg daily starting on day 5 of the menstrual cycle for five days.

Side effects: Dizziness, blurred vision, weight gain, increased appetite, hot flashes, breast discomfort.

MENOTROPIN — HUMAN MENOPAUSAL GONADOTROPIN (HMG)

Trade Names: Pergonal, Menogon, Menopur, Humegon, Repronex

Supplied: Ampoules of 75 IU FSH and LH

Administration: IM or SC

Mechanism: Mimics FSH in inducing follicular growth and LH in aiding follicular maturation.

Dosage: Started on cycle day 2 or 3. Daily or alternative-day dose of 75IU or 150IU until adequate response based upon E2 (estradiol) levels and ultrasound measurement of follicle size.

(For male infertility, menotropin 75 or 150 IU may be

given two or three times weekly or in daily dose along with HCG, or 1500 to 2500 IU, two to three times weekly for at least three to four months to stimulate spermatogenesis.)

Side Effects: Irritability, change in mood, weight gain, increased appetite, multiple gestation, ovarian hyperstimulation, nausea and vomiting, fever, joint pain, skin rash, and local reactions at site of injection. If ovarian hyperstimulation is suspected, menotropin is stopped and HCG is withheld. Treatment should be abandoned if there is no response in three weeks.

FOLLICLE STIMULATING HORMONE

Trade names:

Purified urinary FSH — Metrodin, Normegon, Orgafol, Urofollitropin

Highly purified urinary FSH — Fertinex, Metrodin HP

Recombinant human FSH — Gonal-F, Puregon, Follistim

Supplied: 50, 75, 150 IU ampoules (Puregon available in pen injector)

Administration: IM or SC

Mechanism: Stimulates follicular development for induction of ovulation.

Dosage: Starting on days 2, 3, or up to the 5th day of cycle, 50 to 150 IU every day, increasing by 37.5 or 75 IU if necessary for a maximum dose of 750 IU per day. Response is measured by E2 blood levels and ultrasound response. HCG is given the day after cessation of FSH.

Side effects: Irritablility, mood changes, breast discomfort, weight gain, irritation at injection site, ovarian hyperstimulation syndrome, and multiple pregnancy.

HUMAN CHORIONIC GONADOTROPIN (HCG)

Trade names: Pregnyl, Profasi, A.P.L., Chorigon

Supplied: 2500 or 5000 IU

Administration: IM

Mechanism: In women, HCG serves as a substitute for LH to stimulate ovulation after clomiphene, HMG, or FSH. In men, HCG promotes secretion of gonadal steroid hormones by stimulating production of androgens by the interstitial cells of the testes (leydig cells).

Dosage: After ovulation induction, 5000 or 10,000 IU is given IM when E2 levels and follicle size are deemed adequate.

For luteal phase support, 1500 to 2500 IU is administered two to four times during the luteal phase until menstruation or confirmed pregnancy. Sometimes continued throughout the first ten weeks of pregnancy.

Alternatively, 2500 IU may be given on days 3 and 6 after embryo transfer in IVF.

In men, 1500 to 5000 IU two to three times a week for six to nine months.

Side effects: Pain at injection site, fatigue, irritability, headache, weight gain, and excessive hair growth.

GNRH ANALOGUE

Trade names: Synarel (nafarelin acetate), Suprefact (benzalkonium chloride)

Supplied: Nasal solution 200 mcg/spray

Administration: Nasal spray

Mechanism: GnRH analog that acts on the pituitary gland to decrease release of FSH and LH, thus decreasing ovarian stimulation, lowering circulating estrogens, and improving symptoms associated with endometriosis. Also used as a down-regulator of the menstrual cycle before IVF.

Dosage: 1 spray per nostril two times a day beginning between days 2 and 4 of menstrual cycle for a maximum of six months for endometriosis. Or, one spray of 200 mcg , six times a day for down-regulation starting on day 21 of the menstrual cycle.

Side effects: Headaches, mood changes, insomnia, nasal irritation, hot flashes, reduced libido, vaginal dryness.

TRIPTORELIN EMBONATE

Trade names: Decapeptyl, Diphereline

Supplied: Disposable, pre-filled syringes

Administration: Monthly IM injection

Mechanism: Down-regulation of the pituitary gland before IVF.

Side effects: Same as above.

GNRH ANTAGONIST

Trade names: Cetrotide, Ganirelex, Orgalutran

Supplied: 0.25 or 3 mg

Administration: SC

Mechanism: Inhibition of premature LH surges in women undergoing controlled ovarian stimulation. Prevents ovulation before medically desired.

Dosage: On day 6 or 7 of FSH administration, for one to five days. Can be given at the same time as FSH, but preparations should not be mixed and different injection sites are to be used.

Side effects: Local skin reaction (irritation, redness), headache, nausea.

PROGESTERONE

Trade name: Gestone

Supplied: 50 mg/ml or 100 mg/ml

Administration: IM

Mechanism: Luteal phase support requiring progesterone which is normally secreted by the ovaries to prepare the endometrium to accept and hold the implanted embryo.

Dosage: 25 to 100mg daily from the onset of ovulation or day after embryo transfer for a period of two to six weeks.

Side effects: Itchy rash, irritation at injection site. [Professor Ehud Margalioth, head of the IVF department at Shaare Zedek hospital, Jerusalem, recommends warming the solution to body temperature before injection and using a warm compress on the injection site for fifteen minutes afterwards.] Additional side effects of all progesterone agents include dizziness, irregular bleeding, breast tenderness, and depression.

Trade name: Utrogeston

Supplied: 100 mg capsules

Administration: By mouth

Mechanism: Luteal phase support.

Dosage: 100 mg capsules three times a day.

Side effects: See above.

Trade name: Biphaston

Supplied: 10 mg tablets

Administration: By mouth

Mechanism: Same as above.

Dosage: One tablet, twice a day.

Side effects: See Gestone.

Trade name: Crinone gel

Supplied: Bioadhesive vaginal gel

Administration: Vaginally

Mechanism: Treatment of progesterone deficiency.

Dosage: One to three times daily.

Side effects: Abdominal pain, perineal pain, constipation, depression, breast enlargement.

[Other trade names of progesterone include: Progestogen, Gesterol, Progestilin, Clinone, Depolut]

GLUCOCORTICOID

Trade name: Dexamethasone

Supplied: 0.5 or 2.0 mg tablets

Administration: By mouth

Mechanism: In women, exerts effect to reduce overabundance of male hormones in the blood stream.

Dosage: 0.5 mg at bedtime, with increased dosage as needed to achieve desired results.

Side effects: Weakness, allergic reactions (hay fever, itching), weight gain. Should withdraw gradually from use.

ENDOMETRIOSIS TREATMENT[1]

Trade names: Cyclomen, Danocrine

Supplied: 50, 100, or 200 mg capsules

Administration: By mouth

Mechanism: Gonadotropin inhibitor that suppresses the pituitary-ovarian axis and inhibits estrogenic effects, thereby reducing the size and discomfort of endometrial implants.

Dosage: 100 to 400 mg two times a day for up to nine months.

Side effects: Dizziness, headaches, sleep disorders, nausea, vomiting, diarrhea, change in appetite, weight gain, decrease in breast size, flushing, sweating, menstrual irregularities, oily skin or hair, deepening of the voice, and excessive hair growth (hirsutism).

1. See also GnRH Analogue for endometriosis treatment.

ANTICOAGULANTS[2]

Aspirin (acetylsalicylic acid)

Trade names: Ecotrin, Cartia, Tevaprin, Micropirin

Supplied: 75, 100, 325, or 500 mg tablets

Administration: By mouth

Mechanism: Besides its analgesic and anti-inflammatory properties, aspirin given in pregnancy impedes clotting by preventing platelet aggregation. For prevention of repeated miscarriages.

Dosage: One tablet per physician's recommendation.

Side effects: Gastrointestinal bleeding (report any rectal bleeding or vomiting of blood immediately to your doctor), gastrointestinal distress, prolonged bleeding time, bruising, rash, abnormal liver function.

Enoxaparin sodium (low-molecular weight heparin)

Trade names: Lovenox, Clexane, Fragmin

Supplied: 20, 40, or 60 mg in pre-measured syringes

Administration: SC

Mechanism: A low-molecular weight heparin derivative that prevents overproduction of clotting complexes in the treatment of thrombophilia, thereby improving circulation to the placenta. Given in order to prevent recurrent miscarriages.

Dosage: 1mg/kg SC, or 40 mg SC once daily, from diagnosis of pregnancy until delivery.

Side effects: Bruising, bleeding gums, nosebleeds. To avoid irritation at the injection sites, rotate sites of administration. [Professor Ehud Margalioth recommends applying ice to the site for five minutes prior to injection and for fifteen minutes following the injection to virtually eliminate irritation from the injections.]

---

2. Blood thinning medications.

HYPERPROLACTINEMIA

Bromocriptine mesylate

Trade names: Parlodel, Parilac

Supplied: 2.5 or 10 mg

Administration: By mouth (can also be administered vaginally)

Mechanism: Inhibits the secretion of prolactin.

Dosage: 1.25 to 2.5 mg by mouth daily; can increase up to 10mg per day.

Side effects: Nausea, vomiting, constipation, abdominal cramps, dizziness, fatigue, nasal congestion. Side effects can be minimized by slowly building tolerance toward the required dose of 2.5 mg, twice daily, by taking the medication with milk or food and starting initially at bedtime.

Cabergoline

Trade name: Dostinex

Supplied: 0.5 mg tablets

Administration: By mouth

Mechanism: Same as Parlodel.

Dosage: One dose, twice a week, with a maximum dose of 4.5 mg per week.

Side effects: Same as above.

Lisuride

Trade name: Dopergin

Supplied: 0.2 mg tablets

Administration: By mouth

Mechanism: Same as Parlodel.

Dosage: One dose per week.

Side effects: Same as above.

INSULIN RESISTANCE

Metformin

Trade name: Glucophage

Supplied: 500 or 850 mg

Administration: Tablet by mouth

Mechanism: Facilitates insulin's action in the body. Given to women whose bodies are resistant to insulin action, which interferes with fertility.

Dosage: 1500 to 2000 mg daily.

Side effects: Diarrhea, abdominal pain, nausea, vomiting, reduced appetite. Take with food to avoid stomach upset.

EXPLANATION OF RELEVANT TERMS AND PROCEDURES

Types of Drugs

Analogue: A drug or compound that is similar in structure but has a different effect.

Agonist: A drug that stimulates a response.

Anatagosist: A drug that blocks a response or competes for the same action.

Units of Measure

mg – milligram

mcg – microgram

IU – international units

pg/l – picogram per liter

cc – cubic centimeter (1 cc = 1 ml)

ml – milliliter

Guide to Injections

◆ **SC – Subcutaneous.** This is an injection given under the skin. Subcutaneous needles are usually short and thin. It is not recommended to inject more than 3cc of medicine at one time subcutaneously. More than this amount requires rotation to another site. The most common places for SC injection are the upper arm, thigh, or abdomen.

Steps for injection:

- Wash hands with soap and water
- Clean site for injection with alcohol or alcohol/septadine solution
- Allow to dry
- Grasp skin or stretch the skin between two fingers of non-dominant hand
- Quickly plunge the needle into the skin at a 45-degree angle
- Pull back slightly on the syringe to make sure there is no blood (if there is a return of blood, discard syringe and solution and start again; if there is no blood return, continue to next step)
- Slowly inject medication (about 1cc:5 seconds)
- Quickly remove needle
- Rub gently with alcohol pad and apply warm compress if desired

◆ **IM – Intramuscular.** This is an injection given in the muscle. Intramuscular needles are usually longer and larger than subcutaneous needles. It is not recommended to inject more than 5cc at one IM site. Intramuscular sites can be rotated between the upper arm (deltoid muscle), the lateral thigh (greater trochanter muscle), or the upper buttocks (gluteus maximus).

Steps for injection:

- Wash hands with soap and water
- Clean site for injection with alcohol or alcohol/septadine solution
- Allow to dry
- Stretch the skin between two fingers of non-dominant hand
- Quickly plunge the needle into the skin at a 90-degree angle
- Pull back slightly on the syringe to make sure there is no

blood (if there is a return of blood, discard syringe and solution and start again; if there is no blood return, continue to next step)

- Slowly inject medication (about 1cc:5 seconds)
- Quickly remove needle
- Rub gently with alcohol pad and apply warm compress if desired

No one enjoys getting a shot, and its also hard to give someone you love or even yourself an injection. Try these suggestions to make it less unpleasant:

- Apply ice for two to three minutes, immediately prior to swabbing with alcohol.
- After the injection, use very warm water on a cotton ball or even apply a hot water bottle to the injection site; this will reduce irritation and help disperse the medication throughout the tissues. If redness, irritation, or swelling at the site of injection persists, contact your health care providers.

To dispose of the needles and syringes appropriately, use an empty plastic bottle or large coffee can as a "sharps container" and refer to your doctor or clinic for instructions on disposal. Never throw used syringes or needles straight into the trash.

Appendix C
Glossary of Medical Terms

-A-

ABLATION: separation or detachment; removal or destruction by cutting.

ABORTION:

Spontaneous: a pregnancy loss during the first twenty weeks of GESTATION.

Habitual: when a woman has three or more MISCARRIAGES.

Incomplete: an abortion after which some tissue remains inside the UTERUS and a DILATION AND CURETTAGE (D&C) must be performed to remove the tissue and prevent complications.

Missed: the FETUS dies in the uterus but there is little bleeding or cramping and a D&C will be needed to remove the fetal remains and prevent complications.

Therapeutic: a procedure used to terminate a pregnancy before the fetus can survive on its own.

Threatened: spotting or bleeding that occurs early in pregnancy that may or may not progress to spontaneous abortion.

ACROSOME: the enzymes in a SPERM's head that allow it to make a hole in the coating around, penetrate, and fertilize, the EGG.

ADHESION: scar tissue occurring in the abdominal cavity, FALLOPIAN TUBES, or inside the UTERUS that can interfere with transport of the egg and implantation of the EMBRYO in the uterus.

AGGLUTINATION: clumping together of SPERM due to infection, inflammation, or antibodies.

AGONIST: a drug or other substance that causes an expected response.

AMENORRHEA: the absence of menstruation. Primary amenorrhea refers to a woman who has never menstruated. Secondary amenorrhea refers to a woman who has menstruated at one time, but who has not had a period for six months or more.

AMNIOCENTESIS: a procedure performed around week 17 in pregnancy. A small amount of amniotic fluid is withdrawn from the AMNIOTIC SAC through the mother's abdomen by means of a long syringe for microscopic analysis to rule out chromosomal abnormalities.

AMNIOTIC SAC: the bag of water (amniotic fluid) within the UTERUS which holds the FETUS.

ANALOG: a drug or other compound that acts like another substance.

ANDROGENS: male sex hormones such as TESTOSTERONE and DHEAS.

ANDROLOGIST: a physician/scientist who specializes in male fertility.

ANOVULATION: the absence of OVULATION.

ANTAGONIST: a drug or muscle that has an opposite action or competes for the same thing.

ANTIBODIES: chemicals made by the body to fight or attack foreign substances entering the body. Normally they prevent infection; however, when they attack the SPERM or FETUS, they cause INFERTILITY. Sperm antibodies can be made by either the man or the woman.

ANTIGEN: a substance that causes ANTIBODIES to form.

ARTIFICIAL INSEMINATION (AI): placing SPERM into the VAGINA, UTERUS or FALLOPIAN TUBES through artificial means instead of by COITUS; usually injected through a CATHETER or CANNULA after being washed. This procedure is used for both donor (AID) and husband's (AIH) sperm.

ASHERMAN'S SYNDROME: a condition where the uterine walls adhere to one another, usually as a result of uterine INFLAMMATION.

ASPERMIA: the absence of sperm and semen.

ASPIRATION: suctioning of fluid; for example, the removal of fluid from a FOLLICLE to retrieve an EGG.

ASSISTED HATCHING (AH, AZH): thinning out the ZONA PELLUCIDA prior to transferring the EMBRYO into the UTERUS.

ASSISTED REPRODUCTIVE TECHNOLOGY (ART): several procedures employed to bring about conception without sexual intercourse:

IUI, IVF, GIFT, ZIFT.

ASTHENOZOOSPERMIA: low SPERM MOTILITY.

ASYMPTOMATIC: having no symptoms.

AUTOIMMUNE: an immune reaction against one's own tissue or cells.

AZOOSPERMIA: absence of SPERM in the EJACULATE.

Obstructive azoospermia: the result of obstruction in either the upper or lower male reproductive tract (EPIDIDYMIS, VAS DEFERENS, SEMINAL VESICLES, or ejaculatory ducts). Sperm production may be normal, but the obstruction is preventing the sperm from being ejaculated.

Non-obstructive azoospermia: there is no production of SPERM due to a genetic or anatomical abnormality.

-B-

BASAL BODY TEMPERATURE (BBT): body temperature at rest that can be charted to predict OVULATION.

BETA HCG (BHCG) TEST: blood test to detect pregnancy, referred to as "*Beta.*" Measures the amount of HUMAN CHORIONIC GONADOTROPIN (HCG), a HORMONE released by the PLACENTA. Elevated beta levels can be detected as early as a week after FERTILIZATION.

BIOPSY: the removal and examination of tissue, cells, or fluids from the body.

BLASTOCYST: an EMBRYO in an early stage of development — the first five days after fertilization.

BLASTOMERE: one cell in the BLASTOCYST stage of early fetal development.

BLIGHTED OVUM: a pregnancy that stops developing very early on. Upon ULTRASOUND, the AMNIOTIC SAC will appear empty.

-C-

CANDIDIASIS: yeast infection.

CANNULA: a medical instrument: a hollow tube used for INSEMINATION.

CAPACITATION: a process that SPERM undergo as they travel through a woman's reproductive tract, enabling them to penetrate the EGG.

CATHETER: a hollow, flexible tube used to aspirate or inject fluids.

CENTRIFUGE: a machine that separates materials with different densities by spinning them at high speed. Used in sperm washing.

CERCLAGE: a surgical stitch (suture) used to keep the CERVIX from dilating prematurely.

CERVICAL CANAL: the cylindrical passageway between the VAGINA and the UTERUS.

CERVICAL MUCUS: a viscous (thick, gummy, or sticky) fluid plugging the opening of the CERVIX. At midcycle, under the influence of estrogen, the MUCUS becomes thin, watery, and stringy to allow SPERM to pass into the UTERUS.

CERVICAL SMEAR: a sample of the cervical mucus examined microscopically to assess the presence of ESTROGEN (FERNING) and white blood cells, indicating possible infection.

CERVICAL STENOSIS: a blockage of the CERVICAL CANAL because of a congenital defect or as a result of complications from cervical procedures.

CERVICITIS: inflammation of the CERVIX.

CERVIX: the bottom section of the UTERUS; the gateway between the uterus and the VAGINA. Dilates during labor and delivery to allow the baby to be born.

CHEMICAL PREGNANCY: a pregnancy where HCG levels are detected, but the pregnancy is lost before a heartbeat is seen on an ultrasound. This is a very early miscarriage, often before the woman misses her period.

CHLAMYDIA: a common bacterial sexually transmitted disease that can lead to PELVIC INFLAMMATORY DISEASE (PID).

CHOCOLATE CYST: a CYST in the OVARY that is filled with old blood due to ENDOMETRIOSIS.

CHORIONIC VILLUS SAMPLING (CVS): a BIOPSY of the PLACENTA that is used to check for genetic abnormalities in the FETUS. An alternative to AMNIOCENTESIS that can be done between the ninth and eleventh week of pregnancy.

CHROMOSOME: structures in the cell that carry the genetic material (genes/DNA) the messengers of heredity. Humans have forty-six chromosomes, twenty-three from the EGG and twenty-three from the SPERM.

CLEAVAGE: cell division(s) of the fertilized EGG that results in the BLASTOMERES and changes the ZYGOTE into a multicellular EMBRYO.

COITUS: sexual intercourse.

COLOSCOPY: use of a magnifying scope for close examination of the CERVIX for abnormal cells.

CONCEPTION: the fertilization of an EGG by SPERM that leads to the creation of a new being.

CONE BIOPSY: a surgical procedure used to remove precancerous cells from the CERVIX.

CONGENITAL ADRENAL HYPERPLASIA: a congenital condition resulting in the overgrowth of the adrenal gland, characterized by elevated androgens (male hormones), which suppress the PITUITARY GLAND.

CONGENITAL DEFECT: a birth defect, acquired during pregnancy.

CONTRAINDICATION: a reason not to use a particular drug or treatment.

CONTROLLED OVARIAN HYPERSTIMULATION (COH): also called *superovulation*, the use of fertility medications to stimulate growth of multiple FOLLICLES for OVULATION. See also HORMONE STIMULATION.

CORPUS LUTEUM: yellow-pigmented structure that forms from the ovarian FOLLICLE following OVULATION that produces PROGESTERONE to prepare and support the uterine lining for IMPLANTATION.

CRYOPRESERVATION: freezing quickly and then storing SPERM or EMBYROS for later use.

CRYPTORCHIDISM: when one or both TESTICLES fail to descend into the SCROTUM. Also called UNDESCENDED TESTICLES.

CYCLE DAY: the days of a woman's menstrual cycle, day 1 being the start of the period.

CYST: a fluid-filled sac.

-D-

DIETHYLSTILBESTROL (DES): a synthetic ESTROGEN prescribed for women in the 1950's through the early 1970's to prevent miscarriage. However as a result, many male and female FETUSES exposed IN UTERO to this drug developed numerous deformities. DES was banned in the United States in 1971.

DILATION AND CURETTAGE (D&C): a procedure that dilates the CERVIX to allow the physician to scrape out the lining and remove the contents of the uterus. The procedure can be used to diagnose or treat abnormal bleeding or terminate an unwanted pregnancy. It is also used to remove any remaining tissue after a MISCARRIAGE.

DONOR EGG: EGGS donated by one woman to another.

DYSMENORRHEA: painful menstruation.

DYSPANEUNIA: painful or difficult COITUS.

-E-

ECTOPIC PREGNANCY: a pregnancy located outside of the UTERUS, usually in a FALLOPIAN TUBE.

EDD: estimated due date. An at-term delivery is from 37 to 42 weeks after the last menstrual period (LMP).

EGG (OOCYTE): the female reproductive cell.

EGG RETRIEVAL: a procedure used to obtain EGGS from ovarian FOLLICLES for use in ART.

EJACULATE: (noun) the SEMEN and the SPERM released from the penis at climax.

EJACULATION: the ejection of SEMINAL FLUID from the male.

ELECTROEJACULATION: a controlled electric stimulation to induce ejaculation.

EMBRYO: the early product of conception, so termed up until eight weeks after fertilization.

EMBRYOLOGIST: a scientist who specializes in EMBRYO development.

EMBRYO TRANSFER (ET): placing an EGG that was fertilized outside the UTERUS into a woman's uterus or FALLOPIAN TUBE.

ENDOCRINE GLAND: an organ that produces HORMONES.

ENDOCRINE SYSTEM: system of glands including the hypothalamus, PITUITARY, THYROID, and adrenals.

ENDOMETRIAL BIOPSY: a diagnostic procedure, done after day 21 of the menstrual cycle, where a sample of the inner lining of the UTERUS is taken for microscopic analysis to determine the effects of PROGESTERONE on the ENDOMETRIUM.

ENDOMETRIOSIS: a condition where shreds of ENDOMETRIUM are misplaced and adhere to the pelvic organs, causing pain and affecting fertility.

ENDOMETRIUM: the inner lining of the UTERUS.

EPIDIDYMIS: a coiled, tubular organ attached to and lying on the TESTICLE, in which developing SPERM complete their maturation and develop swimming capabilities.

EPIDIDYMITIS: inflammation of the EPIDIDYMIS.

ESTRADIOL (E2): principal ESTROGEN produced by the OVARY, responsible for female secondary sex characteristics. Supports growth of the FOLLICLE and development of the uterine lining.

ESTROGEN: a female HORMONE produced mainly by the OVARY from puberty to menopause.

-F-

FALLOPIAN TUBES: tubes on either side of the UTERUS with openings at one end into the UTERUS and at the other end into the cavity over the OVARY. SPERM normally meet the egg in the fallopian tube, the site at which FERTILIZATION usually occurs.

FALLOSCOPY: visual examination of the inside of the FALLOPIAN TUBE by way of a flexible CATHETER inserted through the CERVICAL CANAL.

FERNING: a fern leaf pattern characteristic of dried cervical MUCUS on a microscopic slide that is indicative of OVULATION.

FERTILIZATION: the penetration of the EGG by the SPERM and fusion of generic material to result in the development of an EMBRYO.

FETUS: a term used to refer to a baby in utero during the period of GESTATION between eight weeks and term.

FIBROID (MYOMA OR LEIOMYOMA): a benign tumor of the uterine muscle and connective tissue.

FIMBRIA: finger-like projections at the end of the FALLOPIAN TUBE nearest the OVARY that wave the EGG into the tube.

FIMBROPLASTY: reconstructive surgery to repair the FIMBRIA.

FOLLICLE STIMULATION HORMONE (FSH): a PITUITARY hormone that stimulates SPERMATOGENESIS and follicular development. Elevated FSH levels are indicative of GONADAL failure in both men and women.

FOLLICLE: a fluid-filled sac in the OVARY which contains an egg that is released at OVULATION.

FOLLICULAR PHASE: the pre-ovulatory portion of a woman's cycle during which a FOLLICLE grows and increasing levels of ESTROGEN cause the lining of the UTERUS to develop.

FRUCTOSE: The sugar that SPERM use for energy. Produced by the SEMINAL VESICLES.

-G-

GALACTORRHEA: clear or milky discharge from the breasts associated with elevated PROLACTIN in the blood.

GAMETE: a reproductive cell: SPERM in men, the EGG in women.

GAMETE INTRAFALLOPIAN TRANSFER (GIFT): an ART in which the EGGS are retrieved and immediately mixed with the SPERM and injected through LAPAROSCOPY into a woman's FALLOPIAN TUBES for IN VIVO (natural) FERTILIZATION.

GENETIC COUNSELING: advice offered by experts in genetics on the detection, consequences, and risk of chromosomal and genetic disorders.

GESTATION: fetal development in the UTERUS from IMPLANTATION to birth.

GESTATIONAL DIABETES MELLITUS (GD, GDM): a temporary impairment of the ability to process sugar (diabetes) which develops during pregnancy.

GLAND: an organ or structure that produces or secretes essential body fluids or substances.

GONADOTROPIN RELEASING HORMONE (GnRH): a HORMONE which controls the production and release of GONADOTROPINS. It is secreted by the HYPOTHALAMUS and enables the PITUITARY to secrete LH and FSH.

GONADOTROPIN RELEASING HORMONE AGONIST (GnRHA): an AGONIST for a HORMONE capable of stimulating the TESTICLES to produce SPERM or the OVARIES to produce EGGS.

GONADOTROPIN RELEASING HORMONE ANALOG (GnRH ANALOG): synthetic HORMONES similar to the naturally occurring GONADOTROPIN RELEASING HORMONE.

GONADOTROPINS: HORMONES that control reproductive function: FOLLICLE STIMULATION HORMONE (FSH) and LEUTENIZING HORMONE (LH).

GONADS: the glands that make reproductive cells and sex hormones: TESTICLES, which make SPERM and TESTOSTERONE, and OVARIES, which make EGGS (ova) and ESTROGEN.

GRANULOSA CELLS: a layer of cells within an ovarian FOLLICLE.

-H-

HABITUAL ABORTION: repeat MISCARRIAGES (three or more).

HAMSTER TEST: a test of the ability of SPERM to penetrate a hamster EGG. Also called *Sperm Penetration Assay (SPA).*

HIRSUTISM: overabundance of body hair.

HORMONE: a substance secreted by various glands that stimulate certain bodily functions.

HORMONE STIMULATION:the use of HORMONES to effect certain reproductive functions. Also referred to as COH (CONTROLLED OVARIAN HUPERSTIMULATION).

HUMAN CHORIONIC GONADOTROPIN (HCG): a hormone produced in early pregnancy by the PLACENTA. Can be given by injection to trigger OVULATION in women and stimulate TESTOSTERONE production in men.

HUMAN MENOPAUSAL GONADOTROPIN (HMG): combination of hormones FSH and LH, which is extracted from the urine of post-menopausal women. Used to induce OVULATION.

HYPERGLYCEMIA: high blood sugar.

HYPERINSULINEMIA: overproduction of INSULIN.

HYPERPLASIA: thickening of the ENDOMETRIUM or the CERVIX that can lead to abnormal, pre-cancerous cells.

HYPERPROLACTINEMIA: condition in which the PITUITARY GLAND secretes too much PROLACTIN. Prolactin can suppress LH and FSH production, reduce male sex drive, and directly suppress ovarian function.

HYPERSTIMULATION / OVARARIAN HYPERSTIMULATION SYNDROME (OHSS): a potentially life-threatening side effect of OVULATION INDUCTION with injectable fertility medications.

HYPERTHYROIDISM: overproduction of the thyroid HORMONE by the THYROID GLAND that can interfere with OVULATION.

HYPOGLYCEMIA: low blood sugar.

HYPOGONADOTROPIC HYPOPITUITARISM: low PITUITARY GLAND output.

HYPOTHALAMUS: the part of the brain, adjacent to the pituitary, that regulates hormonal production by releasing GNRH, enabling the PITUITARY GLAND to release LH and FSH.

HYPOTHYROIDISM: when the THYROID GLAND produces an insufficient amount of thyroid hormone, which can interfere with fertility.

HYSTEROSALPINGOGRAM (HSG): an x-ray of the UTERUS and FALLOPIAN TUBES after the injection of a radio-opaque dye through the CERVIX to test for malformations and blockage.

HYSTERECTOMY: surgical removal of the UTERUS.

HYSTEROSCOPY: a procedure in which the doctor checks for uterine abnormalities by inserting a fiber-optic scope through the CERVIX. Minor surgical repairs can also be done.

-I-

ICSI — INTRA-CYTOPLASMIC SPERM INJECTION: a procedure in which a single sperm is injected into the EGG to enable FERTILIZATION from a man with very low sperm counts or with non-motile sperm.

IDIOPATHIC INFERTILITY: "unexplained infertility," when no cause for INFERTILITY can be found after substantial testing.

IMMATURE SPERM (GERMINAL CELL): a SPERM that has not matured and gained the ability to swim. In the presence of illness or infection such sperm may appear in the SEMEN in large numbers.

IMMUNE SYSTEM: the body's defense mechanism against any injury or invasion by a foreign substance or organism.

IMMUNOBEAD BINDING TEST (IBT): test done to detect antisperm ANTIBODIES.

IMMUNOTHERAPY: a controversial medical treatment for an immune system disorder that involves transfusing donor white blood cells, usually from the husband, into a woman who has had recurrent miscarriages.

IMPLANTATION: the embedding of the EMBRYO into the lining of the UTERUS.

IMPOTENCE: the inability of the man to achieve or maintain an erection and to ejaculate due to physical or emotional problems.

IN UTERO: within the UTERUS.

INCOMPETENT CERVIX: a weakened CERVIX which opens prematurely during pregnancy and can cause the loss of the FETUS.

INCOMPLETE ABORTION: a miscarriage where some tissue has passed from the body, but some fragments of the pregnancy remain in the UTERUS.

INFECTION: the state or condition in which the body or a part of it is invaded by a microorganism or virus.

INFERTILITY: the inability to reproduce. Usually diagnosed in couples after one year of sexual relations without the use of birth control.

INFLAMMATION: swelling, redness, heat, and pain caused by injury such as infection or tissue trauma.

INHIBIN: a male feedback HORMONE made in the TESTICLES to regulate FSH production by the PITUITARY GLAND.

INHIBIN B: secreted by the GRANULOSA CELLS of the OVARIES. Low levels of the HORMONE are implicated in impaired OVULATION and lower pregnancy rates.

INSEMINATION: the introduction of SPERM into the woman.

INSULIN: a HORMONE produced by the pancreas to metabolize blood sugar (glucose).

INSULIN RESISTANCE (IR): overproduction of INSULIN in relation to glucose which can lead to weight gain and OVULATION difficulties.

INTRAMUSCULAR (IM): the method by which a medication is given by needle into the muscle.

INTRATUBULAR INSEMINATION (ITI): artificial insemination where washed sperm is deposited into the fallopian tubes .

INTRAUTERINE INSEMINATION (IUI): a relatively "low-tech" ART which deposits washed SPERM directly into the UTERUS, bypassing cervical MUCUS and depositing the sperm more closely to the FALLOPIAN TUBES, where FERTILIZATION occurs. Used to bypass hostile cervical mucus and to overcome sperm count and sperm MOTILITY problems.

IN VITRO FERTILIZATION (IVF): Latin for "in a glass"; fertilization takes place outside the body in a small glass petri dish.

IN VIVO FERTILIZATION: Latin for "in the living body"; fertilization takes place inside the body.

-K-

KALLMAN'S SYNDROME: a congenital HYPOTHALAMUS dysfunction that disrupts the production of SPERM and the development of secondary sexual characteristics.

KARYOTYPE: the chromosomal characteristics of a cell.

KARYOTYPING: a chromosomal analysis to determine if a cell (or FETUS) carries an abnormality.

KLINEFELTER'S SYNDROME: a genetic abnormality in which a male has an extra X-chromosome, resulting in INFERTILITY. (46 XY is a normal male. A man with Klinefelter's has 47 XXY.)

-L-

LAPAROSCOPY: visualization of the inside of the abdomen or pelvis using special thin telescopes called laparoscopes. The instrument is inserted through a small incision below the navel; one or two other punctures may be made through which additional instruments can be inserted and manipulated. In women, the OVARIES and outside of the FALLOPIAN TUBES and UTERUS can be visualized and repaired without large abdominal incisions.

LAPAROTOMY: abdominal surgery.

LEIOMYOMA (FIBROID): a benign tumor of the UTERUS.

LEYDIG CELLS: the cells in the TESTICLES that make TESTOSTERONE.

LH SURGE: the sudden release of LUTENIZING HORMONE (LH) that causes the FOLLICLE to release a mature EGG.

LUTEAL PHASE: postovulatory phase of a woman's cycle; the CORPUS LUTEUM produces PROGESTERONE, which in turn causes the uterine lining to secrete substances to support the IMPLANTATION and growth of the early EMBRYO.

LUTEINIZED UNRUPTURED FOLLICLE (LUF) SYNDROME: the failure of a FOLLICLE to release the EGG even though a CORPUS LUTEUM has formed.

LUTEINIZING HORMONE (LH): the HORMONE, produced and released by the PITUITARY GLAND, that triggers OVULATION and stimulates the CORPUS LUTEUM to secrete PROGESTERONE in the female and to stimulate TESTOSTERONE production in the male.

-M-

MENARCHE: the time when a woman has her first menstrual period.

MENOPAUSE: the time when a woman stops having menstrual periods.

METRODIN: an injectable drug consisting of pure FOLLICLE STIMULATING HORMONE (FSH), used to STIMULATE OVULATION.

MICROSURGERY: a surgical technique employing specially designed instruments which is performed under the high-power optical magnification of an operating microscope.

MICROSURGICAL EPIDIDYMAL SPERM ASPIRATION (MESA): a surgical procedure whereby SPERM is extracted from the EPIDIDYMIS with the aid of a microscope.

MISCARRIAGE: spontaneous ABORTION or pregnancy loss.

MORPHOLOGY: the study of form and structure, such as assessing the shape of SPERM during SEMEN ANALYSIS.

MOTILITY: the quality or state of movement, such as the forward swimming motion of SPERM.

MUCUS: a viscid, slippery secretion.

MULTIFETAL GESTATION: a pregnancy with two or more FETUSES.

MYOMECTOMY: surgical removal of a uterine FIBROID tumor.

-O-

OBSTETRICIAN/GYNECOLOGIST (OB-GYN): a physician who specializes in the treatment of the female reproductive tract and pregnancy.

OLIGOMENORRHEA: infrequent and irregular menstrual cycles.

OLIGOSPERMIA: an abnormally low number of SPERM in the EJACULATE.

OOCYTE: the immature OVUM, the unfertilized GAMETE or sex cell (EGG) produced in the OVARIES each month which contains the genetic information to be transmitted by the female.

OOCYTE RETRIEVAL: a surgical procedure to collect the EGGS contained within the ovarian FOLLICLES, assisted via laparoscopic or ultrasound-guided visualization through which a needle is inserted into the follicle, the fluid and egg are aspirated into the needle, and then that mixture is placed into a medium-filled culture dish.

OVARIAN CYST: an enlarged pocket of fluid on the OVARY.

OVARIAN FAILURE: the inability of the OVARY to respond to HORMONE STIMULATION.

OVARIAN RESERVE: the biological survival time of an individual's OOCYTES (ovarian function); diminished ovarian reserve, which may be reflected by elevated FSH levels, correlates with reduced chances for success following OVULATION INDUCTION or IN VITRO FERTILIZATION.

OVARIAN WEDGE RESECTION: surgical removal of a portion of a POLYCYSTIC OVARY to produce OVULATION.

OVARY/OVARIES: the sexual glands of the female which produce the HORMONES ESTROGEN and PROGESTERONE, and in which the OVA are developed.

OVULATION: release of a mature EGG from the ovarian FOLLICLE, usually occurring on day 14 of a 28-day menstrual cycle.

OVULATION INDUCTION/CONTROLLED OVARIAN HYPERSTIMULATION (COH): pharmacologic stimulation of the OVARIES to increase the development of multiple FOLLICLES, and as a result, multiple EGGS.

OVUM (SINGULAR) / OVA (PLURAL): the female reproductive cell released from the OVARY during OVULATION.

-P-

PAP SMEAR: removal of cells from the surface of the CERVIX to study microscopically, usually to rule out cervical cancer.

PARTIAL ZONA DISSECTION (PZD): a predecessor to ICSI in which a ZONA PELLUCIDA, or shell surrounding a woman's EGG, is opened, using either a chemical solution or a sharp instrument, in order to allow easier access for SPERM.

PATENT: the condition of being open or accessible.

PELVIC IMMFLAMMATORY DISEASE (PID): an infection of the pelvic organs that causes severe illness that may lead to tubal blockage and pelvic ADHESIONS.

PENIS: the male organ of sexual intercourse.

PERCUTANEOUS EPIDIYMAL SPERM ASPIRATION (PESA): withdrawing sperm through the EPIDIDYMIS by means of a small needle for use with IN VITRO FERTILIZATION with ICSI.

PERINATOLOGIST: a doctor specializing in treating the FETUS/baby and mother during pregnancy, labor, and delivery.

PERGONAL (HMG): a medication that mimics the actions of the HORMONES LH and FSH to induce follicular growth and maturation of the OVA in women and to stimulate SPERM production in men.

PITUITARY GLAND: located behind the brain, it is referred to as the "master gland." The pituitary is stimulated by the HYPOTHALAMUS and controls all hormonal function.

PLACENTA: a spongy structure formed in and adhering to the inner lining of the UTERUS, through which the FETUS derives its nourishment.

POLYCYSTIC OVARIAN SYNDROME (PCO, PCOS, OR STEIN-LEVENTHAL SYNDROME): a condition found in women who do not ovulate, characterized by excessive production of ANDROGENS and the presence of CYSTS in the OVARIES.

POLYP: a growth or tumor, usually benign, on an internal surface of an organ.

POLYSPERMY: FERTILIZATION of the EGG by more than one sperm.

POST COITAL TEST (PCT) OR SIMS-HUBNER TEST: a microscopic examination of the cervical MUCUS performed several hours after intercourse to determine compatibility between the woman's mucus and the man's SEMEN. Parameters such as the presence of SPERM, its number and MOTILITY, are observed.

PRECLINICAL PREGNANCY (CHEMICAL PREGNANCY): a pregnancy that is detected on the basis of a positive BHCG blood test, before there are physical symptoms.

PRE-EMBRYO: a fertilized EGG in the early stage of development prior to cell division.

PREIMPLANTATION GENETIC DIAGNOSIS (PGD): microscopic examination of one cell taken from an EMBRYO in order to test for chromosomal abnormalities before EMBRYO TRANSFER in IVF.

PREMATURE OVARIAN FAILURE (POF): the cessation of OVULATION and menstruation before the age of 40.

PRE-MENSTRUAL SYNDROME (PMS): emotional and physical disturbances that occur after OVULATION and usually end with menstruation.

PRIMARY INFERTILITY: the inability of a couple to achieve a first pregnancy.

PRODUCTS OF CONCEPTION (POC): tissues resulting from a

pregnancy, such as the EMBRYO and PLACENTA.

PROGESTERONE: an ovarian hormone produced by the CORPUS LUTEUM after OVULATION. It thickens the lining of the UTERUS to prepare it to accept IMPLANTATION of the fertilized EGG. It is also produced by the PLACENTA during pregnancy.

PROLACTIN: a pituitary HORMONE that stimulates milk production in breastfeeding women. Excessive production in non-lactating women can lead to INFERTILITY.

PROSTAGLANDINS: HORMONE-like substances found throughout the body in men and women that cause muscle contractions and uterine spasms.

PROSTATE GLAND: the male gland encircling the URETHRA that produces one-third of the fluid in the SEMEN.

PYOSPERMIA: the presence of white blood cells in the SEMEN, indicating possible infection or inflammation.

-R-

RECURRENT PREGNANCY LOSS (RPL): repeated MISCARRIAGES numbering three or more.

REPRODUCTIVE ENDOCRINOLOGIST: an OB/GYN doctor who specializes in the treatment of hormonal disorders that affect reproductive function.

RETROGADE EJACULATION: EJACULATION backwards into the bladder instead of forward through the URETHRA.

RETROVERTED UTERUS: a uterus that is tilted back toward the rectum.

REVERSAL: a term referring to undoing a sterilization procedure such as a TUBAL LIGATION or VASECTOMY.

-S-

SALPINGECTOMY: surgical removal of the FALLOPIAN TUBE(S).

SALPINGITIS: inflammation of the FALLOPIAN TUBE(S).

SALPINGOSTOMY: a surgical incision made in the FALLOPIAN TUBE, usually to repair a tube or to remove an ECTOPIC PREGNANCY.

SCROTUM: the sac of skin and thin muscle containing the man's TESTICLES, EPIDIDYMIS, and VAS DEFERENS.

SECONDARY INFERTILITY: the inability of a couple to achieve a second or subsequent pregnancy.

SECONDARY SEX CHARACTERISTICS: the physical qualities formed under the stimulation of the sex HORMONES (TESTOSTERONE or ESTROGEN), signifying the passage through puberty. In the man, low voice, body and facial hair; in the woman, breast development, hair distribution, wider hips.

SELECTIVE REDUCTION: an intentional reduction (ABORTION) in the number of FETUSES in women with MULTIFETAL GESTATION.

SEMEN / SEMINAL FLUID: the EJACULATE containing SPERM and secretion from the TESTICLES, PROSTATE, and SEMINAL VESICLES.

SEMEN ANALYSIS: the study of fresh EJACULATE under a microscope to count the number of SPERM per millimeter or cubic centimeter, to check their shape and size (MORPHOLOGY), and to note their ability to move (MOTILITY).

SEMEN VISCOSITY: the liquid flow or consistency of the SEMEN.

SEMINAL FLUID: see SEMEN.

SEMINAL VESICLES: the paired glands at the base of the bladder that produce SEMINAL FLUID and FRUCTOSE.

SEMINIFEROUS TUBULES: the network of tubes in the TESTICLES in which the SPERM are formed, mature, and move toward the EPIDIDYMIS.

SEPTUM: a dividing wall or membrane between bodily spaces or masses of soft tissue, such as a uterine septum (divided UTERUS).

SERTOLI CELLS: testicular cells responsible for providing nourishment to the spermatids (immature SPERM). Secretes INHIBIN, which regulates FSH production by the PITUITARY GLAND. When stimulated by FSH, the Sertoli cell initiates SPERMATOGENESIS (sperm production).

SEXUALLY TRANSMITTED DISEASE (STD): an infectious disease transmitted during sexual relations.

SONOGRAM: ULTRASOUND.

SONOHYSTOGRAM: an ULTRASOUND in which saline is injected into the UTERUS to detect any uterine abnormalities.

SPERM: the male GAMETE or sex cell that contains the genetic information to be transmitted by the male; also known as spermatozoon (plural-spermatozoa).

SPERM AGGLUTINATION: SPERM clumping caused by ANTIBODY reaction or by INFECTION.

SPERMATIC CORD: the cord suspending the TESTES, composed of veins, arteries, lymph vessels, nerves, and VAS DEFERENS.

SPERMATOGENESIS: SPERM production.

SPERM BANK: a place where SPERM are kept frozen in liquid nitrogen for later use in ARTIFICIAL INSEMINATION.

SPERM COUNT: the number of SPERM per milliliter of EJACULATE; also called sperm density or sperm concentration.

SPERM PENETRATION ASSAY (SPA): a test of the ability of the SPERM to penetrate a hamster egg that has been stripped of the ZONA PELLUCIDA (outer membrane). Also called the *Hamster Test*.

SPERM WASHING: a laboratory technique that separates SPERM from SEMINAL FLUID in preparation for use in assisted reproduction (ART).

SPINNBARKEIT: the stretchability of cervical mucus; the stringy quality that occurs at midcycle under the influence of ESTROGEN. A parameter of measurement during a PCT.

SPLIT EJACULATE: a method used to concentrate the SPERM (sample) for INSEMINATION. The ejaculate is separated into two portions: the first portion which is rich in sperm, and the second portion which contains mostly seminal fluid.

STERILITY: an irreversible condition that prevents conception.

STERILIZATION: a surgical procedure designed to cause INFERTILTY, such as a TUBAL LIGATION or VASECTOMY.

SYNTHETIC: made through artificial means.

- T -

TESTES (TESTIS OR TESTICLE = SINGULAR): the two male sexual glands contained in the SCROTUM. They produce the male HORMONE TESTOSTERONE and the male reproductive cells, the SPERM.

TESTICLE: see TESTES

TESTICULAR BIOSPY: a minor surgical procedure used to take a small sample of testicular tissue for microscopic examination.

TESTICULAR SPERM EXTRACTION (TESE): an open BIOPSY where a small piece of testicular tissue is removed through a skin incision. SPERM are then extracted from a biopsied SEMINIFEROUS TUBULES.

TESTICULAR TORSION: when the TESTICLES twists on itself, cutting off its own blood supply. Causes extreme pain, and requires immediate surgical repair to reduce damage to the TESTICLE.

TESTOSTERONE: the male HORMONE responsible for the formation of secondary sex characteristics and for supporting the sex drive. Testosterone is also necessary for SPERMATOGENESIS.

THYROID GLAND: the endocrine gland in the front of the neck that produces thyroid HORMONES to regulate the body's metabolism (T3 and T4).

THYROID RELEASING HORMONE (TRH): a HORMONE synthesized in the HYPOTHALAMUS that stimulates synthesis and release of THYROTROPIN (TSH).

THYROID STIMULATING HORMONE, THYROTROPIN (TSH): a HORMONE produced by the PITUITARY GLAND that promotes the growth of the THYROID GLAND as well as stimulates it.

TUBAL EMBRYO TRANSFER (TET): the placement of an EMBRYO inside the FALLOPIAN TUBE after IN VITRO FERTILIZATION.

TUBAL LIGATION: surgical sterilization of a woman by obstructing or tying the FALLOPIAN TUBES.

TUBOPLASTY: plastic or reconstructive surgery on the FALLOPIAN TUBES.

TURNER'S SYNDROME: the most common genetic defect contributing to female fertility problems. KARYOTYPING reveals that this woman either has only one (45X) chromosome instead of two, or has a structural abberation on one of the (46XX) chromosomes.

-U-

ULTRASOUND: a diagnostic test using high-frequency sound waves to create pictures of internal body structures. Also referred to as *sonogram.*

UNDESCENDED TESTICLES (CRYPTORCHIDISM): the failure of the TESTICULES to descend from the abdominal cavity into the SCROTUM by one year of age.

URETHRA: the tube that allows urine to pass between the bladder and the outside of the body. In the man this tube also carries SEMEN from the area of the PROSTATE to the outside.

UROLOGIST: a physician specializing in the male and female urinary system and the male reproductive tracts.

UTERUS (WOMB): the hollow, muscular female reproductive organ that hosts and nourishes the FETUS during pregnancy.

-V-

VAGINA: the female organ of sexual intercourse; the birth canal.

VAGINISMUS: a spasm of muscles around the opening of the VAGINA, making penetration during intercourse either impossible or very painful. Most often psychological in origin.

VAGINITIS: an inflammation of the VAGINA caused by yeast, bacteria, or trichomonas.

VARICOCELE: varicose veins in the SCROTUM that causes swollen vessels surrounding the TESTICLES that elevate the temperature of the SCROTUM. Can often interfere with male fertility.

VAS DEFERENS: a pair of thick-walled tubes through which the SPERM move from the EPIDIDYMIS to the ejaculatory duct in the PROSTATE. These tubes are severed during a VASECTOMY performed for birth control.

VASOGRAM: an X-ray examination of the VAS DEFERENS involving the injection of dye.

VENEREAL DISEASE: any INFECTION that can be sexually transmitted, such as chlamydia, gonorrhea, ureaplasma, and syphilis. Many of these diseases interfere with fertility.

VIRUS: a microscopic infectious organism that reproduces inside living cells.

VISCOUS: a fluid which becomes thick, gummy or sticky.

VULVA: the female's external genitalia.

-Z-

ZONA PELLUCIDA: the protective outer membrane surrounding the EGG.

ZYGOTE: the fertilized EGG which had not yet divided.

ZYGOTE INTRAFALLOPIAN TRANSFER (ZIFT): an assisted reproductive technique (ART) in which EGGS are removed from a woman's OVARIES and fertilized with the man's SPERM in a lab dish, and then the resulting ZYGOTES are transferred into the woman's FALLOPIAN TUBES.

Appendix D
Glossary of Hebrew Terms

AHAVAS YISRAEL: lit., "love of Israel," i.e. love of one's fellow Jew.

AKEIDAH: Abraham's binding of Isaac on the altar.

AMIDAH: lit., "standing"; the SHEMONEH ESREI prayer, which is recited while standing.

AMORA'IM: (Aramaic) one of the Sages whose opinions comprise the Gemara.

ANAN: a cloud.

AVEIRAH/AVEIROS: sin(s).

AVOS: the forefathers.

AVRAHAM AVINU: Abraham our father.

BA'AL TESHUVAH: a formerly non-observant Jew who becomes observant; a penitent.

BEIS HAMIKDASH: the Holy Temple in Jerusalem.

BEREISHIS: the book of Genesis.

BITACHON: trust in God; faith.

BNEI YISRAEL: the Children of Israel.

BRIS: lit., covenant; the circumcision ceremony.

CHAZAL: a Hebrew acronym for "Our Sages of blessed memory."

CHESED: lovingkindness.

DAF YOMI: lit., "a daily page"; the program wherein a *daf* (two sides) of GEMARA is learned daily, allowing one to complete the entire TALMUD in seven and a half years.

DUDA'IM: mandrakes (see BEREISHIS 30:14).

GEMARA: commentary of the Mishnah (together they comprise the TALMUD); a volume of the TALMUD.

HAKADOSH BARUCH HU: the Holy One, blessed is He (i.e. God).

HAKAFOS: the seven rounds of dancing with the scrolls of the Torah, performed in the synagogue on the Festival of SIMCHAS TORAH.

HALACHAH/HALACHOS: Jewish law(s).

HASHGACHAH: Divine supervision and providence.

HISHTADLUS: effort.

KIDDUSH HASHEM: the sanctification of God's Name; martyrdom.

KIYUM OLAM: the continuation and maintenance of the universe.

KOHEN: a descendant of Aaron the High Priest, and a member of the priestly tribe.

MA'ASEH YIUSH: a hopeless gesture; doing something you know won't help.

MASHIACH: the Messiah.

MAZAL TOV: "Congratulations!"

MENTSCHLICHKEIT: (Yiddish) common courtesy; being an upstanding and decent person.

MIKVEH: a ritual bath.

MITZVAH/MITZVOS: commandment(s); righteous deed(s).

MOSHE RABBEINU: Moses our teacher.

MUSSAR: Torah ethics and values.

NIDDAH: the condition of menstrual impurity.

OHNESS: forced transgression of a commandment, where the transgressor is not held accountable for the sin.

ONAN: one of the sons of Yehudah, who sinned by practicing coitus interruptus (see BEREISHIS 38:7,10); the sin of spilling one's seed in vain.

PARASHAH: the weekly Torah portion.

PIRKEI AVOS: Ethics of the Fathers, a tractate of the Mishnah.

PRU URVU: "Be fruitful and multiply" (BEREISHIS 1:28), the first commandment in the Torah.

R"L: an Aramaic acronym for *Rachmana litzlan,* "May the Merciful One save us."

RUACH HA-KODESH: lit., "the holy spirit"; a lower degree of prophecy; Divine inspiration.

SEDER: lit., "order"; the Passover night ceremony when the family gathers to recount the story of the Exodus from Egypt and to eat a festive meal together.

SEFER: a book; a holy book.

SEGULAH: a supra-logical action which has practical effects.

SHALOM BAYIS: domestic harmony.

SHECHINAH: the Divine Presence of God.

SHEMONEH ESREI: lit., "eighteen"; the eighteen blessing of the AMIDAH prayer.

SHEMOS: the book of Exodus.

SHEVA NEKI'IM: the "seven clean" days a woman counts from the end of her menstrual period until she immerses in a MIKVEH.

SHIDDUCH: a marital match. Sometimes used colloquially to mean any relationship between two parties.

SHIR HASHIRIM: the book of Song of Songs.

SHUL: (Yiddish) a synagogue.

SIDDUR: the prayer book.

SIMCHAH/SEMACHOS: joyful occasion(s).

SIMCHAS TORAH: a joyful Festival in honor of completing the annual cycle of the reading of the Torah.

TALMID CHACHAM: a Torah scholar.

TALMUD: the basic corpus of Jewish law (200 B.C.E.–500 C.E.) consisting of the Mishnah and GEMARA.

TANACH: an acronym for the entire Bible, i.e. the Torah, the Prophets, and the Writings.

TEFILLAH: prayer.

TEHILLIM: the book of Psalms.

TZADDIK: a righteous, pious man.

TZADEKES: a righteous, pious woman.

TZEDAKAH: charity.

VEHIGADETA LEVANECHA: "And you shall tell your child" (SHEMOS 13:8); the MITZVAH of retelling the Exodus from Egypt on Passover night.

VESAMACHTA BECHAGECHA: "You shall rejoice on your Festival" (Deuteronomy 16:14); the MITZVAH to rejoice on the Jewish Festivals.

YOM TOV: lit., a good day; a Jewish holiday or Festival.

ZNUS: promiscuity.

ZOHAR: the basic work of Kabbalah written by Rabbi Shimon bar Yochai.

Appendix E
Selected Bibliography

This bibliography is a partial list of suggested readings and of our source material. Classic rabbinic literature and responsa of halachic authorities are not included.

ENGLISH SOURCES

Anasti, J.N. and Flack, M.R., "The Use of Gonadotropin Receptors in Premature Ovarian Failure." *Journal of Clinical Endocrinology and Metabolism,* 80:824, 1995.

Apfel, R. J. and Fisher, S. M., *To Do No Harm: DES and the Dilemmas of Modern Medicine.* New Haven and London: Yale University Press, 1984.

Bergman, S.H., *Medic,* vol. 28, no. 6. Herzliya, Israel: Shirol Publications, November – December 1999.

Bick, Ezra, "Ovum Donations." *Tradition,* vol. 28, Fall 1993, pp. 28–45.

Bleich, David, *Bioethical Dilemmas: A Jewish Perspective.* Hoboken, NJ: Ktav Publishing, 1998.

Bleich, David, *Contemporary Halachic Problems,* vol. IV. Hoboken, NJ: Ktav Publishing. 1976.

Bleich, David, "Test Tube Babies," in Fred Rosner and David Bleich (eds.), *Jewish Bioethics,* pp 80-85. New York: Hebrew Publishing Company, 1979.

Bleich, David, "The Concept of Refu'ah Bedukah." *Tradition,* vol. 25, 1989.

Brandstreet, Karen, *Overcoming Infertility Naturally.* Pleasant Grove, Utah: Woodland Books, 1995.

Carcio, Helen A., *Management of the Infertile Woman.* Philadelphia and New York: Lippincott, 1998.

Carson, Sandra Ann, M.D. and Casson, Peter R., M.D., with Debrah

J. Shuman, *Complete Guide to Fertility*. The American Society for Reproductive Medicine. Chicago: Philip Lief Group Inc., Contemporary Books, 1999.

Cramer, D.W., "Epidemiology of Endometriosis," in E.A. Wilson (ed.), *Endometriosis*, pp. 5 – 22. New York: Alan R. Liss Inc., 1987.

De Crespigny, Lachlan, with Rhonda Dredge, *Which Tests for my Unborn Baby?* Oxford: Oxford University Press, 1991.

Domar, Alice D. and Lesch Kelly, Alice, *Conquering Infertility*. New York: Viking, 2002.

Feinstein, Moshe, *Darash Moshe*. New York: The Foundation for the Publication of Rav Moshe Feinstein's Writings, 5750.

Finkelstein, Michal and Baruch, *B'Sha'ah Tovah: The Jewish Woman's Clinical and Halachic Guide to Pregnancy and Childbirth.* Jerusalem: Feldheim Publishers, 2001.

Flancbaum, Louis, M.D., *And You Shall Live by Them.* Pittsburgh: Mirkov Publications, 2001.

Frankl, Victor, "The Meaning of Suffering," in Levi Meir (ed.), *Jewish Values in Bioethics*, pp. 117–123. New York: Human Sciences Press, 1986.

Fujusana, M. and Yazazki, T., *Archives of Andrology*, 47:191–194, 2001.

Glazer, Ellen Sarasohn, *Experiencing Infertility*. San Francisco: Jossey-Bass Publishers, 1998.

Goshen-Gottstein, Tamara, "The Souls that They Made," in Ora Wiskind-Elper and Susan Handelman (eds.), *Torah of our Mothers*. Jerusalem: Urim Publishers, 2000.

Gray, John, *Men Are from Mars, Women Are from Venus*. London: Thorsons, 1993.

Grazi, Richard V., M.D., *Be Fruitful and Multiply*. Jerusalem: Genesis Jerusalem Press, 1994.

Jakobovits, Immanuel, "Halacha Survey — Adoption," *Tradition*, vol. 3, 1961.

Kahn, Susan Martha, *Reproducing Jews*. Durham, NC: Duke University Press, 2000.

Landau, Barbara, *Essential Human Anatomy and Physiology*, second edition. Glenview, Illinois: Scott, Foresman and Company, 1980.

Martin, D.C., "CO_2 Laser Laparoscopy for Endometriosis Associated with Infertility." *Journal of Reproductive Fertility*,

31:1089, 1986.

Mazor, M., *Emotional Reactions to Infertility*, p. 43. Paper presented at the 133rd annual meeting of the American Psychiatric Association, San Francisco (1980).

Miller, Manya DeLeon, *The Complete Fertility Organizer*. New York: John Wiley & Sons, 1999.

Peters, A. J. and Lloyd, R.P., "Prevalence of Out-of-Phase Endometrial Biopsy Specimens." *American Journal of Obstetrics and Gynecology*, 73:88, 1992.

Prager, Dennis, *Think a Second Time*. New York: Regan Books, 1995.

Rackman, Emmanuel, "Jewish Medical Ethics and Law," in Levi Meir (ed.),. *Jewish Values in Bioethics*. 150-173. New York: Human Sciences Press, 1986.

Register, Cheri, *Living with Chronic Illnesses*. New York: Bantam Books, 1987.

Resolve Staff, *Resolving Infertility*. Oxford, MD: Amaranth, Harper Resource, 1999.

Rosner, Fred, "Artificial Insemination in Jewish Law," in Fred Rosner and David Bleich (eds.), *Jewish Bioethics*, pp. 105 –117. New York: Hebrew Publishing Company, 1979.

Rosner, Fred, *Modern Medicine and Jewish Ethics*. Hoboken, NJ: Ktav Publishing, 1986.

Rosner, Fred and Tendler Moshe, *Practical Medical Halachah*. Hoboken, NJ: Ktav Publishing. 1990.

Shannon, Marilyn M., *Fertility, Cycles and Nutrition*. Cincinnati: The Couple to Couple League International, 1990.

Shapiro, David S., "Be Fruitful and Multiply," in Fred Rosner and David Bleich (eds.), *Jewish Bioethics*, pp. 59 – 85. New York: Hebrew Publishing Company, 1979.

Sharfman,Yigal, *Selected Studies in Medical Ethics*. Jerusalem: The Chief Rabbinate of Jerusalem, The Department of Medicine and Halachah, 5754.

Speroff, Leon, Glass, Robert H., and Kase, Nathan G., *Clinical Gynecologic Endocrinology and Infertility*, sixth edition. Philadelphia: Lippincott, Williams and Wilkins, 1999.

Steinberg, Avraham, M.D., *Encyclopedia of Jewish Medical Ethics*. Jerusalem: Feldheim Publishers, 2003.

Steinberg, Abraham, M.D., "The Meaning of Suffering: A Jewish

Perspective," in Edmund D. Pellegrino and Alan I. Faden (eds.), *Jewish and Catholic Bioethics*, pp. 77–81. Washington, DC: Georgetown University Press, 1999.

Subak-Sharpe, Genell J., M.S. (ed.), *Columbia University College of Physicians and Surgeons Complete Guide to Pregnancy*. New York: Crown Publishers, Inc., 1988.

Tendler, Moshe, "On the Interface of Religion and Medical Science: The Judeo-Biblical Perspective," in Edmund D. Pellegrino and Alan I. Faden (eds.), *Jewish and Catholic Bioethics*, pp. 106–113. Washington DC: Georgetown University Press, 1999.

Tendler, Moshe, "Population Control: The Jewish View," in Fred Rosner and David Bleich (eds.), *Jewish Bioethics*, pp. 97–104. New York: Hebrew Publishing Company, 1979.

Tendler, Moshe, *Medical Ethics*. New York: Committee on Religious Affairs, Federation of Jewish Philanthropies of New York, Inc., 1975.

Tendler, Moshe, *Pardes Rimonim*. New York: The Judaica Press, 1977.

Tuchman, Hyman, "Halacha Survey – Adoption." *Tradition*, vol. 3, 1961.

Zimmerman, Chaim, *Torah and Reason*. Jerusalem, 5739.

Zohar, Yael, "Stories of Visitation of Barren Women in the Bible: A Literary-Philosophical Analysis" (Masters Thesis). Bar Ilan University, 1997.

Zoldbord, Aline P., P.D., *Men, Women, and Infertility*. Don Mills, Ontario: Lexington Books, 1993.

HEBREW SOURCES

אבן שושן, אברהם, המלון החדש. ירושלים: קרית ספר, 5726.

סופר, אברהם, נשמת אברהם, חלק אבן העזר. ירושלים, 5755.

גינזברג, יוסף שמחה, "הפריית מבחנה והזרעה מלאכותית — הוראת כ"ק הרבי מליבואויטש." אסיא, חלק ד'.

זנד, זאב, בנים, פתח תקוה, 5754.

יעקובוביץ, עמנואל, הרפואה והיהדות. ירושלים: מוסד הרב קוק, 5726.

כ"ץ-לוין, יעל, "העקרות באגדה" (תעודה), כרך 13, עמ' 79-134.

אוניברסיטת תל אביב, 5757.

לוריה, אורית, ילדים עושים מאהבה. כפר סבא: הוצאת אריה ניר, 2000.

סולוביצ'יק, יוסף דוב, איש אמונה. ירושלים: מוסד הרב קוק, 5741.

רוזן, דויד, בטח בה'. ירושלים: המוסד לעידוד לימוד התורה, 5753.

שטינברג, אברהם. אנציקלופדיה הלכתית רפואית, כרך א, ה. ירושלים: המכון לחקר הרפואה על פי התורה ליד המרכז הרפואי שערי צדק, 5748.

שמואלביץ, חיים, שיחות מוסר, ישראל, 5740.

Appendix F
Biographies of Rabbis

The following are brief biographies of some of the main Rabbis who are quoted in this book. They are listed by their acronyms or by the books that they authored, since that is the way they are familiar to most of our readers and that is the way they appear in the book.

Achiezer — **Rabbi Chaim Ozer Grodzinski.** He was the leading Rabbi of Vilna at the beginning of the twentieth century. He was born in Vilna in 1863 and died right before the Nazi takeover of Lithuania in 1940. His responsa appear in his book *Achiezer*.

Alshich — **Rabbi Moshe Alshich.** He was born in Turkey in 1507 and died in Tzefas in 1593. He sat on the *beis din* (Jewish court of law) of R. Yosef Karo and wrote a book of Biblical exegesis on the Torah.

Auerbach, Rabbi Shlomo Zalman. He was born in Jerusalem in 1910. He learned in Yeshivas Eitz Chaim in Jerusalem and was the rosh yeshiva of Yeshivas Kol Torah. He was known for his expertise in technology and halachah. He wrote many halachic essays, as well as the resposa *Minchas Shlomo,* which deals with modern and agricultural problems. He died in 1995.

Bach — **Rabbi Yoel Sirkish.** 1561–1640. He is called the Bach based on his commentary on the *Tur* called the *Bayis Chadash.* He lived in Poland and was the Rabbi of Brisk and Krakow.

Beis Shemuel — **Rabbi Shemuel ben Ari Shraga Feivush.** He is known as the Beis Shemuel, the name of his commentary on the *Shulchan Aruch.* He lived in Poland in the seventeenth and eighteenth centuries. He became the Rav of Fiorda in Ashkenaz in 1691.

Chazon Ish — **Rabbi Avraham Yeshayahu Karelitz.** Known as the Chazon Ish, which was the name of his scholarly set of books that spans the wide spectrum of halachah. He was born in Lithuania in 1878 and moved to Eretz Yisrael in 1933. He settled in Bnei Brak. Although he never held an official position, many scholars considered him to be the authoritative *posek* in Israel. He also published some *igros*, glosses on R. Chaim Soloveitchik on the Rambam, and a small book on *hashkafah* called *Emunah u'Vitachon*. He died in 1953.

Feinstein, Rav Moshe. He was born in Belarus in 1895. He studied under his father, R. Dovid Feinstein. He held rabbinic positions in Europe, came to America in 1937, and was the rosh yeshiva of Yeshivas Tiferes Jerusalem. He was considered the greatest halachic authority in America and answered questions from people from all over the world. His responsa, *Igros Moshe*, spans eight volumes and deals with many topics, especially modern problems and medical questions. He also published halachic essays in journals and wrote *chiddushim* (novellae) on the Talmud called *Dibros Moshe*, as well as a book of Torah exegesis called *Darash Moshe*. He died in 1986. Hundreds of thousands attended his funeral in Jerusalem, for he was loved and respected by the entire Torah community.

***Gra* or *Vilna Gaon* — Rabbi Eliyahu ben Shlomo Zalman.** ("Gra" is the acronym for Gaon Rabbi Eliyahu.) He lived in Vilna from 1720 to 1797 and was considered the leader of Vilna Jewry. He wrote glosses on the *Shulchan Aruch* and other books including Kabbalah, but all his works were published after his death. There are many wondrous stories about his dedication to Torah learning.

***Har Tzvi* — Rabbi Tzvi Pesach Frank.** He was the former Rav of Jerusalem. He was born in Kovno in 1873. He moved to Eretz Yisrael in 1893 and continued learning in Jerusalem. He died in 1960. He wrote the book of responsa *Har Tzvi*, which deals with modern problems and agricultural laws of the land.

Igros Moshe. See Feinstein, Rav Moshe.

Karo, Yosef. See *Shulchan Aruch*.

***Malbim* — Rabbi Meir Leib ben Yechiel Michel.** 1809–1879. He was born in the Ukraine and was Rav in communites in Germany and Romania. He wrote a comprehensive commentary on the Tanach.

Meshech Chochmah — **Rabbi Meir Simchah of Dvinsk.** He was born in 1843 in Lithuania and in 1888 became the Rav of Dvinsk, a position he held until his death in 1926. In the year 1906 he was offered the position of Rav of Jerusalem, but preferred to stay with his community. He stood at the top of a Rabbinic federation. He wrote the *Meshech Chochmah* on the Torah and the *Ohr Same'ach* on the Rambam's *Mishneh Torah.*

Minchas Yitzchak — **Rabbi Yitzchak Yaakov Weiss.** Born in Poland in 1902 and died in Israel in 1989. He was the head of the Yeshiva in Munkatcz, Hungary, and afterwards was a *dayan* (rabbinical judge) in Romania for twenty years. In 1948 he moved to England and was head of the *beis din* (rabbinical court) in Manchester. In 1970 he moved to Israel and became the head *dayan* for the *Eidah Chareidis.* His responsa is called the *Minchas Yitzchak.*

Mishpetei Uziel — **Rabbi Ben Tzion Uziel.** He was born in Jerusalem in 1880 and in 1921 became chief Rabbi of Soloniki. Two years later he became the Chief Rabbi of Tel Aviv and in 1939 became the Chief Rabbi of Israel. He wrote the responsa *Mishpetei Uziel* between the years 1935 and 1950. He died in 1950.

Netziv — **Rabbi Naftali Tzvi Yehudah Berlin.** He was born in the city of Mir in Russia in the year 1817 and died in Warsaw, Poland, in the year 1893. He was the rosh yeshiva of the Yeshiva of Volozhin, which is considered the prototype for modern-day yeshivas. He wrote many works, including the responsa *Meishiv Davar,* a commentary on the *sheiltos* of Rav Hai Gaon, a commentary on the Talmud, and a commentary on the Torah called *Ha'amek Davar.*

Rambam — **Rabbi Moshe ben Maimon.** He was born in Spain in the year 1138 and died in 1204. He lived in Morocco, Eretz Yisrael, and Egypt. He was the personal physician of the ruler Salach A-din in Egypt. He wrote a commentary on the Mishnah in Arabic and the philosophical work *Guide for the Perplexed.* He wrote many other works; a foreword to the Mishnah and a foreword to chapter *Chelek* in tractate *Sanhedrin* are among his many writings. His most important works were *Sefer haMitzvos* and the *Yad haChazakah* (the *Mishneh Torah*), which is on the complete Oral Law.

***Ramban* — Rabbi Moshe ben Nachman.** He was born in Spain in the year 1194 and died in 1270. He was the leading Rabbinic figure in Spain and was forced to leave that country after a public ideological debate with Pablo Cristiani. He arrived in Jerusalem and was influential in reviving Jewish life there. He wrote commentaries on the Torah and the Talmud as well as many essays on Jewish thought and Kabbalah. His commentary on the Torah is considered essential.

***Rashi* — Rabbi Shlomo (ben) Yitzchak.** Rashi is also an acronym for *Rabban shel Yisrael,* which means Rabbi of Israel. Rashi was born and lived in France. He lived from 1040 to 1105, and was the leading Rabbi in Europe. He had three daughters, whose sons became the *Ba'alei Tosafos* and the leaders of European Jewry. His comprehensive commentaries on the Bible and on the Talmud are considered the most essential. His commentary is basic, yet profound. It is the first commentary referred to and is studied by both young children and mature scholars. Rashi's commentary on the Talmud is printed on the side of the text.

***Rif* — Rabbi Yitzchak haKohen Alfasi.** He lived from 1013 to 1103, in Fez (Morocco) and Spain. The Rif is considered one of the most influential halachic authorities. He wrote what scholars throughout the ages consider the first and foremost commentary on the Talmud. It is printed in the back of the Vilna edition of the Talmud, and is studied regularly by Talmud and halachah students to this day.

***Rosh* — Rabbi Asher ben Yechiel.** He was born around the year 1250 in Germany and died in Spain in 1327. He was a student of the Maharam of Rottenberg. Because of the anti-Semitic climate in Europe he moved to Spain. After the passing of the Rashba, the Rosh was considered the greatest Rabbinic authority in Spain. He wrote a commentary on the Talmud, a Tosafos on the Talmud, and thousands of responsa.

***Shulchan Aruch* — Rabbi Yosef Karo.** Also know as the Beis Yosef or Maran or the *Mechaber*. He was born in Spain in 1488 and died in Tzefas (Safed) in 1575. He left Spain because of the Inquisition and moved to Turkey, where he learned Torah. He moved to Eretz Yisrael in 1536. His major work was the *Beis Yosef,* which is a commentary on the *Tur*. Based on that book, he compiled the *Shulchan Aruch*, which consists of the halachic conclusions of the *Beis Yosef*. He came to most of his conclusions based on the majority opinion between the Rif, the Rambam, and the Rosh. This was a highly controversial method of rendering halachic conclusions, yet today the *Shulchan Aruch* is the basic code of Jewish law. He also wrote the *Kesef Mishneh* on the Rambam. He wrote a book of responsa and also wrote on Kabbalah.

***Taz* — Rabbi David Shemuel haLevi.** He is called the Taz based on his commentary on the *Shulchan Aruch*, the *Turei Zahav*. He was the son-in-law of the Bach. He wrote other works, including a commentary on Rashi on the Torah called *Divrei David*. He lived in Poland and was the *Av Beis Din* (chief rabbinical justice) of Lvov, and taught Torah in Krakow. He also moved to other Polish cities. He died around the year 1672.

Teitelbaum, Rabbi Yoel Moshe. Born in 1888, he was part of a Hungarian Chassidic dynasty, and was more commonly known as the Satmar Rebbe. In 1928 he became the Rav of the city of Satmar, and at the end of the Holocaust was brought to Israel for a short time. After that he moved to Williamsburg, New York, where he strengthened his Chassidic following. He wrote a book called *Vayoel Moshe*, where he explains his anti-Zionist philosophy. He also published some *igros* in various publications.

***Tiferes Yisrael* — Rabbi Yisrael Lipshitz.** 1782–1860. He was Rav in Germany in a few places, including Danzig. He is known mostly for his commentary on the Mishnah called the *Tiferes Yisrael*.

Tosafos. It literally means "additions," as it is a compilation of Ashkenazi commentary on the Talmud spanning the twelfth and thirteenth centuries. It is printed alongside the Talmudic text, opposite the commentary of Rashi.

***Tur* — Rabbi Yaakov ben Asher.** 1276–1340. He was born in Germany and moved to Toledo, Spain, as a young boy with his family and his father the Rosh. He wrote the *Arba'ah Turim* ("four columns"), commonly known as the *Tur*. It was a revolutionary work in its time; it established a new order for learning halachah, as the author brought down different opinions if there were halachic disputes. The order and style established in the *Tur* became the order and the style of the *Shulchan Aruch,* which is still used today as the standard halachic code.

Rabbeinu Tzadok haKohen. 1823–1900. He lived and learned in Lublin. He was one of the leaders of the Chassidic movement. He wrote many books on Chassidic thought, including *Pri Eitz Chaim, Tzidkas haTzaddik,* and *Daver Tzaddik.*

Tzitz Eliezer. See Waldenberg, Rabbi Eliezer.

Waldenberg, Rabbi Eliezer. Author of the *Tzitz Eliezer.* He was born in 1917 and was a chief *dayan* (rabbinical judge) in Jerusalem. His massive responsa, the *Tzitz Eliezer,* deals with a tremendously wide range of topics, including laws for the modern state of Israel and many medical questions.

***Yaavetz* — Rabbi Yaakov Emden.** He was born in 1697 and died in 1776 in Germany. His father and teacher was the Chacham Tzvi. He wrote many works, including the *Siddur Beis El* and *Responsa Yaavetz.* He was very controversial and his famous dispute with Rabbi Yonasan Eibeshutz divided the Jewish world in Europe.

***Yaskil Avdi* — Rabbi Ovadiah Hodiyah.** He was born in Jerusaelm in 1890. He published the first volume of his resposa, *Yaskil Avdi,* in 1931. The eighth volume appeared after his death, in the year 1983. He was the rosh yeshiva of Yeshivat Beit El and served as a *dayan* (rabbinical judge). He died in 1969.

Yosef, Rabbi Ovadiah. Former Chief Rabbi of Israel. He was born in Iraq in 1920 and moved to Eretz Yisrael at the age of four. He learned in the Old City of Jerusalem and received rabbinical ordination from Rabbi Ben Tzion Uziel, the chief Rabbi of Israel at the time. In 1947 he became the Chief Rabbi of Egypt, and in 1950 he returned to Israel. He wrote the responsa *Yechavei Da'at* and *Yabia Omer,* among other halachic works. He is the spiritual leader of the Shas party in Israel.